GENTEEL PARTISAN: *Manton Marble,* 1834–1917

GENTEEL PARTISAN: *Manton Marble*, 1834–1917

GEORGE T. McJIMSEY

THE IOWA STATE UNIVERSITY PRESS, AMES

GEORGE T. MCJIMSEY is Assistant Professor of History, Iowa State University, where he has taught since 1965. He holds the B.A. degree from Grinnell College, the M.A. degree from Columbia University, and the Ph.D. degree from the University of Wisconsin. Before coming to Iowa State, he taught at Portland State University, Portland, Oregon. At Iowa State he teaches courses in nineteenth-century American political history and does research in the same area, with special reference to the state of New York.

Composed and printed by
The Iowa State University Press

First edition, 1971

International Standard Book Number: 0-8138-1105-8
Library of Congress Catalog Card Number: 79-126164

To some very special McJimseys:

Harriet, Joseph, Robert, Marianna, and Sandra

CONTENTS

PREFACE

SHORTLY after I had begun to work on this biography, someone remarked to me that Manton Marble's name was not exactly a household word. Although this book will not likely make it one, I do think it will show why Manton Marble is worth writing about. From 1862 to 1876 Marble edited the *New York World,* which most people acknowledged as the single most important spokesman for the Democratic party. Together with his intimate friends, August Belmont, S. L. M. Barlow, and Samuel J. Tilden, he shaped his party's response to the issues of the Civil War and Reconstruction eras. During Grover Cleveland's first term, he undertook a special diplomatic mission and so influenced Secretary of the Treasury Daniel Manning that in practice he held the office unofficially. In 1892 he managed David B. Hill's campaign for the presidential nomination.

Marble's importance transcends his associations. As a disciple of the French economist Henri Cernuschi, he used his influence with Manning and Hill to promote international bimetallism. His failure to have his program adopted suggests that though theoretically sound, international bimetallism was not politically viable in the late nineteenth century. His efforts on its behalf, however, provide a fresh perspective on monetary controversies that historians are coming to examine with growing interest.

Marble's personal history is also significant. He shared many characteristics with the "genteel reformers" of his day. He read widely, wrote essays on literature, philosophy, and political economy, and declared it the duty of the press to educate the masses in the principles of good citizenship. He lived by a code of personal honor and loyalty that made his friendships true and lasting and his friends' confidences secure. He looked for intelligence and moral character—"manhood" he called it—in political leaders and yearned for the chance to be an independent force in public affairs. Indifferent to the plight of the less fortunate in his society, he confined his associations to those of his own social class and made sure that only "gentlemen" were admitted to his club.

But such gentlemanly independence was not to be his. Circumstances dictated that in order to influence public affairs he would have to be a partisan Democrat. And partisanship demanded that he risk his principles, his social sensitivities, and even his honor. Marble tried to minimize the risks and by the 1880s had succeeded remarkably. In his campaign for international bimetallism he masterfully shaped his principles to fit the political realities. Indeed, so well did he keep his basic principles intact during these years that one may suspect that the only difference between himself and the genteel reformers was his partisan commitment. He was willing to accept the risks of partisanship, they were not.

In the end Marble's crusade for international bimetallism failed. That failure, too, is instructive. Try as he might, Marble could not make his cause relevant to the many social and economic problems of his day. Farmers angered by high freight rates, workers oppressed by low wages and degrading working conditions, and middle-class Americans frightened by their protests could see little to gain from an international agreement to coin gold and silver at a single ratio. Nor, it should be noted, could professional politicians, unaccustomed to considering novel ideas. Marble's life shows how easily the genteel intellectual, partisan or not, could be led to advocate simple cure-alls that more often than not reflected at best their own parochialism and at worst their ambition to be more influential than their colleagues.

In writing this book, then, I have sought to accomplish two purposes. I have tried to tell an important part of the story of the Democratic party in the latter nineteenth century and to reveal the psychological and social pressures that played upon a man who tried to be genteel and partisan at the same time.

I am pleased to thank those who have helped me along the way. Professor Richard N. Current suggested the topic to me and expertly supervised its preparation as a doctoral dissertation. Professor Joseph F. Wall read the entire dissertation and offered many helpful suggestions for its revision. I am especially grateful to have the opportunity to thank Professor Wall not only for his help with this work but also for stimulating my interest in history during my undergraduate years. He is a fine teacher and a fine man. My colleague, Professor Hamilton Cravens, examined my treatment of the "swallowtails" with great insight and offered advice that improved it markedly. Two other colleagues, Professor Walter Rundell, Jr., and Professor Richard N. Kottman, also offered helpful advice and encouragement. All have contributed to this book's strengths and not its weaknesses.

For research assistance I am indebted to Marianna McJimsey, who painstakingly examined the Manton Marble scrapbooks in the University of London. Thanks go also to her husband, Professor

Robert D. McJimsey, for winning the Fulbright Scholarship that made her research possible. I owe a special debt to Margaret R. Butterfield of the Rush Rhees Library of the University of Rochester for uncovering the letters written by Marble to Dr. Martin B. Anderson. Without her help this book could never have assumed its present form. I am also grateful for the help provided by the staffs of the Library of Congress Manuscript Division, the New York Public Library, the New York Historical Society, the New England Deposit Library, the New York State Library, the Henry E. Huntington Library, the Iowa State University Library, and the State Historical Society of Wisconsin. A grant from the American Philosophical Society enabled me to examine the S. L. M. Barlow MSS, where I found many valuable items.

Indispensable typing and clerical assistance was provided by Mrs. Edna Henry, Mrs. Wilma Bryant, and my wife, Sandra McJimsey. To one whose own clerical skills are at best primitive their assistance bestowed the gift of sanity.

PART ONE

The Artist

CHAPTER ONE

The Education of an Artist

WHEN the leisure of old age permitted him to reflect upon his life, Manton Marble seldom spoke of his ancestry. He could have said a good deal about it, for if his forebears had not contributed brilliantly to his country's history they had contributed substantially. Since their arrival in New England in the 1650s, the Marbles had established and developed various Massachusetts towns. Marble's own father, Joel, had contributed to the pioneering tradition by working to improve public education in Worcester, Massachusetts, and in Albany, New York. But the son never mentioned any of this in his personal correspondence, and when he submitted his life sketch to *Who's Who in New York,* he noted only that Marble Ridge near Andover, Massachusetts, was named for a great-grandfather and that a grandfather had fought in the Revolution.[1]

Perhaps if space had allowed he would have said more, but it was appropriate that he did not. He had derived little from his family traditions. Most of the Marbles had been yeomen and artisans. Samuel Marble, of the first American generation, had been a bricklayer and his son, Freegrace, a mason. Thaddeus, grandson of Freegrace, had been a scythe maker, and his son, John Putnam, had kept a general store and had been associated in the manufacture of boots and shoes. The descendants of Freegrace's third son, Malachi, managed the family farm near Sutton until moving to Worcester in 1841, where young Edwin T. Marble began his apprenticeship in cloth manufacturing. A mere glance at the record should have shown that a literary critic, newspaper editor, politician, and political economist owed little to such a heritage.[2]

Although Marble never tried to explain how his career had come to diverge so radically from the family norm, the records suggest an answer. They show that his father was the youngest of ten children born to Deacon Solomon Marble (himself a farmer near Millbury, Massachusetts). They suggest that in his early twenties Joel Marble left Millbury and became the first of his family to move to Worcester.

There he met and married Nancy Coes, daughter of the town blacksmith, and began his career as a school teacher. In 1836 he was steward of the Worcester Manual Labor High School, which the Baptist Church had established to provide young men with an education in return for their labor. So it was as a school teacher's son that on November 16, 1834, Manton Malone Marble entered the world.[3]

In 1840 Joel Marble and his family moved from Worcester to Albany, New York. The reasons for the move are obscure, but he may well have learned of the recent expansion of the city's public school system, which two years earlier had added nine new buildings at a total cost of nearly $119,000. Whatever the reason, the move determined that young Manton would grow up apart from the New England environment of his ancestors.[4]

Upon arriving in Albany, Joel Marble took the job of teacher at District No. 2 public school, directly across from the State Capitol. No record remains to tell what Joel Marble taught or to reveal the quality of his teaching. At his death, however, he was remembered as a stern but kindly man, devoted equally to the improvement of his students and of the school facilities. He was also remembered as a firm believer in public education and as one of the first to advocate putting the Albany schools under a single board of education and abolishing tuition payments in order to provide educational opportunities for all Albany children.[5]

Among Joel Marble's pupils was his own son, and it was from his teaching that his son's ambition began to form. When the federal census taker visited the Marble household in 1850, he recorded that young Manton had decided to become an "artist."[6]

His parents shared his ambition, so when Manton completed his public school education, he entered the distinguished Albany Academy. Enrolled in the Academy's "Classical and Higher Mathematical" curriculum, he studied algebra, geometry, trigonometry, calculus, and nautical astronomy, and read Juvenal's *Satires,* Cicero's *De Officiis,* Demosthenes' *Graeca Majora,* and Sophocles' *Oedipus Tyrannus.* His tastes ran toward the classics, and at the end of the term he joined some classmates in presenting a gift to his professor of Greek and Latin.[7]

His artistic impulse, it seemed, was a literary one, and he indulged it by joining Phi Mu Alpha, the academy's literary society, and by entering the poetry contest of the Albany Young Men's Association. The first produced the joy of spirited, eager discussion, the second a prize for a poem entitled "Visions: The Arctic Discoverer," and a unanimous invitation to be the poet at the next Fourth of July celebration.[8]

His literary career thus launched, the young artist turned toward selecting a college to complete his formal education. In 1852 Joel Marble's salary brought home $650 per year, not enough to provide his son with a first-class education of any kind. As a result, the issue fell to the Marbles' close friend, General John F. Rathbone, Albany stove manufacturer and philanthropist.[9]

The Rathbones and the Marbles were Baptists, and their friendship may well have grown from their attending the Emmanuel Baptist Church on Pearl Street. The General had been Manton's Sunday school teacher and had developed a strong interest in seeing to it that the youth maintained "a consistent Christian life." "Let not a day pass," he would remind his young pupil, "without devoting some portion of it in securing the favor of the 'All Wise God.' Let those by whom you are surrounded know that you are a Christian—and let your influence be a blessed one."[10]

Rathbone was also a trustee of the Baptist seminary of the University of Rochester. Formerly Madison University in Hamilton, New York, the school had moved following a religious controversy, taking with it a faculty of many eminent scholars. With a majority of Baptist trustees and a pledge to "inculcate a pure morality, and the great truths and duties of Evangelical Christianity" it seemed just the school for a young artist.[11]

So in January 1853, after taking a special examination, Manton entered the second term of the sophomore class. His college experiences in many ways paralleled those of other college students, then and since. He became homesick, complained about the food, and joined a fraternity. He also studied hard. Lacking self-confidence, he tried to compensate by working long hours. Only fragile health and General Rathbone's insistence persuaded him to reduce his study schedule, and only then to something less than eleven hours per day.[12]

The Rochester curriculum fitted the "artist's" ambition. It was a curriculum designed to develop the reasoning and artistic faculties so that he would acquire a "balanced" intellect. Scientific studies disciplined him to think logically, while the classics furnished examples to guide his artistic tastes. Intended to prepare young men for law, medicine, and divinity, the curriculum also provided graduates with the attitudes and knowledge to cut a proper figure in genteel literary circles, and this no doubt attracted an aspiring artist.[13]

But curricula were only what men made them, and for Manton Marble no one made more of Rochester's than the man who arrived in the fall of 1853 to become the school's new president. Martin Brewer Anderson, born in New England, had had considerable experience in college teaching and had spent three years as editor of the *New York Recorder,* a weekly Baptist newspaper, published in New York City. Stern and humorless, he yet managed to win the respect and devotion of many students, including young Manton Marble, who would later refer to him as "the wisest counsellor of my youth."[14]

Dr. Anderson counseled most effectively in his required course in moral philosophy. Offered during the senior year, the course was designed to encompass all knowledge within the framework of moral order. Anderson used Francis Wayland's *The Elements of Moral Science* and various writings from the common-sense school of Scottish philosophy to illustrate the sources of moral understanding. These works began by positing a moral order created by God and hidden from man's senses. It followed that man had to fall back on his conscience or inner experience to discover the principles of Right and Wrong. Consequently the morality of an act resulted from the intentions that inspired it and not from its observable effects in the world. Nevertheless, Dr. Anderson tried to direct his students toward discovering "some great and worthy purpose for the good use of man."[15]

But the service of man was never enough for so orthodox a Baptist as Dr. Anderson. While editor of the *Recorder,* he had distinguished himself by opposing a movement within the Baptist church to revise the translation of the Bible. In announcing his opposition he had declared: "We publish the *Recorder* to advocate orthodox Baptist principles, not any one of the thousand systems of which the world is full, and which we believe to be destructive of the best interests of the human soul. We have positive convictions on the subject of religion. We thank God that we are not a modern liberal. We are not of those who care not 'whether a man worship twenty gods or one.'" As one of his students observed, Dr. Anderson believed that Christ spoke to him out of the Bible, and he could not disassociate obedience to Christ from loyalty to the Word.[16]

To this combination of religious orthodoxy and social service Dr. Anderson added pride in the American nation and its manhood. He believed that American civilization had achieved the Good Life, and he sought to defend and to strengthen it at every turn. He opposed unrestricted immigration, which threatened to corrupt the nation with "debased elements." He defended the classical curriculum as an "indigenous growth" and scoffed at those reformers who sought to incorporate professional schools in the American college curriculum as purveyors of "German" ideas. The training and discipline of a classical education, he argued, endowed the student with his American manhood, without which he could never succeed in professional life. "A true man," lectured Dr. Anderson, "is the noblest product of earth; a nobler thing than a clergyman, a physician, an advocate or a merchant. Let us shape our educational system to make men."[17]

The whole direction of such beliefs was toward restraint and discipline. Basically, Dr. Anderson believed that because man's better nature would never control, it was necessary to control his nature for the better. Anderson's belief in individual conscience and individual manliness was real enough, but it was a conscience tutored by the Word of God and a manliness disciplined by a classical education. His influence on Manton Marble was profound. Shortly after graduation, Marble wrote him: "I never felt so much under obligation to any person (my parents excepted) as I do to you, and if I shall ever live to attain to a noble manhood it will be mainly owing to the impulse you gave me when in college, and to the regard which makes the effect of that impulse perpetual."[18]

Dr. Anderson also advised his students about their careers, and it was on his suggestion that Manton decided to become a journalist. In order to gain experience in the profession, Manton apprenticed himself to the *Rochester American,* edited by Chester P. Dewey, son of Chester Dewey of the university faculty.

In the *American* Manton found Dr. Anderson's philosophy translated into conservative Whiggery. Continually the paper called for restraints upon the men who were dividing American society over the slavery issue. The abolitionists, it believed, should learn to respect the Constitution and its laws. Although the *American* opposed the institution of slavery and openly attacked the Fugitive Slave Law, the Kansas-Nebraska Act, and southern sentiment to annex Cuba, it revered the Constitution too highly to tolerate any civil disobedience by the abolitionists. Following the Anthony Burns riot in Boston, where a federal officer had been killed trying to return a captured fugitive to his owners, the *American* attacked the abolitionists for "standing in the desecrated temple of Liberty—polluting its floor with their ensanguined feet, and brandishing the axe from which drips the gore of a man struck down to death in the performance of his duty as an officer of the law." Unless the abolitionists learned their duties to the law, the *American* warned they would be guilty of treason.

If the *American* would civilize the abolitionists by teaching them to respect the law, it would civilize the slaveholders by educating them. Believing that only "degrading ignorance" perpetuated slavery, it called for all states to devote their public lands to common schools. A rising standard of public education in the South would show the slaveholders "the superiority of enlightened and free industry, as compared with any unenlightened, slave labor."

Common schools that turned slaveholders into freedom-lovers would also turn foreigners into true patriots. So the *American* argued in opposing former Governor William H. Seward's defense of parochial schools. Pointing out that the New York school laws had purged the common schools of the "taint of Sectarianism," the paper opposed the effort to promote any religious denomination through education. It noted that some persons had claimed foreign students were handicapped in the common schools by their inability to understand English, but replied that such students should merely defer their education until they could understand the language. "The sooner they forget the languages and customs of monarchical Europe, the sooner they will become good American citizens." For the aim of American education was to "teach Americans the language of America, and leave them free to follow the religion of their fathers or to abandon it as they choose."

Education had its limits, however, and the *American* thought they ran out before they reached the free Negro. Noting that free Negroes in the North met with a hostility that combined prejudice with cruelty, the *American* advocated their colonization in Africa. Citing legal disabilities placed upon the Negro in northern states, including New York's restriction of the suffrage, it speculated that an increased Negro population in the North might force a reestablishment of slavery. It could only conclude that "freedom, in this country, does not bring to Negroes its appropriate blessings" and hope that in Africa they might be free to live as men: erect, independent, and equal.[19]

On the *American,* Manton worked as a correspondent, reviewed books, and wrote feature articles and editorials, all unsigned and now unidentifiable. His work was well received, however, and Dewey was always ready with kind words of praise and encouragement. Thus the young journalist would hear that his letter was very much liked and that one reader said it was the best thing the editor himself had ever written. He would be encouraged to write as often as possible in order to gain confidence and a claim upon a good position in the future. He would be reassured that puns were perfectly acceptable, and that "the worst generally receive the most applause." Above all, his timid hopes would receive support with the assurance that he would always have "a first class seat" on the *American.*[20]

To deepen his knowledge of public affairs, Manton supplemented his regular studies with reading in history and political theory. Apart from his recollection, there remains little to tell of his efforts. He recalled that his junior year oration stated the theme of Milton's *Areopagitica,* an eloquent appeal for freedom of the press. His commencement oration dealt with the Italian republics, and at the same ceremony he received the President's Prize for the best senior essay, a work entitled "The Ancient and the Modern Idea of the State."[21]

After graduation in July 1855, Marble returned home. Although his formal education had been completed, his future was by no means clear. He had decided to become a journalist, but he had not even thought much about where he would like to begin. Furthermore, his literary interests remained strong enough to conflict with a journalistic career. Questions and conflicts would challenge him throughout the next five years, as he struggled in his quest for a career and the attainment of a noble manhood. ✣

CHAPTER TWO

A Peg in the Universe

IT WAS NATURAL that Marble should have thought of returning to Rochester to begin his career. His years at Rochester had been rewarding and secure, and a summer's illness had reinforced his usual timidity. So it seemed to him that if success was possible for him anywhere it would be in Rochester, where his many friends would deal gently with his early mistakes and would assist him with advice and encouragement. He also worried about being able to return to scholarly pursuits and thought the "very atmosphere" of Rochester would make him a student once more. Above all, however, he wanted to end the uncertainty he felt about his future. As he wrote to Dr. Anderson, he was far less concerned about *when* he started to work than *where*.[1]

But it turned out that Rochester held no immediate opportunities for him. Accordingly, with much trepidation and a bundle of recommendations so impressive that they embarrassed him, Marble followed Dr. Anderson's advice once more and set out for Boston. Happily, he found his fears were unjustified. He quickly received a trial with the *Boston Journal* as theatrical critic, an offer from the *Boston Advertiser* to make up congressional reports and to write occasional book reviews and theatrical notices, and an unspecific guarantee from the *Boston Traveller* that a job would be open for him in the near future. Although it did not gratify his tastes exactly, he thought the *Journal*'s offer the best. The paper boasted the second largest circulation in the city, its politics were "straight-out Whig" and its reputation "highly respectable."[2]

Before he had even begun, Marble found himself promoted to assistant editor. His theatrical reviews had so impressed the *Journal*'s owner, Charles O. Rogers, that he was offered the job without further trial. The position afforded him a chance to perform a variety of tasks, including reporting, item-collecting, and reviewing. He received a starting salary of $500 per year, and Rogers assured him that he would not hesitate to raise the pay before the year was out. Thus

Marble returned home to celebrate his twenty-first birthday a happy young man. He was also a dedicated young man, promising Dr. Anderson that "it will be my endeavor to repay you by proving myself deserving."[3]

After nearly a month Marble was pleased to find that he could spend most of his time writing book notices. His literary interest still strong, he hoped to find some way to combine it with a journalistic career. Gradually he lost interest in the other responsibilities of his position, somewhat to the dismay of his editor-in-chief, James A. Dix. "He says," Marble reported to Dr. Anderson, "that I can never succeed as a political or news editor, but in literary matters he has unlimited confidence in me."[4]

Clearly, Marble was not yet suited to the varied duties of an assistant editor, so early in 1856 he left the *Journal* to become an assistant librarian at the Boston Athenaeum, the city's finest library. His only ties to journalism were as book reviewer for the *Boston Traveller*.

Everything seemed to be working out splendidly. He would be a literary scholar. Through literature he could achieve a comprehensive understanding of human affairs and thus attune his intuition to the moral order of the universe. Indeed, he had found that by merely reflecting upon the amount of knowledge contained upon the library's shelves he had broadened and strengthened his sympathies and had come to feel somehow ennobled and serene. As he put it: "The infinity of human relations and the omnipresence and omnipotence of Deity have been made more apparent to me than ever before. I never used to be able to *realize* how the present would seem trivial and yet be the sphere of an active and widely sympathetic life, but that problem is all solved now and I know what it is to be intensely *in* the world and yet not *of* it." At last the way seemed open for him to attain the noble manhood he sought so earnestly.[5]

Once again, however, circumstances altered his course. The rewards of the Athenaeum fell below his expectations, and at the same time a new opportunity presented itself. Impressed with his work on the *Traveller,* its owner, Roland Worthington, offered Marble the job of editor-in-chief. Marble accepted, and on October 1, 1856, assumed his new duties.[6]

In its politics the *Traveller* espoused the type of conservative Whiggery that Marble had been so long associated with. It denounced abolitionists and slaveholders alike and hoped that natural economic forces would bring an end to slavery. Until such forces asserted themselves, however, it urged all men to abide by the laws protecting slavery. Its conservatism also carried it to speak approvingly of the nativist American Party, which it thought appealed to all "freedom-loving" men with sentiments that "commend themselves to all sons of America." Marble characterized the *Traveller*'s political posture as "Republicanism peppered with Americanism" and noted that "we all agree in this matter, thank fortune."[7]

Marble devoted himself to his new job with characteristic intensity, sleeping only four to six hours a night and at the same time trying to keep up with his literary interests. At times fatigue brought spells of depression, and he worried that he would never come into his own as a journalist but would remain a creature of "mere versatility and adaptiveness." Through it all, however, he was becoming convinced that his future lay in journalism and that the *Traveller* would be his vehicle of success. Even John F. Rathbone, who had so often worried about his lack of self-confidence, noted the change and even felt constrained to caution him against too much self-pride in his accomplishments.[8]

But in these years nothing in Marble's life remained the same for long. He had been editor-in-chief scarcely six months when the owners decided upon a new course for the *Traveller.* Hoping to sweep the paper into the forefront among the Boston dailies, Worthington consolidated the *Traveller* with three lesser dailies, adopted a new format, and changed the paper's politics to independent Republican. Last of all, he demoted Marble to literary editor and replaced him with the young and successful editor of the *Springfield Republican,* Samuel Bowles.

At first Marble welcomed the reduced responsibility and the chance to devote more time to literary subjects. He also thought the new arrangement would make the *Traveller* the leading Boston daily. *"Now,"* he declared to Dr. Anderson, "I feel as though I had a future."[9]

The immediate future belonged to Bowles, however, and Marble's prospects soon became uncertain again. Marble chafed under the criticisms of Bowles, who proved a stern overseer. In his book notices Marble consistently maintained an elevated moral tone, which Bowles disliked and sought to have him eliminate. Although usually a loyal and willing subordinate, Marble refused to budge when a moral issue was involved. So Marble wrote his own reviews, while Bowles had others written to suit his own ideas. As time passed, Marble became convinced that Bowles was "unprincipled," and Bowles retaliated by allowing less space for literary notices. "Why has the literary department of the *Traveller* been so meagre of late?" inquired Rathbone, adding "I have always feared that your position with your co-editors would not be as pleasant as when you were alone."[10]

Although Bowles had little success in changing Marble's reviews, he was able to work a revolution in the *Traveller*'s politics. Strongly antislavery, he openly attacked the Fugitive Slave Law as a threat to free institutions, religious conviction, and "the better nature of man." Completely rejecting the paper's earlier nativism, he supported Nathaniel P. Banks, the Republican candidate for governor, against the Know-Nothing incumbent, Henry J. Gardner. He even went so far as to suggest that Democrats and Old Whigs support Gardner so the people could see "the overwhelming importance of the slavery issue."[11]

Faced with such changes, Marble quite naturally hesitated when Worthington announced a financial reorganization and offered him a chance to buy some of the new stock. Marble believed that the *Traveller*'s ultimate success was assured by Bowles's ability to "ride with the wind," but he did not look forward to working under a man who allowed him so little freedom. He also realized that the paper had not been an immediate financial success and would not likely show much profit for two years. Once again at loose ends, he thought of returning to Rochester or of making a new start in the West with a paper in Keokuk, Iowa. He even considered leaving journalism altogether to make a career in "business." Confused and discouraged, he wrote to Anderson and Rathbone to see what they thought he should do.

Both men advised Marble to stay with the *Traveller,* but not to commit himself indefinitely by purchasing stock. His only alternative, Rathbone suggested, would be to seek a position in New York City. To Marble that seemed preferable to remaining in Boston, so in December 1857 he resigned from the *Traveller* and left Boston.[12]

Before going to New York City, however, he embarked on a lecture tour. His desire for literary culture had led him to seek companionship among Boston men of letters and he had become friends with George Hillard and Thomas Bailey Aldrich. Since it was customary for such men of literary taste to deliver public lectures, Marble imitated them as a matter of course. His lecture, which he may well have developed from his study of ancient and modern political theory, dealt with the utopias of Plato, Aristotle, Cicero, More, Hobbes, Bacon, Campanella, Hall, and Berkeley. He entitled it "Castles in the Air."[13]

Marble made his first appearance in Albany, where he spoke before the Young Men's Association. The lecture was well attended and described by some as the best of the season. Frederick W. Seward, who attended the performance, contributed a letter of recommendation. Thus encouraged, Marble obtained the aid of C. P. Dewey in arranging further engagements. He continued the tour through February, meeting with favorable comments and enjoying himself immensely. For a time he may have considered leaving journalism for the lecture circuit. At any rate, George Dawson, the editor of the *Albany Evening Journal,* was soon urging him to get back into "editorial harness. . . . *That* is your vocation [Dawson admonished him]. No one, by tastes, habit and education is better fitted for it."[14]

In March 1858 Marble returned to harness in New York City as a member of the *Evening Post.* Politically, his choice seemed strange, for the *Post* had long spoken for the radical wing of the New York Democratic Party. Still, the *Post* had a distinguished literary reputation, and probably of greater importance, now employed his former editorial mentor, C. P. Dewey.[15]

John Bigelow, the assistant editor, was looking for a man to write short editorial notices, which would "get out the naked facts from exchange and the times and by a few words of comment give them an interpretation, a significance, and a complexion." He gave Marble a short project, liked his work, and offered him the job. Marble realized the difficulty of the task and confessed to Dr. Anderson that "I go with fear and trembling." His years in journalism had given him a measure of confidence, however, and he felt some audacity and excitement at the prospect of success with a distinguished metropolitan newspaper. "I feel," he declared, "as if this were the hole to which in the universe's adjustment I am to officiate as the peg."[16]

As it turned out, Marble adjusted easily to his new surroundings and soon was writing nearly all the book notices and turning out three or four editorials a week. He enjoyed his companions in the editorial rooms and thought they liked him, though he thought he worked harder than many of them. Bigelow was so pleased with his work that he did not require him to go out as a reporter and drew up a new contract, expressing the "highest opinion" of his abilities.[17]

Once safely established on the *Post,* Marble turned to his own self-improvement and professional advancement. In those days it was customary for young men interested in broadening themselves intellectually to travel, either to Europe or to the western United States, preferably to both. Since his early college days, Marble had been interested in the American West and for a time had considered moving to Iowa. He also became interested in the Canadian Northwest, where a few years earlier a gold strike in the Fraser River region of British Columbia had set loose a sudden rush of population. Editor-in-chief William Cullen Bryant thought a western trip would help him professionally and encouraged him to go. Although Marble was determined not to become part of the gold rush, he thought a trip to the Northwest would help him intellectually and would reinvigorate his fragile health. Thus in the spring of 1859 he decided upon a trip to Fraser River.[18]

Before leaving, Marble contracted with *Harper's Monthly* to furnish illustrated articles of his trip, and in return received a $300 advance to cover his traveling expenses. Bryant also assured him that he could continue to write for the *Post* at $10 a column. His financial problems solved, Marble set about procuring the necessary equipment and arranging his passage west. An inexperienced frontiersman, he faced his journey with some apprehension. He tried to joke about it to Dr. Anderson, declaring that "if the Indians don't scalp me, I shall put money in my purse." But he closed his letter on a note which belied his humor: "If I go and do not return, goodbye, and may God reward you for all your kindness to me."[19]

On his western adventure Marble accompanied an expedition of gold-seekers and scientists who were looking for a new overland route from Minnesota to British Columbia. The expedition planned to proceed northwest from St. Paul, through the middle lakes region of Minnesota to the Red River of the North, thence northward to Pembina on the Canadian boundary and westward to the Rocky Mountains. The group left on the tenth of June, and after six weeks it was clear they were moving too slowly to achieve their goal before snowfall. Realizing this, Marble and a traveling companion decided to continue as far west as possible, return southward through the Turtle Mountains and the Devil's Lake region of Dakota Territory, and arrive back at Pembina in time to strike northward for a short visit to Ft. Garry and Selkirk. They traveled as far west as Ft. Ellice, near the junction of the Assiboine and Qu'Appelle rivers in western Manitoba before starting their return. They then completed their itinerary and by the first of October were back in Minnesota, ready to return to their homes.

During the western trip Marble quickly adjusted to the inconveniences of camp life. He mastered the daily routine and praised the "uneducated wisdom" and skill of the guides. He grew to savor the food so that by the end of the trip he was telling the *Post*'s readers that he preferred buffalo tongue to anything served at Delmonico's.[20] He rode on the buffalo hunts and wrote dashingly of how his blood boiled, his "mind sat apart," and his heart trembled during the chase. He was also enchanted by the West's natural beauty, which he described during his first watch on the Mississippi:

> Over the whole sky clouds were flying to the south, in thick billows, through the upper air, and in whiter flecks of foam below. In the west the full moon was going down, now completely hidden from sight, and now bursting through the rifts with a sudden light. In these moments the white tents gleamed, and the thick darkness which hung over the river, the forests of green trees upon its western bank, and upon the islands between, suddenly passed away, revealing their sharp outline against the sky, the rounded graceful masses of foliage, broken here and there by a giant trunk leafless, the memorial of some storm and its swift lightning stroke.

Other experiences he filtered through attitudes formed years earlier. Suspicious of Catholicism, he described the charitable work of the nuns at Selkirk as "inspired elsewhere than at Rome, and at sources long foresaken [*sic*] by the successors of St. Peter." Convinced of the moral value of formal education, he delighted in a companion who could exclaim upon sighting a buffalo herd, "Viands for a regiment of hungry gods, brought to us in the pockets of Jupiter's old coat," and attributed the frontiersman's lack of education to lawlessness, improvidence, and indifference.

From these experiences Marble drew up a picture of the ideal frontiersman as one who combined formal education with practical skill and an adventurous spirit so that he could master the wilderness without degenerating into savagery. In Joe Rolette of Pembina, he found the closest approximation to his ideal. As Marble described him, Rolette possessed great physical strength and a practical skill taught by more than twenty years of life on the frontier. Inside, however, Rolette was a "man of character, educated in New York." Bold and self-assertive, he was at the same time generous and public spirited. Although occasionally given to overindulgence in strong spirits, he would undergo months of total abstinence "for the sake of his wife." These, Marble thought, were the traits of a true man, one who had gained his permanent place in the order of the universe and who could assert his own manhood, fearing no one but himself. Rolette was indeed Marble's idea of a man of character.[21]

Before leaving for the West, Marble had confided to Dr. Anderson that he hoped things would be different in the *Post*'s editorial rooms when he returned. Evidently they were not, for by December 1859 he was looking for another job. He soon learned that Alexander Cummings and J. R. Spalding were gathering a staff to publish an independent, religious newspaper in the city. Such a project appealed to him, and in January he offered his services. After taking time to consider his application, Spalding hired him on the editorial staff of the *New York World*.[22]

What can be said of the young man who in 1860 stood on the threshold of a distinguished career in journalism and in politics? All his acquaintances testified to his broad scholarly interests and to his quick and subtle mind. They lauded his energy and determination and agreed that he would work loyally for his employer. They commented approvingly upon his refined literary taste and his ability to conduct the literary department of a newspaper. William Cullen Bryant also found him competent to handle political journalism. All noted that he mixed well with his associates and that his personal life was above reproach. Without hesitation they predicted a distinguished career for him.[23]

Unquestionably Marble's interests were principally literary. He contributed reviews and articles to leading magazines and preferred to spend his time in literary journalism. He also enjoyed demonstrating the polite culture his education had taught him to value by filling his letters to Dr. Anderson with literary allusions and by sprinkling his prose with quotations in Latin and Greek. He sought his friends among men of literary culture and judged his associates by their literary taste. He became dissatisfied with his job at the Boston Athenaeum mainly because he considered the head librarian "no scholar, almost illiterate."[24]

Along with his literary interests went the study of metaphysics. At Rochester he had studied the works of Sir William Hamilton, the leader of the Scottish philosophers, and after graduation he continued to read Hamilton and tried to defend him against his critics. "I have just been reading again," he reported to Dr. Anderson, "Henry James's article on Sir William in Putnam for 1853. Perhaps it is presumptuous but I think I could answer it fairly. It used to bother me a great deal, but I have kept pegging away at it, as Tutor Wayland used to say, and with a good result. . . . If anyone were to refute the theory of the conditioned [he concluded], I couldn't help becoming almost a Pyrrhonist."[25]

Throughout these years Marble held steadily to his Baptist faith. He never speculated upon theological questions, but accepted the fundamental principles of his faith and used them as weapons against immorality. Like Dr. Anderson he could not think of religion apart from scripture and was ready to attack anyone who suggested there might be substitutes for religion in one's life. Early in 1857 he affirmed the principles of his belief in reviewing a book of poems by Richard Henry Stoddard. Although he praised the book as a whole, he went out of his way to attack a piece entitled "Carmen Naturae Triumphalae," in which Stoddard had written:

> Creation is enough for me:
> I will not look
> On creed or book,
> Or aught beside the earth and skies;
> There is no need
> Of book, or creed
> To teach a man, and make him good and wise.
> . . . .
> No need of stoled priests, and chanting friars
> Censers, and incense smoke, and altar fires;
> No need of crucifix and beads,
> No need of sacred bread and wine,
> Of hymns, and psalms, and prayers supine.

"It is a fact," Marble declared, "that this is simply profanity—disguised under a poetical covering. We choose to believe that the Sacred Scriptures show the only way to life—that nature can never obviate the necessity of revealed religion, that Christ instituted the Sacraments, that he commanded men to follow in his footsteps and obey his commandments. If poetry is found which contradicts this, we can only lament such prostitution of the 'vision and the faculty divine.' . . . We hope Mr. Stoddard has written these particular poems as it were unwittingly—unknowing of the fearful abyss to which their doctrines inevitably tend."[26]

Marble's devotion to the Baptist church was more than allegiance to its creed. His letters show a continued concern for the institution of the church and for its historic traditions. He especially honored the Baptist tradition of religious freedom, derived from Roger Williams.

When he reviewed Samuel Greene Arnold's *History of Rhode Island,* he spent the major part of his review praising Williams's contribution to religious freedom in America. Williams, he claimed, was unique among religious dissenters because he fought not merely for a greater measure of toleration but for "man's inalienable right to abstract and absolute liberty of conscience." Marble believed that such a noble principle well deserved an honored place in his country's heritage and indeed declared that America "holds it for a watchword and a secret of its imperial greatness."[27]

Marble was also ambitious. In one sense he was ambitious for professional success which would make his own life secure and allow him a sufficient income to provide for his aging parents and for the education of his younger brother. In another sense he was ambitious to justify Dr. Anderson's faith in him. That kind of success, however, demanded more than mere professional distinction; it demanded no less than the achievement of the "noble manhood" the good doctor so highly honored. Marble never stated his conception of manhood systematically, though he came close to it in describing his reaction to the Boston Athenaeum. He seems to have sought to broaden his knowledge of human affairs so that he could understand the moral order of the universe. Such understanding, he felt, would give him knowledge of his own identity and would at the same time show him how he could best serve his fellowman. Possessing such a moral perspective—as he put it, "*in* the world and yet not *of* it"—he could stand alone, fearless and self-determined, yet dedicated to principles that transcended his own self-interest.

But manhood required more than self-awareness; it required action. It required him to learn the techniques of survival and mastery in his environment so that he might assert himself in the world. And it would require him to balance that self-assertion with a true devotion to moral principle. Such a balance Marble had found in Joe Rolette, and it was with the Joe Rolettes of the world that he yearned to count himself.

In 1860 it appeared that Marble had accomplished part of his ambition. He had learned to stand fast for principle. The first person he referred to as a "man" was the Massachusetts antislavery Senator, Charles Sumner. Marble's conservative Whiggery predisposed him to dislike Sumner, yet upon meeting him he was thoroughly captivated. "Such a man!" he exclaimed to Sumner's private secretary. Later, he explained to Dr. Anderson, "I was impressed with the purity of his aims. I may be deceived in this, but it seemed to me beyond doubt that he entered politics and stays in them solely on a sentiment and as the representative of it, and that he would feel no mortification in failing of a re-election—which is a test."[28]

Tests, indeed, made men, and it would tell much, if after having faced his own tests, Manton Marble would be able to say the same of himself.

PART TWO

The Entrepreneur

CHAPTER THREE

Adjustments to Time and Space

IN THE 1860s the press of New York clustered near Printing House Square in lower Manhattan. Of the many press buildings the most imposing was the *New York Times* Office, which had been built near the end of the previous decade. Just up the street from the *Times*, at 35 Park Row, editor-in-chief James R. Spalding was able to lease space for the *World*. Thus the *World* would begin its career in the center of things. "No better situation in New York," Spalding proudly informed his newly hired night editor, Manton Marble.[1]

Unquestionably, the site would do—but would Spalding? His credentials were less compelling. Certainly there was no doubt about his experience; for years he had written editorials for James Watson Webb's *Courier and Enquirer*. Nor was there any doubt about his abilities. A man of considerable literary and historical learning, he could hold his readers by his polished and forceful prose. To his writing he also brought a strong moral conviction, rooted in a quiet, yet fervent, Christian faith.

These, however, were not necessarily the talents of a journalist, much less an editor-in-chief. In fact, Spalding had entered the profession almost inadvertently, when his series of articles about his European travels attracted popular attention and praise. Throughout his career, his attitudes and habits remained those of the essayist. He wrote at his leisure with little thought to deadlines or schedules. Indeed, he could often be found wandering about the streets, carelessly dressed, contemplating great ideas, and recognizing no one. At an early meeting of the *World*'s editorial staff, he astonished his colleagues by suggesting they write up their political articles three weeks in advance in order to have them ready for the first issue.[2]

Had Spalding been alone in founding the *World*, the paper might never have gone to press. But the real founder of the journal was Alexander Cummings of Philadelphia. To the enterprise Cummings brought over twenty years of journalistic experience, mostly acquired in the Quaker City, where he had helped to found the *North Ameri-*

can and the *Evening Bulletin.* His role with the *World* was that of publisher and business manager, while Spalding headed the editorial department. His religious and political views were fundamentalist and conservative. A devout Methodist, he held his beliefs so strongly that one of his subordinates once accused him of being a "Jumper" or "Holy Roller." Politically, he was a conservative Republican with nativist sympathies. A convinced protectionist, he was a close friend and associate of Simon Cameron, the Pennsylvania Republican boss, and for many years had served as his emissary and confidant. In founding the *World,* however, he sought primarily to establish a religious daily newspaper.[3]

In the winter of 1859–60 Cummings had set out to raise the capital to launch his project. By May he had raised $100,000 from some of the city's leading citizens, representing all Protestant denominations. While he was accomplishing this, Spalding and Marble were recruiting the *World*'s staff. In this project they succeeded admirably. When the paper was ready to go to press, it employed such noted writers as Richard Henry Stoddard, Edmund Clarence Stedman, Thomas C. Evans, Richard Grant White, George Perkins Marsh, Ivory Chamberlain, and David Melliss. With such an exceptionally talented staff, it easily rivaled the leading journals of the city.[4]

Cummings and Spalding had hoped to begin publication in the spring of 1860, but mechanical difficulties put it off until the middle of June. Shortly before the first issue appeared, the *World* advertised widely in the New York papers. Although there is no evidence to show who wrote the advertisement, it may well have been Marble; for it so perfectly expressed his ideas that it practically summarized his journalistic ambitions.

The advertisement began by announcing that the *World* had originated in the belief that the time had come for "living Christianity to assert itself in secular journalism more positively than it has yet done." Although the *World* would support no religious doctrine, it would show the "authority and efficacy" of Christian principles in practical life. Its news coverage would provide up-to-date stories of all moral, religious, social, political, literary, and industrial events, both foreign and domestic, while refusing "to pander to corrupt tastes," and excluding "everything unfit to be read in a pure household."

Especially, it would report all that concerned "mental progress and culture." It would aim to promote the interests of education and to give special attention to new publications, inventions, discoveries, and works of art. Here again its criticisms would "faithfully expose infidelity and immorality, wherever lurking in the current publications of the day."

In politics the advertisement professed to see good and bad in both parties and declared it would never lend itself to party service.

Instead it promised to select from the nominees of both parties the men best qualified to serve the public good. In judging the candidates, however, it indicated it would follow Whiggish principles. It promised to keep true to the doctrines of the Founding Fathers: "that slavery is a moral, social and political evil; yet withal one that can be safely and effectually treated only by those who have a legislative and legal jurisdiction over it." It called for strict adherence to the division of powers between state and federal government, opposing any federal efforts to plant slavery where it did not exist or to uproot it where it did. Also, it promised to stand behind the Constitution and the Union and to present calm appeals to allay sectional hostilities. Its political program, in short, appealed to the traditionalism, constitutionalism, and rationalism derived from the old Whig party.[5]

On June 14, 1860, the first copies of the *World* appeared on the streets. A New Yorker purchasing a copy on that day would no doubt have had some difficulty in distinguishing it from most of the other papers. It followed the major New York dailies in presenting a quarto sheet of eight 6-column pages. Advertisements took up the greatest single share of the space, over 30 percent. The reader had to turn to the third page before encountering news items and articles, which included a review of the *Origin of Species.* The next page presented the latest domestic news, mostly political items and lengthy reports of the proceedings of Congress. The religious theme appeared in a one-column summary of the "Farewell Address" of a prominent cleric.

Page five contained the editorials, led by a strongly worded article by George Perkins Marsh, praising the movement for Italian unification and the progress of democratic institutions abroad, and attacking Congress and the American press for failing to lend support to such movements. Among the columns of advertising that dominated the remaining pages were several articles on science, art, literature, and the latest commercial intelligence.[6]

In its tone and style the *World* seemed distinguished principally by its restraint. It excluded all theatrical advertisements and handled police and crime news with care. Because it was not as yet a member of the New York Associated Press and thus had to rely entirely upon its own correspondents, its news stories were a bit behind the leading papers. Its articles, however, revealed a spirit and talent that, if nothing else, promised that the paper would make good reading. If the beginning fell somewhat below its advertising claims, it at least showed signs of hope for the future. Within three weeks, Marble was reporting an "unprecedented" circulation of 30,000, declaring that "we have never printed less than 25,000."[7]

"The *World* is a Protestant paper," an early edition proclaimed, "and will not disguise or do violence to its convictions." The journal was true to its word. Prayer meetings, church attendance figures, noteworthy sermons, and theological controversies were dutifully reported. Crime news was suppressed and theatrical advertisements banned. Catholicism was charged with hindering Italian unification and the progress of democracy throughout the world. Advertisements requesting "Protestants" for domestic help were accepted.

The *World* was also a nativist paper. German protests against the laws closing theaters and taverns on Sundays were labeled "an insult to the moral sense and public virtue of the city." A sharp line was drawn between "a decent respect and due obedience to the national convictions and time-honored statutes of the land" and the importation of "foreign vices."[8]

In politics, while continually professing its independence, the *World* followed a conservative Republican course. Considering the political sympathies of its editors, no other course could have been possible. Spalding had worked for the Whig *Courier and Enquirer,* Cummings was a political ally of Simon Cameron, and one of the principal editorial writers, Ivory Chamberlain, had helped Millard Fillmore campaign for president in 1856. When he thought about it, Marble was also a Whig.[9]

It was no surprise, then, that during the secession crisis the *World* spoke for reason and moderation by calling all Americans to stand by the Constitution and the Union. Although it had professed neutrality in the presidential election, it had freely predicted Lincoln's victory and had welcomed it as an antidote for disunionism. Playing up the role of the Old Whigs in electing Lincoln, it did its best to provide a conservative ideology for the president-elect. The goals of the Republican party, it declared, should be to maintain both the letter and the spirit of the Constitution and to steer between the secessionists and the abolitionists. "The Constitution is neither a proslavery nor an anti-slavery instrument; and to pervert it to either end would be alike a political wrong." Thus the paper called upon northerners to renounce party spirit and to treat the seceded states with generosity.

To accomplish these ends, the *World* believed the federal government should abolish the spoils system and support economic improvement in the South. The rapacious desire for office, it declared, had caused unscrupulous politicians to pander to sectional prejudices. For every important office there were at least a score of aspirants who would exaggerate and distort any issue in order to win the place. To replace the spoils system the government should allow minor officials to be elected in local districts and should permit them to hold office during good behavior. To mollify the South, it should improve transportation on the Mississippi River, reclaim flooded land, build levees, construct a canal from the Great Lakes to the Mississippi, and construct a southern Pacific railroad. Thus did the *World* attempt to employ the ideology of Clay and Webster to restore sectional unity, hoping that the rewards of economic expansion would turn North and South from their rush toward conflict.

Although the *World* pleaded for compromise, it made clear its own hostility toward slavery. In an editorial entitled "Why the North Abandoned Slavery," it went out of its way to attack slavery as a moral wrong. Denying that the North had abandoned slavery merely because it had become unprofitable, it asserted that "man's moral convictions are the deepest and most enduring part of his nature" and that antislavery was "a great moral movement," prompted by the public conscience. Thus it warned that while public duty forced the North to respect the South's domestic institutions, the North would never consent "to degrade itself by renouncing the humane sentiments and conscientious convictions which led it to abolish slavery within its own jurisdiction." In defending its position it even went so far as to denounce the Crittenden Compromise for allowing slavery to expand south of 36°30′. "No danger to the Union, no earthly consideration could, for one moment, have justified such a betrayal of principle."

But if morality was important, so was social order, and the *World* believed the Union was essential to order. Thus it argued that secession was but another name for anarchy. If the South must have concessions to protect slavery, she would have to obtain them through constitutional processes and not through lawless rebellion. The *World* would even concede that secession was constitutionally possible, but believed that the South had chosen to attack the Constitution. Against such action, the *World* marshaled all the rhetoric of its Whiggish morality to pronounce its awful judgment:

> Faction never took a shape of more completely detestable selfishness, or more utterly destructive tyranny. The great law-abiding North will not give way to it. They will not consent that the blessed Liberty of their fathers shall be made hopeless, interminable license. Come what may, they intend to meet the responsibilities God has devolved upon them—to act worthily of their fathers, and faithfully to coming generations.[10]

While the *World* thus prepared its readers to accept the crisis it claimed to abhor, it was experiencing a crisis of its own. In the editorial rooms, things had rapidly gone from bad to worse. The first problems had arisen over control of the paper's editorial policy. According to the original plan of organization, Spalding was to be the editor and Cummings the publisher and business manager. They were in effect equal partners, however, since both men acted as the Executive Committee of the board of trustees. Cummings at once demanded editorial authority equal to Spalding's and refused to leave Philadelphia until he received it. While Cummings sulked in Philadelphia, Spalding was proving to be spectacularly incompetent as editor-in-chief. Not only was he neglecting his duties but he was refusing to allow anyone to undertake them for him. Thus in its formative months, the *World* wallowed, leaderless.

As night editor, Marble fell heir to Spalding's follies. He tried manfully to keep the paper going, working eighteen hours a day and seldom getting to bed before sunrise. He soon found, however, that in Spalding he had met his match. Spalding neither corrected copy himself nor allowed Marble to correct it, forcing Marble to correct the proofs. He assigned Marble to hire a city editor and reporters, and when the job was nearly finished brushed them aside and hired others. When the city editor he hired proved to be incompetent, he refused to fire him. Trying his best to be a loyal subordinate, Marble refrained from challenging Spalding openly. He burned inwardly, however, and to Dr. Anderson he confided his displeasure. "The idiots that are here, you should be astonished that they make so good a paper."

Most likely Spalding was only running true to form: preoccupied and careless. But Marble was not disposed to let him off so easily. Acknowledging the editor-in-chief's incapacity and eccentricity, he still charged him with a "monstrous egoism" that left him incapable of seeing the best interests of the paper. It was characteristic of one tutored in the doctrines of moral philosophy to make such a charge, for unselfishness and public service were that system's cardinal virtues. Unfortunately, however, Marble's attitude caused him to overlook Spalding's real virtues and to support Cummings, whose ambition outdistanced Spalding's by a considerable margin.

The *World* needed executive leadership, and Marble thought that Cummings had it. "His *drive* is very vigorous," he explained to Dr. Anderson, "his foresight and judgment good. He always accepts ideas on their merits and will learn from anybody, having no fear of weakness or indecision of character before his eyes." He also noted that Cummings had expressed confidence in his own "tact and executive ability," and had favored giving him greater authority on the paper.

Since Marble believed it was in his own interest to keep Cummings with the *World,* he tried his best to prevent a rupture between him and Spalding. But Cummings, keeping his hand in the *Evening Bulletin* to protect himself, in the event of just such an occurrence, refused to come to New York until Spalding either reorganized the staff or gave Marble the authority to reorganize it. He also reiterated his demands for an equal voice in editorial policy. Having assumed the responsibility for hiring the staff, Spalding refused to listen to Cummings. By early July 1860, tempers were raw and the atmosphere charged. "The crisis must come," Marble declared to Dr. Anderson, "and very soon."

Although he could not know it, Marble was witnessing only the first of many crises that would plague the *World* in its first two years. Marble, in his desire to find executive leadership for the *World,* was coming to hold entrepreneurial virtues in higher and higher esteem. While looking upon Spalding's egoism as his principal weakness, he was also quick to note that the editor-in-chief lacked such indispensable qualities as "organizing power, tact in dealing with men, and adjustment to time and space." The artist, it appears, was acquiring a new dimension to his character. Within a few months, such an "adjustment" would become almost instinctive.[11]

By the end of the year, the *World* faced not only managerial problems but also a serious financial crisis. A new press used up $30,000 of the original capital. Circulation and advertising declined. Late in November, the trustees demanded that the price be increased from one to two cents, and soon afterward rumors sprang up that the paper was for sale.[12]

Although the rumors were not quite accurate, a reorganization was in progress. In an effort to recoup their losses, the trustees approved a new issue of stock and in the process Cummings attempted to seize the paper from Spalding. By that time, many of the trustees had lost confidence in Spalding, and when he refused to subscribe his share of the new stock they decided to get rid of him. Early in April 1861 they removed him from the editorship and replaced him with Cummings. The board of trustees was itself reorganized to exclude both Spalding and Cummings, but Cummings retained unconditional powers as editor-in-chief.

When all these changes had been made, there still remained the matter of the unsubscribed stock. At once Cummings sought to use it to increase his control. Even before the trustees had confirmed his editorial powers, he began negotiations with Thurlow Weed in an effort to bring the famous editor-politician into the company. On a number of occasions Cummings had acted as Simon Cameron's representative in deals with Weed and had come to know the Albany editor well. As a fellow member of the conservative wing of the Republican party, Cummings knew that Weed desired to connect himself with a New York City journal, from which he could return the fire of Horace Greeley's radical *Tribune* at close range. Weed's political connections and reputation in New York journalism would also prove invaluable assets to the struggling *World.* Thus Cummings offered most generous terms, including a discount on the stock, a fixed salary, and a commission on any new advertising Weed secured.

The negotiations failed. Although Weed strongly desired to go to New York, he hesitated to leave Albany until he had found a suitable editor for his *Evening Journal.* Since his associate editor, George Dawson, had accepted the Albany postmastership and his partner, Frederick W. Seward, had gone to Washington to assist his father, no one seemed available. Interestingly enough, Weed told the *World* trustees that he would come to New York if Marble would replace him in Albany, but the trustees would not agree to it.

While Cummings was seeking to consolidate his power, Marble was rising in the organization. Considering Cummings the better businessman, Marble had supported him in his struggle with Spalding. Appreciating Marble's support and recognizing the young man's abilities, Cummings appointed him managing editor. Marble's abilities had also impressed the trustees, especially Francis N. Bangs, a New York lawyer. Marble developed a warm personal friendship with Bangs, who kept him informed about the actions of the board and promoted him with the other members. Marble apparently needed little promoting, however, for when the trustees sought to reorganize the staff they consulted him alone and followed his suggestions to the letter. When the negotiations with Weed fell through, Marble further strengthened his position by persuading his friends to purchase the unsubscribed stock.[13]

Marble's growing importance in the organization brought him moments of concern. Although eager for professional success, he worried lest his rise be construed as selfish ambition. After some thought, he succeeded in rationalizing his success by attributing it to chance. He had neither planned nor expected, for example, that Bangs and the other trustees would trust him so thoroughly. As he recalled, he had actually offered no suggestions about the editorial department, but the trustees still had removed the men he considered incompetent. Thus he could write to Dr. Anderson that he was not responsible for the changes and could conclude that "no one can accuse my ambition of selfishness or injustice."[14]

When the reorganization was over, Cummings and Marble had emerged as the principal figures on the *World*. Generally, the two enjoyed good personal relations. Marble approved of Cummings's management and realized the importance of his political connections. In return Cummings performed personal favors for Marble, especially helping his younger brother, Frank, obtain an appointment at West Point. The two held similar political views, and with the exception of a slight difference over the Morrill Tariff the columns of the *World* revealed no disagreement between them.[15]

Cummings, however, failed to impress the trustees. Throughout his connection with the *World*, he remained active in politics, often spending entire weeks in Washington to support Simon Cameron's interests in the Lincoln administration. Shortly after the war began, he became involved in one of Cameron's favorite projects, purchasing supplies for the army. So much did this job engage his energies that he hired Thomas McElrath of the *Tribune* out of his own pocket to handle the responsibilities of publisher. Eventually, Cummings's conduct came under the eyes of the trustee businessmen and lawyers, who saw his extracurricular activities as bad management.

Cummings's position was further weakened by the failure of the reorganized paper to pay its way. In part the failure resulted from the generally depressed state of business, which caused advertising revenues to fall off. Also the cost of telegraphic correspondence and extra reporters to cover the war occasioned an untimely increase in expenditures. "Not a daily here pays now," Marble reported to Dr. Anderson, adding that "a week ago the *Herald* had two columns of *'bogus'* ads." But Marble told only half the story, for the *World* continued to suffer from its religious restraint and from its inability, as a nonmember of the Associated Press, to supply its readers with up-to-date news. To make matters worse, the paper lost the services of its most able editor during the month of May, when Marble's health failed from overwork. Cummings, of course, bore the responsibility for such misfortunes.[16]

In growing desperation, Cummings persuaded the trustees to try another reorganization. It was decided to drop the *World*'s religious character and to merge it with the *New York Courier and Enquirer,* a conservative Republican paper also in financial straits. Negotiations were probably begun sometime in May and concluded by late June. Cummings did his part by using his political influence to persuade Lincoln to appoint the *Courier and Enquirer*'s editor, James Watson Webb, minister to Brazil.[17]

On July 1, 1861, the *World* announced the merger and officially became the *World and Morning Courier and Enquirer.* The new paper, declared the lead editorial, would unite the strong features of both old papers. The *Courier and Enquirer* had long been distinguished for its commercial coverage, while the *World* had led in general, political, literary, scientific, and agricultural news. In politics the paper promised to remain independent but to uphold the Lincoln administration "in this great crisis of the nation's fate." Not a word was said about religion.[18]

In the reorganization that accompanied the merger, Cummings's power declined. The new organization was capitalized at $300,000, with 200 shares going to the *World* and 100 to the *Courier and Enquirer.* The *World* placed four men on the new board of trustees, the *Courier and Enquirer* two. George H. Andrews of the *Courier and Enquirer,* however, was named president of the board with what Marble described as "large supervisory functions." One of the *World*'s trustees was appointed treasurer, and Thomas McElrath, who had successfully managed the *Tribune* years earlier, was appointed publisher; both appointments were blows to Cummings's influence. Largely at Marble's insistence, Cummings was retained as editor-in-chief, principally because of his political connections. A special bylaw, however, declared that in case of any disagreement between Cummings and McElrath the latter would have the final decision. Marble was retained as managing editor and was now given the same salary as Cummings.

Marble also benefited in other ways from the new arrangements. The reorganization effectively prevented Cummings from strengthening his own influence. Henceforth, aside from McElrath, Marble was the only highly placed person with extensive journalistic experience. It was to Marble's advantage that Cummings remained as editor-in-chief, for the latter's prolonged absences on political business allowed the managing editor great discretion in determining editorial policy. Marble also benefited from Bangs's remaining on the board of trustees. Within a month, Andrews expressed his pleasure with Marble's work, and the board continued to consult him about changes in the staff and general organization.[19]

In the following weeks the *World*'s financial status improved somewhat, but not enough to show a profit. This was the end for many of the stockholders, who began advertising their shares for sale. Late in August the *World* as much as admitted its weakening financial condition by declaring that its liabilities would have to be met within "a very limited period."[20]

At this point, John R. Ford, the head of a New York publishing house and the *World*'s principal stockholder, brought about another reorganization. In return for his increasing his investment, the board of trustees assessed all the paper's liabilities against the outstanding stock and required the old stockholders to pay the assessment before exchanging their holdings for new stock. Many seemed more willing to take a loss than to sink any more money into what appeared to be a dying concern.[21]

Hence Ford's efforts did little to relieve the financial crisis. Early in December the trustees called an emergency meeting to confer with Marble and McElrath about reducing expenses. "I am sorry to write you thus," Ford declared to Marble, "but we must act prompt or the paper goes to protest." The meeting resulted in a few dismissals, including that of Cummings as editor, but accomplished little else.[22]

Without new infusions of capital the *World* continued to fail. Since Ford had the most to lose, he remained at the head of the board of trustees while others sold out. So intent were the investors upon saving their money that the board did not even appoint a successor to Cummings. Marble did what he could to keep the paper going and to find financial support. Together with the remaining trustees, he sought out a number of wealthy and influential men, including Thurlow Weed, A. T. Stewart, Commodore Vanderbilt, Hamilton Fish, Governor William Sprague of Rhode Island, and David Hoadley, but none was willing to risk money in a business of the *World*'s reputation. One of Marble's friends even considered his appeals a bit silly. "I hold your letter as a literary curiosity," he wrote, "it may be of some commercial value as an autograph in future days—perhaps Mme. Tussards or Barnum may want to label it to a statue in the 'horrid murder' department of their collections."[23]

During these weeks of struggle and frustration, Marble was moving toward a decision. As managing editor of the *World* he in effect controlled the editorial policy of a paper that lacked only capital to assure its success. Should the paper fail, his ambition and hope might well be dashed. At last he decided to stake his future on the success of the *World.*

Where to find the necessary financial support? The political situation was pointing him toward an answer. Disturbed by the growth of radicalism in the Republican party, he was becoming more than ever convinced of the need for a conservative journal in New York City. He thought his salvation might lie with "*liberal* Democrats" who would carry the *World* through its crisis and join with it in leading the way to a reconstruction of political parties and the Union.

At that moment, in March 1862, Marble was actually less concerned about the *World*'s role in American politics than about its need for new leadership. Noting that under his management the paper had lost only $200 in the first two months of 1862, he contended that an investment of $30,000 "would accomplish much, $50,000 everything." Yet the prospects were dark. Ford was a "fidgety fool," whose timidity might kill the paper, and the other trustees were Radicals. So it seemed essential to place the *World* in the hands of "others who were strong in purse and principles. . . . If I do not do something of this sort, I fear the paper will fall into Ford's hands or into Cummings's who is scheming for it."[24]

Early in April when the board of trustees resolved to stop the paper, Marble took decisive action. He purchased Ford's controlling interest for $33,000, giving a mortgage on the whole business in return, and he promised to raise $100,000 or return the paper to the trustees for sale. Cummings, trying to regain power in the organization, undertook to outbid Marble but could not raise enough capital. For the moment he was forced to stand aside, while the young editor tried his luck.

In the first few weeks of his management, Marble's luck was bad. He was able to raise $75,000 from "just the right men," but by mid-May his chances for success seemed to have evaporated. Twice he had failed to meet the deadline for completing the contract, and the trustees had refused another extension. His ambition apparently blighted, he prepared for his fate with resignation but without regret. "Perhaps I tried to accomplish too much, but I should take the same risk again. I would give my right hand to succeed but failure stares me in the face."

He still had one last appeal to make. In desperation he sought out Thurlow Weed and Governor Sprague. To Weed he offered half the stock in return for the remaining $25,000. He relied upon Sprague to guarantee his own share and hoped that Ford would continue to support him in case Sprague refused. Although Weed's friends encouraged him by declaring that the Albany editor planned to leave the *Evening Journal,* they could make no promises, and the editor himself was in Great Britain on a mission for the Lincoln administration. In the meantime trustees and creditors were pressuring him, and Cummings was lurking in the background, "biding his time to give me a throw," Marble supposed. To his friend Samuel Greene Arnold it seemed that all was lost. "You have 'fought a good fight,'" he wrote Marble, "and deserve to win, but we have both lived long enough to know the difference between desire, dessert, and success."[25]

Somehow Marble suddenly managed to reverse his fortunes. On May 23 he reported to Dr. Anderson that he had completed the purchase of the *World* and no longer had to deal with trustees, stockholders, or "Mr. Cummings, who is *out.*" He did not reveal his benefactor, though he declared that no help had come from Weed's friends. He said only that he now controlled the stock and could dispose of it in any way he chose.

The struggle had been long and harrowing. Now that it was over, Marble took time to contemplate his future. There had come over him, he reported to Dr. Anderson, "the very natural desire to insure beyond contingency the success of the paper and increase the value of that portion of the stock which I shall in any event retain." Regarding the proposed combination with Weed, "I must confess that I strongly incline to the alliance of which I then spoke as a choice of prudence and as one which *in the long run* would give me more money, more power, wider political and personal connexions and larger opportunities of doing good work in and with the *World* in the long future than any other which is now feasible or which would gratify a shorter-sighted ambition." Gone were Marble's devotion to principle and his desire to comprehend the moral order of the universe. The artist had endured his first test and had emerged from it an entrepreneur.[26]

This, then, was the man who in the spring of 1862 set out to secure the fortunes of the *World.* Now the success of the paper and his personal ambition were inseparably joined, and the combination led directly to a political alliance. Only through such an alliance could the paper hope for security in those financially troubled times. So one institutional loyalty led to another, making Marble at each step more a man *of* the world.

Marble's political instincts guided him toward the conservative wing of the Republican party. Shortly before weathering his first financial crisis, he had placed the *World* in the conservative camp by urging all conservative Republicans to support Lincoln against the Radicals. "President Lincoln is a good conservative," the *World* declared. "The platform on which he was elected is essentially conservative; and it strikes us as an unwise experiment to throw away two such important advantages, and run the risk of finding a new rallying point for conservative men." After the war the danger to sound government would come from unreasonable demands by the South or from "rampant radicalism" within the Republican party. Both dangers could be overcome if the party remained conservative and devoted to preserving the Union and the Constitution.[27]

Fearing that controversy in the North would abet the rebellion, Marble urged a conservative approach to the war's most divisive issue: emancipation. Supporting Lincoln's program of gradual, compensated emancipation, the *World* also suggested a colonization program that by transporting only the younger slaves would rapidly diminish slave births and allow for the gradual introduction of machine technology on southern plantations. When Congress rejected such an approach by passing the Second Confiscation Act, the paper called upon the president to enforce it only in battle areas and to grant pardons generously once the war was over.

Indeed the *World* hoped that in victory the North would be broadly generous. Horrified by proposals to treat the defeated Confederacy as conquered territory, it called for a war only to reestablish the authority of the Constitution and a peace that would allow loyal Southerners to adopt state constitutions and laws *"as they existed before the breaking out of the rebellion."* Even the Confederate leaders ought not to suffer political disabilities, lest the North create a mass of "sullen, disfranchised people" open to foreign intrigues.[28]

Thus, while declaring its political independence, the *World* supported the Lincoln administration and the conservative Republicans. If Marble was to maintain such a position in the spring and summer of 1862, however, two things would be necessary. First, the administration would have to avoid doing anything to offend his conservatism. Second, the Republican party would have to find a place for the *World* in its patronage system. The search for those strong in "purse and principles," begun by Marble in March, would determine the ultimate fate of his paper. In the end the Republican party would prove lacking on both counts.

Although the *World* generally approved of the principles of the Lincoln administration, it did have its reservations, especially regarding the financial policies of Secretary of the Treasury Salmon P. Chase. Nothing disturbed it more than the secretary's support of the issuing of $150 million in paper money. Even before the "greenbacks" appeared in circulation, the paper had opposed their issue and urged the administration to meet its expenses through taxation. Denying that a shortage of specie existed and declaring that "the people want and must have a speedy return to specie payments," it had demanded that the administration adopt a policy of "taxes first, loans next, and

Treasury paper last." After the greenbacks appeared, it only increased its attacks on them and on the secretary. On July 10 when the price of gold had risen to 116¼ and sterling sixty-day bills to 129, it brought forward its own program to restore the nation to "sound money." The government should issue no more legal tender notes until bank note circulation had been reduced. In the meantime, it should pay all expenses with certificates of indebtedness. As long as the market rate for money remained high, it should authorize the assistant treasurers in large cities to receive cash on deposit at 5 percent instead of 4 percent and should allow the assistant treasurer to sell securities at rates corresponding to the New York market quotations. Only if these expedients failed, should it expand its legal tender issues.[29]

Another major concern arose over the activities of Secretary of War Edwin M. Stanton. When Lincoln appointed Stanton in January 1862, the *World* welcomed him, praising Stanton's efficient, decisive behavior and picturing him as the outstanding member of the cabinet. Its ardor soon cooled, however, as Stanton began devoting his impressive energies to projects it despised; for it soon became apparent that the secretary believed in tightening military censorship of the press and that, horror of horrors, he was an abolitionist.

Late in January Stanton began his attack on garrulous news coverage by sponsoring a bill to place telegraph lines and railroads under military control. A month later he followed with an order forbidding newspapers to publish information about military operations and threatening violators with confiscation. Throughout the country the reaction was immediate and unanimous. The *World* voiced a typical sentiment when it declared: "It is not possible that this free government is thus prepared to adopt the first necessity of military despotism. This is the people's war. . . . There must be freedom of information, and freedom of speech. And so there will be, even though it rains interdicts." Much to its satisfaction, Stanton revoked the order.[30]

Still, the secretary's efforts to preserve military secrecy continued to bedevil newspaper editors and correspondents. Although seldom successful, his efforts nevertheless strained the ingenuity of the working press and provoked much animosity. To outwit the secretary, many reporters sought protection and information from the generals in the field. For the most part, the generals, often harried by political enemies, personal rivalries, or professional incapacities, welcomed them as useful public relations agents, and perhaps in a few cases, as builders of historic reputations.

In the spring and summer of 1862, no northern general seemed in greater need of an understanding editorial page than General George B. McClellan, the commander of the Army of the Potomac. Since first assuming command, McClellan had found himself in a delicate position. A Democrat, known to be politically ambitious and opposed to abolition, he faced the hostility of the Radicals in both Congress and the cabinet. Especially did he incur the hostility of Secretary Stanton, who found him lacking in every major category of political and military wisdom.

The *World* sympathized with McClellan and admonished his critics to remain silent until he had been tested in battle. Grateful for such words from an independent Republican journal, McClellan responded by welcoming the *World*'s correspondent, Edmund Clarence Stedman, and by instructing his aide, General Fitz-John Porter, to supply him with inside information. Porter, who was also grateful to the *World* for similar favors, was happy to oblige. His first reports included details of the plan to capture Richmond and the observation that the men in the ranks were so devoted to McClellan that they had stopped reading the *Tribune*. Warmed by such news, Marble at once published three successive editorials in praise of McClellan.[31]

Once the lines of communication were firmly established, Porter reported directly to Marble. On March 17 he sent news that the army, strong and confident, would march on Richmond as soon as Yorktown was taken. "But," he warned, "treason is at work and the abolition element is working with Southern rebels to produce dissensions and break up our army." And the chief traitor was Secretary Stanton.[32]

Throughout the campaign Porter played upon the themes of McClellan's brilliance and Stanton's duplicity. It was Stanton who had caused fatal delays by dividing counsels within the army and who had withheld McDowell's needed reinforcements. On June 20, in the wake of many sickening military reverses, Porter raised the question, "Does the President (controlled by an incompetent Secretary) design to cause defeat here for the purpose of prolonging the war to have a defeated General and favorite (McDowell) put in command—a general whom the army holds in contempt and laughs at—and has no confidence in?" This was one explanation; but there was also another. "I believe," Porter went on, "one reason for Stanton's acts is when this army enters Richmond many of the volunteers will say that the Government must not make this an abolition war—that they must act to restore peace—and quickly but not by compulsory measures [in order] to give some hole through which the rank and file of the enemy may return and not have their property confiscated." Marble, also an opponent of emancipation, pondered the weight of such charges and the next day called for "a hundred thousand more soldiers . . . this very hour." On July 4, after Malvern had become history, the *World* announced: " 'Tried and found wanting' is the damning verdict which the nation pronounces against the men to whom the President has intrusted for them the administration of the war. . . ."[33]

Although his suspicions of the Lincoln administration were growing, Marble still sought a place for the *World* within the Republican party. After the crisis of May, he began negotiations with friends of

Thurlow Weed. From the beginning, however, difficulties arose. On May 27 he learned that it would be impossible to form a combination of investors willing to support Weed. His informant even suggested that success was possible only if Weed was kept out altogether. Marble, however, was not content to accept such advice, and he traveled to Albany to present his case personally after Weed had returned from Europe.[34]

The negotiations stalled, however, and Marble's financial position weakened. In 1862 Weed was under severe attack from the Radicals. During that summer, when Marble needed help at once, the Radicals were gaining strength and preparing for their victory in that fall's state convention. Such signs indicated that if the *World* attached itself to Weed it might remain in political isolation and cut off from patronage. Also, Weed's financial condition was uncertain. Although he was to emerge from the Civil War a wealthy man, the profits from his ventures had yet to be realized. No doubt in 1862 his credit had been stretched to the limit, so that he would have hardly jumped at the chance to risk his money in so shaky an enterprise as the *World*.

Adding to Marble's troubles that summer was the generally depressed state of the newspaper business. Conditions had not improved noticeably from the previous year, and even the *Herald* and the *Tribune* were complaining of rising expenses and declining incomes. Especially were they distressed by the rise in the price of newsprint, which more than doubled in the year. Marble later attributed his financial difficulties to this added expense. Probably more dangerous, however, was the intense competition inspired by the economic situation. As business declined, the newspapers competed for sales with increasing savagery. The *Tribune* ridiculed the *World* for its lack of principles and denounced its "scurrilous assaults on individuals," presumably referring to attacks on Greeley and Stanton. Early in May the *Tribune* even suggested that the *World* had formed an alliance with the Tammany Hall Democracy. Letting the principles fall where they might, the *Herald* joined the attack by reminding its readers of the *World*'s association with Alexander Cummings, suggesting that Cummings's speculative schemes while procuring war supplies for Simon Cameron still influenced the *World*'s policies. This charge especially disturbed Marble, because he believed it damaged his credit. When the *Times* picked up the charge, he wrote a strongly worded letter to its editor, Henry J. Raymond, declaring that except for "a very small proprietary interest" Cummings had no influence with the *World*. "In the present distracted state of the nation," he concluded, "newspaper quarrels are of all things most disgusting and impertinent, nor are they very welcome to my taste which at all times would lead me when treated with perhaps unintentional injustice to exhaust every opportunity for candid and if possible friendly explanation and reparation, before resorting to other means of redress." He left it to Raymond's imagination as to what the "other means" might be. Raymond apologized.

By that time, however, the situation had so deteriorated that only money and not apologies could save the *World.* Circulation was steadily declining, debts were mounting, and Ford, anxious over his investment, was declaring that if Weed did not provide support he would foreclose and sell the paper for whatever it would bring. Desperately, Marble sought to persuade Weed to join him, proposing that he arrange a loan to tide the paper over until a final settlement could be reached, but Weed continued to stall. Early in August the two had a final meeting. Weed reported that Lincoln and Seward had asked him to return to Europe and declared that Marble would have to wait until he returned. Perhaps, he suggested, Marble might consider whether his task was not, in fact, hopeless. Disheartened and angry, Marble broke off negotiations. A few days later he also learned that Governor Sprague "had too many irons in the fire" to come to his aid. The Republican party, already grown weak in principles, had shown him an empty purse.[35]

Marble later remembered the next few weeks as a "desperate struggle." On August 15 the *Herald* crowed that "the wicked *World* . . . is about to come to an end. The bankers and bullionists who have been supporting the *World* lately . . . now refuse to contribute any more money to sustain it, on the ground that it has no circulation and less influence." Evidently the *Herald* knew whereof it spoke, for faced with the destruction of his ambition and hope, Marble had decided upon a new course. On August 16 the young entrepreneur made his way to the offices of the prominent New York lawyer and Democrat, S. L. M. Barlow.[36] ✣

CHAPTER FOUR

Apprentice Democrat

LIKE MANTON MARBLE, Samuel Latham Mitchill Barlow was a native-born New Englander who had come to New York City to seek his fortune. Unlike Marble, he had found it by 1862. Admitted to the bar in 1849, within a few years he had become one of the city's most successful corporation lawyers. His firm, Bowdoin, Larocque and Barlow, served the city's wealthiest merchants with a skillful diplomacy that usually settled disputes before they came before the court and the censuring eyes of the public. The partner most responsible for gaining the firm its reputation was Barlow, whose success was reflected in his standard of living. He spent his summers with his wife and two children on his estate in Glen Cove, Long Island, and the rest of the year in a brownstone mansion on the corner of Madison Avenue and Twenty-third Street, where he entertained prominent members of the city's genteel upper class. He raised blooded cattle and show dogs, collected paintings, acquired one of the city's finest personal libraries, dabbled in American history, and played an expert game of whist.

He also played a shrewd game of politics. A life-long Democrat, he belonged to the conservative, upper class, or "swallow-tail," wing of the city Democracy, in which, as in his legal career, his was the art of the compromiser. During the 1840s and '50s, he devoted his best energies to keeping the national Democracy united. He opposed Martin Van Buren's Free Soil flirtation in 1848, supported the nominations of Buchanan and Breckinridge in 1856, and strove desperately to prevent the rupture at the Charleston Convention in 1860. Through such efforts he gained wide acquaintance with the nation's leading politicians, including John Slidell, Judah P. Benjamin, John Breckinridge, and Montgomery Blair. Perhaps his closest political and personal friend, however, was George B. McClellan. During the war the two exchanged numerous letters, all showing great mutual trust and admiration. Undoubtedly the *World*'s faithful support of the general did much to induce Barlow to aid Marble in those desperate August days.

In obtaining Barlow's aid, Marble needed all the persuasions available. Aside from a brief meeting a few months earlier, the two were perfect strangers. Lacking personal knowledge of the *World*'s financial condition, Barlow at first refused to grant Marble's request for assistance. Marble persisted, declaring that unless he could raise $2,000 at once, the paper would fail. After half an hour, Barlow finally agreed to the loan, and Marble left the office, restored, as he later recalled, to "peace and salvation."[1]

The exact terms and conditions of the loan are not known. Although Marble may not have specifically committed himself to the Democracy, he did increase his attacks on the Lincoln administration within two weeks of receiving the loan. The issue that he seized upon was the policy of arbitrary arrests. Since the suspension of the writ of habeas corpus, the administration had imprisoned numbers of persons for subversive activity. Outspoken critics of the administration, most frequently Democratic editors, suffered most. Jealous of its freedom, the press looked with suspicion upon such arrests, and the Democratic press attacked the administration for its "tyrannical" actions. Until late August, the *World* complained about the arrests, but for the most part seemed willing to accept them as a necessary evil. On August 30, however, Marble published the first of a series of sweeping condemnations of the arrests. Citing examples of men arrested merely for mildly criticizing the administration, the *World* declared that the government was imperiling its moral power. "American nature, cradled in liberty," it warned, "and ever habituated to freedom of thought, speech, and action, cannot long endure this repressive policy. However much it may suit the crouching serfs and unquestioning dupes of the old world, it is out of its place in this land." When ten men engaged in procuring substitutes for the draft were arrested, the paper intensified its attacks and kept them up until the men were released a week later. Marble later attributed a sudden and heartening rise in the *World*'s circulation that fall to these editorials.[2]

The *Tribune,* however, sensing a more practical explanation, attributed the *World*'s sudden popularity to its having found favor "among a certain class of men." True enough, while Marble was excoriating the administration, Barlow was setting about to secure support for the *World* within the Democratic party. By the middle of September he had accomplished his task. In the final settlement Marble sold three-fourths of his interest for $60,000, plus $12,000 to cover his outstanding debt and $15,000 for immediate expenses. A share equal to Marble's went to Barlow, and the rest was divided among John Anderson, a prominent tobacconist; Hiram Cranston, the proprietor of the New York Hotel; and Fernando Wood, mayor of New York and boss of the Democracy's Mozart Hall. Marble remained as editor, removable for cause at three-months notice, at an annual salary of $3,500. He also received full authority to organize the staff and to conduct editorial policy. Although final arrangements with Ford were not completed until the end of September, the agreement was declared in effect as of September 1.[3]

While the negotiations were in progress, the *World* steered between the Democratic and Republican parties. Although sharply critical of the administration, it hesitated to endorse the Democracy wholeheartedly. In part its attitude may have resulted from Marble's uncertainty about the negotiations and from Ford's concern that the Democracy might forsake the *World* after the fall elections. Thus when the Democratic state convention assembled on September 9 the *World* adjured it to "rise above narrow party views." The Democracy should make a broadly based conservative appeal to "friends of constitutional liberty, who love the Union and favor a vigorous prosecution of the war." But, the *World* cautioned, the recent history of the Democracy had shown little evidence that it could rise above mere party views and ends.[4]

It is difficult to state confidently that the *World* was expressing an independent opinion. The New York Democracy had, in fact, decided to make just the sort of appeal that the paper now advocated. Hoping to attract the support of conservative Republicans who had become discouraged by military failure and the administration's drift toward radicalism, the party had contrived to have the Constitutional Union party, representing the "Silver-Gray" Whigs, meet in nearby Troy at the same time it held its own convention. At its own convention it demonstrated its willingness for an alliance by nominating a Constitutional Unionist as its candidate for clerk of the Court of Appeals. The *World* applauded the nomination as political wisdom. The platform also showed a desire to attract conservative Republicans by reaffirming support for the Crittenden Compromise, calling for liberty of speech and press, and denouncing arbitrary arrests.

The rest of the party ticket, however, included only party regulars, with Horatio Seymour receiving the gubernatorial nomination. An outspoken conservative, Seymour had consistently called for a union based upon sectional compromise and conciliation instead of one imposed by the force of a strong central government. Strongly opposed to emancipation, he had gone so far in 1861 as to declare that the South should be allowed to secede rather than be forced to give up slavery. His nomination suggested to the conservative and independent *Herald* that the Democracy had not freed itself from narrow and reactionary partisanship. Voicing similar suspicions, the *World* reserved its judgment until the Republicans had made up their ticket. In the meantime it suggested that the Democracy might broaden its popular appeal by dropping its party name.[5]

Marble was still hoping that the Republicans would follow a conservative course. Specifically, he hoped the Republicans would nominate War Democrat John A. Dix for governor and would adopt a platform repudiating all radicalism. But such was not to be. In a convention dominated by the Greeley forces, the Republicans nominated the abolitionist James S. Wadsworth and enthusiastically endorsed Lincoln's preliminary emancipation proclamation. The convention ended all hopes of Marble's cooperating with the Republicans. On September 29 the *World* declared that all who voted for Wadsworth had to believe that the war could be won only by resorting to emancipation. To do so, conservative Republicans would have to abandon their principles, and judging from the support Dix had received in the convention, there were many who could not abandon them. Thus, the *World* declared, the election would turn on the single issue of emancipation. For Marble there could be neither doubt nor hesitation. True to his conservative Republicanism and Whiggery, he committed his paper, and his career, to the Democratic party.[6]

Others on the *World* were unwilling to accept Marble's decision. Soon after the *World*'s policy became clear, Spalding resigned to take a place with the *Times*. "I have no alternative," he wrote, "in fidelity to my own convictions." H. L. Wayland, Marble's former tutor at Rochester and at the time the paper's correspondent at Port Royal, also resigned because he thought Marble's decision neither "wise, patriotic, nor humane." "Well!" Marble declared to Dr. Anderson, "you can imagine the ocean of pen and ink abuse and the continent of 'God bless yous.' "[7]

He had taken an important step, but had it brought him nearer to a noble manhood? He thought it had, and amid the recriminations, abuse, and excitement he explained his reasoning to Dr. Anderson. Although acknowledging the importance of the financial crises, the frustrated negotiations with Weed, and his own ambition and fears, he declared that his decision had been based upon principle. Admitting that he had abandoned the Lincoln administration "with profound regret," he declared that he could see "no other logical consequence to all that the *World* has been saying for a year than that and no other hope for the Union, for our liberties, than in the success of a conservative—yes, even the success of the Democratic party, by whose organization and votes alone a conservative party could hope to achieve a practical success." Assuring Dr. Anderson that "the detestable past of that party is dead past resurrection," he predicted that "accessions from conservatives of other names and creeds, and events must leaven it."

Some of his associates troubled him. He disliked Fernando Wood and Judge George Barnard, whom he considered a "scamp." Still, Barnard would help the *World* financially by permitting it to advertise foreclosure sales and Wood would "run the Democratic machine here now, as long as he lives." Such men, in other words, had their usefulness.

With Barlow, however, it was a different story. Here was a man after Marble's own heart. Barlow's "culture, breadth and very large acquaintance with affairs and men" qualified him as a fine example of noble manhood. "He has not one fanatical streak in his head," Marble declared, "and has a great deal of red blood in his veins."

Thus from his own point of view, Marble's course remained true and pure. His political principles had, indeed, suffered little, and he could well believe that the addition of such conservative Republicans as himself would improve the Democracy. True, he had first approached the Democracy out of financial necessity, but if he had been able to keep the *World* solvent through September without appealing for aid, the Republican convention would have given his party loyalty a severe test and might have turned him to Seymour anyway. As it was, everything had turned out well. In Marble's words, "the hour struck, the opportunity came. I seized it. . . . interest seemed to me for once to coincide with duty."[8]

During the campaign, the *World* continued its attacks upon the Lincoln administration. As it had indicated following the Republican convention, emancipation was the principal issue. The *World* attacked the Radicals as enemies of law and order and charged that their schemes would merely prolong and embitter the fighting. Chase's greenback policies received an occasional denunciation, and arbitrary arrests were held up against Stanton. Interestingly enough, the paper attacked the president himself only indirectly. Perhaps because he thought Lincoln was at heart still a conservative, Marble hoped he would respond to a Democratic voice strengthened by conservative republicanism.

Because of its party affiliation, however, the *World* had to introduce a new theme into its editorial policy: the need for an opposition party. The rationalization presented neatly fit the conservative republicanism of its editor. A well-organized and patriotic opposition party, according to the *World,* would force the administration into a more sensible and effective prosecution of the war. Also, without such a party, the only avenue open to the administration's opponents would be violent revolution. Thus a loyal opposition would safeguard constitutional and social order by providing a peaceful way to change men and measures. It would also train men for public leadership so that political change could bring to power men with a proper knowledge of their civic duties. "Peaceful, loyal, and constitutional opposition is the proper prophylactic against the treasonable revolutionary resistance that is already threatened in radical quarters."[9]

While he was rationalizing his new loyalty, Marble was also finding his way among the leaders of the New York Democracy. August

Belmont, prominent financier and chairman of the Democratic National Committee, contributed money, suggested editorial topics, and helped Marble gain admission to the exclusive Century Club. Seymour appeared for several conferences, as did such party regulars as Charles O'Conor, John McKeon, Richard O'Gorman, Royal Phelps, and James Brooks. As Marble's associations with such men increased, many of his former friends expressed their concern. John R. Ford, ever nervous about his mortgage on the *World,* worried lest Stanton suppress the paper and thus injure its credit. Samuel Greene Arnold, former Whig governor of Rhode Island and close personal friend, cautioned Marble to stay with the Constitutional Union conservatives, warning that "the genuine old Democracy is the Vallandigham school—that will appear by and by."[10]

Perhaps because of such counsels, Marble kept the *World* officially independent during the campaign. Certainly he had no desire to become identified with copperheadism. Early in the campaign he revealed his own concern by appealing to Barlow to buy up Fernando Wood's share of the *World.* After the October elections, the *World* rejoiced in the defeat of the arch-copperhead, Clement Vallandigham, declaring that it had resulted from his "personal unpopularity and secession sympathies." Vallandigham's defeat proved to the *World* that Democratic gains elsewhere did not indicate any popular antiwar sentiment, but only the public's opposition to radicalism. To bolster such a conclusion, Marble continually looked for signs of an alliance between the Democracy and conservative Republicans. He quickly checked into a rumor that John A. Dix and Thurlow Weed were negotiating with the Democracy, only to find it false. When the Democratic ticket scored an impressive victory in the November elections, he assured Dr. Anderson that "the Democratic leaders owe the triumph to the unpledged, unbought conservatives of every former name and creed."[11]

Yet Marble's own independence was waning, his involvement with the Democracy growing. The policies of the Lincoln administration and the financial support of the Democracy made that inevitable. Also, in the months following the election, the Democratic leaders moved to tie the *World* even more closely to the party. The impetus behind the move came from the upstate or Albany Regency wing of the party. Led by Dean Richmond and Erastus Corning of the New York Central Railroad, the Regency was in the process of mending a serious split that had occurred between itself and the city Democracy. In the earlier years of Martin Van Buren's ascendancy, the Regency had been represented in the city by the *New York Evening Post,* whose working-class liberalism had appealed to the rank and file of Tammany Hall. During the 1850s, however, Van Buren's influence had declined, and the *Post* had transferred its liberalism to the Republican party and the cause of antislavery. At the same time the Regency leadership had passed to a group of railroad executives and western land speculators who possessed few noticeable sympathies for the working class. Such changes severed the ties between the Regency and the city and inspired Fernando Wood to launch a drive to capture the state party. In 1859 Wood had failed to displace the Regency, but had won the mayoralty and control of the city Democracy. During the campaign of 1862, Wood had cooperated with the Regency, but his ambition to control the party remained strong.[12]

The Regency clearly needed to rebuild its strength in the city. A newspaper such as the *World* presented a ripe opportunity. During the campaign, the *World*'s circulation improved markedly, rising, according to Marble, to 20,000 by the middle of October. Although a continuing rise in the cost of newsprint wiped out possible profits, Marble was able to declare by December that the *World*'s losses were far less than those of any other city journal. "Consider the rise in price to 3 cents and the future of the country," he declared, "and tell me if peace comes ever, if this is not the best newspaper property in America."[13]

As Marble's income rose, so did his ambition. His letters to Dr. Anderson show that he never modified his desire to control the *World* by himself. In his financial arrangements with the Democracy he had insisted upon determining the *World*'s editorial policy and had seen that the largest shares of stock went to himself and to Barlow. Early in October he asked Barlow to buy out Fernando Wood so that he and Barlow might control a majority of the stock themselves. Later he may have purchased an extra share from Barlow; he reported to Dr. Anderson in December: "I have been wide awake, as I was able, and have so placed it now, and have secured to my own absolute control such a large portion, that my stock with that of any one of the present stockholders would make a majority." He had also maneuvered to make himself president of the company and of the board of trustees. He then considered his position so strong that "even the infidelity of my most intimate friend" could not remove him. "It is a hard lesson in life," observed the young entrepreneur, "but I have learned it, to take even such precautions against all men except perhaps three." He even wondered about those three, for he assured Dr. Anderson that as soon as he was able he would buy up a majority of the stock for himself.[14]

Thus, early in his career the lines of tension in his life were established. For if Marble's ambition pointed the way toward an independent and noble manhood, it also created strains between himself and his party. While he was making plans to establish his independent control of the *World*, the Regency was deciding that the paper should merge with the Regency's upstate organ, the *Albany Argus*. Barlow had long favored the merger, and after the election

Richmond, Seymour, and the other party leaders joined him. Their plan called for the *Argus* to purchase all of the *World*'s stock and for the two papers to share in making editorial policy. In December they approached Marble with their plan. Horrified by the proposal, Marble stalled the negotiations until he could be sure he would "keep the whip hand" in the final transaction. In the meantime he turned his attention to buying out Cranston and Anderson.[15]

Nothing came of the merger until the summer of 1863. By June Calvert Comstock and William Cassidy of the *Argus,* concerned perhaps by the activity of Fernando and Benjamin Wood, who established their own newspaper to intensify their drive to control the party, had conceded most of Marble's demands. They agreed that Marble would remain as editor-in-chief of the *World* and would determine editorial policy. They continued to differ with Marble, however, over the financial arrangements. All agreed that the new company should be capitalized at approximately $100,000. Comstock and Cassidy proposed that the money be raised by consolidating the two papers and selling the stock to outsiders. Fearful that such an arrangement might jeopardize his control of the paper, Marble refused to accept it. Instead he proposed that the *Argus* be transferred to the *World* in exchange for one-fourth of the stock and that the necessary cash subscription be secured by not less than $30,000 in scrip, bearing 1 percent interest and payable at the option of the company. An additional $10,000 would be borrowed on the obligations of the company for working capital. Such an arrangement would leave Marble and Barlow in control. Explaining the plan to Comstock and Cassidy, Barlow declared that Marble desired to control "the preponderating interest" and "his friends are all anxious that he should control."[16]

With Marble and Barlow united against them, Comstock and Cassidy had no alternative. In the final settlement, the *World*'s stock was distributed in accordance with Marble's wishes. Marble and Barlow each received 9/32, Comstock 8/32, and John Anderson 6/32, thus confirming the control of Marble and Barlow. On Comstock's suggestion, the scrip was entrusted to a prominent railroad lawyer and Regency stalwart, Samuel J. Tilden.[17]

As soon as the merger had been completed, Marble launched an ambitious campaign to capitalize on it. He sent circular letters to prominent Democrats throughout the country, asking them to return names of active party men in each postal district. These men would form clubs to distribute the *World* and would send political information from their districts. To make the *World* a clearinghouse for party information he also requested the name, post office address, and political affiliation of each newspaper in the agent's county. Thus by the summer of 1863, Marble had decided to cast his lot with the national Democracy. From that time on his ambition would depend upon the ability of the party to rebuild its forces and upon his own ability to lead the rebuilding. Upon these two goals would depend his ambition for worldly success and for a noble manhood. Clearly, it was time for the young editor to begin his political apprenticeship in earnest.[18]

At the moment it appeared that Marble had decided wisely. From many quarters he was receiving praise for the *World*'s services to the Democracy. S. S. ("Sunset") Cox, Democratic Congressman from Ohio, wrote him that many Ohioans were requesting copies of the *World*. "Your splendid articles," he declared, "have made an era in journalism." Marble's Albany correspondent, William H. Bogart, reported similar praise for the *World*'s editorials, and an upstate journal characterized Marble as among "the most scholarly, forcible, and ready writers of the day." Early in February 1863, Marble joined with prominent Democratic businessmen and lawyers to found the Society for the Diffusion of Political Knowledge to spread party propaganda throughout the country. With increasing frequency, the Republican papers referred to the *World* as the voice of the Albany Regency.[19]

The elections of 1863 were thus the first political event to find the *World* openly committed to the Democracy. As such, they afforded Marble the first lessons of his political apprenticeship. They involved him, for the first time in his life, in the complex and delicate art of maintaining party unity under the most trying of circumstances. The Democratic successes in the elections the previous fall had given new hope to the copperheads, who, led by Clement Vallandigham and Fernando Wood, sought to assert their influence on the party by turning it against the war. Because Marble and the Regency both favored a vigorous prosecution of the war, they sought to check the copperheads. The question was, however, whether they could accomplish it without wrecking the party.

The best solution would be to achieve a compromise that would unite the party without leaving the voters in hopeless confusion over its principles. This could best be accomplished if the two factions could forget about their differences and stress their agreements. The peace issue aside, there was actually much in Vallandigham's program that the Regency could approve. Vallandigham had consistently opposed the war because he believed it allowed the Lincoln administration to increase the powers of the central government and thus to undermine the liberties of the American people. His familiar slogan, "the Union as it was and the Constitution as it is," appealed to principles of states rights and personal liberty that the Regency could heartily endorse. Seymour, for example, had sought to make an issue with Lincoln over the arbitrary arrests and had urged Marble to play upon the issue as often as possible. Also, both Vallandigham and the Regency opposed emancipation. And Congress had recently obliged with another issue by passing the first conscription act in American history. Thus when Vallandigham toured New York in March, the

Regency had solid grounds for hoping they might persuade him to de-emphasize his peace sentiments. After conferring with him, they came away believing they had succeeded.[20]

More than party unity depended upon the ability of the Regency to accomplish its task. The Republican press was using copperheadism to smear all Democrats, including the Regency and the *World.* The instant a Democrat called for peace the Republican press made him a spokesman for his party. It was the job of the party organization to keep such men quiet. Failing this, it was the job of the party press to make him seem insignificant. With such men as Vallandigham and Wood in the party, the *World* was in for a busy time.[21]

In explaining away the peace men, the *World* employed three arguments. First, it simply denied that such men existed. When Vallandigham and the Regency conferred, the *World* announced that Republican charges of Democratic disloyalty were wholly unfounded. The Democracy's only crimes, it declared, were having carried several of the most important states in the last elections by opposing unconstitutional arbitrary arrests and emancipation. Thus it dismissed Republican charges as politically inspired. Second, it declared that the peace men were an insignificant minority within the party. Following a large peace rally sponsored by Fernando Wood, it declared that "a majority of the Democratic party are resolutely opposed to peace." Until the South consented to rejoin the Union, "there is nothing for negotiation to stand upon, and peace is impracticable." Thus it assured both the loyal men of the North and the followers of Fernando Wood that "we have no desire to repress the growth of the small wing of the Democratic party that has declared for peace." Third, it attempted to submerge the peace issue beneath the more popular one of free speech. From time to timc it defended the right of the peace men, as free Americans, to speak their minds. "If Mozart Hall, or any other body of Democrats," it declared, "dissent from the war planks in the platform, it is their right to do so, and to attempt to secure the adoption of a platform more in accordance with their present views."[22]

In politics, however, free speech has been a weak defense for despised views; men have not often won elections simply because they spoke their minds. They have had a much better chance if they have been kept from speaking, for of all the silences, an enforced one is the most golden. This, at any rate, seems to have been Vallandigham's theory, for upon returning to Ohio he openly defied the orders of the district commander, General Ambrose Burnside, by delivering a series of vicious attacks upon the Lincoln administration. On May 5 he was arrested by Burnside, tried before a military tribunal, and convicted of violating the orders.

His arrest galvanized the Democracy. Factional disputes were forgotten and all other issues cast aside as the party rose to protest the wanton violation of free speech. In editorial after editorial the *World* tore apart the flimsy legal pretext for the arrest, warned the American people of the administration's growing "despotic power," and praised Vallandigham's courage. So hotly did it denounce the arrest that it occasionally went beyond its traditional conservatism. On May 9 it praised a mob of Vallandigham's supporters, who had gathered in Columbus to threaten to free their hero by force. "When free discussion and free voting are allowed," it declared, "men are not tempted to have recourse to violence and relief of bad rulers. You may stigmatize these irregular avengers as a 'mob,' but there are times when even violence is nobler than cowardly apathy." On May 11 it even approached advocating the cause of peace itself. "If nobody, while a war lasts, were permitted to advocate peace," it declared, "wars would be interminable." In a few months Marble would have cause to regret such partisanship.[23]

As the Democracy rallied behind him, Vallandigham set about to make the most of his opportunity. In Ohio his friends at once launched a drive to win him the party's gubernatorial nomination. From his cell in Cincinnati he labored to keep himself the center of national attention. He sent Marble letter after letter, praising New York's support for his cause, suggesting refinements in the *World*'s attacks upon the administration, and promising "an important paper or two" for publication. Through it all, he supported the Union, the Constitution, the Democracy, and above all himself. "Wherever I am," he assured Marble, "you will hear from me."[24]

Vallandigham's arrest thus gave the peace movement a respectability it might otherwise have lacked. Quick to take advantage of that fact, Fernando Wood convened his followers at Cooper Institute, where he attacked the administration and the Regency, praised Vallandigham, and recommended a negotiated settlement between North and South. Only then did Marble realize the political importance of the situation. Stung by the abrupt return to factionalism, the *World* at once resumed its delicate task of playing down the peace issue while maintaining party unity. Noting that Wood's meeting in no way spoke for the state organization, it warned against dividing the party. When the Ohio Democracy nominated Vallandigham as its candidate for governor, it assured its readers that Democrats would support him not because of his peace sentiments but because of his martyrdom for free speech.[25]

The Regency was fighting desperately to silence the peace men when the July draft riots shook the nation. No event gave the Republicans better cause to attack the Democracy than did the week of looting and racial violence that accompanied the attempt to administer conscription in New York City. Nor did any event so alienate from the Democracy the conservatives who had brought the victories of the previous year.

The *World* had joined Governor Seymour in opposing the Conscription Act, denouncing it as a threat to states rights and American democracy. The act, in taking control of military recruiting away from the state governors, had opened the door to centralized military despotism. Before putting the act into effect, Lincoln should reassure the people by removing the Radicals from his cabinet and by allowing the Supreme Court to rule on the act's constitutionality. On the day the act went into effect in the city, the *World* denounced the administration for failing to encourage voluntary enlistments and suggested the act represented "an oligarchic conspiracy plotting a vast scheme of military servitude."

It is, of course, impossible to estimate precisely the effect of the *World*'s editorials upon the draft rioters. It is clear, however, that once the riots had begun, the paper offered the rioters ambiguous advice. On the second day of the riots, its lead editorial expressed regret over the bloodshed and the destruction of property, but made it clear that the rioters' objects were noble. The administration had framed an act "never tolerable to a free people, unconstitutional beyond any manner of doubt in its provisions if not in its very nature, offensive and most unwise in the method of enforcement, discriminating between rich and poor, unfair, onerous, and most oppressive here where the attrition of discontent was at its height. . . . Does any man wonder that poor men refuse to be forced into a war mismanaged almost into hopelessness, perverted almost into partisanship. Did the President and his cabinet imagine that their lawlessness could conquer, or their folly seduce a free people?" Such words could hardly be expected to calm impassioned tempers. For all its own partisanship, the *Evening Post* came close to the truth when it charged that the *World* encouraged the rioters.

The political pressures upon the *World* and the Regency were, of course, immense. The riots had broken out at a time when the administration was gaining support because of the recent victories at Gettysburg and Vicksburg and when it could plausibly argue that more men would enable the union forces to crush the rebellion once and for all. A rising peace offensive within the Democracy was threatening to split the party and to discredit it publicly. In such circumstances, political wisdom pointed the Regency toward maintaining party unity by appeasing the peace men and by continuing to attack the administration's conduct of the war. But at that moment it would seem that the Regency allowed its partisan needs to overcome its civic responsibilities.[26]

The riots supplied the Republican press with one more bit of evidence that the Democracy opposed the war, thus helping to keep the peace issue in the forefront as the parties entered the fall election campaign. As deftly as possible, Marble continued to trim between the factions. When Vallandigham escaped from his exile in the Confederacy and appeared at Niagara Falls to report that the rebels were determined to continue the war, but would seek reunion once it was over, the *World* praised his *unionism* and declared him "triumphantly vindicated." It also attacked the administration for failing to send out peace feelers to encourage unionist sentiment in the South, suggesting that Lincoln sought to prolong the war in order to use a swollen federal patronage to keep the Republicans in power. On the eve of the Democratic State Convention, however, it called for honest elections of delegates so that the peace men might be denied an excuse for bolting the party.[27]

As the campaign progressed, Marble received reports of growing Democratic strength. Reports from Ohio assured him that Vallandigham's prospects were bright and that only the soldier vote could defeat him. Seymour reported that the New York party was united and confident and that such administration blunders as a recent suspension of habeas corpus ought to help the Democracy. "We have everything to hope from the folly of our opponents," he declared.[28]

Perhaps it came as something of a shock, then, when the fall elections brought Republican victories. Beginning with the September elections in Maine and carrying through the October elections in the Middle West, the country witnessed a swing back to the Republican party. As the New York elections neared, Marble confessed "grave doubts" over the Democracy's chances for success. On election day his doubts were realized as the Republican ticket swept the state.[29]

His first campaign had proved a failure. Disheartened and angry, Marble charged the defeats to the peace men. As a martyr for free speech, he declared, Vallandigham had been a strong candidate, but as the foremost peace advocate he had proved a liability. If the Ohio Democracy had nominated a war Democrat, "no one doubts that Mr. Brough would have been defeated. . . . It is the war which the people have endorsed, and beyond an endorsement of the war these elections have no significance." Clearly, so long as the war lasted, no party could succeed without supporting its vigorous prosecution. Not even Vallandigham's rationalizations could dissuade him. For Manton Marble, peace was no longer an issue.[30]

Nor was it any longer an issue as to whom would carry the Regency banner in the coming presidential election. Since his removal as commander of the Army of the Potomac, General George B. McClellan had become the center of Regency attention. During 1863 amid the mounting offensive of the peace men, the Regency had urged McClellan to step forward as their leader. Seymour and his friends invited the general for consultation. In Ohio, S. S. Cox, concerned over Vallandigham's popularity in the party, urged McClellan to seek the gubernatorial nomination and asked Marble to give the general a boost in the *World*.[31]

So far as Marble was concerned, McClellan was a perfect choice. The two had met shortly after McClellan's dismissal from command, and a warm friendship had grown between them. McClellan showed Marble his dispatch books and personal correspondence, confirming in both their minds the general's virtue and Stanton's duplicity. Convinced of McClellan's loyalty to the union and of his military genius, Marble was also convinced of his pure character and noble manhood. "He is as pure-hearted, single-minded a man as lives," he reported to Dr. Anderson, "and has a moral elevation of character unobtrusive and real which you would soon see and admire." The general was even "very modest."[32]

Despite the urgings of his political friends, McClellan spent the year 1863 out of the political limelight. Although ambitious, it seems that he hesitated to emerge into active political life. There were, of course, sound reasons for his decision; too early a start would have given his opponents a chance to organize against him. Still, McClellan's hesitancy probably resulted more from another consideration, his lack of political experience. Basically, he viewed politics with the professional soldier's bewilderment and distrust. Unskilled in political negotiation and maneuvering, and certain only of his own historic greatness, he constantly feared that "the managers" were out to use him for their own ignoble purposes. Facing a Democracy split between war and peace factions, and not always certain who spoke for which, he declined overtures from strangers and spent his time with such trusted friends as Marble and Barlow. He summed up his attitude toward politics quite accurately, when he declared to Barlow that "if the miserable intriguers think that they can use me for their purposes I will soon show them that they have mistaken their man—I am sick of the whole thing."[33]

For the most part, McClellan's friends respected his wishes. On only one occasion did they compel the general to declare his principles in public. The occasion arose when the Pennsylvania Republican party declared that McClellan supported its gubernatorial candidate, Andrew G. Curtin. To the general's friends it was obvious that if he ignored the claim he would risk losing the support of many Democrats. They advised him to declare his principles in a statement supporting the Democratic candidate, George W. Woodward.

On October 13 McClellan published a letter supporting Woodward and opposing both the Republicans and the peace Democrats. He was supporting Woodward, he declared, because the Pennsylvanian favored "the prosecution of the war with all the means at the command of the loyal states until the military power of the rebellion is destroyed." He also praised Woodward for favoring a policy "in consonance with the principles of humanity and civilization, working no injury to private rights and property not demanded by military necessity and recognized by military law among civilized nations." In short, the war should be fought only to restore the Constitution and the supremacy of national law. The *World* published the letter, adorning it with praise for McClellan's vision of "national honor, victory, unity, and peace." Although the Republicans at once tried to use the letter to link McClellan to the peace movement, the Pennsylvania Democracy enthusiastically welcomed his support. "The people's eyes are turned all one way in their search for the candidate who will win in 1864," Marble wrote McClellan. "I am greasing the axis of the *World,* which I hope will keep rolling long enough to witness what Old Abe called the Salvation of the Lord."[34]

In the early months of 1864, salvation seemed to draw nearer. In February the Democratic State Convention selected a McClellan delegation to the national convention, but for strategic purposes refrained from endorsing him openly. The Lincoln administration also remained conveniently vulnerable to the *World*'s charges of violating civil liberties. In May open warfare broke out between Lincoln and the Radicals with the passage of the Wade-Davis bill and the assembling of the Cleveland convention, which nominated John Charles Fremont as the Radical candidate for president.

For other reasons as well, May was an eventful month in Marble's life. For its soft breezes carried not only the scent of a Democratic victory but also the fragrance of romance. After many months of a courtship characteristically filled with much introspection and many self-doubts, Marble had found himself worthy of the love of Delia Bishop West, and the two had set the date. The romance no doubt had been sweetened by Marble's memories of his happy college days, for Delia was a Rochester girl, and the marriage was to be performed by Chester Dewey, Marble's former professor and father of his first employer on the *Rochester American.* The ceremony was planned for May 19.[35]

Then on May 18 federal troops, commanded by General John A. Dix, seized the *World* and suppressed its publication. The suppression resulted from the *World*'s publication of a forged presidential proclamation, announcing the failure of Grant's Richmond campaign and a national day of "fasting, humiliation, and prayer" and calling for 400,000 additional draftees. The forgery was the work of Joseph Howard, Jr., of the *Brooklyn Eagle.* Believing his income ill suited his abilities, Howard was hoping to use the proclamation to drive up the price of gold so he could make a speculative killing. Careful checking by most of the dailies exposed the hoax before their papers went to press, but at the *World* and the *Journal of Commerce,* as luck would have it two of the most prominent spokesmen for the Democracy, the night editors allowed it to slip by. Thus on the morning of

May 18, those two papers appeared on the streets with an unwanted "exclusive."

When news of the hoax reached Washington, the administration wasted little time in ordering stern measures. Stanton immediately ordered General Dix to close down the offending journals and to arrest the editors, Marble and William C. Prime. While this was happening, news of the hoax became general, and frantic efforts were made to withdraw the printed copies from circulation. Marble personally rushed to the docks to reclaim outbound copies of the *World,* going so far as to confiscate even the purser's copy. Such activity convinced Dix that the two papers had taken no part in the conspiracy, and he hesitated to carry out Stanton's orders. But the orders remained in force, so at 9 P.M. his troops entered the offices of the *World.* When the soldiers first appeared, the editors on duty, George Wakeman and David Goodman Croly, did not realize what was going on and kept on with the business of getting out next morning's edition. They soon found out, however, and next morning there was no edition.[36]

About the time the troops were occupying the *World*'s offices, Sam Barlow learned that a warrant had been issued for his arrest. He was in the midst of preparing for a trip to Fort La Fayette when Charles Halpine of the *Citizen* appeared and asked him to accompany him to Dix's headquarters. The two left at once and on the way picked up Marble and Prime. By the time they all arrived, they were told that the arrest order had been countermanded "on the urgent representation of General Dix, Thurlow Weed, and others who knew the facts" and they were free to go. Thus ended Marble's harrowing wedding eve.[37]

The affair created a great stir among the city press, all of which rallied to the side of their suppressed colleagues. In an open letter to Lincoln, the managing editors of the *Tribune, Express, Sun,* and *Herald* defended Marble and Prime. Once again, Stanton found himself being denounced for suppressing freedom of the press. In his diary Secretary of the Navy Gideon Welles conceded that the affair had seriously injured the administration.[38]

Once certain that he was in no danger, Marble wanted to make sure that the administration received its due. So he put off his marriage long enough to prepare a blistering attack on Lincoln and Stanton. The day the *World* reappeared, it carried his thoughts on "Freedom of the Press Wantonly Violated." Reviewing the facts of the case, Marble emphasized his innocence of unlawful intent and attacked the president for violating the Constitution. Comparing Lincoln to Charles I and accusing him of political partisanship, Marble declared the president would have acted differently if the affair had involved either the *Times* or the *Tribune.* Referring darkly to Howard's membership in the church of Henry Ward Beecher and to his association with the Republican press, he suggested the whole business might, indeed, have been a conspiracy—of Republican manufacture. "For the purpose of gratifying an ignoble partisan resentment," he accused the president, "you have struck down the rights of the press, you have violated personal liberty, subjected property to unjust seizure, ostentatiously placed force above law . . . and thus, and by attempting to crush the organs of free discussion, have striven to make free elections impossible, and break down all the safeguards of representative government."

It was an able campaign document, and the Society for the Diffusion of Political Knowledge included it in the Democracy's campaign handbook. Once he had completed his work for press and party, Marble traveled to Rochester, where on May 25 he and Delia at last became husband and wife.[39]

It is impossible to estimate the effect of the suppression upon the presidential campaign. One of its definite results, however, was to strain relations between Marble and Governor Seymour. Ever since the *World* had become associated with the Democracy, the two had been cool toward one another. Marble never spoke of Seymour with the warmth he bestowed upon Barlow, McClellan, or later, Samuel J. Tilden. His notes to the governor were always perfunctory and lacking in the wit and charm so characteristic of his personal correspondence. It also appears that Seymour reciprocated Marble's feelings. At one time he even went so far as to accuse Marble of misrepresenting him in the press.[40]

Because Marble considered the suppression of the *World* an assault upon his honor, he demanded that Seymour take strong measures on his behalf. When the governor waited four days before entering the controversy, Marble became furious. "Can the chief magistrate of the State of New York be relied upon to support by all the power necessary to accomplish the result, the proper legal measures to restore to us the possession and use of our property?" he demanded. "This is the plain question. Will you give it a plain answer?" Seymour's friends assured Marble that he would, and the governor himself answered by instructing District Attorney A. Oakey Hall to lay the case before the Grand Jury. When the jury refused even to investigate the affair, Marble was outraged. He then declared that Seymour should have ordered the state militia to remove the federal troops from the *World*. Instead, the governor had not acted, and Marble had been forced to obtain help from "Republican influences" to have them withdrawn. In fact, Marble charged, the governor had *consistently* failed to protect individual rights from federal suppression.[41]

Clearly, Marble's case was weak. Although Seymour had acted slowly, he had taken the proper course in appealing to law rather than to armed force. With the draft riots still a fresh memory and

Republican charges of Democratic treason and disloyalty appearing in the press almost daily, a clash between state militia and federal troops would have been political suicide. Moreover, though Seymour had done little to revoke the arrest order or to remove the troops, Marble had not done much himself. Barlow's account, which shows that the order had been revoked before he, Marble, and Prime arrived at Dix's headquarters, suggests that Marble owed his freedom less to his own efforts than to a Republican change of heart. Because, however, Marble identified freedom of the press with freedom for his personal ambition, he could not tolerate even the slightest hesitancy or circumspection on the governor's part.

Thus at a time when the Democracy sorely needed unity for the coming presidential election, Marble allowed his personal ambition to create a rift between him and Seymour. This was especially unfortunate, since the unsatisfactory progress of the Union forces in the Confederacy had given new momentum to the peace men, who were threatening to split the party wide open unless their principles were adopted. The reappearance of Vallandigham had also provided the peace movement with dramatic and vigorous leadership that promised trouble for the McClellan forces at the national convention.

During the summer Marble's suspicions of the Regency leadership grew as it appeared that the Albany men were leaning toward the peace camp. With a McClellan delegation to the national convention already selected, with peace sentiment growing among the upstate Democracy, and with Fernando Wood threatening to split the party, the Albany leaders decided to conciliate the peace men. The first evidence of their policy appeared late in June, when they supported a proposal to postpone the national convention from July 4 to August 29. The peace men had favored the postponement, hoping that the military stalemate would cause a rise in peace sentiment throughout the country. While rejecting this belief, the Regency leaders did hope that the military situation would alienate public opinion from the administration and would widen the split in the Republican party. Thus they tried to rationalize that the postponement would be of no value to the peace men. From Albany, William Cassidy reported to Marble that "the peace men had little or nothing to do with the decision" to postpone.[42]

Marble and his friends strongly opposed the postponement. Barlow feared the postponement would "lose much valuable time" and would give Vallandigham an opportunity to cause "serious trouble." McClellan, always suspicious of anything suggesting a political deal, feared that "the managers" were about to sell him out to the peace men. When he learned of the decision to postpone, he was so disgusted that he thought of withdrawing from the race altogether.[43]

Events quickly proved that Marble and his friends had the better foresight. Capitalizing on the delay, the peace men launched a determined offensive. While Marble, Barlow, and McClellan watched in horror, Vallandigham and Wood openly campaigned for peace before large, enthusiastic crowds. By the middle of August, peace sentiment had grown so strikingly that the *Argus* seemed on the verge of embracing the movement. By the time the convention assembled, McClellan was being beseiged by requests that he make some public concession to the peace men. Fighting for his political life in Ohio, S. S. Cox suggested that McClellan come out for "peace and union" and remain silent on the desirability of continuing the war.

In the midst of such pressures, Marble remained constant in his opposition to the peace men. When Fernando Wood assembled a large peace convention in Syracuse on August 18, the *World* condemned the meeting and claimed that the Democracy was still united against the peace faction. In his private correspondence, Marble declared to an interested stranger from Wisconsin that "the Chicago Convention will make a fatal error if any part of its platform shall in such wise declare for peace as to cripple the hands of the administration we hope to elect either in making war or negotiating peace."[44]

While they were fighting the assaults of the peace men, Marble and the Regency were busily preparing a strategy to defeat them in the convention. By the time the convention assembled, they had laid plans to grant them as little as possible while still maintaining party unity. Their strategy called for nominating McClellan for president and a border state representative, such as James Guthrie of Kentucky, for vice-president, thus securing a ticket that would stand for a vigorous prosecution of the war. To keep the party united, the platform would ignore the peace issue entirely and make reunion the rallying cry.[45]

Although not an official delegate, Marble accompanied the New York delegation to Chicago. Upon arriving, he quickly ascertained the forces at work. The convention favored McClellan's nomination, but a split in the Kentucky delegation made Guthrie's nomination doubtful. The perfidious Seymour seemed to be courting the peace men, perhaps in hopes that he might receive the nomination himself. Realizing that Seymour might thus cause trouble in the New York delegation, Marble wired Barlow to ask whether McClellan still wished to put up a fight. When Barlow's reply was delayed, he wired excitedly, "I can't believe you such a damned fool as to suppose I spoke of myself otherwise than as representing Richmond and Tilden—I tell you that every other card will be needed today and tomorrow." Barlow at once replied, telling Marble to keep up the fight for McClellan and reminding him to keep his temper.[46]

Despite the determined efforts of the peace men, it soon became evident that nothing could prevent McClellan's nomination. Accepting the inevitable, Seymour withdrew his name and the movement behind him collapsed. Two days before the convention assembled,

Marble assured Barlow that McClellan's nomination was certain. Delighted, Barlow told the general: "It is plain to me that but for Richmond, Tilden, and Marble, the peace men, the Lincoln men, and Seymour men, would have had it all their own way." He concluded, "As it stands now, if we win, we win everything."[47]

Barlow was overoptimistic. As Marble predicted, McClellan received the nomination, but the peace men included the famous "war failure" plank in the platform and nominated Vallandigham's associate, George H. Pendleton, for vice-president. Although Marble took no part in writing the platform, he reported the heated fight between the war and peace factions on the committee and predicted "result probably against us." At the time, however, the platform did not concern the McClellan men so much as the nomination of Pendleton. Before the balloting for vice-president had begun, John Douglas told Marble that he thought the ticket and the platform "perfect." As the balloting progressed, however, it became apparent that it would be impossible to nominate a war Democrat. The peace men skillfully used McClellan's 1861 order suspending the Maryland state legislature to keep the Northwest from supporting Guthrie and then pressured the easterners into accepting Pendleton. The vice-presidential nomination so horrified Richmond and Tilden that they declared McClellan ought to resign from the ticket.[48]

But that would not do; so it was decided that McClellan would counter the force of the peace men's victory in his letter accepting the nomination. In such an enterprise, the general, unskilled in the techniques of intraparty warfare, needed all the help he could get. He conferred with Marble and his other New York friends and changed his mind three times before accepting a final formula. The final draft, of course, followed the lines of the platform Marble and Barlow had hoped the Democracy would adopt at Chicago. It called for the party to stand fast for the Union and to subordinate questions of peace or war to that end. Marble praised it as "exactly right."[49]

The campaign gave Marble his first practical experience in party administration. Too new to the game to take part in forming policy, he worked with the Central Campaign Committee distributing campaign literature. He helped establish a special committee of prominent Democrats to attend to fund-raising, newspaper commentary, legal problems, public speakers, soldier voting, and to recruiting a special detective force "for obvious reasons and purposes." He also cleared requests for funds and speakers and kept track of the various disbursements required. It was a demanding job, requiring constant attention to detail, and as usual, he wore himself out performing it.[50]

He also took time to defend his honor. In the midst of the campaign, a Republican journal in Albany printed a series of articles pointing out his Republican past and charging him with failing to repay the loans that had sent him through college. When he learned of the articles, he drafted a letter for John F. Rathbone to issue in his defense. Skirting the issue of his political allegiances, he declared that from his earliest days his political opinions had "tended to a fixed, perhaps an excessive, conservatism," which he had not changed. Reviewing his career with the *World,* he noted that he had saved the paper from bankruptcy "two or three times," and that when all his former supporters had given up, he persevered until he had "built up the *World* into the leading and powerful organ of a great party." As for the loan, it had long since been paid back with interest. If the letter exaggerated a bit and was somewhat false to the facts, it was at least true to its author's ambition. It revealed for all to see the new elements in his conception of noble manhood.[51]

So for Marble the campaign was strenuous, exciting, and as for all the Democracy, unsuccessful. Following the election, he retired to Newport to rest and to reflect a moment or two on his experience. In the thirty-first year of his life and the second of his political apprenticeship, he still felt the need to think through events and to interpret their significance. Instead of addressing his remarks to Dr. Anderson, he now addressed them to McClellan: the candidate was replacing the teacher.

"It is hardly possible that one who takes politics so much to heart as I do," Marble began, "should permit our defeat last Tuesday to sever silently the intimate political relations of the previous months." Passing lightly over the lost contracts and patronage, he declared that he would make no "sinister allusions . . . to your conduct in exciting my hopes with a contingent promise of the keepership of the Montauk Light-House, already promised explicitly to both Barlow and Prime." For him the significance of the election lay in the principles it affirmed. It showed, he believed, that it would be difficult to restore constitutional government in the North, "because the North in its secret soul is still stubborn and stiff-necked in its refusal of constitutional rights to those who saw its temper and sought a lawless and wicked remedy." Here lay the explanation for the Democratic defeat. Without a change of heart by the North, even a victory would have been "transient, temporary, and lacking in all that made success worthy to be fought for, or worthy to be won." He refused to despair for the Republic, but neither could he hope.

Still, he hoped that McClellan would take from the contest at least one important consolation. "No man ever had truer friends than you have, General, or firmer to do and dare. You cannot point to any flinching anywhere, General, among us. . . . You have found them game to the last—all the same *impavidi*." Thus he assured the candidate that "so long as I conduct a public journal or participate in political affairs it will be a solid satisfaction and source of pride for me, to remember that my earliest responsible direction of the *World* was marked by the record of your achievements in the Peninsular campaign, and by battles with the enemy in your rear; to have advocated the election to the Presidency (my first advocacy); and to have cast my ballot (my first vote) for you, to whom my esteem goes hand in hand with an affectionate regard."[52]

It was a notable statement, if only because it showed that for all his commitments to the world of affairs and men, Marble had not yet strayed far from that youthful moment of idealism in the Boston Athenaeum. ✣

CHAPTER FIVE

Two Barnburner Elections

MARBLE'S POLITICAL APPRENTICESHIP continued through 1865 and 1866. His first two years in the Democracy had taught him the inner workings of his party. He had met its leaders, learned of its factions, witnessed its procedures, and participated in running its machinery. It remained for him to experience negotiations with the enemy as the Democracy strove to recruit sufficient Republican support to regain its prewar ascendancy. The political complexities of the postwar years afforded ample opportunity for such negotiations. Once he had learned that art, his party would have taught him all it could, and he would be on his own.

When the war ended, there was little doubt as to Marble's position on reconstruction. As he declared in his postelection letter to McClellan, he favored a generous and speedy restoration of the Union. Throughout the war, the *World* had also supported such a policy. It was largely because of this that the paper consistently opposed emancipation. According to the *World,* emancipation would both prolong the war and complicate the peace. Pointing out in 1863 that the national government lacked proper constitutional authority to free the slaves, it predicted that emancipation could be carried out only by treating the South as conquered territory. But both international law and custom, it declared, accorded the national government no such authority. In a civil war the victor was required to abide by the terms of the existing Constitution, which in this case prohibited tampering with the rights of private property. For the national government to act otherwise, it would have to assume that the southern states had in fact seceded from the Union and were thus no longer protected by the guarantees of the Constitution. Since the national government refused to assume this, it would have to restore the southern states to the Union without emancipating their slaves. Indeed, the *World* declared, once the war had ended it would be necessary for the national government only to grant pardons and amnesty to the leaders of the rebellion. Since the North's great aim was to restore the Union as quickly as possible, the national government would have to be generous with its pardons.[1]

The *World*'s arguments placed the Democracy on strong ground legally and politically. While offering a consistent rationale for its traditional principles of states rights, they also appealed to conservative Republicans who supported a vigorous prosecution of the war and opposed emancipation. They were not, however, foolproof, as became quite evident when the Republican party proposed to abolish slavery by amending the Constitution.

The Democracy found the Thirteenth Amendment a perplexing issue. When the amendment was introduced in the spring of 1864, the Democratic minority in the House of Representatives succeeded in delaying its consideration until after the fall elections. When Congress reassembled in December, however, the situation was, if anything, worse. The Lincoln administration, wholly committed to the amendment, had won reelection, indicating that opposition might bring political annihilation. Also, Secretary Seward had organized a powerful lobby to pressure recalcitrant Democrats into supporting the amendment. At the same time it appeared that emancipation was rapidly becoming an accomplished fact. In the Confederacy, advancing northern armies were leaving freedmen in their wake, and reports were circulating that Jefferson Davis had decided to free the remaining slaves in order to use them in military service. Thus it was beginning to appear that emancipation could no longer be considered a vindictive or Radical measure. But if the forces supporting emancipation were strong, so were the forces opposing it. In Congress the peace men, led by Fernando Wood and George Pendleton, declared they would never vote for the amendment, and their sentiments echoed in the copperhead press. Such sentiments, expressed by a faction that had proved so formidable in the recent national convention, could not be ignored.[2]

To some Democrats it seemed that the best way to deal with the situation would be to support the amendment in order to eliminate the issue from politics. Such a course would allow the party to accept the inevitable death of slavery, while leaving it free to develop other issues for the future. S. S. Cox, a war Democrat serving as a lame-duck representative from Ohio, put the question squarely to Marble: "Would you make judgment by default against states in rebellion flagrant—by voting the constitutional amendment abolishing slavery; or would you for party purposes now, vote to *eliminate* the slavery question out of our politics for the purpose of future success?"[3]

Marble believed that emancipation could still serve as a viable issue for the Democracy. In its editorials on the amendment, the *World* declared the party's "antecedents and associations, as well as its respect for the Constitution as it stands" forbade its becoming an abolition party. It could neither support an amendment that deprived the states of their traditional control over their domestic institutions nor could it favor any policy that would merely prolong the war and forestall a speedy restoration of the Union. Indeed, it believed restoration would be hastened if the administration promised to protect slavery once the fighting had stopped.

The *World,* however, was by no means consistent in its views. Although it opposed the amendment, it declared that the Democracy despised slavery and that the war had so damaged the institution as to assure its eventual collapse. Marble hoped to have the issue both ways: on the one hand favoring the end of slavery and on the other opposing the Republican method of accomplishing it. Such a formula was well calculated for the moment. In keeping with the traditional conservative hope that emancipation would come about through "natural forces" rather than governmental coercion, it offered antislavery Republicans a reason for leaving their party without abandoning their opposition to slavery. Thus while opposing the amendment, the *World* could also declare that emancipation could no longer be an issue between the parties.[4]

But even such clever strategy as this could prove dangerous, for it gave the peace men an opportunity to capitalize on the issue. Using the Democracy's hesitancy to support the amendment as their chance to dramatize their party leadership, the peace men launched an all-out attack on the amendment. In the House, Fernando Wood and George Pendleton denounced the amendment as an attempt to wipe away the divine distinction between the white and black races and denied that Congress possessed the authority to approve any constitutional amendment interfering with the internal affairs of the states.

The issue thus reintroduced the intraparty factionalism that had proved so demoralizing for the past two years. As usual the Regency wanted no part of the fight. As early as December 20, Dean Richmond and Horatio Seymour promised one of Seward's lobbyists not to advise Democratic representatives to oppose the amendment. On January 23 Richmond suggested to Marble that the party would do well to leave the question alone and to allow "each member of Congress to vote according to his own disposition." He declared, "There is reason to apprehend that the peace men may undertake to make difficulty on this question, and as the party is not yet worked up to comprehend that slavery cannot long be an element in politics, the safest way would be to keep as clear as possible of it."[5]

S. S. Cox was reaching similar conclusions. On January 13 he reported to Marble that attacks by the peace men on both the amendment and the war Democrats had made it impossible to kill the amendment with a quiet vote. Indeed, the copperhead offensive had almost convinced Cox that it would be "best to vote for the thing as it stands." He asked Marble, "What object have I, or you, looking to the near future, as well as the remote—in being tied to this body of death?"[6]

Such advice had its effect. On January 17 the *World* replied to the peace men by upholding the power of Congress to abolish slavery by constitutional amendment. On January 26 one of Seward's confidants reported to his chief that Marble had promised to write an article declaring that the amendment was not to be considered a test of party loyalty. Although the article never appeared, the *World* did at least remain silent on the question, thus implying that Democratic representatives could vote as they chose. The article probably never appeared because to the end Marble opposed the amendment. Just after its passage, Cox, who had voted in the negative, declared that a letter from Marble had arrived "just in time to settle the effervescence of my mind" on the question. Nevertheless, the *World*'s silence had shown that the young editor had learned one of the basic lessons of party journalism.[7]

With the emancipation question settled, Marble hoped the Democracy would rebuild its fortunes upon its traditional economic principles. During the debate on the Thirteenth Amendment, the *World* campaigned to reduce the national debt, to eliminate the greenbacks, and to abolish the protective tariff. Immediately following the passage of the amendment, it declared, "the sun of liberty is set; we must now light up the candles of industry and commerce." Upon these principles the Democracy should stand fast.[8]

But such principles could prove valuable only in the proper political context, and in the months following the end of the war and the death of Lincoln that context was confused and volatile. Factions within both parties began drives to reorganize the major parties. In New York the Regency sought to win the support of President Andrew Johnson and dissident Republicans. The Regency also hoped to isolate the peace men, effect a generous peace with the South, and with the help of grateful southern votes build a coalition that would dominate national politics for the long future. Such a course involved many complex and delicate decisions. The forming of alliances was especially tricky. How far could the Regency afford to go in supporting the new president without placing itself entirely in his hands? What groups in the Republican coalition should it attempt to attract, and what issues would be most appealing? Throughout 1865 and 1866, the Regency struggled to make the right choices, and when the ballots had been counted, found it had made the wrong ones.[9]

In the spring and summer of 1865 the Regency watched Andrew Johnson closely to see if his actions merited its support. Johnson had just assumed the presidency when Barlow opened negotiations with Montgomery Blair, Lincoln's one-time postmaster general and a conservative Republican, who was attempting to recoup his political fortunes by building a Johnson party. During the negotiations Barlow let Blair know that the Regency would support the president if Johnson would liquidate military rule in the South, allow the southern states to decide questions of Negro suffrage and civil rights for themselves, and defend the right of the southern states to the earliest possible representation in Congress. By September the negotiations had progressed so satisfactorily that Tilden could pay the president a personal visit and Barlow could report that Johnson "promises all that we could ask." Although the exact nature of the presidential promises is unclear, they were sufficient to convince the Regency that Andrew Johnson was worth supporting.[10]

The agreement between Johnson and the Regency was reached on the eve of the Democratic State Convention. By the time the delegates assembled in Albany, everything was prepared to place the New York Democracy squarely behind the president and to bid for the support of conservative Republicans. The Regency's first step was to exclude Wood's peace faction from the proceedings. Then the convention adopted resolutions, which had been drafted in the *World*'s offices following Tilden's conference with Johnson, endorsing the president's reconstruction policy, applauding the death of slavery, and calling for a speedy restoration of the Union. Traditional Democratic principles appeared in the resolutions supporting states rights and the obligation of the national government to pay off the national debt.

The Regency's nominations for state offices also showed how it hoped to build a majority coalition behind the president. Heading the ticket as the nominee for secretary of state was Henry W. Slocum, a conservative Republican. War Democrats, who had cooperated with the Republican party during the war, were accorded the nominations of John Van Buren for attorney general, Lucius Robinson for comptroller, and Martin Grover for the court of appeals. The ticket was thus designed to appeal primarily to former Democrats and secondarily to dissatisfied conservative Republicans. That fall, however, the conservative Republicans were far from dissatisfied. Instead of accepting the Democracy's invitation for an alliance, Thurlow Weed skillfully maneuvered himself into the leadership of a Republican State Convention that adopted resolutions and nominated candidates almost identical to those of the Democracy. Speaking for the conservative Republicans, the *New York Times* denounced the Democratic convention as a "Falstaffian assumption of magnanimity—this cheap virtue of dropping all scandalous by-gones for the public good." Making the best of a disappointing situation, the *World* claimed that "the Republicans are checkmated."[11]

One Republican journal, however, had nothing but praise for the Albany convention. The *Evening Post* complimented the Democracy on its wise course. "They let the dead bury the dead," the *Post* declared, "they cut loose from the two-faced policy of Seymour; they heartily take the war and its debt upon their shoulders; and they nominate for candidates men who have been either distinguished in the war, like General Slocum and Patrick, or distinguished for their loyal support of the war, like Robinson and Grover."[12]

The *Post*'s statements must have heartened the Regency, since the journal spoke for the important "Barnburner" faction. In the 1840s the Barnburners had emerged as a significant group within the Democratic party. At that time they represented the party's radical wing, led by Martin Van Buren and Silas Wright. Others prominent in its ranks were John Van Buren, John Bigelow, William Cullen Bryant, John A. Dix, Preston King, David Dudley Field, and Samuel J. Tilden. Ideologically, the Barnburners considered themselves the true heirs of the plain republicanism of Jefferson and Jackson. Dedicated first and last to individual freedom, they opposed special privilege and corporate power in all its forms. Although especially concerned about limiting the activities and powers of government, they also lent their energies to such causes as free trade and antislavery. They formed the backbone of Martin Van Buren's Free Soil Party in 1848, and many were among the early supporters of the Republican party.[13]

In 1865 the Barnburners still considered themselves the true Democrats. Only they had remained faithful to the party's principles by opposing the expansion of slavery and supporting emancipation. They still clung to the old Democratic faith that government and society existed only to protect the rights of the individual citizen. Speaking for the Barnburners in 1865, the *Post* summed up this philosophy, which it named "the rights of man":

> It means that every man has a natural right to the free and unobstructed development of his capacities; a right to the unrestricted expression of his thought and the genial exercise of his affections; a right to labor when and where he pleases, or to pursue happiness according to his own conceptions of happiness; and a right to participate in all the blessings and opportunities of an orderly social state, and in the direction of those of its powers which affect his own destiny. In other words, free thought, free speech, free action, and free and equal political institutions are his imprescriptible inheritance, which no government has a right to take away, but which every government is bound to secure and protect. These rights, indeed, are above all government, being the end for which it is the means, the object which alone sanctions the existence of government, the prime purpose for which institutions are formed, and society itself exists.[14]

It appeared, then, that the Barnburners had differed with the Regency chiefly on matters of principle. Now, however, since the Regency seemed willing to renounce the peace men and to accept emancipation, they could find little to prevent their reuniting with their old comrades. Indeed, there was much in the Regency's program they could heartily endorse. The Albany convention's resolutions favoring free trade and the payment of the national debt drew upon the great principles of Jeffersonian economic thought; its support of states rights and civil liberties drew upon the Jeffersonian political philosophy. To many it appeared that there was about to be a reunion between the two factions. On the day the *Post* acclaimed the Albany convention, the *Herald* shrewdly observed that "there are strong indications of a return to the Democratic fold of all those Silas Wright, Barnburner and Freesoil Democrats who a few years since went over to the Republican party. It looks very much like the commencement of a reunion of old associates, long separated, and a reconstruction of the party from one end of the state to the other."[15]

During the campaign the *World* shaped the issues to appeal to Barnburner principles. The economic, political, and constitutional aspects of reconstruction, it argued, were interrelated. The national government's first obligation was to pay off the national debt. So long as the government kept troops in the South and thus prevented a restoration of the Union, northern capital would not be invested in southern development. Without such investment, the southern economy would languish. And until prosperity returned to the South, the government could never raise sufficient revenue to pay off the debt. Thus only when the federal troops were withdrawn could the country return to plain, economical government.

In his letter accepting the nomination for comptroller, the former Barnburner Lucius Robinson also appealed to his former allies to return to the Democracy. Noting that opposition to slavery had been the only issue uniting the Barnburners and the antislavery Whigs, Robinson emphasized that the two groups had "differed radically upon most other questions of government and especially upon those of finance, public economy, and legislative purity." Now that slavery was dead, the cause for the alliance had disappeared, and the existing Republican party should be dissolved. Indeed, Robinson declared, on the remaining issues of states rights, economy in government, and payment of the debt he had no faith in a Republican party led by Thurlow Weed. "Those who are aware of his notorious lobby operations and the manner in which he has enriched himself whilst the country was bleeding at every pore," he declared of Weed, "can judge the propriety of clothing him with all power." When it published Robinson's letter, the *World* emphasized its own agreement and added that "all who have ever been intelligent enough to be Democrats from principle, must see that the old Democratic doctrines were never so applicable as now; and as the slavery issue is obsolete, the time has fully come for fulfilling the pledge made by the Free-Soil Democrats nine years ago."[16]

Despite such efforts, the *Evening Post* refused to endorse the

Democratic ticket, and as the campaign wore on, turned strongly against the Democracy. The *Post*'s attitude showed the shortcomings of the Regency's appeal and illuminated the central issues of the reconstruction controversy.

When Robinson's letter appeared, the *Post* decided to put the Regency to the test. Charging that the Democracy was "even more retrograde and conservative of evil now than it was in 1856," it called upon the party to testify to its purity on the two great issues of the hour. First, did the party approve of the Thirteenth Amendment, "the grand closing act of the war?" Second, did it "in obedience to the whole drift and pressure of democratic doctrine, instinct, and feeling, favor impartial and equal suffrage, not as a federal imposition, nor in states where it has no power to act, but in states where it can and may act with perfect propriety?"[17]

The queries showed how little ground actually existed for an alliance between the Barnburners and the Regency. In emphasizing states rights and economic policy, the Regency had evaded, so far as the Barnburners were concerned, the crucial issues of reconstruction. True, the Regency had accepted the Thirteenth Amendment and had even urged the southern states to ratify it in order to be restored to the Union as rapidly as possible. But on the question of Negro suffrage the two were diametrically opposed. On the very day the *Post* raised its queries, the *World* published a blistering attack upon Negro suffrage. Declaring that Negro rule in Haiti and Jamaica had brought only chaos and poverty, the *World* charged that only the ignorant, vengeful, or politically corrupt advocated the principle. Earlier it had quoted approvingly the statements of Governor Perry of South Carolina that " 'this is a white man's government, and intended for white men only.' " It was small wonder, then, that as election day neared, the *Post* could only conclude that the Democracy's "newspaper organs are still filled with the old virus of pro-slaveryism. Forgetting few of their old prejudices, they learn little from the progress of events."[18]

While the *Post* could not endorse the Democracy, it found itself uncomfortable within the Republican party. The Barnburner distrust of Seward and Weed stretched back many years, and the coming of peace had done little to set it to rest. "You know," wrote David Dudley Field to James R. Doolittle in 1866, "the extreme repugnance which the *barnburners* of this state have to Mr. Seward; a repugnance which I doubt if it is possible to overcome." The Radical Republicans were only slightly more attractive. Although the Barnburners agreed with the Radical stand on Negro suffrage, they were horrified by the Radical desire to impose suffrage by federal force and by most of the Radical economic program. It was not surprising, therefore, that throughout the campaign the *Post* called for a reorganization of the parties.[19]

As the election approached, the party system in New York contained three major groups: the Democracy under Regency leadership, the Republicans under Seward and Weed, and the Barnburners under the guide of the *Evening Post.* Unwilling to give up its principles, each group turned its attention toward Andrew Johnson. If the factions could not agree with one another, they might gain a decisive advantage by winning the support of the president. During the campaign, however, Johnson refused to commit himself. Each faction attempted to interpret the president's actions to suit its own interests. When the president addressed a group of Negro militiamen, the Radical *Tribune* pictured him as committing the federal government to helping the freedmen attain full citizenship. The *Post* viewed him as endorsing the principles of human equality. The *World* saw him as condescending to an inferior race. Each gave the president's speech high praise.[20]

As it turned out, the election itself settled little. Although the Republican ticket carried the state with a majority of 27,000 votes, it had little opportunity to capitalize on its victory. For within four months Johnson's veto of the Freedman's Bureau Bill had shaken the political alignments more forcefully, causing yet another faction to emerge in New York. Now the Radicals, led by Greeley's *Tribune,* appeared. Thus was shattered the victorious Republican coalition of radicals and conservatives. In this context, the politicians returned to the building of new alliances.[21]

While the Regency coaxed Johnson along, the *World* outlined its larger strategy. The Regency ultimately hoped for a rupture between the president and the Republican majority in Congress. Once that had occurred, Johnson would naturally gravitate toward the Democracy, taking some of his Republican supporters with him. To encourage such an outcome, the *World* freely predicted a clash between the president and Congress and played up any evidence of friction. When the House passed a bill granting a limited Negro suffrage in the District of Columbia, it commented that "if the Republican party wishes to insult the President, it was no business of the Democrats to enable them to . . . palliate the insult." Lest the Republicans realize the Regency's plan and unite against the president, it pretended that the Democracy was seeking no advantage from the controversy. The Democracy, it claimed, sought no favors from the president and no alliances with disaffected Republicans. "The Democracy is opposed to every coalition, either with the President, or with any portion of the party that elected him." Following Johnson's veto of the Freedman's Bureau Bill, however, it pointed out that "Mr. Johnson never pretended to be anything but a Union Democrat" and predicted that "the same class of voters to whom [the Republicans] appealed in nominating him for Vice-President, will follow his political fortunes." A few days later, it observed that "there is opened before the so-called conservative Republicans the most encouraging prospect ever offered a political minority."[22]

But not all conservative Republicans were welcome. The Regency especially distrusted the followers of Seward and Weed. Many times the Regency had been victimized by Seward-Weed maneuvers, one as recently as 1864, when Weed had formed an alliance and then welched on it. A similarly long-standing hostility between Seward-Weed and the Barnburners also ruled out any effort to attract both to the Regency camp. The previous October, Barlow had urged Johnson to divorce himself from Seward and Weed so the Regency could ally with the "Radicals," who were the men of "real brains and power in the State" and who were "sound on the great questions of popular government; of civil liberty; of responsibility of the President and his Cabinet for unlawful assumption of power." Barlow also warned that the South would never accept a party containing the secretary of state and his followers.[23]

It was in the service of this strategy that Marble was called upon to advise the president on an important matter of patronage. Since October 1865 the office of collector of the port of New York had lain vacant. Until Johnson's veto of the Freedman's Bureau Bill, the Regency men had urged the president to fill the post with one of their number. After the veto, however, when it appeared that the president was moving toward their position, they counseled him to appoint "his own man." On March 10 Samuel J. Tilden and Marble wrote to Montgomery Blair, explaining their position. They both argued strongly against Johnson's appointing a Seward-Weed Republican. Declaring that "more than three-fourths" of the Republican organization in New York opposed the president, Tilden warned Johnson not to rely upon that party for support. Instead "the President must appeal to the *whole people*" by appointing someone who would support him regardless of party. Nor would it do for the president to appoint a Seward-Weed Republican in hopes that some alliance might be forged between that faction and the Democracy. It would be the "height of folly," said Marble, for the president to give the collectorship to "mere traffickers in office . . . who are as far from being able to consolidate the Republican party in his support, as they are from being able to persuade the Democratic party into cooperation with them." A month later Johnson followed the advice by nominating for the office the politically neutral Henry A. Smythe.[24]

With the president thus placed above the factional turmoil, the Regency men turned to building an organization to support him. The National Union Convention, which assembled August 14 in Philadelphia, was the product of their labors. The convention sought not only to reconcile northern conservatives with southern unionists but also, and more importantly, to reconcile Barnburners, conservative Republicans, and regular Democrats. The appointment of conservative Republican James R. Doolittle of Wisconsin as president of the convention and Barnburner John A. Dix as temporary chairman symbolized the effort, while behind the scenes Dean Richmond, Montgomery Blair, and Samuel J. Tilden worked to secure the Regency's influence. To complement this movement on the state level, Richmond and Weed arranged to combine forces in a Union Convention, which would nominate Johnson candidates for state offices.[25]

Although many hailed the National Union movement as an effort to construct a new party, it was clear that the Regency had no such idea. These men merely sought accessions to their own organization. As the correspondence of prominent Democrats makes clear, the Regency allowed the conservative Republicans to appear to lead the movement, but only so that they might increase the gulf between the conservative Republicans and the Radicals. After the organization had been completed, they aimed to be sure that, as Fitz-John Porter declared, "democratic principles would rule."[26]

Ill health prevented Marble from attending the Philadelphia convention, but after an initial hesitation, the *World* gave the meeting its hearty endorsement. No sooner had the meeting adjourned than Marble and his friends were hard at work trying to carry its principles into effect. From the beginning they considered the Barnburners their most important problem. During the summer the *Post* had shown itself willing to be enticed from the Republican party. On July 25 the *Post* openly declared its opposition to Republican efforts to increase the power of the central government. "They have aimed to leave nothing to the states," it declared, "nothing to that local government which is our greatest safeguard against despotism. They will make of the federal government, if they have their way, as overshadowing and all-devouring a monster as the government of Napoleon is in France." Also, the *Post* had greeted the Philadelphia convention as a sign that "northern and southern secessionists" were at last willing to recant their past errors.

But the hope that the *Post* gave in one sentence it took away in the next. The convention, it declared, "may not be of the slightest use to the Democratic party. That party, if it wishes to rule the country, must not depend upon Philadelphia conventions; it must depend upon the enunciation and defense of sound and liberal principles . . . if it defends the rights of every man freely to speak, to labor, and to trade, everywhere, it will compel victory—because it will deserve it." At the same time other Barnburners were expressing private doubts about the Philadelphia convention. "In talking with our people about the Phila. convention," David Dudley Field reported, "I am met with this objection; it is a Seward and Weed concern; or Seward and Weed are getting it up; or, if we go into it, we shall have to bear all the odium of those names, whether they actually control the movement or not."

Thus as the state convention approached, the Barnburners remained unconvinced of the need for the proposed alliance. August 25 found Barlow writing frantically to Smythe to arrange his patronage in such a way as to reconcile the conservative Republicans and the Barnburners, "where two-thirds of our strength is to be found." "What an easy fight we would have both to put the party in power and to reform it," John Van Buren wrote to Tilden on August 31, "if only those *Evening Post* Barnburners would come back and take the lead."[27]

It was at this critical juncture that fate dealt the Regency a lethal blow. On August 25 Dean Richmond, who had taken the lead in negotiating the alliances, died at Tilden's home in Gramercy Park. "He breathed once or twice very softly and very slow—and then—it was all over," reported William Henry Hurlbert to Marble. "I never saw a more quiet death." That moment of quiet, however, vanished at once, as the living, leaderless Regency sought desperately to effect a consistent policy. Richmond, it seems, had died without telling anyone of his plans for the convention, not even mentioning the name of the gubernatorial candidate. In the two weeks between his death and the opening of the convention, rumors were everywhere. Some said that Seymour and Augustus Schell, leader of the "hardshell" Democrats, had decided to support John Ganson. Others declared that Richmond and Weed had agreed on Henry C. Murphy. Others believed Murphy had no western support and that either John A. Dix or John T. Hoffman, the mayor of New York City, would be strong candidates. On August 29 Joseph Warren of Buffalo summed up the situation with masterful understatement, when he wrote Marble that Richmond's death had left the party "a little in the dark."[28]

Amid the conflicting rumors, demoralizing factionalism, and rising panic, Marble searched for a solution. By early September he had made up his mind. Believing that Johnson's controversy with Congress over admitting the southern states provided the basic issue of the campaign, he concluded that the principal task remaining was to "prevent the disintegration or demoralization of the Democratic organization." Marble believed that the task could be accomplished if the convention nominated a man "whose Democracy is as indisputable as the Sermon on the Mount." Running down the list of possible candidates, he evaluated the strengths and weaknesses of each. Hoffman and Murphy he dismissed as lacking any appeal outside the party; both were too easily associated with Tammany Hall, Hoffman lacked experience, and Murphy had achieved no public distinction. The other two prominent candidates, Sanford E. Church and John A. Dix, he found wanting on different counts. He had no specific objection to Church, a party leader for many years, but thought he would be more valuable as head of the state committee or as collector of the port, "a place which our success in November would make us demand of Mr. Johnson for him and *get*." While admitting that Dix, a former

Barnburner, would attract many Republicans to the ticket, he could not support him for personal reasons. Dix's role in suppressing the *World* left a bitter memory, and Marble was not willing "to make haste to charge him again with executing laws which but lately he trampled under foot."

Still, Marble recognized the need to attract "outside accessions," namely the Seward-Weed Republicans and the Barnburners. He thought the former's loyalty could be gained by the promise of the lieutenant governorship. The Barnburners, however, were a more difficult problem. Recognizing their importance and recalling the Regency's failure to attract them in the last election, Marble declared that "this fall we must capture all that remain." It was here, he believed, that the gubernatorial nomination became crucial.

The Democracy had to find a gubernatorial candidate who would rally the regular forces, withstand the intrigues of Seward and Weed, and win over the Barnburners. For this demanding role Marble recommended Samuel J. Tilden. Noting that Tilden's successful career as a corporation lawyer had gained him the friendship of many wealthy businessmen, Marble declared he would attract important financial contributions. Besides, Tilden's years of relative political inactivity had left him free of factional ties, making it easy for the party to unite behind him. Most important, Tilden's prewar association with the Barnburners would win over Bryant and the *Evening Post.* Emphasizing the importance of the Barnburners, Marble doubted that "anything short of the nomination of Mr. Tilden would stir them to take a vigorous part in the contest."[29]

Thus did Marble respond to the political crisis. There was a good deal of merit in his proposal. Tilden did, in fact, possess the advantages attributed to him and undoubtedly would have made a strong candidate. His candidacy would have especially attracted the *Evening Post,* since he and Bryant were close friends. Certainly there is good reason to credit Marble with a degree of political sophistication in his choice; the apprentice had learned fast. One must always wonder, however, whether the choice resulted entirely from Marble's political sophistication. For it is equally important to note that Tilden moved in the same circles of upper-class city Democrats as Marble and that the two were in the process of becoming fast friends. Indeed, in later years Marble would hold Tilden in an esteem that approached reverence. Thus it is equally possible to conclude that bewildered by the factionalism of the moment, Marble sought his answer in familiar surroundings and among his friends. And the answer that he found revealed him as not so much the master of factionalism as the victim of it. Nor did he realize, as he waited for the convention to assemble, that that factionalism had yet to run its course.[30]

The Democratic convention assembled September 11 in Albany. By that time Tilden, who had succeeded Richmond as state chairman, had worked out an arrangement with Weed whereby the two would support Dix for the nomination. Not everyone was satisfied with the arrangement, however, and the Democracy remained sufficiently divided to provide the moment of opportunity for one last faction to make itself felt. Since the elections of 1865, William M. Tweed had been looking forward to increasing his power in the Democratic party. In that year Tweed had succeeded in electing his close associate, John T. Hoffman, mayor of New York City. Hoffman's ability and popularity suggested that he might well become the first city Democrat since DeWitt Clinton to move from the mayor's office to the governor's mansion. To the ambitious Tweed it was vital that Hoffman make such a move, since under state law the state government exercised great powers over the city. Dean Richmond's death gave Tweed just the chance he needed.[31]

In the convention Tweed had an easy time. He first made a deal with the ever-accommodating Weed to divide the first two places on the ticket and then turned his Tammany toughs against the bewildered Regency. Faced with the Boss's determined cohorts, Tilden decided not to put up a fight. On the first day parliamentary juggling delayed the proceedings until Dix's supporters could be persuaded to withdraw his name. On the second day Hoffman received the nomination by acclamation. Tweed then allowed Weed's candidate, Robert H. Pruyn, to receive the nomination for lieutenant governor. The platform, in addition to reaffirming the principles of the Philadelphia convention, endorsed Tweed's demand for home rule in New York City.[32]

Nothing could have served the forces of factionalism better than the Albany proceedings. Hoffman's nomination clearly violated the spirit of compromise necessary to construct a Johnson party in the state. Once again the factions were free to consult their own best interests. The *Evening Post* was the first to decide. Deprecating the convention's partisan spirit and charging that Hoffman had cooperated with the peace men during the war, it declared that the Democracy would have to repent its past sins before it could claim public support. Then it heartily endorsed the Republican state ticket, noting that the gubernatorial candidate, Reuben H. Fenton, had been "a Barnburner Democrat, of the *Evening Post* school, brought up in the policy of Jackson and Van Buren." Throughout the campaign, the *Post* also maintained that its support of Negro suffrage had caused it to support the Republican ticket. Still it admitted its discomfort in a party that relied so much upon the power of the central government. As election day neared, the *Post* informed its readers that "we much prefer . . . a more moderate policy than some prominent Republicans advocate . . . but the country has no choice; it must declare for men who, whatever their mistakes, are at least faithful to liberty and union."[33]

It took the conservative Republicans only a little longer to come to the same decision. Although the *Times,* the spokesman for Seward and Weed in the city, gave Hoffman a guarded endorsement following the convention, it soon changed its course. On October 2 it came out wholeheartedly for the Republican ticket. By election day only Weed and a few of his followers remained loyal to the Albany ticket.[34]

For Marble, of course, there was no alternative. Never once did the *World* waver in its opposition to Negro suffrage or in its demands that the southern representatives be seated immediately in Congress. Embittered by the desertions from the conservative coalition, the journal denied that the Democracy had ever thought seriously of forming a new party—which, of course, was partly true.[35]

But not even the bravest rhetoric could cover over the feelings of disappointment and loss. That summer, even before the Philadelphia convention, such feelings had been fostered in Marble in a peculiarly savage fashion. During the commencement week meeting of the Rochester University alumni, someone proposed Marble's name for the president of the organization. Although Marble was clearly the most distinguished graduate of the university, hostility flared at the mention of his name. Amid charges that the famous editor sympathized with treason, and amid much talk of "our blood-stained heroes," his name was withdrawn. One may only guess how deeply the affair wounded the young man, who had taken so much of his ambition and so many of his values from his years at Rochester. The following year, when he authorized the alumni organization to draw upon him for whatever sum was necessary to complete the memorial to the university's Civil War dead, he requested that his name not be considered for any office in the organization. When the alumni, "unanimously and by acclamation," chose him to be their orator at the next year's commencement, he declined with curt formality.[36]

With the November elections, Marble's political apprenticeship came to an end. During the four years of his training, he had acquainted himself thoroughly with the men and the ideas that guided the New York Regency. More importantly, he had acquainted himself with the Regency's principles of party organization and operation.

Those principles were simple. They began with loyalty to the New York party, and from that all the rest followed. (1) Party unity must be maintained. Regency men were not bolters. As their dealings with the peace men revealed, they could maneuver and argue against their opponents, but would not desert them. (2) New recruits must assume a subordinate role. During its negotiations with President Johnson and its wooing of the Barnburners, the Regency had sought to strengthen itself without relinquishing its power. (3) Ideas are political weapons. Although professing an ideology of states rights, free trade, and hard money, the Regency was notably flexible when it came to specific issues. Emancipation might be bad in principle, but if it would help the party win outside recruits, it was all right. On obviously divisive issues within the party the Regency was usually willing to say nothing. If peace was divisive, it should be left out. The party should proclaim only what all its factions could agree to. Unity was the important thing, and unity was obtained not by debating principles but by conciliating groups. As he battled the peace men in 1863 and 1864 and sought to entice the Barnburners in 1865 and 1866, Marble learned those principles. His letter to Joseph Warren in September 1866 revealed his ability to recognize the elements of a given political situation and to propose a course of action consistent with Regency thinking.

And the man who described a politics of maneuver and party loyalty to Joseph Warren had earlier described a politics of principle and personal fidelity to George B. McClellan. Even earlier he had demonstrated the skills and attitudes of entrepreneurship. He was reaching the balanced perspective he had lacked when he first joined the *World*. If he could attain security and independence in his personal life, he would be prepared to make use of it. ❖

CHAPTER SIX

Success

A POWER such as no other journalist in America possesses," Sam Barlow wrote of Marble in 1868, "and a personal position, growing daily, but already placed beyond the reach of calumny, and which no paper can destroy or even seriously impair." Although an extravagant estimate, it was close to the truth. By that year Marble's entrepreneurial struggles had brought him rewards that came to few who ventured a career in New York politics and journalism. Wherever one looked, the signs pointed to a young man who had arrived. He was happily married and the father of two small children, a girl, Delia, and a boy, Frank. Successful in business, he was enjoying his most profitable year as editor of the *World*. He was in the process of joining the elite of New York's society by purchasing a four-story brownstone mansion on upper Fifth Avenue. Even the circles of the nation's cultural elite were opening up to him, as evidenced by an invitation from Andrew D. White to become a trustee of the newly established Cornell University. Well might the casual observer credit the report that he planned soon to retire from journalism to lead a life of gentlemanly inactivity.[1]

Marble's acceptance into New York's high society modifies the generalization that men of new wealth usually found themselves social outcasts. He dined frequently at Delmonico's, enjoyed summer holidays at Newport, patronized the opera, and surrounded himself with the artifacts of conventional upper-class taste. In 1867 John Fiske estimated Marble's library at nearly 2,500 volumes, housed in a "luxurious room." Two years later, when Fiske visited Marble in his Fifth Avenue mansion, he found the decor "magnificent." "The floors are everywhere made of varied woods, like Gordon McKay's music room," he declared, "and the book shelves in the library are supported by columns of splendid marble and *lapis lazuli;* there are also many beautiful bronze statuettes." In 1867 Marble first appeared as one of the managers of the charity ball, an affair sponsored by the *"crème de la crème"* of New York society.[2]

Marble's associations and social position established him in the "swallow-tail" wing of the city Democracy. Composed largely of wealthy merchants, bankers, and lawyers, who filled the party's coffers and dominated its national councils, the "swallow-tails," as Henry Adams observed, "played the game [of politics] for ambition and amusement" but with goals "considerably larger than those of the usual player." Their aims were principally to maintain their prominence in the nation's economic order and to keep America safe from the radicalism of western farmers, labor reformers, and the immigrant masses. During the years of Marble's rise to prominence, they succeeded reasonably well, generally controlling the state organization and holding their own in Tammany Hall, the city machine. In national politics, as the election of 1864 showed, their success was less complete. Still, they were powerful enough to be classed as part of the nation's social and political elite.[3]

Although the full social history of the swallow-tails remains to be written, an examination of twenty-three prominent members may suggest their salient characteristics. These men served on the first managing committee of the Manhattan Club, which was formed in 1865 as a Democratic counterpart to the successful Union League Club. Among the managers were most of Marble's close friends—Barlow, Belmont, Tilden, Charles O'Conor, William Butler Duncan, William C. Prime, and George Ticknor Curtis—and Marble himself. They were a remarkably homogeneous group. Their average and median age was forty-nine, and eighteen (78 percent) fell between the ages of thirty-five and fifty-five. With only one exception (Belmont) they were native born, either in New York State (52 percent) or in New England (44 percent). Like Marble, most of them had come to New York City to establish their careers. Only 26 percent had been born in the city. Not only were they native born, but they were also old stock. Twelve of the sixteen for whom information is available came from families that had first reached America in the seventeenth century. Although the evidence is less conclusive, it appears that most were born into comfortable, if not affluent, circumstances. Fourteen investigations revealed information about the father's occupation. In nine instances the father was a professional man: teacher, lawyer, physician, journalist, or minister. Three were merchants or manufacturers, one a wealthy landlord, and one a ship-captain. Whatever their occupation, however, the fathers were able to provide their sons with educational advantages. Fourteen (61 percent) of the sons had attended college and three others had attended secondary school. Not surprisingly, most had entered the professions. Sixteen (70 percent) had received legal training, and of these, thirteen had become lawyers. Two others had entered journalism, so that fifteen (66 percent) were professional men. The remaining eight held positions in banking, commerce, and industry.[4]

The typical swallow-tail leader was an old-stock, native-born

American in his late forties. Born into comfortable circumstances, he had received a good education and had left home to seek a professional career in New York City. Such a portrait omits much. It does not reveal the precise influence of family support in building their careers, nor does it describe what each faced in pursuing his goals. Nor does it reveal the truly distinctive features of the swallow-tail elite. Many New Yorkers who were not swallow-tails shared these social characteristics. What really distinguished the swallow-tails was their loyalty to the Democratic party. The value of their social portrait lies in showing the comfort and privilege that could cause them to think of themselves as an elite within their party and in showing how Manton Marble, an old-stock, well-educated, native-born New Englander who had come to the city to seek success in the profession of journalism, could be accepted as part of that elite.

It must be emphasized that the swallow-tails were a political elite. They were Democrats, heirs to Martin Van Buren's Albany Regency, and it was their duty to keep their party united, vital, and powerful. Essential to their mission, and to their identity, was party loyalty. Occasionally a swallow-tail would show flashes of independence. Following the call of the National Union Convention, August Belmont considered giving up the Democratic organization and announced that he wished "only to do what is best for the country." Edwards Pierrepont, one of the original managers of the Manhattan Club, later became attorney general in the Grant administration. And even Marble would show some party independence. But such behavior was exceptional. More characteristic were Barlow's evaluation of the National Union Convention as "merely the stepping stone to a final consolidation with the democrats," Marble's search for a "Sermon on the Mount Democrat" for the gubernatorial campaign of 1866, and Belmont's own shift from opposing Stephen A. Douglas in 1856 to supporting him in 1860. In 1874 it was enough for Tilden to refuse a loan to the *World* because the paper "did not fill the requirement of the party."[5]

Party loyalty also required the ability to maneuver. Faced with the extreme political factionalism of the 1860s, the swallow-tails had to maneuver to survive. So they maneuvered, shaping issues to suit their institutional needs, mastering the techniques of behind-the-scenes negotiation and attack. Their performance during the early years of reconstruction was typical. Confronted with a unique political problem that raised fundamental constitutional, social, and ethical questions, they responded with proposals to ally with Barnburners and conservative Republicans, to reshuffle the president's cabinet membership and patronage distribution, to eliminate the slavery issue by passing the Thirteenth Amendment, and to create a front organization, the National Union Party.

So as Henry Adams noted, the swallow-tails knew how to play the game. They were not, however, mindless organization men. Although the demands of maneuver and loyalty closely circumscribed their principles, they did not eliminate them. The swallow-tails shared certain assumptions about the good life and the means for securing it. In their philosophical moods, they extolled the freedom of the individual citizen. A good society, they believed, allowed people to decide things for themselves. Because they were lawyers, they looked to the Constitution to sustain individual freedom. By interposing the power of the individual states between the national government and the citizen, the Constitution accomplished this great purpose. "Have you ever reflected upon what it is that preserves constitutional liberty, in our internal condition," asked the noted constitutional lawyer and historian, George Ticknor Curtis, "what it is that stands as a barrier against the mere physical force of this nation, and protects the rights of minorities and sections from being crushed beneath the same power that can make itself so formidable to the external world? Beyond all question, it is the States, with their separate political rights, their local institutions, their admitted control over their domestic affairs." Whatever challenged that constitutional structure, whether it be southern secessionists or Republican centralizers, challenged individual freedom and the future of American democracy.[6]

Swallow-tail economic theory squared with its constitutional theory. Individual decision-making, unfettered by governmental interference and regulated only by the law of supply and demand, was their ideal. Aside from helping the law of supply and demand to function by enforcing the obligation of contract, guaranteeing a stable currency, and safeguarding private property and the free market, the government had little to do. It was by appealing to such ideas that the swallow-tails had hoped to entice the Barnburners back into the Democracy, believing that around such principles most good Democrats could rally.

Two Republican economic policies most agitated the swallow-tails: high taxation and paper money. During the campaign of 1868, Samuel J. Tilden attacked excessive federal taxation before a group of up-state farmers. Noting that American government had grown more costly than the imperial, despotic regimes of Europe, he called for a choice of new men and new measures. The existing system of taxation, he declared, had perverted American government from the "simple and cheap machinery" envisioned by the Founding Fathers. It had put labor in a "strait-jacket," clogged "the processes of production," repressed "invention and improvement," and encouraged dishonesty and fraud by placing "a penalty of the forfeiture of all their business upon whole classes unless they will evade the public revenue. . . . We must arrest this system, or all that has made this country great and glorious, and that has distinguished it from the empires of the Old World in the beneficent operation of our political and social system . . . will have disappeared."[7]

Paper money was no less nefarious. As university students the swallow-tails had read scholarly works that held a currency of unvarying, "intrinsic" value to be a prerequisite of economic progress, condemned issues of irredeemable paper money as immoral evasions of just obligations, and denounced greenbackers as "charlatans and quacks." As life-long Democrats, many of them had learned to honor the "hard money" ideology that had inspired Andrew Jackson's anti-bank animus. They believed that like high taxation, irredeemable paper money taxed the productivity of capital, robbed the laborer of his due reward, and turned the economy over to unscrupulous speculators in paper values. As residents of New York City and close friends of its business leaders, they were outraged by a monetary system that increased the risks of doing business in the nation's commercial and financial capital.[8]

As the 1860s wore on, the swallow-tails saw their ideas come under increasingly heavy attack. Faced with a Republican party that raised tariff rates, issued multitudes of greenbacks, suppressed their newspapers by military force, and sought to employ Negro votes to overwhelm their planter allies, with William M. Tweed and his hoards of docile immigrants who challenged their local leadership, and with western peace men who challenged their national leadership, they looked about desperately for protection. For stripped of its high-flown, abstract rhetoric, the only individual freedom the swallow-tails cared about was their own.

Nothing better illustrated the course of swallow-tail thinking during the 1860s than their evaluation of city politics. In an environment so varied in its economic, ethnic, and ideological life, constantly undergoing change, and too poorly organized to effect much integration, the problems of government seemed beyond comprehension. Such complexity presented the New York elite with challenges that the traditional techniques of political democracy seemed incapable of meeting. In the winter of 1869–70, when Tweed was consolidating his power in the city and the state, the *World* discussed the problem in an illuminating series of editorials.

In rural and small-town America, the paper noted, "where amusements and diversions are few, and everybody knows everybody," people participated widely in politics. The problems of government were simple and the citizens were able to inform themselves about the issues and the candidates. In New York City, however, few people were inclined to concern themselves with politics. "The operations of the municipal government are so vast and multifarious," the *World* explained, "that few citizens have leisure or capacity to study them in detail; and those who are best qualified for such a task are overburdened with private business and too glad to spend the little leisure they command in social relaxation or attendance on public amusements." Hence the city government could easily fall into the hands of corrupt politicians, who by mastering the details of party manipulation could run the city for their own profit.

Certainly the city government reflected the city's diverse social environment. Under the charter of 1857, the administration had been divided among the mayor and a series of boards, either popularly elected or appointed by the governor. Completely independent of the mayor's authority were the almshouse, the board of education, the comptroller, the corporation counsel, and the police, fire, and health departments. Local taxes were imposed by the popularly elected county board of supervisors, which represented a larger constituency than the city proper. Such a system of government had been imposed upon the city by a Republican-dominated state legislature for obviously partisan purposes. The result was administrative chaos. "Was there ever," inquired an observer in 1866, "such a hodgepodge of a government before in the world?"

The *World* agreed and called upon the state legislature to provide the city with a more unified system of government. Especially did it call for an increase in the powers of the mayor, by abolishing the board of supervisors and giving the mayor the power to appoint and to dismiss all department heads. The *World* also recommended increasing the mayor's salary, so that he might devote all his energies to the tasks of government. Although such reforms would not touch the city's social fragmentation, it would at least focus the voter's attention upon a single official and give the majority a chance to effect a thorough housecleaning at a single election. Centralized, responsible government seemed essential if democracy was to survive.[9]

The *World* also assumed that proper leadership would ameliorate the city's governmental ills. To be effective, leadership would have to be given the power to coordinate the city's many administrative departments. Should the mayor receive such power, the *World* declared, he would be able to serve as the people's agent in public affairs just as the lawyer served as their agent in private affairs. A full-time mayor, trained in the science of administration, would assure those citizens who were too much concerned with their private affairs to watch their government closely that public problems would be met with honesty and ability. "What the citizens of a great metropolis cannot do themselves," the *World* stated, "they must depute some competent person to do for them."

Naturally enough, the *World* also assumed that leadership would come from the city's successful business and professional men. Declaring that the "best qualified" citizens were too busy to take an interest in government unless it was made worth their while, it reemphasized its demand that the mayor receive adequate compensation for his services. It also urged that the mayor be made ineligible for reelection, in order to discourage professional politicians from seeking the office.[10]

Marble had good reason to believe that the "best qualified" citizens wished to take charge of the city government. In 1865 he had joined other prominent swallow-tail Democrats in establishing a gentleman's political club. The idea for such an enterprise had first been discussed among the members of the Democratic Executive Committee during the election of 1864. Inspired largely by the success of the Union League Club, which provided a home for upper-class Republicans and snubbed the applications of upper-class Democrats, they decided to retaliate. As many of the swallow-tails later recalled, it had been difficult for Democrats to maintain their social prestige during the Civil War. Attacked as copperheads and traitors, snubbed by their Republican friends, and classed with the Irish ruffians and draft rioters, they faced a social isolation that troubled them deeply. As one recalled, "it was not fashionable to be a Democrat."

McClellan's defeat so demoralized the party that for a few months the project was set aside. In the spring of 1865, however, it was revived and carried through. Meetings were held at the offices of Marble, Douglas Taylor, and Augustus Schell to work out the details. The project attracted so much support that by mid-July Marble had been asked to frame a constitution for the club. In the fall the group secured the Benkard House on the corner of Fifth Avenue and Fifteenth Street. Described as "a very handsome building," with a fifty-foot frontage and a large garden in the rear, the house provided excellent facilities for the organization, which on Marble's suggestion was named the Manhattan Club.[11]

From the first the club sought to include only the social elite of the New York Democracy. To guarantee an exclusive membership, the club charged an initiation fee of $150, plus yearly dues of $50. Of the original members, none seemed more concerned with maintaining an elite membership than did Marble. His constitution provided that only two blackballs out of the twenty-five votes of the permanent managers would disqualify an applicant. In 1910 Douglas Taylor recalled how frequently Marble had declared that "it was necessary to keep it a high-toned club" and that Marble had "exerted his great influence to have only gentlemen admitted."[12]

Late in December 1865, the *World* announced the birth of the Manhattan Club in an editorial that Marble may have written. The Union League, it declared, had demonstrated the need for a counter social club to preserve freedom of political opinion. It was hoped that the Manhattan Club would provide such a service and would also tone down the bitterness of political debate and raise the level of discussion so as to create a new mutual respect between the parties. The political clubs of England, declared the editorial, had forced men to learn "self-command and self-restraint" in their daily social relations, and "the tone at once of political manners and of political morals is insensibly elevated by the elevation of the social atmosphere in which political measures are matured and carried out." A class of men so organized and so disciplined could provide the leadership necessary to guide public opinion by sharpening the issues and by providing the rules for political debate. Politics would then be freed from vindictive personal attacks and the clamor and chaos of "irresponsible majorities."[13]

In short, the Manhattan Club would serve as a school for the political elite. It would define the terms of political discourse and would create a political climate congenial to the sensibilities of the upper class. By removing sordid personal attacks from politics it would allow friendship and honor to become a bond between political leaders and would permit them to concentrate upon administering the great principles of government. Also it would deny the political boss the power to overwhelm his betters by controlling irresponsible majorities. It would make politics truly safe for the swallow-tail.

During these years Marble's personality revealed itself clearly. At its center was his desire to attain that sense of vocational competence and ideological certainty that he and Dr. Anderson had known as a "noble manhood." As he sought that goal, he revealed the traits that would distinguish him for the rest of his life.

During his years in New York, Marble's spirit was strengthened by a growing sense of vocational competence. Many of the uncertainties of his Boston years no doubt had arisen from an uncertainty of vocation. To the young artist, smitten with literary ambitions, the attractions of the Athenaeum or the lecture circuit were strong and real. Not until he joined the *World* did he begin to gain confidence in his editorial abilities. "If the paper outside of the Editorial columns has been tolerable," he informed Dr. Anderson, "it is owing to my labor." All that was "striking" in the city columns had resulted from his suggestions and the work of the one reporter he had placed in the department. Indeed, Cummings was urging Spalding to turn over his "managing part" to Marble, and Marble thought it was a good idea. Also encouraging were Weed's suggestion that Marble replace him in Albany, the trustees' show of confidence in his abilities, and his successful maneuverings to save the paper.[14]

Supplementing his ability to handle business affairs was his ability to handle men. Marble usually treated his associates with tact and sympathy. His letters of recommendation testified to his loyalty and cooperativeness, and Marble himself agreed. He despised Bowles's policies but never challenged his authority. Spalding's behavior he endured in silence. "My place was to yield," he told Dr. Anderson, "and I have yielded, and begun again in another place and another way." When it appeared that Cummings might leave the *World* rather than endure Spalding's incompetence, Marble did his best to reconcile them. It was his "constant care to prevent an open rupture" between the two. As the weeks passed, he noted Cummings's confidence in his "tact and executive ability." When he assumed the editorship, Marble treated his subordinates with generosity and consideration. When Edmund Clarence Stedman resigned his reportorial duties late in 1861, he told Marble: "you have discharged the nice responsibilities of your management [so] as to secure the best of both my friendship and working ability. . . . My late associates will say the same." Years later St. Clair McKelway departed, recalling "only kindness and consideration in my official and personal contact with you for *four* years." Shortly before broken health and spirit forced him from the paper, Jerome B. Stillson commented to Barlow that Marble's friendship "through all these trials has been as steadfast and tender as a man's could be."[15]

As the years passed, Marble's confidence inspired pride in his accomplishments. When he drafted the letter for General Rathbone to issue in defense of his career, he credited himself with having "built up the *World* into the leading and powerful organ of a great party." When he prepared a sketch of his career for an English periodical, he recalled that he had reorganized the journal's staff, given "prominence to able discussions" of political economy, "boldly increased its expenses for news," and determined its political course. The *World* "has been very successful," he concluded, "has wide circulation in New York and through the States and is the leading Democratic and Free Trade journal."[16]

His optimism also increased. It seemed that success always lay just ahead. Only in the months following his graduation from college and during his controversy with Bowles did he express doubt about his future. In each new situation he found opportunities for advancement and self-improvement. The *Boston Journal* offered the chance for "much profitable study" and the Athenaeum an "enlargement of ideas—a widening and strengthening of sympathies which is more and deeper than the mere poetical." A few months with the *Traveller* convinced him that it "can and will be made *the* New England paper," and Bowles's arrival strengthened the conviction. He faced his first assignment with the *Evening Post* confident that he had at last found his place in the universe.[17]

Although his trials with the *World* severely challenged his optimism, his feeling of competence persuaded him to go forward. Indeed, the darker things looked, the more determined he became to succeed. During the spring of 1862, his letters to Dr. Anderson balanced fears of failure with details of new plans and strategies. When at last he had saved the paper, his optimism returned. That fall he was predicting that "in ten or twenty years, if I live and can work as I hope to, the *World* will be at the head of the American Press in circulation and influence."[18]

He harbored no regrets. He had always done the right thing. The controversies and disappointments had been someone else's fault.

Bowles had been unprincipled, Spalding incompetent and egotistical, Cummings a schemer. Seymour could have sent the state militia to free the *World* from federal suppression "without the slightest danger of an armed collision." In May 1862, when it appeared that his efforts to save the *World* would fail, he found nothing in himself to blame. "I can reproach myself with nothing undone," he wrote. "Perhaps I tried to accomplish too much but I should take the same risk again." Amid the reproofs accompanying his entry into the Democracy, he informed Dr. Anderson that "at any rate I am fully persuaded in my own mind."[19]

He had so little to regret principally because he had been consistent. At every turning point, advantage and principle had gone hand in hand. When charges arose that he had once been a Whig and had joined the Democracy out of financial necessity, he hotly denied them. His father had been a Jacksonian Democrat, the Whig party was dead by the year he reached his majority, his first political act was to persuade a publisher not to support Fremont, and his political views had always expressed "a fixed, perhaps excessive, conservatism." Indeed, he had purchased the *World* "in order to change its political character and had refused to be a party to an arrangement for continuing it in the same political course." All this he would say, omitting only that he had been a Whig and had joined the Democracy out of financial necessity.[20]

As such statements suggest, an important trait in Marble's personality was self-protection. Ever wary of threats to his career and character, he quickly lashed out when they appeared. Whatever form they took—Bowles's literary censorship, Spalding's administrative fumbling, Comstock and Cassidy's ambition to share the editorship of the *World*, Seymour's timidity—his response was always the same, a blaze of anger and a stern refusal to yield. When the *Tribune* referred to the *World* as a "Secessionist Contemporary," Marble branded the words "false and libelous" and demanded "as an act of justice that the calumny be publicly retracted . . . at once." There was "no rule of honorable journalism, no license of decent political warfare" that could "tolerate" such "aspersions." He did not propose to submit to them "now or hereafter."[21]

Nor would he permit others to share his power. His efforts to buy out his partners and his hesitancy to merge the *World* with the *Argus* showed how zealously he guarded his independence. To Horace Greeley he asserted that he had "always retained and [did] retain a controlling share of [the *World*'s] stock." He was "and [had] been its sole, responsible and uncontrolled Editor." Samuel Greene Arnold understood. "Marble has an insane desire to be a 'Reel Editah,' " he told Barlow, "and like Issachar or Reuben, or one of the Israelitist dozen . . . 'is joined to his idols—let him alone.' "[22]

Although not insane, Marble's desire was both compelling and envious. Nothing attracted him more than the independence of the great journalists of the city. They were impervious, he felt, to the attacks he had to endure. Although he despised the *Herald* for attacking the *World* during its financial crisis, he craved the reputation of its editor, James Gordon Bennett. "Half the singular power of Bennett with the people," he observed, "comes from this that they judge him with no ambition save what the *Herald* embodies and discount nothing but that. We aim at marks as different as are the *World* and the *Herald* of today but in this respect I desire to be his peer." In 1873 Marble paid Bennet the supreme compliment of offering to purchase the *Herald* from him.[23]

No one so inspired Marble's envy as Horace Greeley. Marble hated Greeley for having attacked the *World* during its financial crisis. "When it would have saved me mental pain and pecuniary anxiety I discovered that I could expect nothing from the *Tribune*'s fairness, justice, or generosity." But more than that bothered Marble. During an exchange of letters over a number of issues, including Marble's Whiggish past, Marble suddenly launched a curious attack upon his fellow editor. Greeley had complained that the *World* had violated journalistic ethics by attacking him by name. Marble thought the complaint absurd. "I confess to having learned from a close observation of your career that personal prominence was grateful to you," he replied. "Studied uncouthness and elaborate eccentricity are your daily confession that you desire notoriety even at the cost of some contempt." Furthermore, he was "driven to infer" that Greeley "started in life with a determination to have principles and achieve pecuniary success and that now in your age you find you have failed to do either."[24]

That he should have closely observed the career of one he so detested was revealing enough; but to have drawn such conclusions was even more so. Years later, when defending himself against charges of too much independence from his party, Marble would argue that such eccentricities added to his influence—and would cite Greeley as an example. Also, it is noteworthy that his attacks on Greeley's failure to have principles and to have achieved financial success came near the end of a letter in which he had doctored the record to conceal his Whiggish past and at a time when his own financial success was far from certain. It seems that in attacking Greeley's ambition and failure he was also attacking his own.

An outstanding student of the subject has defined personal identity as "the perception of the selfsameness and continuity of one's existence in time and space and the perception of the fact that others recognize one's sameness and continuity." Although he obviously yearned for such a perception, Marble did not achieve it. As he approached the core of his ambition, his life revealed inconsistencies and failures that he could not face. So by condemning them in others and by altering the historical record, he denied their existence.[25]

For the most part, such defenses worked adequately. Although he never came fully to believe in his integrity and independence, Marble did not allow feelings of inadequacy to dominate his life. To be sure such feelings informed many of his prominent traits, especially his persistent optimism, self-righteousness, and defensiveness. Without such traits he would have had to accept some unacceptable truths, and his manhood would have appeared far less noble than he desired. Another trait that helped was risk-taking. Rather than face failure, he would strive on until he had reached the limits of his ingenuity. Then if he failed, he would blame someone else. His efforts to save the *World* from financial collapse testified eloquently to his risk-taking character. Also useful was jealousy of those rivals who succeeded in realizing his ambition. Not only Horace Greeley, but in later years the Mugwumps, those independent men of principle so influential in the politics of the Cleveland administration, earned a hatred that exceeded the demands of political competition. Throughout his life, however, such traits merely colored his behavior without affecting his fundamental motives. With perhaps two exceptions, the course of the *World* during the campaign of 1868 and his actions in Florida during the disputed election of 1876, they played no important role in the major decisions of his life and never affected the outcome of those decisions.

It was in the formation of another trait that Marble's feelings of inadequacy contributed significantly to his personality. Lacking the confidence necessary for true independence and self-determination, Marble turned to those who seemed to have achieved such goals and in their service sought to attain his manhood. To those persons he was a true friend.

Marble's friendship was not the intrusive, compulsive sort. Rarely did he force himself on his friends and then only for just cause. Nor did he seek to win them by attracting public attention to himself. Scorning extravagance and display, he limited himself to the society of his family and friends. In 1864 he chose to be married in a simple ceremony performed by his former professor, Chester Dewey, at the home of his bride's relatives in Rochester. Marble struck the only note of extravagance by paying Dr. Dewey $50, nearly ten times the professor's usual fee. Probably, however, Marble desired less to display his wealth than to show his affection for Dr. Dewey and for his alma mater. In 1873 a student of New York society described Marble as "a sort of journalistic recluse and valetudinarian, dining occasionally with his political friends, but seldom appearing in public." Marble himself jokingly claimed he cultivated "the 'simplex munditus' " in his dress and manners.[26]

Indeed, Marble's friends were most likely attracted by the man himself. His wit and charm were inescapable. Young Lucy Rathbone's gift of orange marmalade inspired the sparkling reply: "Some men are vulnerable in their patriotism, some can be wounded in their pride, and some in their possessions. As for me I am weakest at the point of contact with orange marmalade." After a children's party at the Marble home, Mrs. August Belmont learned that her daughter's "manners and behavior won [my nieces'] hearts" and that "my own son, my Absalom! was so entirely devoted to a pretty girl in a pink silk that he utterly forgot to make his morning 'reverences' to the father of his being." And Sam Barlow would be bombarded by passages like this description of a July day at the Newport beaches:

> De profundis clamo!
> Out of the burning depths I call and cry unto thee. You are wooing Cloacina, but I am making love to the mermaidens under the translucent wave. They comb their hair, gazing in handglasses, but anon smile upon me, wiggle their finny funny tails, and lead me to the watering grottoes! I myself am the votive offering, naked as born. Consider what exuviae are those which you deposit upon the altar of your goddess.—For shame![27]

Those who called on him for assistance found him willing. When Mrs. Barlow asked his help in passing a bill to appropriate funds for a children's nursery and hospital, he used his influence in the state legislature and accomplished it. When the young essayist and historian John Fiske sought his aid, Marble gave him a job with the *World* and used his influence with Andrew D. White to help him obtain a teaching position at Cornell. "Marble is a very warm-hearted, affectionate fellow," Fiske wrote his wife.[28]

Few persons profited more from Marble's friendship than Louisa Arnold, wife of Samuel Greene Arnold of Rhode Island. The Arnolds maintained a cottage at the fashionable vacation resort of Newport, and hardly a summer passed without a visit from the young editor. Deeply religious and committed to her home and family, Louisa found in Manton Marble many qualities to enjoy and admire. Again and again she commented on the way her children took to him, reporting that little Nina asked to part her hair on the side "that she may look like Mr. Marble" and that all the children loved him better than their own uncles. She appreciated the interest he took in their upbringing, thanking him for his suggestions on their guidance. Nearly all her letters concluded, "all the children send love."

Louisa also appreciated Marble's interest in her. During his visits, she would sit quietly while he sang and whistled familiar hymns. Such moments, she would write, brought her more spiritual peace than a Sunday in church. When she was away, she would remember him through the books, largely on religious subjects, he sent her. So highly did she regard him that she credited him with helping her overcome a natural shyness. "I am willing to pass for what I am," she announced to him on her thirty-fifth birthday, "learn all I can, contribute my mite to society, and thus try to fill as far as in me lies the place appointed me by God. . . . You, my dear friend, have done much more than you imagine toward bringing me to this point and I wish you to know what benefit your perhaps unconscious influence has been to me and I shall always feel grateful for it."

In return for such advice and inspiration, Louisa often advised Marble about his own moral character. Marble's personal vices were few, consisting of a taste for an occasional glass of wine or whiskey and a craving for Havana cigars. His vocabulary of basic Anglo-Saxon, somewhat meager, never appeared in feminine company. On only one occasion did Louisa actually reprimand him for his behavior. The incident occurred on an August evening in 1865 when Marble, apparently suffering from an overindulgence in wine, avoided her and a lady companion by slipping into the sanctuary of the den. When he later denied having avoided them, she scolded him for prevaricating and demanded that he promise "*never again* to let the gratification of an appetite get the better of your judgment." Marble took the advice with good humor, labeled the note "The Chateau '64 Letter!!" in honor of the address of the Arnold's cottage, and undoubtedly promised to mend his ways. There is no evidence that he ever again drank to excess. Louisa accepted his apology in similarly good spirits, and from then on signed her letters "Chateau '64."[29]

Marble's relations with August Belmont were especially close and, indeed, demanding. Although one of America's most prominent financiers and politicians, Belmont continually craved the praise and loyalty of his friends and was always ready to suspect them of treachery. Again and again he would tell Marble of personal slights upon his honor or position and would demand that his young friend stand by him. For example, when he prepared a defense of his diplomatic career by collecting his correspondence for publication, he urged Marble to read through the material and to select the letters most appropriate for publication. "I feel an envious desire," he declared, "that you should see why I feel so keenly the want of candor and fairness with which my private and official character has been treated not only by our political opponents but also by our own party." Dutifully, Marble complied with the request.[30]

Marble matched his loyalty to his friends with loyalty to his family. When he first came to New York, his father had retired from teaching to become superintendent of the Albany Orphan Asylum. Advancing age had dictated the change, and Marble realized that his family soon would have to rely upon him for financial support. Without hesitation he determined to supply their needs. He agreed to pay for the education of his younger brother, Frank, and assisted his father in purchasing a farm in Westchester County, where the kindly old man lived out his retirement years. Although his papers are strangely free of family correspondence, they show that to the end he gave generously to secure their ease and comfort.[31]

Marble's attitude toward his brother, Frank, provides the only direct insight into his family loyalty. In assuming responsibility for the boy's education, Marble determined that he should approach his studies with a dedication that would match his own. Believing in discipline and authority, he took it upon himself, with the aid of Dr. Anderson, to plan Frank's education. Quite naturally, he sent his brother to Rochester, no doubt hoping that the boy would enjoy the same success and guidance he had experienced. If in his first year Frank proved himself worthy, Marble thought of rewarding him with an appointment to West Point.

It was essential, however, that Frank prove himself. So when the young man's performance at Rochester fell short of expectations, Marble determined at once to discipline him. He set the West Point appointment aside, declaring to Dr. Anderson that "if he didn't succeed in Rochester I could never help him to a failure at West Point." Frank's failures, he felt, showed a lack of respect and responsibility. "His injustice to himself in making so little of what costs so much is degrading," Marble declared, "and his injustice to me I won't tolerate." Concluding that Frank required further guidance, he sent him back to Rochester for another year.[32]

Marble was a true friend not only because friendship afforded an opportunity for service but because it afforded an opportunity for self-fulfillment as well. In the service of others he found himself most able to stand fast for principle. Marble usually pictured his friends as men of principle. Barlow had "culture, breadth, [and] a very large acquaintance with affairs and men." McClellan was "as pure-hearted—single-minded a man as lives" and had "a moral elevation of character unobtrusive and real." Tilden's "Democracy [was] as indisputable as . . . the Sermon on the Mount." Not surprisingly, when he reflected on the significance of the election of 1864, he found it in devotion to principle and loyalty to friends.[33]

During these years Marble's principles evolved to their final form. Gradually, the religious and metaphysical interests of his youth gave way to an ideology that more satisfactorily interpreted his experience. As he struggled to save the *World* from bankruptcy, his religious beliefs changed. His commitment to the Baptist Church weakened, and he grew to doubt the principles of his early faith. As his doubts became explicit, Louisa Arnold sought to reassure him and to guide him back to the faith. She urged him to read sermons and to join a church in the city. But she could not persuade him. Time and again he confessed to her that he would give anything to be "a consistent Christian," but he had no faith. He refrained from joining any congregation and in June 1864 officially withdrew from the Baptist Church. Although at the time he affirmed a belief in the general truths of Christianity, he declared he could no longer "in conscience continue to subscribe to some of the articles of faith which when I was baptized commanded my youthful assent."

Nor did he ever return to the church. Four years later his friend and colleague, William Henry Hurlbert, was so startled to hear Marble described as a good churchman that he reported the incident with the exclamation: "This is a fact! I said, 'Yes, *I* thought you a little disposed to ritualism—but that you really felt the peace and good order of the whole body to be more important than any questions either of discipline or of liturgy.' "[34]

Having broken with his church, Marble paid little attention to religious matters. Only once again did he mention the subject. In April 1875 the *World*'s managing editor, Jerome B. Stillson, suffered the loss of his wife and child in childbirth. "I can wish you every help in this darkness," Marble wrote him in sympathy, "friends, kinsfolk, religion, philosophy, 'the mild and gentle sympathy of nature,' if they are helps." But in a personal aside, which he crossed out in the first draft of the letter, he showed how far he had come from his youthful faith. "Religion, philosophy may come to your aid. Me they never helped." On the question of life after death, Marble showed a guarded skepticism. Only those who accepted the scriptures as a trustworthy account of actual events, he said, could believe in eternal life. Those who subjected them to "the common standards of literary and historical criticism" were forced to resist "the most powerful bribe and the most secret seduction which can address the heart of man. . . . To those who find such faith impossible, it can profit little to imagine a future life, which, lacking every warrant while also incapable of any disproof, adds no substance to the moral law and no substance to the shadow of hope. Yet being unprofitable it might also be most precious to a sore heart."[35]

Such fragmentary evidence suggests that Marble's religious crisis resulted from skepticism about his church's theology rather than from a general loss of faith. He continued to believe in the omnipotence of God and the ethical teachings of Christianity, while rejecting sectarian dogma. Perhaps as he involved himself in the diverse and changing world of affairs, he found his Baptist faith incapable of guiding him from day to day. And as his ambition for noble manhood became ever more intimately a part of that world of affairs, he was forced to turn from religion to seek a philosophy that would be of more use.

The search led to Herbert Spencer. Although the demands of Marble's career reduced the time available for reading philosophy, he still kept up his interest in the subject. When the first volumes of Spencer's *Synthetic Philosophy* appeared in America in the early 1860s, he read them and found them to his liking. When John Fiske first met Marble in 1864, he found the young editor "an excellent Spencerian."[36]

Although Marble took philosophy seriously and occasionally tried his hand at formal analysis, there seems little doubt that his attraction to Spencer resulted from the circumstances of his career. His struggle to save the *World* had introduced him to the competitive environment of New York journalism, and his battles with Spalding and Cummings had sharpened his competitive instincts and will to survive. The perilous months of mid-1862 had, by his own admission, fixed his attention upon wealth, power, personal and political influence, and other prerequisites of worldly success. By 1864 he did not need Herbert Spencer to convince him that only the fittest survived; his own career had been proof enough.

If Marble had good reasons for believing that competition was man's natural activity, he had equally good ones for accepting the rhetoric of rugged individualism. His own ambition drove him toward a noble manhood of independence and self-determination. Louisa Arnold thanked him for helping her achieve greater self-confidence. August Belmont sought his help in defending his own character. And the other swallow-tails, threatened by war-inspired hostilities and suspicions, appealed to Jeffersonian constitutionalism to protect their independence. Indeed, the Democracy's celebration of Jeffersonian doctrines strongly influenced his social thinking. In 1868 he neatly linked politics to philosophy by informing Dr. Anderson that "questions of currency, banking, trade-unions, cooperation and finance generally, and the relations of these to the state are, as it seems to me, all happily solved by the political philosophy of which Jefferson and Herbert Spencer are the best expounders I have read. Freedom—the least for the state to do, the most to the individual—is likewise the axiom here."[37]

In later years Marble would have the opportunity to apply his beliefs in a variety of roles: political strategist, political economist, presidential adviser, and ex officio secretary of the treasury. In the late 1860s, however, he was first a journalist, who, he believed, filled a dual role. The journalist was first "a merchant of news," buying his product everywhere and selling it wherever it was not supplied. "Enterprise and industry get him, and other merchants, success and honor, and of like kind. Probity has the same reward in public confidence. Shrewd and far-sighted combinations bring to the merchant of news—or of flour, or of pork—profit and credit." The journalist was second a trustee and steward for expressing and molding public opinion, seeking "through all conflicting private interests, solely the public general good." Therein his work was "allied to the statesman's [and] the politician's."

Public opinion, Marble believed, was not "popular caprice. . . . The daily ups and downs of the mercury in the thermometer are not the annual mean of temperature." Public opinion was, instead, "the eminent dominant power in the modern free state," the modus operandi of democracy. The press promoted democracy by diffusing intelligence among the people and by teaching them to form political combinations. By seeking out and revealing all, it brought "all society to bear upon the individual," hindered "the committal of that which is indefensible, and [made] men seek for sure ground of action, and a plausible defense of every act."

The press advanced individual freedom. It raised "the standards of merchants, manufacturers, and artisans by exposing to a wider competition the goods, or the skill, in any market." It thus fulfilled the purpose of the modern state, in which "the individual—his rights, relations, interests and liberty—have come to be the common aim of every change."

The press educated the masses for citizenship. Through its columns the masses conversed with the world's great statesmen and learned "the higher arts of government. . . . By and through the press our false democracy is made to approximate to the true democracy. The unheard of and disfranchised minorities make themselves heard through it."

By giving voice to the masses, the press insured that legislation would follow "the general sense of a community." By identifying the interest of the state and the interest of the people, the press helped to insure "security . . . confidence in humanity . . . [and] yielding obedience to law. . . . How its gentle compulsion has made almost all men, each one to himself, a vindicator and officer for the enforcement of law!"[38]

While Marble was putting the *World* into the service of this version of swallow-tail ideology, he was also striving to succeed as a "merchant of news." Marble realized that journalistic success depended upon good business sense. His early years with the *World* had taught him that "as a mere merchant of news there are demanded of the journalist the same industry, enterprise, and foresight which give success in mercantile life." Hence the journalist had to learn to gauge public opinion as well as to guide it—so that he might sell his wares at a profit. By the end of 1868, Marble could count himself a successful journalist. Not only was he recognized as a powerful member of the New York Democracy but in circulation and earnings his paper stood among the leading New York dailies. As a merchant of news, he had shown himself to be as good as the very best.[39]

The *World*'s popularity resulted in part from the high quality of its news coverage. During the first five years of Marble's editorship, the paper presented its readers with an ever-broadening range of topics. The emphasis upon religion disappeared altogether and with it the restraint that had discouraged sensationalism. By the end of the decade, readers had become accustomed to, and no doubt attracted by, such column headings as: "CHAPTER OF HORRORS. *A Father Stabs his Two Sons and Attempts to Commit Suicide.* MADDEN'S DYING STATEMENT. *Cool Suicide of a Love-Sick German.* Double Murder in Philadelphia. A Man Murders His Mother-in-law in Massachusetts. A ROW IN THE KITCHEN. & c., & c., & c."[40]

But even more importantly, the *World*'s news coverage expanded to bring its readers a fairly complete picture of American society. By 1867 it had emerged as a fully-developed modern newspaper, taking all society as its field of coverage. During that year it appeared weekly in "triple-sheets," twelve-page editions devoted largely to topics of local interest. Although advertising, politics, and editorial comment continued to dominate its contents, readers could find expanded coverage of cultural, educational, labor, and agricultural affairs. Typical stories dealt with working conditions of factory girls in Massachusetts, New York's streetcar pickpockets, Negro life in the city, night life, Prince Albert's visit to Canada, and the Oxford-Harvard boat race.[41]

To prepare such stories, the *World* acquired a distinguished corps of reporters and editorial writers, many of them young men destined for brilliant careers. In 1865 Marble hired Montgomery Schuyler, whose history of American architecture would later mark him as an authority in that field. A year later St. Clair McKelway began a career that he would carry to distinction as editor of the *Brooklyn Daily Eagle*. Already on hand were Jerome B. Stillson, who had made a name for himself with a brilliant account of Sheridan's Valley Campaign, and George W. Adams, an old Washington hand and well-respected professional. Soon A. C. Wheeler would join them to cover social events as the lively, charming "Nym Crinkle."[42]

The heart of the paper, however, lay with its chief editors, Marble, Ivory Chamberlain, William Henry Hurlbert, and David Goodman Croly. One would like to know more about Marble's precise role in managing the *World*. There is no account of his daily routine, so it is difficult to estimate the amount of time he devoted to supervising directly the putting out of the paper. His correspondence makes clear, however, that he controlled all important decisions regarding editorial policy and acted as final judge in all intramural controversies. But aside from that, the record is too fragmentary to yield a more complete picture of his life as a practicing journalist.

Nor is much known of the daily lives of the other editors, though their attitudes and general contributions to the paper are clear enough. Ivory Chamberlain had joined the *World* in 1862, after many years as a school teacher and journalist in up-state New York. He had entered journalism in the mid-1850s in Buffalo, where his political editorials attracted the attention of ex-President Millard Fillmore. The two became friends, and in 1856 when Fillmore ran as the American Party's candidate for president, Chamberlain prepared his campaign biography. On the *World* Chamberlain served as the chief editorial writer on political affairs. Like Marble, he found the transition from conservative Whiggery to Democracy an easy one, and he became a devoted partisan. "The old Democratic leaders," he declared to Marble, "were men of great political sagacity and thorough knowledge of popular feeling, and I should sincerely regret to see the Democratic party swinging round on to the old Whig ground."

Most likely, however, it was less Chamberlain's partisanship than his literary skill that attracted Marble. Because he wrote with great difficulty, Chamberlain greatly valued proper style and skillful argument. He would spend hours discussing style with his fellow editors and would never miss an opportunity to start an argument, usually for the fun of seeing if he could maintain an untenable position. Such qualities no doubt strongly attracted Marble, whose literary career had taught him to value style, wit, and ingenuity.

Throughout his career Chamberlain suffered greatly from a malady described as "dyspepsia." The disease had forced him to give up teaching, and during his last years with the *World*, seriously impaired his writing. In order to relieve the pain, he began to drink heavily. In 1872 he confessed to Marble that he felt compelled to drink in order "to do any work at all." From that year until he left the *World* in 1875, David Goodman Croly recalled, "I do not think Chamberlain ever wrote an editorial article unless he was so far under the influence of liquor that he might fairly be called drunk." Marble must have known of Chamberlain's condition, but he allowed him to remain on the staff and seems never to have reprimanded him.[43]

Although in many respects similar to Chamberlain, William Henry Hurlbert added his own peculiar traits to the editorial staff. Hurlbert had also joined the *World* in 1862, fresh from a South Carolina prison, where he had been placed for denouncing slavery. That after such an experience he should have joined a Democratic paper might have created some doubts about his judgment. Still, his journalistic credentials were impressive. Like Chamberlain, he had begun his career in the mid-1850s, when he joined the staff of *Putnam's Magazine*. He had also served as drama critic for *Albion* and as a reporter and editorial writer for the *New York Times*. Again, one may imagine that it was his literary skill that attracted Marble, for in addition to his experience in journalism Hurlbert had won acclaim as a poet and playwright. Irresistibly charming, he was known as a brilliant and popular table talker and as a close friend of the famous lobbyist, world traveler, gourmet, and social lion, "Uncle Sam" Ward. Compulsively aggressive in his social relations, he became Marble's most prolific correspondent, deluging his editor-in-chief with hundreds of notes in a round, sprawling, nearly illegible script. His undated letters alone comprise an entire volume in the Marble papers. One cannot imagine Marble's being able to withstand such a man.

But Hurlbert also had his weakness. Seldom has the estimate "brilliant but eccentric" seemed more appropriate. Running through his life was a whimsical streak that made him almost wholly unpredictable. During his college days, for example, he had changed his name from "Hurlbut" to Hurlbert when a printer misspelled the name on his calling cards. Before turning to literature and journalism, he had preached as an unordained Unitarian minister and had composed a number of popular hymns. Always given to display, he boasted of being the only newspaper editor capable of working on as many as three editorials simultaneously, writing alternate pages for the typesetters. Because he liked to travel in international society, he spent months at a time away from the *World* writing series after series of feature articles. Thus life with him, while always entertaining and often exciting, was a bit mystifying. Still, Marble seemed more than willing to accept the risk.[44]

Chamberlain and Hurlbert helped make the *World* a newspaper of literary distinction. It was the managing editor, David Goodman Croly, who was most responsible for making it into a modern newspaper. As a boy Croly had left his native Ireland for the United States where he worked as a silversmith before becoming a reporter on the *Evening Post*. As his journalistic ambitions rose, he traveled to Rockford, Illinois, where he attempted to establish his own daily newspaper. The effort failed, however, and he returned to New York in time to join the original staff of the *World*. From the beginning it seems that Marble recognized Croly's abilities. When it appeared the paper's financial difficulties might cost Croly his job, Marble helped to keep him on and to advance him to city editor. When Marble assumed control of the paper, he appointed Croly managing editor.

Time and again Croly justified Marble's confidence. From him came the ideas for feature articles and news stories that moved the *World* toward modern journalism. Although almost entirely self-educated, he was able to converse knowledgeably on the most advanced ideas in theology, medicine, social and political theory, and psychology. Early in his career, he became fascinated with the positivist religion of humanity espoused by the French philosopher, August Comte, and by the end of the 1860s was establishing Comtean churches in the city and founding journals dedicated to spreading Comtean ideas. With his wife, Jane Cunningham, he also championed the women's rights movement and a number of other popular reforms. As managing editor of the *World* his agile, inclusive mind was his greatest asset. "To be with him," recalled St. Clair McKelway, "was a liberal education in the art of suggestion, in the work of subject getting, in the knack of topical expansion." Those staff members who sat fascinated by his incessant, rambling discourses on the topics of the day soon came to refer to him as "The Great Suggester."

In later years those staff members would recall the differences between Marble and Croly, emphasizing the many ways in which Marble restrained and suppressed the talents of his managing editor. They would claim that Marble's short-sightedness and conventionality kept Croly from pushing the *World* to the pinnacle of modern journalism and so caused the paper's eventual failure. Specifically, they charged Marble with trying to make the *World* into a vehicle for an elite class, thus throwing away the chance to gain widespread popularity. Writing in the age of Pulitzer, St. Clair McKelway would declare that if Croly had been allowed to guide the *World* it would have become "that matchless purveyor for the small wants of mankind and that extraordinary exponent of the ethical and practical opinion of the people which the paper, since its re-creation under its existing control, has proved itself to be." And in our own day the foremost authority on the history of American journalism would suggest that Marble intentionally tried to keep the paper's circulation low because he believed that there were only 20,000 intelligent readers in the city.[45]

On the surface there were good reasons for making such charges. Croly's long and fervent pleas for changes in the *World*'s format, news coverage, and editorial policies went largely unheeded. His support of such causes as labor reform, women's rights, and positivism were scorned by his Spencerian editor-in-chief. When he finally left the paper in 1872, Marble celebrated the end of "the detestable Comtism, women's rights trash and all the ismical gabble which I have had to fight down for years."[46]

It is by no means clear, however, that the contrast between Marble and Croly was so sharp as the latter's partisans have made it. Despite their differences, the two were far from adversaries. Marble appreciated Croly's talents and generously rewarded them. In 1864 when Croly sent Marble a series of "ultimatums" threatening to resign unless his salary was raised, Marble responded with a raise so generous that it left the voluble managing editor speechless. "I gratefully accept your generous offer," he replied after some time, "and will satisfy my conscience in accepting the money by trying to earn for its paper at least four times as much." Four years later another ultimatum brought a similar response, this time made retroactive for the preceding year. As before, Croly promised to redouble his efforts to repay his editor's generosity.[47]

It also seems that the contrast between Croly the reformer and Marble the reactionary has been overstated. Despite Croly's enthusiasm for labor reform and the emancipation of women, it was he who perpetrated the famous "miscegenation hoax" of 1864. In 1863 Croly and George Wakeman prepared a pamphlet advocating racial intermarriage and circulated it to prominent abolitionists for their comments. After the subject had been widely discussed in the abolitionist press, they rose in horror to defend the purity of the white race. As a result, "miscegenation" (a word Croly himself coined) became a much-discussed topic during the presidential campaign.[48]

In other significant ways Croly revealed the conservative side of his nature. In 1866, for example, he suggested to Marble that the *World* change its format to emulate such fashionable European journals as the *London Pall Mall Gazette* and the *Paris Fuelliton*. He proposed that the *World* enlarge to sixteen pages, raise its price to ten cents per issue, and cater to men of taste and refinement. To emphasize the change, the *World* should abandon the tradition of anonymous journalism and should display feature articles by such literary figures as E. C. Stedman, Richard Henry Stoddard, Richard Grant White, George Alfred Townsend, Gail Hamilton, and James Parton. "The taste of the times," Croly declared, "is towards great expense, as the experience of theatres, great public restaurants, and the caterers to public taste in all departments of mercantile enterprise shows that the wealthy and more cultured class demand *not the cheapest but the best articles irrespective of cost*. People who pay 50¢ a glass for their brandy, and 25¢ for their cigar, will not hesitate to expend a dime for the best, handsomest, and ablest paper in the metropolis."

Croly offered these suggestions in October 1866, when public opinion was clearly turning against the Democracy. Perhaps impressed by the ability of the *Herald* and the *Times* to escape public censure by changing their political allegiance, he also urged Marble to show greater political independence. The *World*, he declared, ought to continue to advocate Democratic principles, but ought at the same time to remain aloof from the party organization. "It must be obvious," he remarked, "that the vehement partisanship of the paper has had the effect to excite an opposition that has led the public to overlook the remarkable editorial ability of its columns."[49]

In principle there was little in Croly's program that would have caused Marble to disagree. Marble might well have questioned, however, whether such a course would have been compatible with the situation of a metropolitan daily newspaper. Increased price and an obvious social and cultural bias would certainly have limited circulation and no doubt caused a reduction in advertising revenues. Also the expense of paying distinguished literary men for signed contributions and of increasing the size of the journal to sixteen pages would have added substantially to production costs. In the competitive world of New York journalism it is doubtful if the *World* could have survived as a daily newspaper. It is interesting to note that a few years after he offered these suggestions Croly himself complained of the financial drain caused by the high salaries paid Chamberlain and Hurlbert.[50]

In the matter of political independence, however, Marble agreed with Croly and acted in accordance with his advice. After 1867 the *World*'s editorial columns proclaimed the paper's intention of remaining independent of the party organization. On two striking occasions the *World* directly challenged the party. In the presidential campaign of 1868, it suggested that the party's vice-presidential candidate withdraw from the race, and in 1870 it launched an attack on the Tweed Ring. In neither instance, however, did the *World* gain in prestige or popularity. Both incidents, in fact, alienated powerful supporters and seriously damaged the paper's financial condition. By 1871 Croly had reversed himself and was urging Marble to show more loyalty to the party organization.[51]

These examples indicate, then, that the contrast between Marble and Croly was exaggerated by journalists who were grateful to their former managing editor for inspiration and advice. To drive the point home, it is appropriate to note that much of the *World*'s success resulted directly from Marble's leadership. It was Marble who directed the most daring crusade undertaken by the *World* in the 1860s, when he successfully defied not only the nation's most popular newspaper, the *Herald,* but also the nation's most powerful newspaper organization, the New York Associated Press.

Ever since he assumed control of the *World,* Marble had sought to challenge the *Herald*'s place in New York journalism. Jealous of the *Herald*'s position as the circulation leader among the city dailies, he also harbored a personal grudge because of its attacks on the *World* during its financial crisis in 1862. Throughout the first four years of his editorship, plans for "that *Herald* fight" were frequently discussed. Croly especially championed the idea as a way of increasing the *World*'s circulation.[52]

In the summer of 1866, the long awaited opportunity arrived. With much fanfare, the New York papers announced the opening of the Atlantic cable, which would provide Americans with current reports on European affairs. Seeing at once a chance to steal a march on its competitors, the *Herald* set about to monopolize the cable for itself. Stationing its reporters at the cable offices, the *Herald* began to publish special reports from European capitals. By August it was declaring that the cable "has been the medium of bringing us very important news, for which the public is indebted to the enterprise of the *Herald.*"[53]

The *Herald*'s activities brought forth an immediate response from the other New York dailies. At the time, the *Herald, World, Tribune, Times, Express, Journal of Commerce,* and *Sun* were all members of the New York Associated Press, a newsgathering agency whose agreements with the American Telegraph Company and Western Union allowed it to monopolize the collection and the distribution of news. Under the rules of the association, news collected by members was to be provided to all and the expenses jointly shared. The *Herald* technically abided by these rules, sending its European dispatches to the other members and requesting that they share the cost of collecting them. Papers such as the *World,* however, found themselves unable to pay the price, which often was more than twice the rate charged by the steamship companies that brought the news many days later. Often these papers returned the cables to the *Herald* without paying. Technically relieved of its responsibilities to the association, the *Her-*

ald then published the cables as "Special Telegrams to the *New York Herald.*"[54]

Unable to pay for the dispatches, the *World* sought to prevent the *Herald*'s taking advantage of them. At a meeting of the Associated Press, Nat Bangs, the *World*'s publisher, joined with a majority of the members to block the *Herald*'s request that the association pay for the cables. At the same time, the *World* ridiculed the dispatches as unworthy of publication. One dispatch, it reported, announced the sighting of Guy Fawkes' ghost in London. "It is not likely," it concluded, "that any considerable number of readers, even of the *Herald,* can have failed to discern at a glance the shallow and senseless character of these preposterous 'dispatches.' " The *Herald* replied that Marble was a "nincompoop."[55]

The dispute continued into the fall with neither side being able to force a decision. Then in November, an opportunity suddenly presented itself to Marble. For some time the western press had been growing restive under the domination of the New York association, and the close of the Civil War found them ready to assert their independence. Through their own organization, the Western Associated Press, they determined to attack the eastern monopoly. Meeting in Cincinnati on November 19 and 20, the WAP drew up a list of grievances and appointed a delegation to present them in New York.

The revolt came at a bad time for the easterners. On November 5 the New York AP had dismissed its general agent, Daniel H. Craig, and was in the midst of reorganizing its newsgathering facilities. Craig, whose dismissal had resulted in part from his efforts to solve the dispute over the cable dispatches, responded to his dismissal by organizing a rival news agency. The split in the New York association offered the western representatives, Murat Halstead and Horace White, the chance to drive a good bargain for the West. They proposed that the WAP and the AP cooperate equally in collecting and distributing news, each having complete authority in its own section. When the New Yorkers refused, they formally left the AP and began negotiations with Craig.[56]

This was Marble's chance. The *Herald* and a majority of the AP members firmly opposed the WAP. By supporting Craig and the westerners, Marble believed he would gain the support needed to put the *Herald* in its place. As soon as the news of the western revolt appeared, the *World* offered its support and cooperation. It also announced that it was accepting special news dispatches, probably from Craig, that were not available to AP members. Shortly thereafter, it formally announced an offensive and defensive alliance between Craig and the British news agency of Julius de Reuter. Beginning January 1, 1867, its European coverage would include all the news published in the *Times of London.*[57]

Trying to hold its forces together, the AP lashed out at the

World by unanimously suspending its right to AP dispatches. Marble's success now depended upon the determination of the westerners and the ability of Craig. Should either fail, he would be left alone and humiliated. But his allies remained firm. The day before the WAP members met to ratify the actions of their executive committee, Horace White wired Marble: "Give yourself no uneasiness. We are firm and strong and will listen to no compromises." When the members voted to leave the AP, he wired jubilantly: "The Border Ruffians had it all their way. I congratulate you on your complete emancipation from the Ring." The WAP then proceeded formally to join with Craig in establishing their own news association.[58]

Sensing that he and his allies now held the upper hand, Marble pressed the AP for an immediate settlement on his own terms. Warning the AP president, William C. Prime, that his allies were willing to spend any amount of money, he declared that unless a compromise was speedily effected all the papers outside the city would join in the revolt and would ruin the AP. His terms called for an agreement allowing Craig to withdraw from the newsgathering business; permitting the AP and other newspapers to exchange commercial intelligence at low rates; guaranteeing the WAP fair treatment in the quantity, quality, and general distribution of news; allowing the WAP representation in the AP councils; and preventing "unscrupulous violators" of the association's rules from profiting at the expense of the other members. He also demanded the *World*'s reinstatement in the AP, claiming that he had never, in fact, violated the association's rules.[59]

Rather than engage in a costly struggle, the AP decided to negotiate. The final agreement, announced January 11, 1867, gave the rebels everything they wanted. The WAP and the AP received exclusive territorial rights in newsgathering and agreed to share each other's news through specially designated agents. For withdrawing from the newsgathering business and assigning his Reuters contract to the AP, Craig was to be granted exclusive rights to supply commercial intelligence. The *World* rejoined the AP without penalty. It was total victory. "We were tendered everything for which we made war on the Associated Press," Craig declared to Marble.[60]

Marble's war with the AP had proved an unqualified success. He had not only defied the association with impunity but had also forced concessions that deprived the *Herald* of its ability to use the association for its own ends. Nothing better demonstrated his success than the *Herald*'s unwillingness to abide by the new agreement. Within six months that paper had again made special arrangements to receive European news through its own agents and was threatening to withdraw from the association unless the other members went along. The threats rang hollow, however, for though the *Herald* did establish its own foreign news association, it could not improve on the

Reuters service. Also, the *Herald* representatives were forced to endure the embarrassment of sitting at AP meetings and having Marble call their bluff by introducing resolutions to expel them from the association.[61]

The *Herald* fight won the *World* its place in New York journalism. That was half the story of Marble's success as a "merchant of news." The other half dealt with Marble's efforts to buy out his co-owners.

Marble's ambition to become the sole owner of the *World* first became evident when Elon Comstock arrived in New York to share in managing the paper. When the *World* merged with the *Albany Argus* in the summer of 1863, Comstock came to the city to take charge of the *Weekly World,* subject only to Marble's editorial supervision. Upon arriving, however, he found that Marble had prepared an announcement, declaring only that in some unspecified way he was to be associated with the *World.* He also found that Marble did not intend to allow him to edit the weekly. When he suggested that the weekly ought to carry the typeface of the weekly *Argus,* Marble refused to hear of it.[62]

But that was only the beginning for Comstock. In succeeding months he found himself excluded from all important decisions. His political articles were altered without his consent or were omitted altogether. During Marble's absences, Chamberlain supervised the editorial rooms. When Comstock left town for a few days, his desk was removed from Marble's office. By the end of his first year with the *World* he had been relegated to a corner of the publisher's office and allowed only to write agricultural columns for the weekly. All his protests were ignored.[63]

Realizing that he had no future with the *World,* Comstock soon began looking for opportunities elsewhere. His resolve to leave was no doubt strengthened by the decision of his brother, Calvert, to withdraw altogether from the newspaper business. In February 1865, he resigned from the *World.* Sensing that Comstock's departure showed that the *Argus* was losing enthusiasm for the partnership, Marble at once began negotiations to dissolve it. At first William Cassidy, Calvert Comstock's partner in the *Argus,* suggested that he assume his partner's scrip and move to New York to join Marble in editing the *World.* Marble, of course, refused to consider such a proposal. He also refused to allow Comstock to sell only part of his stock and to wait until the rest had risen to par. It was all or nothing. Although the par value of the stock was $25,000, Marble offered only $15,000 and claimed it was more than he had been advised to offer. On June 2, 1865, Cassidy accepted Marble's terms. Soon afterward Marble increased his holdings by buying up John Anderson's 6/32 interest.[64]

By October 1865 only Marble and Barlow held an interest in the

World, Marble holding 7¼ shares, Barlow 2¾. As soon as he had acquired the other holdings, Marble asked Barlow to surrender his. Thus began a long conversation between the two friends. For the most part the talk was remarkably candid, revealing basic attitudes about themselves, their friendship, and their ambitions. In it were tied the threads of personal loyalty and professional ambition, out of which were woven the status of Manton Marble.

Both Marble and Barlow tried to convict the other of bad faith and disloyalty. Reviewing the course of their business relations, Barlow recalled his first meeting with Marble, his initial skepticism about the financial condition of the *World,* his change of heart upon hearing Marble's earnest pleas for help, and Marble's sincere expressions of gratitude. From that first meeting had grown a friendship to which he had on numerous occasions proved himself loyal. He recalled how he had bought out the Woods' interest so that Marble would not have to associate with men he despised, how he had arranged for the investments that kept the *World* from financial failure, and how he had supported Marble's drive to buy out the other stockholders. He also claimed that he had been responsible for Marble's prominence in politics. "You knew comparatively little of politics, state or national, and still less of the leaders of the party," he recalled. "You know them now, and they know you, as the editor of the *World* only to respect you, to counsel with you and to be guided by your judgment." He thought it fair to conclude that Marble owed him much and was being ungrateful in trying to deprive him of his interest in the *World.*

Barlow was honest enough to admit to ambition on his own part. To one so long active in politics, it was natural to want to maintain an interest in his party's leading journal. For nearly ten years prior to his meeting Marble he had worked to achieve power and influence in the party. Now he found his name linked with Marble's in the *World,* and he hesitated to have it removed.

At the same time Barlow tried to convince Marble that his ambition transcended his self-interest. It was true that he had promised to help his friend control all of the stock, but under the circumstances he thought he should be released from his promise. The income he received from his stock, he declared, was vital to maintaining his standard of living and to providing for his family. Emphasizing that loyalty to his family forbade him to sell, he declared that his wife fully supported him in his course. Thus he urged Marble to reconsider his demand.[65]

It was a formidable indictment, against which Marble could muster only a partial defense. He had to acknowledge Barlow's many services to the *World,* declaring that he appreciated them far more than did his friend. Still, he believed he was entitled to full control. Barlow's aid, he said, had been motivated by a desire for speculative gain while his own motives were more lofty. "To you it was healthful and energizing," he declared, "to me it was peace and salvation." To Marble the *World* had become an integral part of his personality, character, and ambition. Unless he could free the paper from the control of others, he would be unable to free his own spirit and would thus be unable to attain a noble manhood. So long as he shared the ownership of the *World* he could never feel able to defend himself adequately against the attacks of his political and journalistic opponents. Barlow's shares, he contended, were no less than a "permanent mortgage" on his life's work. And he hoped to "give a definite measure and term to that mortgage upon my energies, my training, my professional skill and my reputation, which you invite me to submit myself to in perpetuity."

Marble knew that his request revealed a great personal ambition, and he acknowledged Barlow's right to call attention to it. "But you cannot think it unnatural," he replied, "nor esteem me less because my ambition has grown with my growth." Were Barlow a journalist, he would realize the justice of the demand. Indeed, sole ownership of the *World* would purify Marble's ambition by identifying its policies solely with its editor's principles. "Half the singular power of Bennett," Marble argued, "comes from this, that they judge him with no ambition save that the *Herald* embodies and discount nothing but that. . . . You see how it comes from the core of my heart or I would not press it thus, even though the *World* be to you an investment merely, but to me the inseparable mistress of a life's ambition."[66]

When all this had been said, it was clear that neither had changed his mind. It was equally clear that a compromise was necessary. Neither man really relished the controversy, which was endangering their friendship and filling their lives with anxiety. Realizing that Marble's purpose was fixed, Barlow was the first to suggest a possible solution: arbitration by a mutual friend. But Marble would not hear of it. Interpreting Barlow's suggestion as evidence of his willingness to sell, Marble demanded that his friend honor his promise. While he waited for Barlow's reply, Marble had the famous lawyer Charles O'Conor prepare an opinion, which protected him against any claim Barlow might make against the shares he had purchased from the *Argus*.[67]

Left with no alternative save continuing the fruitless argument, Barlow decided early in November 1868 to sell his interest. For two months he and Marble debated the value of the stock, until he gave way on that point also. On January 21, 1869, Marble became sole owner of the *World* and at last custodian of his own manhood.[68]

The purchase of the *World* marked a transition in Marble's life. In 1858 he had entered New York City a young man from the provinces, sustained only by his abilities and his restless ambition. In 1869 he had become sole owner of one of the city's most popular and respected dailies and a man of stature and influence in its society. These accomplishments in many respects satisfied his youthful ambition of attaining a noble manhood.

Now that the enterprise was over, it was necessary to look ahead. Success had been achieved, but to what purpose? Marble knew the answer. Having succeeded as a "merchant of news," he could turn to the tasks of statesmanship: influencing and marshaling public opinion on the great issues of the day. He was ready to begin, for by 1869 he not only knew the issues but also how to resolve them. ✣

PART THREE

The President-Maker

CHAPTER SEVEN

New Departures in Reconstruction Politics

THE NEW YORK DEMOCRACY's strategy for the elections of 1866 had been simple: demand an immediate, unconditional restoration of the former Confederate states; ally with the president; and maneuver to secure enough support from moderate Republicans and War Democrats to carry the election. For a variety of reasons, the strategy had failed. Moderate and Radical Republicans had joined forces behind the Freedman's Bureau Bill, the Civil Rights Bill, and the proposed Fourteenth Amendment. President Johnson's blustering, aggressive "Swing Around the Circle" had diminished public confidence in his personal abilities. The Barnburner Democrats, suspicious of the Democracy's flirtation with Seward-Weed Republicans and unwilling to compromise their support of equal rights for the black man, refused to desert the Republican party. The results were disastrous. Hoffman lost the governor's race to Fenton by 14,000 votes and the Republicans took 20 of 31 congressional seats. Nationally, Republican strength in Congress increased from 142 to 143 in the House and from 38 to 42 in the Senate.

Yet the New York Democrats still believed that it was possible to achieve an unconditional restoration. Apparently, they never imagined that Congress would impose military rule in the South. Writing to James Buchanan shortly after the First Reconstruction Act had passed the House, Marble confessed that before December it had seemed incredible that Congress would institute martial law "from the Potomac to the Rio Grande." The Democracy had believed the southern states could hold out indefinitely against the Radicals. Throughout the election campaign, the *World* had urged the southern states to reject the Fourteenth Amendment, declaring that ratification might lead to further conditions. Opposition, the *World* declared, would in no way harm the South. The southern states would still remain out of the Union, and as the controversy over their restoration remained unresolved, public opinion in the North would turn on the Radicals and would force them to restore the Union unconditionally. "The Radicals," the *World* declared, "must do something. They are responsible for disunion; they can only rid themselves of the responsibility by permitting the Union to restore itself."[1]

Marble found the South eager to heed such advice. In October the Texas legislature overwhelmingly rejected the Fourteenth Amendment. Georgia followed suit in November, and by the first of January seven of the southern states stood together in unanimous opposition. The southern press also followed the *World*'s advice. In opposing Negro suffrage, the *New Orleans Crescent* declared that "there is not hostile power enough on this continent to force upon us a result so inconsistent with our feelings, so adverse to our best interests, so entirely uncalled for, so humiliating to all proper sense of political dignity, and so utterly useless to the class sought to be raised to a level for which they have no fitness, and to which they have no semblance of a rightful claim." In fact, so widespread and so enthusiastic was the southern opposition that one may question whether the *World* actually influenced southern opinion or merely responded to it. As early as October 13, 1866, John Forsyth, editor of the *Mobile Advertiser and Register* and secretary of war under James Buchanan, had outlined just the postelection strategy the *World* was to follow. "The *Herald* and that ilk threaten us with dreadful things if we refuse [to ratify the amendment] and promises much if we consent," he wrote, "but its advice and its menaces are disregarded, and no one believes it has the power to make good its promises. We think we owe it to our friends at the North as well as to ourselves to decline to surrender any of our voting power in Congress, and we owe it to the whole country to refuse all instrumentality in fastening the canker of black suffrage on the voting system." Faced with such an attitude in the southern states, Marble may well have thought it best to follow along and hope for the best. In any event, it appears that the strategy of continued opposition to the Fourteenth Amendment represented majority opinion among both northern and southern Democrats.[2]

Northern and southern Democrats also placed great hopes in Andrew Johnson's determination to continue his opposition to the Radicals. If the president stood firm, exasperated northerners could rally around him to force an immediate restoration. John Forsyth even suggested that Johnson might lead a forcible resistance to the Radicals. "A counter-revolution can alone roll back the advancing mass," he declared to Marble, "and it all depends on the President." Marble was horrified by the prospect of civil war breaking out again, but he fully approved of the president's attacking the Radicals by every peaceful means. In fact, one of the Democracy's greatest fears in the postelection months was that the president might decide to compromise with Congress. Shortly before Johnson was to deliver his annual message to Congress, Ivory Chamberlain and S. S. Cox journeyed to

Washington to survey the situation. Although Montgomery Blair assured them that Johnson would perform satisfactorily, Chamberlain was unconvinced. "It is for our interest to precipitate this fight with the Radicals," he reminded Marble, "and I am apprehensive that Johnson will so manage as to postpone it." He reported that he had inspired Cox to launch "some sort of thunderbolt" once the president delivered his message in order to "set the Radicals on fire and kindle a conflagration." Even if Johnson did try to compromise with the Radicals, the Democracy would have to continue its opposition. "If the President does not give us an opportunity to fight the Radicals in *his* interest," Chamberlain declared, "we must fight both them and him in our own."[3]

For the most part Johnson behaved satisfactorily. In his message he held to his position that the southern states were entitled to immediate representation in Congress. On January 17 he declared publicly that the southern states had nothing to gain by ratifying the Fourteenth Amendment. "I do not believe," he added, "that the people of the whole country will sustain any set of individuals in attempts to change the whole character of our government by enabling acts or otherwise."[4]

The Democracy also hoped the Supreme Court would come to its aid. Especially heartening was the Court's decision in the Milligan Case, holding that in areas where the civil courts were functioning, Congress had no power to declare martial law and to authorize military trials for civilians. Despite the narrowness of a 5–4 decision, the *World* believed the Court could be relied upon to overrule any Radical plan to subject the South to military rule.[5]

With the South, the president, and the Court apparently ready to fight the radicals to the end, the *World* sought to win northern public opinion to its cause. As Chamberlain's letter indicated, the Democracy hoped for some dramatic conflict to break out between the president and Congress in order to rally the public. The issue that seemed most likely to start such a conflict was the Radical effort to impeach the president. During the campaign, Marble had considered the question of impeachment, though it is impossible to determine how seriously. On January 7, however, when the House resolved to investigate the president's conduct to see if grounds existed for impeachment, the issue was out in the open. At once the *World* sought to take advantage of it. "The removal of the President," it declared, "is a party necessity for the Republicans." The longer Johnson blocked the Republican reconstruction program, the greater the likelihood that northern voters would rally to his side. Thus the Republicans faced the choice of yielding to the president or of deposing him at once. Convinced that Republican pride, ambition, malice, and insolence would never permit them to yield, the *World* foresaw impeachment as inevitable.[6]

Obviously, Marble hoped that impeachment would so enrage northern opinion as to cause a great turning away from the Republicans. Also, he may have hoped that Johnson would seize the occasion to intensify his opposition to further reconstruction. At least the *World* seemed to imply this when it declared that Johnson would continue to frustrate the Republicans as long as he controlled the army and refused to enforce Republican legislation. Having said this, the *World* called for the people to rally behind the president. "Nothing can restrain [the Republicans]," it declared, "but vigorous and overwhelming popular demonstrations." Mild opposition merely encouraged the Republicans "by leading them to think they will encounter no resolute opposition."

While the *World* called for public demonstrations, the party leaders undertook to provide them. Across the country Democratic state conventions resolved for a national convention to protest the impeachment, and the National Democratic Association, inspired by Belmont and Charles Mason, the chairman of the National Democratic Resident Committee in Washington, protested Republican schemes and suggested the Democracy might use force to defeat them.

As the party machinery rolled forward, the *World* intensified its attack. Five days after first calling for popular demonstrations, the paper counseled fellow Democrats not to resist Republican efforts to remove the president. If the Senate would agree to give the president a fair hearing, through counsel of his own choosing, the Democracy would commit a "fatal mistake" by attempting to interfere with the proceedings or to resist the verdict. Instead, the party should stand aside and await the response of the American people. "The Republicans," the *World* cautioned its followers, "are apparently about to commit a stupendous blunder. Instead of interposing between them and political suicide, it is the business of the Democracy to take advantage of their folly, when they have gone too far to retreat."

Realizing that a successful impeachment would injure the Democracy so long as it continued to support the president, on the following day the *World* savagely attacked him. From the day of his accession, the *World* declared, Johnson had never acted with the Democracy. By staying aloof he had enabled the Republicans to "shame their rank and file out of any inclination to desert to the Democrats." Had Johnson boldly led the way in the early stages of the reconstruction debate, he could have divided the Republicans. Had he then "countenanced the Democratic party," he could have brought it a large popular following. Instead he had followed his own "peculiar course," thereby maintaining the strength of the Republican party "without in any degree disarming its hostility to him." Clearly, then, no true Democrat had any reason to bemoan the president's impeachment.[7]

In this way Marble fashioned Democratic strategy in the early weeks of 1867. Believing that the Republicans would not impose military reconstruction and that northerners desired above all a speedy restoration of the Union, he no doubt thought his plans had a good chance to succeed. If the Democrats could hold their ground, they could frustrate the Radicals, win over northern opinion, effect an unconditional restoration, and reap the rewards in the next presidential election.

It soon became evident, however, that Marble's strategy had only played into the hands of the Radicals. Committed to working out a reconstruction program and worried that the Democratic strategy might succeed, Republican leaders turned their full efforts upon getting a reconstruction bill through the lame-duck session of the Thirty-ninth Congress. In their haste and anxiety, they shelved the impeachment issue, thus depriving the *World* of a key element in its strategy. As the Republican determination became increasingly evident, new rumors appeared that Johnson had finally decided to compromise with Congress. Apparently unaware that its own denunciations of the president might have encouraged him to seek such a compromise, the *World* declared anxiously that the time for compromise had long since passed. Now that the president had "exasperated the Radicals" and had "educated the South into stubbornness," there was no turning back. Compromise would not win the president new friends; it would only alienate the few friends he still possessed. Such advice, if it had any effect at all, merely served to keep the president inactive during the writing of the Reconstruction Act, so that during a crucial stage of the reconstruction process he gave the Democracy no support. On February 20 Congress at last passed a reconstruction bill and sent it to the president.[8]

The bill divided the South into five military districts, provided for establishing provisional governments, and set forth the conditions the states would have to meet in order to gain readmission to the Union. Principally, it required that the southern states establish Negro suffrage, exclude former Confederate leaders from holding office, and ratify the Fourteenth Amendment.

To Marble the significance of the bill lay not so much in its provisions as in its very existence. Congress had acted, thus defeating his hopes for defeating the Republicans by prolonging a deadlock. Realizing that the bill would certainly become law over the president's veto, Marble began at once to formulate a new political strategy. The Democracy could no longer rely upon the president's opposition or upon southern intransigence to frustrate the Republicans. Nor could it safely rely upon the Supreme Court, since the Republicans had reduced the membership on the Court to seven, thus insuring against the president's appointing conservative replacements. Since the older justices were the more conservative, the Court would soon be in the hands of Radical sympathizers. But even if it had been possible to rush through a successful test case against the Reconstruction Act, little would have been accomplished. The Republicans had shown themselves so determined to enact their own reconstruction program that they would merely continue to exclude the southern states.

Here lay the heart of the problem. Marble had advocated the strategy of deadlock in the hope that an angry North, demanding a speedy restoration, would force Congress to readmit the southern states without conditions. This would have permitted ten Democratic states to rejoin the Union in plenty of time to help elect a Democratic president in 1868. But the Reconstruction Act had changed all that. The Republicans had presented a plan for restoration, and presumably northerners would expect the South to abide by it. The Republicans had seized control of the reconstruction process and now seemed able to use it for their partisan purposes.

Such thoughts ran through Marble's mind as he considered the Democracy's future. As he meditated, he seems to have resolved the problem into the following terms: the Democracy's principal aim was to restore a Democratic South; the Republicans hoped to prevent such a result either by refusing to readmit the southern states or by using Negro votes to create a Republican South; if the Democracy encouraged further resistance, it would merely give the Republicans an excuse for further delay; if the Democracy offered no resistance, Republicans would be able to fashion their majorities in the southern states. There seemed only one way out of such a dilemma. Northern Democrats should accept the Reconstruction Act, thus committing the Republicans to a definite plan of restoration. Southern Democrats should also accept the act, but should try to control the reconstruction process by influencing the Negro vote. Indeed, many southern leaders had seemed willing to accept such a plan. A few weeks earlier Governors Sharkey, Parsons, and Orr had met with Johnson and had worked out a proposal calling for an impartial suffrage in exchange for amnesty for former Confederate leaders. If the southern Democrats succeeded, the Republicans would have no recourse but to restore a Democratic South in time for the presidential election. Thus the time was ripe for the Democracy to adopt a new departure in its reconstruction policy.[9]

Once he had formulated his strategy, Marble set about putting it into practice. On February 21, the day after the reconstruction bill passed Congress, the *World* urged President Johnson to return an immediate veto rather than to use a pocket veto, which would kill the bill for the session. Declaring that a pocket veto would allow the Republicans to drop the bill and to blame the president for excluding the southern states from the 1868 elections, the *World* urged the president to bind the Republicans to their present plan. "This bill, bad as it is," it announced, "is more favorable than any likely to be passed in its stead."

Two days later, the *World* began to outline the strategy for the South. It mainly attempted to persuade the southerners to accept Negro suffrage. Arguing that military rule made Negro suffrage inevitable, the *World* urged the South "to welcome the negro vote *and control it,* [rather] than by ineffectual resistance to sour and exasperate the negro mind, and thus render it as a political tool into the hands of the Radicals." Realizing that many southerners would not easily give up their resistance and also that many northern Democrats wanted that resistance to continue, the *World* presented its plan modestly, referring to it only as an alternative course of action. If the South continued to resist, it would have to maintain white solidarity and perhaps to engage in armed resistance. Honorable though such a course might be, the South should realize that peaceful political action was more likely to succeed. Again and again the *World* emphasized the need to have southern votes cast in the coming presidential election. Only by electing a Democratic president could the South be sure that conservatives would be appointed to the Supreme Court and that legislation repealing the Reconstruction Act would be signed into law.[10]

For a time it seemed that the South was willing to accept the *World*'s advice. Joseph E. Brown, Confederate governor of Georgia, counseled the South to accept the Reconstruction Act. He was soon joined by Governor Patton of Alabama and former Governor Albert G. Brown of Mississippi. Even John Forsyth agreed with Marble. "United ourselves," he wrote, "we can easily manage the negroes." On March 9 the *World* covered its front page with editorials from twenty-five southern newspapers, all agreeing with its strategy.[11]

As the Reconstruction Act went into effect, the *World* continued to urge compliance on the part of the South. As the summer of 1867 wore on, however, and preparations went forward to select delegates to state constitutional conventions, its attitude began to change. By mid-August the *World* was voicing suspicions about the wisdom of Negro suffrage, suggesting that the practice might endanger white property rights. Six weeks later it was denouncing Negro suffrage as a cynical attempt by Congress to impose rule by ignorant savages upon the southern states.[12]

The *World*'s about-face was in part a response to developments in the South. As the military governors assumed their duties, appeals came north from southern Democrats for aid in capturing the Negro vote. From North Carolina Marble learned that Republicans were planning to flood the state with Radical speakers and to organize the Negroes and the "frazzle-end of our whites" in the Republican party. Although the editor of the *Wilmington Daily and Weekly Journal* thought the Democracy could control the convention "even without the Negro vote," he wondered if Marble thought it was still wise to try to win Negro support. The Democratic candidate for governor in Georgia paid Marble a personal visit, bringing a letter of introduction, requesting northern money to finance his campaign. "The *sinews of war*," the letter frankly stated, "are not abundant."[13]

Whether they called for money, for speakers, or only for advice, all the letters showed that leading southerners doubted their ability to carry out the *World*'s strategy. No doubt those feelings multiplied as northern Democrats failed to respond to their pleas. When Marble approached Belmont for financial aid, he received a firm refusal. "I have spent as much and more money for politics and for the South than I had any business to do," Belmont wrote. "It is never too late to mend and I have made up my mind not to sin any more in that direction, even if tempted by so seductive a fellow as you." As their appeals went unanswered and as the Republican organizing drive proceeded apace, southerners gradually came to doubt the good faith of their northern advisers. As early as June 1, a Democratic editor in Maine had urged Marble to sponsor a convention of northern and southern editors to unite the Democratic effort. "You cannot have failed to have observed in your southern exchanges of late," he warned, "expressions of *distrust* of our Northern Democracy."[14]

As the summer passed and no help came from the North, southern Democrats lapsed into inactivity. While Republicans organized and registered thousands of the freedmen to vote for their delegates to the constitutional conventions, Democratic whites refused to stir. Throughout the South there were reports of "appalling apathy" shown by white voters. As voter registrations proceeded, fear of Negro domination only added to the paralysis. By the end of August, the southern Democracy had become so demoralized that Wade Hampton, who had been one of the earliest supporters of the *World*'s strategy, was declaring that it would be better for the South to remain out of the Union and under military rule than for it to be restored under Republican control. By fall the southern Democracy had decided almost unanimously to boycott the state elections.[15]

While southerners were turning away from Marble's advice, northerners were also suggesting another course. The drive to establish Negro suffrage in the South had inspired similar movements in the North. In 1867 New York, Ohio, Kansas, and Minnesota considered Negro suffrage and in each case either postponed or rejected the proposition. In June the issue came before the New York State Constitutional Convention. Under the constitution of 1846, New York had allowed Negroes to vote if they owned $250 in property. In 1867, however, the Republican majority, led by Horace Greeley, sponsored a measure bestowing the franchise upon all male citizens twenty-one years of age or older and a resident of the state for one year prior to the election. The Democracy opposed the measure. William Cassidy presented a report on behalf of the existing provision and Samuel J. Tilden asked the convention to submit the issue to a popular vote. Although the convention finally adopted the Republican measure, it did not do so until after the November elections, thus denying the voters the opportunity to vote on the question. The Democracy charged the Republicans with gross hypocrisy. "If the Republicans are really in favor of negro suffrage," the *World* declared, "why did they refuse to submit it as a constitutional amendment?"[16]

In the meantime the *World* was warning its readers of the dangers of Negro domination in the South. On October 4 it declared that the only way to save the country from "actual negro control" was to defeat the Republican party in the North. "A sweeping Democratic victory in the North, united with the nearly unanimous vote of the Southern whites, will give us the victory." It would be especially disastrous for the Democracy to fail in the 1868 presidential election, since a Republican victory would lead to more Radical truckling to the Negro interest. When Ohio defeated a Negro suffrage amendment by over 50,000 votes, the *World* completely reversed its position of six months earlier and made opposition to Negro suffrage its principal campaign issue. "Negro suffrage is the hinge of the whole Republican policy," it announced, "it is what they most value in the Reconstruction laws; it is the vital breath of the party." To impose Negro suffrage on the South, while rejecting it in the North, was "a gross absurdity and monstrous injustice." The Ohio election had renounced the principle and exposed the efforts to force it on the South as "a piece of hypocritical tyranny."

The response to Negro suffrage in both North and South was thus forcing Marble to adopt another departure in his political strategy. No doubt the circumstances tempted him to return again to the strategy of deadlock. But he resisted the temptation, perhaps because it had already failed once. He may also have noticed that the *Evening Post,* the spokesman for the crucial Barnburner faction, continued to support Negro suffrage. If the Democracy hoped to win back enough Barnburners to fashion a Democratic majority in the state, the party could not content itself merely to oppose Negro suffrage.

On October 21 Marble presented another departure. Accepting the southern decision to remain aloof from the reconstruction process, he called upon northerners to return more Democratic victories in the state elections to show the Republicans the errors of their program. If the Democracy carried the northern states it could thwart Radical Reconstruction. Although the Republicans would still control Congress, the northern Democrats would be strong enough to check their schemes. By surrendering their states to Negro control, the southern whites would make their Republican state governments "contemptible." A northern public, unwilling to accept Negro rule in either North or South, would then presumably force the Republicans in Congress to offer the South more lenient terms. Marble believed the Republicans would be willing to restore the southern states in return for a constitutional amendment guaranteeing the freedman's civil rights. Perhaps Negro suffrage might come after the freedman had prepared himself for it, but for the moment he would have to submit to a government by white men.[17]

The fall elections went as well as Marble could have hoped, returning Democratic majorities in Pennsylvania, Connecticut, and New York and seriously reducing Republican majorities in Ohio, Maine, and Massachusetts. Kansas and Minnesota also joined Ohio in voting down Negro suffrage. In New York the Democratic ticket swept the state with a majority just under 48,000 votes. Although the general apathy attending such off-year elections and the influence of other issues such as the exposures of Republican corruption contributed to the Democratic victory, Marble could well believe that he had taken the proper stand on Negro suffrage. Perhaps his offering an alternative to Negro suffrage had in fact brought some of the Barnburners back into the Democratic fold. At least the *World* indicated as much when it declared that "we are indebted for this magnificent and manifold triumph to citizens who have not, for the last few years, acted in the Democratic party."[18]

In the weeks following the elections, Marble developed his compromise strategy more fully. On November 13 the *World* offered a comprehensive proposal for reconstruction and restoration. It called for a bipartisan national convention of leading southerners and northerners. The southerners, it suggested, might show their good faith by accepting a limited Negro suffrage, which in a generation would become universal. In return, the northerners might accept constitutional amendments requiring a two-thirds vote to pass appropriation bills, limiting the president to one 6-year term, and granting him an item-veto. While its readers pondered such suggestions, the *World* continued to urge the southern states to guarantee Negro civil rights.[19]

Marble's fellow Democrats accorded his suggestions a mixed response. Such hidebound conservatives as James Buchanan and George Ticknor Curtis thought the party ought not to risk division by presenting its own program but should confine itself to opposing Negro suffrage and to preaching traditional Democratic constitutionalism. The ever-cautious Tilden thought the *World* should remain silent on Negro suffrage until the New Yorkers had voted upon it. Then, if suffrage was approved, the Democracy could appeal for Negro votes.

A few southerners favored the *World*'s suggestions. John Forsyth declared that Alabama Democrats had at last decided to appeal openly for Negro votes. W. N. Haldeman, editor of the *Louisville Courier,* approved Marble's position and requested the *World*'s aid in removing civil disabilities from Kentucky Negroes.

Although there were signs of hope in these responses, the overall picture was still unfavorable. Most of the party leaders, instead of accepting Negro suffrage and bidding to restore the southern states as quickly as possible, were still determined to fight the Radical state constitutions and to rely upon northern Negrophobia to sweep the Democracy back into power. Early in 1868 Alabama Democrats set the pattern for the South by boycotting the referendum on their new constitution. In the Midwest, former copperheads adamantly refused to countenance Negro suffrage. Faced with such attitudes, Marble could not long continue to support his compromise strategy. Soon, compromise proposals disappeared from the columns of the *World,* and the paper returned to pointing out the horrors of Negro domination in the South and to urging all southern whites to boycott the elections to ratify their state constitutions. Returning to its deadlock strategy, it declared that passive resistance by southern whites would force the Republicans to maintain military rule, which in turn would so enrage northern opinion that the Republicans would be swept from office in the presidential election. So far as the northern Democracy was concerned, Negro suffrage would remain a partisan issue.[20]

Many northern Democrats had refused to give up the suffrage issue because the alternative was so unattractive. Shortly after the elections of 1866, some party spokesmen in the Middle West had called upon the Democracy to accept Negro suffrage and to concentrate its fire upon the Republican economic program. Chief among these was Wilbur F. Storey of the *Chicago Times.* Storey urged his party to become again a "progressive and aggressive party" by concentrating on such economic issues as the tariff and currency reform. Following the passage of the Reconstruction Act, which discredited the deadlock strategy, Storey's approach gained considerable support. In March 1867 the *World* suggested that the party turn to the economic hardships imposed on the workingman by Republican financial policies. It was in Ohio, however, that Storey's advice became most popular. There, Washington McLean, editor of the *Cincinnati Enquirer,* came forward with a proposal to pay the national debt in greenbacks. When it seemed that McLean's idea was gaining widespread approval in the state, the less inflationist Democratic leadership appropriated and modified his program. The final product, known as the Pendleton Plan after its sponsor, George H. Pendleton, was cleverly contrived to appeal to both moderate and radical agrarians. Instead of proposing to pay the entire national debt in greenbacks, the plan proposed to pay only the $338 million principle of the 5–20 bonds held by the national banks. While this was being done the Treasury should use the $18 million in gold annually saved by not paying interest to the national banks, add the $48 million in gold received from customs revenues, and convert the total into a sinking fund of $92 million in greenbacks, with which to pay the rest of the debt. A political masterpiece, the plan combined western hostility toward eastern bondholders and the national banks with inflationist hopes for an expanded money supply. Veteran political observers agreed that it was largely responsible for the strong showing of the Ohio Democracy in the 1867 elections.[21]

Although the plan horrified the leaders of the New York Democracy, they treated the Pendleton Plan cautiously in public. Realizing the plan's western appeal, they hoped to avoid a party split that would endanger their chances in the presidential election. Thus when Pendleton complained to Marble about unfair treatment in the eastern press, Marble wrote an editorial on his behalf. Arguing that the plan would not really inflate the currency, he concluded that it could not injure the public creditors. If the Treasury was to pay the 5–20s in greenbacks, he declared, the loss to the holder would be 7 percent. But with the price of gold at 140, the bondholder would receive 7.2 percent interest in coin. If a person bought 5–20s today and three years later received payment in greenbacks, his interest would amount to 6 percent, enough to allow him to recover his entire investment. Thus the public creditor had no reason to fear that the Pendleton Plan would mean repudiation. Indeed, since the 5–20s were presently selling at 106, "precisely the price they would be worth if payable in currency," the bondholders actually *expected* to be paid in greenbacks. Ignoring the probability that the bondholders had invested with higher hopes than of just breaking even, Marble concluded that they opposed the Pendleton Plan for no selfish motive. Rather, they opposed it out of a "high sense of national honor and a punctilious regard to the public faith." Although far from an endorsement, the article at least defended Pendleton against charges that he was an all-out inflationist. When he read it, Pendleton said he was satisfied.[22]

Marble's article fairly stated his views on the Pendleton Plan. For him, questions of economic policy could never turn on narrow class or personal self-interest. From his college days he had learned to regard mere acquisitiveness as an unworthy motive, and though he had shown a good deal of it himself, he had always considered it part of his ambition for a noble manhood. Marble had first encountered economic theory in reading Francis Wayland's *The Elements of Political Economy,* which declared that moral principles provided the surest guide to a true science of wealth. Wayland assumed that individual moral character, rather than legislative fiat, would assure prosperity. Thus he opposed bankruptcy laws, which tried to relieve debtors of their moral responsibilities to pay up. Rigid observance of all contracts, he maintained, would hasten the accumulation of capital while also raising moral barriers to extravagance and vice. Convinced of the morality of hard money, he favored a currency of specie or of notes easily convertible into specie.[23]

By 1868 Marble had found Wayland's views reenforced by the teachings of Herbert Spencer, the Jeffersonian and Jacksonian economic tradition, and his friends in the "swallow-tail" Democracy. Generally, he believed the economy worked best when it was left free to be run by men of well-disciplined moral character. He declared to Dr. Anderson:

> There is no science of exchanges except free trade. I can hardly imagine the teaching of anything at all about exchanges of the use and products of men's faculties, in a philosophical and scientific way, which did not demonstrate the saving of labor to all men by freedom in those exchanges. I think it even disputable if the interests of any considerable class, in this country, or in England, France, and Germany can be permanently benefitted by a protective tariff. Individual interests doubtless may profit by them, in certain cases and for short periods of time. That defines protection as plundering and jobbery. The science of jobbery hardly needs a university to expound it.

When he came to apply his principles to the Pendleton Plan, he had no difficulty finding it "unsound in morals and weak in political economy." "Greenbacks are a debt," he asserted, "nothing is paid by mere promises to pay." The government could pay the 5–20s in greenbacks only through taxation or by the printing press. Marble believed the inland revenues would fall below even the lowest estimates, while expenditures would remain high. Hence the government would have to turn to the printing press to carry out the Pendleton Plan. "But Pendleton denies that he proposes inflation to the extent of a single dollar," Marble declared. "Pah!"[24]

Yet there was a more important reason for rejecting the Pendleton Plan. Not only did the plan threaten the national honor and sound morals but also threatened Democratic chances in the presidential election. The elections of 1867 had shown that the Democracy could expect to win in 1868 only if it kept its forces united. But unity seemed unlikely should Pendleton or some other inflationist win the nomination. From upstate New York such well-informed observers as William H. Bogart, the *World*'s Albany correspondent, and Joseph Warren of the *Buffalo Courier* were warning Marble of the danger. "A great many leading men who . . . affect realities," Bogart declared, "consider an attack on national obligations as a blow at their possessions, and they will leave all else to take care of those."[25]

Adding to the threats from the West were threats at home. The party leaders realized that the victories in the recent elections had been achieved with the help of conservative Republicans and "former Democrats." As in 1866, they hoped to incorporate these elements into the Democracy, but also as in 1866, they hoped to avoid having to share power with them. Following the elections, Horatio Seymour warned Tilden that "the time-servers and spoil hunters are seeking to come back to our party, not as penitents, but as leaders. . . . There is a danger that these men may divide those who stood together in the years of trial and trouble." He believed the party already had enough generals and needed only more troops.[26]

Further to complicate matters, the returnees favored hard money. This was especially true of the Barnburners, whom Marble described as "in every philosophical sense Democrats."[27] If the Pendleton men captured the party in 1868, the Barnburners might well be lost again. Thus the old leaders had still another reason to look fearfully upon the Pendleton Plan; it threatened them fully as much as had the peace issue.

In the early months of 1868, the New York Democracy set out to avoid the mistakes of 1864. In January and February meetings were held to appeal to former Democrats and "conservatives" of all kinds to join the Democracy. On March 2 August Belmont, chairman of the Democratic National Committee, issued a letter to the state chairmen, asking them to appeal to "the conservative element throughout the Union which has not heretofore acted with the Democratic party." He suggested the party concentrate on such issues as congressional usurpation of executive and judicial power, and the corruption and mismanagement that had caused burdensome taxation, Negro domination, and continued disunion.[28]

Meanwhile, the New Yorkers asserted their authority in the councils of the National Committee. At the committee meeting in Washington on February 20, they overcame western demands that the national convention be held in St. Louis or Cincinnati and located the meeting in New York.[29]

They also began framing the issues. Practical politics dictated that the Democracy not repudiate the Pendleton Plan. Since, however, the plan could not be endorsed without risking the loss of considerable eastern support, there was only one alternative: the whole issue would have to be dismissed. On January 20 the *World* set out to accomplish this by calling the plan politically inexpedient. Pendleton, it declared, had merely made a logical deduction from "Republican principles of finance." If it was right to pay off private creditors in greenbacks, it was right to pay off public creditors in greenbacks. This had been the logic pursued by the Republicans in the recent congressional elections in Ohio. The Republican strategy seemed based on the belief that there were more debtors than creditors in the country. Yet, the *World* warned, there were in fact "multitudes of voters" who were out of debt and who had no interest in the plan aside from a concern for "the general interest and prosperity of the country." Although politically inactive for the moment, that class would ultimately control the election. The *World* concluded that any party that followed a policy of inflation would only "suffer far more than it would gain."[30]

The Democratic State Convention, which met March 11 in Albany, afforded the New Yorkers their best opportunity to frame the issues. On the first day Seymour and Tilden delivered addresses, outlining the New York strategy. Seymour dealt largely with economic questions. Following the line of the *World,* he insinuated a connection between Republican financial policies and the Pendleton Plan. He charged the Republicans with dividing the nation into hostile debtor and creditor factions by raising the tariff, favoring the New England states in the national banking system, and imposing heavy internal taxes to finance lavish salaries, corruption, and military rule in the South. He also noted that the Republicans had created hostility toward bondholders by exempting them from taxation and by paying them in coin while forcing private creditors to accept greenbacks. To solve the nation's financial problems, he called for a return to hard money. Payment of debts in greenbacks would not only defraud the widows and orphans who held the government bonds, it would also create "uncertainty and confusion," increase the cost of living, and continue the already oppressive burden of taxation. If the Democracy should return to power, however, "sterling coin shall ring again on the counter of the tradesman and glitter in the palm of labor, and gladden the heart of the wounded soldier." Praising the speech, the *World* declared it was just the sort of argument needed to win new men to the Democracy. "Though it is important to kindle the energy of Democrats, it is more necessary to proselyte Republicans."[31]

Tilden's address dealt wholly with the issues of Reconstruction. In various ways he played upon the theme that the Republican policy was dangerously centralizing the power of government. Charging the Republicans with ignoring the opportunities for a speedy and peaceful restoration of the Union, he accused them of attempting to increase their strength in Congress by imposing Negro rule in the South. In their attempt they had trampled upon the rights of the states to control suffrage. Also they had established a costly and tyrannical armed force to maintain their authority. Finally, they had made war upon the executive and the courts. "These changes are organic," Tilden declared, "they would revolutionize the very nature of the government. They would alter every important part of its structure on which its authors relied to secure good laws and good administration, and to preserve civil liberty."

The Republicans were also accused of attempting to change American society. Tilden argued that Americans had traditionally granted political rights only to those who "could be admitted into the family." They had refused "to enter into a partnership in self-government with inferior or with mixed races." Neither Mexicans, Chinese, nor Indians had been considered fit for citizenship. It was unthinkable, therefore, to enfranchise the 932,000 Negro males of voting age, for no one dared risk such a dilution of American society. Only the European immigrants who sprang "from the same parent stock with ourselves" were capable of assimilation. "A man born in the land of our ancestors," he concluded, "may become, in every essential characteristic, a native here almost immediately. A man descended from an African may be, after the lapse of centuries, still an alien."[32]

Although the *World* praised Seymour's speech more than Tilden's, Marble personally approved of Tilden's the more. To Dr. Anderson he declared that "the dominant issues in the November elections will be organic, structural, institutional ones, not financial, nor tariff, nor currency issues." Practical considerations suggested such an approach, since Pennsylvania, a key state, was protectionist. But more importantly, Pennsylvania's vote would be needed so that the Democracy could preserve the structure of representative self-government in the United States. Pendleton's mistake, Marble declared, was not so much his greenbackism as his attempt to elevate "an inferior and unimportant issue," which Marble hoped to dispose of.

Marble believed the Republican party could never adopt "liberal ideas" because, like the old Whig party, its "philosophy of state initiative" forced it to be "the party of class interests, of jobbery." From Jefferson's time onward, they had been "the tariff men, the enlargers of state functions, the limitless directors and oppressors of state liberty and of free individual activity." This philosophy, enhanced by the large war expenditures and the resulting "army of officeholders," had brought the Republicans to their present position as the oppressors of liberty. As he looked over their ranks, Marble could see no important person or persons influential enough to turn them to another course.

Thus it was up to the Democracy to cure the nation's "organic malady" by restoring individual liberty and local self-government. After that, Marble predicted, it would concentrate on free trade, "because [then] it will not hesitate to risk the loss of Pennsylvania and to strike for the great western states." The Democracy would have to take such a course because its "principles, philosophy of politics, its way of looking at things, all tend and constrain it in this direction." There would be difficulties, since the "generations which were educated upon this topic are gone," since the large national debt would obscure the need for free trade, and since the science of political economy had grown up in an age of protectionism. Still, he believed the descendants of the tariff reformers of the 1840s would be the free traders of 1870.[33]

Although such views reflected Marble's political and social education, they also seemed eminently practical. To bring the currency issue before the public would be to risk a serious party split. Thus it seemed wiser, as Marble advised Washington McLean, to exclude the currency question from the platform altogether and to concentrate upon issues, such as states rights, that all could agree upon. McLean replied that though he favored a bold statement on the currency question, he wanted above all to avoid a quarrel with the *World*. Pendleton added his own agreement. Perhaps the lessons of 1864 had, at last, taught the two wings of the Democracy to work together.[34]

With the issues seemingly settled, it remained to find a suitable candidate. In 1864 the easterners had attempted to blur the distinction between the two parties by supporting a popular military man. Such strategy well suited the needs of a party that had been reduced to minority status and that needed to attract outsiders in order to triumph. To many Democrats, including Montgomery Blair, it continued to have a strong appeal. Throughout 1867 Blair sought to focus the attention of the Democracy on Ulysses S. Grant. Still hoping to arrange an alliance between the Democracy and the Johnson administration, Blair believed that Grant would be the proper vehicle for success. For during 1867 Grant seemed to sympathize with the beleaguered president.[35]

For a time Marble and the other New York leaders showed considerable interest in Grant's candidacy. When Wisconsin's conservative senator, James R. Doolittle, pointed to a radical speech by Grant's close friend, General John A. Rawlins, and claimed that Grant had joined the Radicals, Marble refused to believe him. Noting that Grant was "unpracticed in civil affairs," Marble recalled previous occasions on which the general had opposed Radical ideas. He also declared that the Democratic victories in the 1867 elections might have caused the general to turn away from his Radical suitors. Personally, he preferred to wait until Grant had spoken for himself. In the meantime, he thought Doolittle should try to discourage the Radicals by publicizing Grant's conservative statements.[36]

Early in 1868 Grant spoke. When the Senate declared that his appointment as secretary of war violated the Tenure of Office Act, he gave up the office and deserted the Johnson administration. His action convinced Marble that he had gone over to the Radicals. On January 22 the *World* declared that the Democracy could no longer think of nominating him.[37]

But if Grant was unacceptable, so was Andrew Johnson. Since early in 1867 the New Yorkers had given up hope for the president. Unwilling to ally with him until he committed himself to their organization, they refused to support him so long as he kept Seward and Stanton in his cabinet. In March 1867 Marble wrote Montgomery Blair that "a more unapproachable blunderer never had put into his hands the cards of a great game. . . . Cowed by the fear of impeachment, the President has consented to impotence, and chosen the worser part. Chained to Stanton and Seward one wonders which is the body of Death." Later that fall, after a conversation with Tilden, Gideon Welles observed that the Democracy had decided to "cut clear" of the administration. "The President is too much identified with Seward," he wrote, "has been too much advised by him to gain the affections, or even the good will of the New York Democrats."[38]

To some observers it seemed that the New Yorkers were preparing to nominate one of their own men. When the National Committee selected New York City for the national convention, such different observers as the former Barnburner, John Bigelow, and the Pendleton newspaper, the *Cincinnati West and South,* concluded that a move was afoot to nominate Seymour. "Tilden thinks Seymour will run stronger than any man in New York," Gideon Welles recorded in his diary, "he does not look beyond it."[39]

Certainly among the upstate regulars Seymour was a popular choice. During the preconvention weeks, both Joseph Warren and William Cassidy declared their support for the former governor. Tilden, Belmont, Barlow, and Marble, however, had other ideas. Contrary to Welles's belief, these men were looking for a man who could gain necessary Republican votes for the Democracy, and Seymour was too much a party regular to attract such votes. With Grant out of the running, it soon became apparent that the man who best fitted their qualifications was Salmon P. Chase.[40]

Given the circumstances, Chase was an attractive candidate. A Free-Soil Democrat in his early life, he had joined the Republican party because of the slavery issue. Throughout his career, however, he held to his Democratic beliefs in hard money, free trade, and states rights. Although after the war he favored Negro suffrage and civil rights, he was gradually becoming disenchanted with a Republican party that centralized governmental power, kept the Union divided, challenged the Supreme Court, and above all, showed little interest in gratifying his burning ambition to become president of the United States.[41]

Interest in Chase developed rather late among the New Yorkers. On March 14, 1868, just after the meeting of the state convention, the *Atlas,* a small Democratic journal in the city, announced that Chase might be the party nominee. Three days later Marble indicated that he had taken notice of the chief justice, when he declared to Dr. Anderson: "Chase I presume to be a free-trader, but he despairs of moulding his party to liberal views." On March 26 the *World* first discussed the possibility of Chase's candidacy, concluding that his "political principles and personal self-respect" would allow him neither to seek nor to accept a Democratic nomination.[42]

The *World*'s announcement, however, was merely the signal to open negotiations between Chase and the New York Democracy. In the following weeks the two sounded each other out on the issues and tested public opinion. On April 6 Chase wrote his friend and chief supporter in New York, Colonel John Dash Van Buren, to thank both him and Marble for announcing his unavailability. Two days later he wrote Alexander Long of Ohio that "nothing could satisfy me more than to see the Democracy turn away from past issues, and take for its mottoes: Suffrage for all; amnesty for all; good money for all; security for all citizens, at home against military despotism, and abroad against governmental invasion." On April 14 the *World* published Belmont's letter of the previous month, calling for the party to appeal to conservatives who objected to Radical centralization of government, high taxes, "negro supremacy," and continued disunion. On April 19 Chase wrote again to Long, declaring that a Democracy united in opposing military rule and disfranchisement in the South and committed to universal suffrage would receive his support and would carry two-thirds of the southern states. The chief justice and the Democracy were, indirectly at least, talking turkey.[43]

From these exchanges it soon became clear that Negro suffrage was keeping the two apart. On May 28 Hiram Barney, another friend of the chief justice, reported from New York City that the Democrats were talking widely about nominating Chase, since it was "supposed that neither Pendleton nor Seymour can be a successful candidate and neither would object to Mr. Chase. . . . But his views on Negro suffrage are the point of hesitation."[44]

While the New Yorkers hesitated, Chase began to gather support from sources outside the Democracy. On May 7 the *Herald* came out for his nomination. Charles A. Dana of the *Sun* also supported him, and the *Evening Post,* dissatisfied with the Republican stand on Negro suffrage, declared that Chase's nomination on a platform supporting his principles would bring about a dissolution of the parties.[45]

Democrats from outside New York City also increased the chief justice's stock. In May, S. S. Cox of Ohio and Daniel Voorhees of Indiana came out for Chase. Also, the upstate New Yorkers seemed willing, if only for strategic purposes, to boom Chase. Although Joseph Warren, William Cassidy, and Sanford Church favored Seymour, they were so frightened by Pendleton's strength that they conceded the need for "some movement on the part of the New York Democrats." On May 29 Seymour came out for Chase. "This talk of Chase," wrote Joseph Warren to Marble, "can do no harm" and might at least widen the breach between the Radicals and the conservative Republicans. "We will use him well," agreed Church, "but must not think of nominating him."[46]

Marble has left no statement to show his feelings. All the evidence, however, suggests that he sincerely favored Chase's nomination. After the convention, John Fiske, who was close to Marble at the time, wrote his mother: "Marble himself, I know, favored Chase; and Stickney told me that Marble worked faithfully for Chase in the convention." Years later, Belmont, who before the convention had told a friend of Chase that he supported the chief justice "with all my heart," reminded Marble that Chase "was your and my candidate for the Presidency in 1868."[47]

The course of the *World* also suggests that Marble favored Chase's nomination. During the month before the convention, the paper did its best to reconcile Chase and the Democracy on the issues of reconstruction. On June 3 it published its version of an acceptable party platform. Declaring that it had learned "the folly of permitting extreme men to foist upon the party a platform that could not be made acceptable to the people," it called for another departure in reconstruction strategy. Discarding Tilden's racism as an objection to Negro suffrage, it opposed only its imposition by the federal government.

On June 8 it went even further, urging the party to say nothing on the suffrage question. Declaring that Negro suffrage already existed in the southern states and that it could be abolished only by a constitutional amendment, which the Negroes themselves would be able to vote on, it once again urged the Democracy to promote cooperation between southern whites and Negroes. Would an antisuffrage declaration aid the southern whites to regain control of their states? Would Negroes be more likely to vote with the whites if asked to vote for their own disfranchisement? The *World* thought not. "Since we can *do* nothing about negro suffrage," it concluded, "why not practice the dignity of silence and *say* nothing?"[48]

But other party leaders wanted to say something. From around the country they reported that the Democracy had won its recent victories because it had opposed Negro suffrage. Some even threatened to form a third party if the Democracy gave up the suffrage issue to attract Chase. Once again the pressure was too great. On June 15 the *World* wrote off the chief justice. "As he regards negro suffrage as a blessing instead of an atrocious though perhaps irretrievable blunder, we do not see how he and the Democratic party can have any bond of fellowship."[49]

Then politics suddenly lost all importance. Following the birth of a second child in April, his wife, Delia, had failed to regain her strength. For weeks she lay in her room, growing weaker and not responding to treatment. If Marble wrote or received any letters concerning the nature or course of her illness, he destroyed them to erase the memory. All that remains is a telegram, dated June 17, to Dr. Anderson: "Mrs. Marble died peacefully and painlessly today at noon."[50]

"So to me in the middle of a summer day," Marble later wrote, "came out of the sky like the blowing of the resistless winds, whither or whence I know not, this great bereavement and I am desolate." Suddenly he felt empty and alone. He had come to rely upon Delia for moral strength, and without her he felt "orphaned." From a man who had so often sought advice and encouragement, who so anxiously craved success to reassure himself of his manhood, and who believed so deeply in the sentimental verities of his age, such expressions of loss ring true. Perhaps his loss of Delia so threatened his security that it caused him that fall to redouble his efforts to gain total control of the *World*. At the moment of her death, however, it only paralyzed him with grief. Confessing that "sometimes, very often indeed, entire indulgence in the luxury of woe is the chief craving," he fled the city, the newspaper, and the campaign.[51]

During his absence the *World* was itself paralyzed. When a representative of President Johnson visited New York to advance the president's interest with the Democracy, he found "several 'heads' of the concern, and no one of courage to take an independent and impartial stand relative to the selection of a nominee." During the rest of June, the *World* merely repeated its previous statements, urging the Democracy to forget Negro suffrage and greenbacks and to concentrate on the threat Radicalism posed to the separation of powers and to states rights.[52]

By the time Marble returned to the city, Chase's opportunity for the nomination had nearly evaporated. Firmly committed to Negro suffrage, the chief justice had refused to accept the *World*'s terms. Western Democrats not already committed to Pendleton were turning not to Chase but to Thomas A. Hendricks of Indiana. Under pressure from the upstate Seymour faction, Tilden had decided to throw the convention open to favorite-son nominations and to see if anyone developed enough strength to win an early nomination. On the first ballots he directed that New York's votes be given to Sanford Church, who everyone knew had no chance whatsoever. Any movement for Chase would have to come spontaneously from the delegates.[53]

The convention, which opened July 4 in Tammany Hall, must have seemed one long nightmare to Marble. First, the convention approved a platform, which, though following his suggestions on Negro suffrage, approved the principles of the Pendleton Plan. Next, it suffered through twenty-two ballots before nominating the truest of party regulars, Horatio Seymour. Finally, it threw away its suffrage plank by nominating unanimously for vice-president Francis Preston Blair, Jr., who on the eve of the convention had called for the election of a Democratic president who would declare the Reconstruction Acts null and void, "compel the army to undo its usurpations at the South, disperse the carpet-bag state governments, [and] allow the white people to reorganize their own governments." Nothing could have more flatly contradicted the *World*'s campaign strategy. The suffrage and currency issues had been boldly thrown before the voters and the nominee was a party regular unlikely to appeal to either the Barnburners or conservative Republicans. It was 1864 all over again.[54]

Shortly after the convention adjourned, Sam Ward accurately forecast that the Republicans would attack Seymour for opposing the last war and Blair for favoring the next. To counterattack, he urged the Democracy to send Seymour into the field as a "log Cabins and Hard Cider" candidate, hoping that he would create a popular image. Marble, however, showed little interest in the proposal. The summer's events had so dispirited him that he had little interest in anything. After a few feckless efforts to misconstrue the platform as favoring a return to specie payments and to misinform its readers that Blair's election would not affect the course of Reconstruction, the *World* lapsed into indifference. Soon letters were pouring in to Seymour, complaining about the *World* and demanding that it be brought into line. By early September Joseph Warren was openly criticizing the *World* for failing to stand by the financial plank.[55]

To make everything thoroughly uncomfortable, personal dissensions were also rife among Marble and his friends. Belmont began complaining to Marble that Seymour and Tilden were conspiring to remove him from the national committee. Marble had a row with Tilden, and early in October declared that "after such conduct as yours I will promise nothing." At the same time, he and Barlow touched raw nerves over the sale of the *World*. Then came the Republican sweep of the October elections and the *World*'s proposal to change the Democratic ticket.[56]

Rumors of a possible change in the ticket had been circulating since late September. Largely a response to Republican successes in using Blair's statements on Reconstruction to show that the Democracy planned a counterrevolution against Republican governments in the South, they suggested that Blair be replaced. By October, however, they included Seymour also. According to later accounts, Barlow had initiated the movement and had gained the support of Washington McLean's *Cincinnati Enquirer* and John H. Coyle's *National Intelligencer*. Since at the time Barlow referred to the proposed change as "my scheme," there seems reason to credit these accounts. The day after the October elections, Barlow reported to Tilden that "the suggestion that Seymour shall resign, that our convention shall at once re-convene, not later than Monday next; that we shall nominate Chase and [John Quincy] Adams, and elect our ticket . . . takes at the West like wild-fire." Later the same day, Barlow and Tilden met and decided to put off any further action until Seymour could be heard from. The next morning, however, both awoke to find Barlow's plan advocated in substance by the *World*.[57]

Marble had not been a party to Barlow's plan and possibly had not even heard about it.[58] Still he had reasons enough for his action. Grieved and dispirited by the events of that summer and fall, he had no doubt exhausted his patience, and as if to purge himself of his misery, lashed out. If the Democracy was to suffer another defeat, he at least would not share responsibility for it. Thus he decided to call for one last, dramatic departure.

On October 15, under the title "The Youthful, Indomitable Democracy," the *World* surveyed the results of the October elections. Noting the closeness of the vote in several key states, it concluded that a majority of the voters actually favored the Democracy, but had been repelled "by things having no proper connections with the merits of the canvas." These included the military prestige of Grant and the

Republican misrepresentations of Blair. Even Grant's popularity could have been overcome, however, had it not been for the attacks on Blair. Thus it seemed to the *World* that the time had come to "remove or neutralize" the adverse and irrelevant influences in the campaign. "We have still nearly three weeks for action," it declared, "and where so slight a counterpoise would suffice to turn the scale, prompt action . . . will accomplish wonders."

Admitting the possibility of defeat in the coming election, the *World* also called upon the Democracy to set its sights upon victory in the next one:

> This is a young country with a great career before it which no imagination can grasp; a majority of our voters are young men abounding in hope, enterprise, ardor, activity; and the country being in the dawn of a new era, when all minds are filled with expectation and excitement, that party has the best chances of a great future which is most in sympathy with the youthful, irrepressible energies of the nation. A growing nation, like an improving individual, has always something to learn. A political party, which does not advance with the nation, and enter into the fulness of its expanding, exuberant life, is on the declivity which descends to decadence and decrepitude. The Democratic party is full of vigorous, youthful, aspiring elements; similar elements in the other party are yearning to join it, if we have the boldness to build a bridge on which they can cross.[59]

So once again the *World* called upon the Democracy to change its image by forgetting the issues of the war, accepting Radical Reconstruction, and moving on to other issues. It was an appeal that an ambitious, young editor, determined to shape his own political career, ought to have made. Although foolhardy and disastrous as a practical proposal, it was wise and constructive as a guide for future policy. And in the misery of those October days only the future seemed to have any appeal.[60]

Although the editorial did not expressly call for a change in the ticket, it was easily interpreted as doing so. Since the party leaders had not known it was coming, its effect was devastating. While the *National Intelligencer* and the *Cincinnati Enquirer* supported the *World,* Belmont, Tilden, and Augustus Schell hurriedly denied any intention of changing candidates. From all over the country mail flooded into the *World*'s offices, revealing the confusion. Comments ran from "let others be put in nomination that are free from the obnoxious *sayings* and *doings* of Blair," to "you are inimical to all that is dear to a lover of liberty, the rights of labor, and Democratic principles." One upstate subscriber left no doubt of his opinion: "If your office be left standing unburned and unsacked by the outraged Democracy of New York City when this note reaches you, consider it a favor due to the unfortunate fact that *some* others are almost as pusillanimous as your dastardly selves." William Cassidy spoke for most party leaders when he wrote Tilden that "we were completely puzzled with Marble's course. How could he have come out with such an article without consultation?"[61]

The impracticality of the *World*'s proposal was soon evident. Even among those approving a change in the ticket there was no agreement upon a suitable replacement. Suggestions ranged from Chase to John Quincy Adams, Jr., Winfield Scott Hancock, Hendricks, McClellan, and Thomas Ewing. It was thus obvious that a reconvening of the national convention would only bring about the same deadlock that had already given the nomination to Seymour. This, if nothing else, would have made the plan unacceptable to the party leaders. As it became apparent that the National Committee would not consider the *World*'s proposal, its supporters quickly vanished. Soon the paper had returned to its dreary task of defending Blair's inflammatory statements and painting Seymour as a bold party leader. Thoroughly disgusted, Marble sat back and predicted that Seymour would carry only Kentucky and that half the Democrats would vote for Grant.[62]

Election day, however, produced no such disaster. Although decisively beaten in the electoral vote, Seymour ran well, and without Negro suffrage would have captured a majority of the popular vote. The Democracy carried New York, electing John T. Hoffman governor. As Marble studied the results, he may well have wondered whether he would have been wise to remain silent in October. "The beaten party will want a scapegoat," William Cassidy had warned him, "and . . . you have elected yourself the victim."[63]

Still, many consoled and encouraged him. "Cannot we get rid of all the old rubbish of Vallandigham, Pendleton, Seymour, and a dozen others," demanded Belmont, "build up a new party, take hold of new issues, so as to get the people with us and not to remain in the leading strings of the old political hacks?" Such sentiments were echoed by Congressman Michael Kerr of Indiana and Winston Pierce of Indianapolis. Both thought the Democracy should cast off its extremist wing and bid for the support of conservative Republicans and former Democrats. From upstate New York, Allen C. Beach, the lieutenant governor elect, assured Marble that the *World* had not injured the party in the state and those who said otherwise were either "red hot Democrats" or jealous local editors. Such words from the party's national chairman, representatives of a key middle western state, and an upstate leader must have gone far toward easing Marble's mind and giving him courage to continue.[64]

It would seem that Marble's course during the campaign was more an effect than a cause of the Democracy's failure. In the years from the end of the war to the election of Grant, the party's basic problem had been its narrow partisanship. In its negotiations with

Johnson, Chase, and the Barnburners it had demanded almost total submission to its leadership and program. In its choice of candidates it had valued party regularity more highly than the background and attitudes necessary to attract outside support. In its choice of issues it had consistently given in to the most extreme and reactionary positions. At the same time it had been pitifully unable to resolve the differences between its eastern and western wings. The spectacle of McClellan running on a peace platform and of Seymour running on a greenback platform was less the result of artful compromise than of patchwork politics.

The New York leaders bore a heavy responsibility for such a situation. Although in isolated instances they had moderated the worst elements of Democratic extremism, their narrow partisanship had stopped them short of any truly meaningful reform. Bent on maintaining their own leadership and fearful of alienating even the most reactionary extremists, they failed to make the sort of appeals necessary to attract the broad conservative middle of the political spectrum.

It was to Marble's credit that at times he had shown himself to be independent of their influence. Twice since the elections of 1866 he had urged the Democracy to accept Republican Reconstruction and to move on to other issues and candidates. In formulating his policies he had been influenced, undoubtedly, by such friends as Barlow and Belmont. But he had also seen that powerful southern leaders seemed willing to accept his advice and that the Barnburners were anxious for the Democracy to adopt a new course. In seeking to take advantage of these circumstances, he revealed a political sophistication that belied his years. It was a promising beginning for an ambitious president-maker, even though in his first effort he had done more to unmake than to make a president. ✣

CHAPTER EIGHT

Party Independence

FOLLOWING SEYMOUR'S DEFEAT, things could not have looked darker for the "swallow-tail" Democracy. In the national government, the Republicans now controlled both Congress and the presidency, thus having a free hand in their reconstruction program. Even worse, a New Yorker had led the party to defeat, thus further discrediting their national leadership. And in New York itself, where the Democracy had captured the statehouse, the real victory belonged to William M. Tweed's Tammany organization. It was no wonder, therefore, that when the wealthy and influential merchant, Robert B. Minturn, was invited to join the Manhattan Club, he declined. "I distrust the whole Democratic machine," he declared, "and especially do I doubt whether the Manhattan Club will ever form the instrument to mend the ricketty old concern."[1]

If Marble wished to become a power in the Democracy, he clearly had his work cut out for him. Not only would he have to keep the *World* on the course it had advocated during the campaign; he would also have to inspire such leaders as Tilden and Belmont to bolder action. The first task he could accomplish, but the second seemed in doubt. Belmont had come under heavy attack following the election and was spending most of his time fighting for his position as national chairman.[2] Tilden had never shown instincts for leadership, and with Tweed's power increasing with each election, he seemed unlikely to do so.

Still, the early months of the new year found Marble as determined as ever to push the Democracy to a new departure. On January 2 the *World* announced that it intended to be both Democratic and "independent" in politics. Declaring that every political party tended to fall into the hands of a self-serving "oligarchy," it announced that it would keep the party open to new ideas. In this way it hoped to prevent in-breeding in Democratic thinking and to point the way for the party's young men. "Democratic ideas are placed in new lights," it declared, "they are shown to be in harmony with all that is valuable in the progressive spirit of the age; the party is made respectable in the eyes of its opponents, which increases the chances of its gaining proselytes."

With this pronouncement, the *World* continued to press for its new departure. Again it called on the Democracy to lay aside the issues of the war and to concentrate upon those economic issues that would attract Republican voters. The Republicans thus gained could then be used to attract Negro voters. Then the Democracy would be able to repeal the tariff, restore sound money, reinstate the authority of the executive branch of the national government, attack the monopolies and corporations that were corrupting Congress and the states, destroy sumptuary legislation, reduce the army and navy, and restore local self-government. That August the *World* showed the way by beginning to publish a series of free-trade articles by the "Parsee Merchant," J. S. Moore. "There can be no doubt," it reminded its readers, "that apart from the reconstruction and negro questions, the preponderating sentiment of the country is in favor of Democratic principles and measures."[3]

It was in local politics, however, that the *World,* with Tilden's timid support, fought most actively. In December 1868 it began an attack on Tammany Hall's boss, William M. Tweed. Prompting the attack was Tweed's effort to expand his influence in city government into the board of education. Under the city charter the board controlled all appropriations for the city's schools. Since these appropriations totaled approximately $3 million annually, they were too rich for Tweed to ignore. No sooner were the elections over than Tweed moved to replace the incumbent clerk of the board, Thomas Boese, with his stooge, William M. Hitchman. It almost goes without saying that the clerk supervised all the board's expenditures.[4]

For reasons that are not entirely clear, Tweed's move greatly disturbed Tilden. In December Tilden rather hesitantly suggested to Marble that the *World* not print anything against Boese, and that "so far as it leans at all, it should be in the other direction." Marble at once agreed and sent one of his top political reporters to confer with Tweed's associate, Peter B. Sweeny. In the meantime he set the *World* solidly behind Boese. Even when Sweeny assured him that Tweed had no intention of injecting politics into the board, he continued to defend Boese.[5]

In January Marble moved from the defense to a full-scale attack on Tweed and his "ring." On January 5 the *World* charged that "The Ring's faithless and inefficient discharge of public duties, their corruption, their extravagant expenditures of the public moneys without the result of an efficient civil administration, have been the excuse of the Radical legislatures for steadily taking away from the Democrats of the City of New York the control of their local affairs." Declaring that "corrupt and intriguing politics" must be kept out of the schools, it called upon every "honest and intelligent" Democrat to support Boese. On January 13 the board responded by refusing to elect a new clerk. A few weeks later, Marble proudly reported to Dr. Anderson that Boese and Andrew H. Green both credited the *World* with preventing Boese's ejection.[6]

Tweed, however, was not so easily defeated. Realizing that he was facing his first serious challenge from the "swallow-tails," he turned to the state legislature for help. In the Assembly a bill soon appeared, abolishing the existing board of education and replacing it at the next general election with a partially elected, partially appointed commission. In the interim the bill gave the mayor, in this case Tweed's henchman A. Oakey Hall, the power to appoint a new board. Although sponsored by Republicans, the bill was clearly a Tweed project. Quickly the *World* identified it as such.[7]

Boese realized the game was up and resigned. Marble, however, would not give up so easily. Believing that the bill would surely pass, he appealed to Governor Hoffman to veto it. Although he undoubtedly knew that Hoffman was another of Tweed's confederates, Marble may actually have hoped the governor would follow his advice. Earlier in the year he had received a note from Hoffman, thanking him for his advice on a patronage matter and declaring "if I had any doubts, I assure you your letter would go very far to remove them. I shall always be glad to serve you." Still, Marble was wise enough to know the difference between minor patronage favors and major factional disputes, so he used the *World* to impress the governor with the seriousness of the issue. Charging that many legislators were delaying the votes on other bills in order to form a log-rolling combination in case the governor vetoed the school bill, it warned that the true test of party loyalty would be whether or not Democratic legislators supported their chief executive. Assuming that the governor would return a veto, it promised that "no Democratic member who acts with such a ring in opposition to Governor Hoffman, shall escape exposure and chastisement."[8]

Marble soon discovered that in this struggle he was overmatched. No prominent city Democrat supported the *World;* the *Albany Argus* supported the school bill; and the Republicans, sensing the opportunity for spoils, remained loyal to Tweed. Hoffman signed the bill as soon as it passed, and on May 12 a reorganized board elected William Hitchman as its clerk.[9]

Marble's independence stirred the party organization to overt disapproval. In the wake of the affair, he and William Cassidy sharply debated the *World*'s course. Cassidy began by accusing Marble of allowing a petty, personal quarrel to alienate him from his friends and even went so far as to compare the course of the *World* to that of the Radical press. Marble denied any such motive and declared the *World* had employed "careful phrases" in expressing its dissent.

In fact Cassidy's whole attitude disgusted him. Charging that the *Argus* editor seemed anxious to read him out of the party, he warned that he was "not exaggerating the seriousness" of his displeasure.[10]

Cassidy's reply clearly showed the difficulties that confronted anyone who questioned the party's leadership. The whole trouble with the *World,* he declared, was its pretension to independence. Instead of loyally following the party, it was judging the party by its own standards. It was "not a true soldier, imbued with the spirit of the party, not a hearty fellow soldier." Cassidy noted that Marble had argued that Greeley's independence had proved a source of strength. But Marble should remember, Cassidy declared, that "Greeley first earned the right to be wayward by twenty years of devoted partisanship, and his influence is nearly frittered away." Perhaps if the *World* had actually fought for reform, Cassidy could have supported it. But such did not seem to be the case. Instead of attacking Tweed, Connolly, or Sweeny, the paper had attacked Mayor Hall, who was honest, and Governor Hoffman, "whose administration is a turning point in our party history."

"Perhaps it is the highest office of journalism," Cassidy concluded, "to stand aloof and above and independent of, parties and sects and events—and to turn opinion into wholesome channels. But this tone is incompatible with party devotion, or with association with other journals. It [results in] comparative isolation. You must expect adverse critics. Your old associates must be compelled to disclaim your opinions, when they dissent from them; and to deny your leadership."[11]

And dissent they did. On July 5 Lieutenant Governor Allen C. Beach, who had approved Marble's new departure in October 1868, warned Tilden that among the upstate editors "intense bitterness" was arising against the *World.* At a convention of the Democratic editors, many complained that the *World* seemed jealous or contemptuous of its colleagues. So great was their dissatisfaction that Beach found "the country press disposed to oppose anything proposed by the *World.*" He declared, "Something must be done. The rural press of this state, as you know, can by its combined influence exert a far greater pressure on the people than any single sheet no matter how ably it is conducted nor how large its circulation."[12]

When Tilden sent him Beach's letter and included his own warning, Marble was forced to give in. "I will take good care to propose nothing except what you want defeated," he replied. Although admitting to "some contempt for these processes, which is probably not softened by the treatment the *World* has always received," he recognized "the obligations of cooperative work. . . . I know a true friend when I see him [he concluded] in Watertown or Gramercy Park."[13]

Despite his promises, Marble was soon attacking the ring again. This time, however, Tilden could not object, for the occasion was

Tweed's attempt to remove him from the state committee and Belmont from the national committee. Although Marble dutifully defended his friends, he did so with proper restraint. Never once did he set himself above the party. When the *World* spoke of the devious aims and deeds of the Tammany Ring, it carefully contrasted them with "the disinterested purity and steady devotion to principle" of the rural Democracy. It was at this time that the *World* discovered that democratic government and civic virtue prospered most in a rural environment. On September 20 it pointedly warned Tammany that the country leaders were planning to make the fall state convention "a very strong one in point of talents, integrity, and the respectability and standing of its members," and advised them to follow suit in their own selection of delegates.[14]

This time Tammany backed down. Tweed, who had been out of the city, returned and immediately stopped the attacks on Belmont. At the same time, Sweeny approached Hiram Calkins of the *World* to see if the two could make peace. In a subsequent conference with Chamberlain, he agreed that the Tammany newspapers would not only stop attacking the *World* but would also "do all in their power to build up the *World,* and that it should receive the treatment to which an acknowledged party organ is entitled." He also promised that Tammany would not oppose Tilden's remaining on as chairman of the state committee. A relieved Tilden also urged Marble to strike as many bargains with Tammany as possible.[15]

At the state convention, Tweed was the picture of reason and amity. On nearly every issue, including the naming of the state ticket, his delegates divided their votes evenly, allowing the country members to make the final decision. Tilden retained his chairmanship by an overwhelming vote and Belmont remained on the national committee. "The 'hayloft and cheese press' Democracy have checked the Tammany Ring," the *Evening Post* declared, "Seymour and Hoffman have checked Tweed and Hall; Belmont is revenged on his enemies."[16]

Throughout the ensuing campaign, the *World* maintained its truce with Tammany. But when the voters returned heavy Democratic majorities, giving the party control of both houses of the legislature for the first time in a decade, it moved again to discredit Tammany's leadership. The victory, it declared, had vindicated the leadership of the rural Democrats. "They have learned by experience that it is safe to resist the claims of the Tammany leaders and to follow their own judgment. They have found that self-reliance is not a source of weakness, but of strength."[17]

Obviously, Marble was planning to ally with the rural Democracy against Tweed. In the winter of 1869–70, as he looked around for supporters, he also found members of the city Democracy ready to join him. At the state convention Tweed had removed from the senatorial ticket three Tammany incumbents, Michael Norton, Thomas

J. Creamer, and Henry W. Genet. Perhaps he did so to please the rural delegates, since in the last session of the legislature each man had acquired a reputation for shady dealing. After the convention the three convinced Tweed to allow them to seek reelection, and the convention nominees withdrew in their favor. All won their bids for reelection and might have returned peacefully to the fold had it not been for the devious designs of a man named George H. Purser. Purser had coveted Norton's seat and had helped to persuade Tweed to remove him at the convention. When Tweed later changed his mind, Purser organized an anti-Tweed faction within Tammany. To the movement he soon attracted Norton, Genet, and Creamer as well as John Morrissey (an ex-prize fighter and gambler turned politician), Assemblymen Lawrence Kiernan and Peter Mitchell, and ex-sheriff James O'Brien. Held together only by their hatred of Tweed and committed to no discernible principle, their only importance was their considerable political power. Early in 1870 they proposed to put that power in the service of the *World*.[18]

Marble must have searched his conscience a bit before deciding about the proposition. An alliance with such a group could not have strongly attracted a man of his genteel sensibilities. Still, the experience of the previous year had taught him the dangers of too much independence and self-proclaimed purity. And the dissidents shared his dislike of Tweed. So he joined them to form the Young Democracy.

Fortunately for Marble, the alliance was sweetened by the presence of a few friends. Barlow joined as did Lieutenant Governor Beach, who represented the rural Democracy. Belmont, who so despised Tweed that he referred to the boss and his friends as "canaille," refused to soil his hands in the movement. Tilden remained aloof, offering occasional advice through Marble. So concerned was he lest his name be attached to the anti-Tweed movement that he expressly demanded that his support be kept secret. He only wanted it known that he was ready to join any combination that would "stop corruption and give us good government." He had no hesitation, however, about urging Marble to step forward in the movement. "Leadership of a party in a course," he declared, "seems to be [and] is at present your position, and its relations are the more important ones to yourself and to your journal for the moment."[19]

In January and February of 1870, the Young Democracy mapped out its strategy. It was decided that the *World* would not attack Tammany but would only claim that specific members of the ring were trying to use Tammany for corrupt purposes. Also Beach urged Marble not to attack Hoffman, who, though Tweed's confederate, was popular with the rural Democrats. Thus the Young Democracy would not set itself up outside the Democratic party, but would work to capture the party from within.[20]

Everyone knew that the major test of strength between Tweed

and the Young Democracy would come over the proposed reorganization of the city government. It was an open secret that Tweed intended to use the Democratic majorities in the state legislature to enact a new city charter, which would allow him to run the city free from upstate interference. Marble and the Young Democracy had no objection to home rule as such, but they wanted to make sure that Tweed did not profit from it. Thus they hoped to block Tweed's charter, enact one of their own, and then, by controlling Tammany, rule the city.[21]

The battle began February 3, when Tweed's charter first appeared in the legislature. On its face, the charter met the Young Democracy's standards, principally because it created a strong mayor. It provided that the mayor would appoint the heads of major departments, and that together with the comptroller, commissioner of public works, and president of the park department, he would serve on a special board to supervise all expenditures. To guarantee the board's tenure, the charter provided that its members could be removed only by impeachment, requiring a charge by the mayor and conviction by the Court of Common Pleas. It retained the County Board of Supervisors, of which Tweed was currently the head, but reduced its powers.[22]

As soon as the charter appeared, the Young Democracy and the *World* attacked it. Offering amendments and suggestions for its improvement, they called for abolishing the Board of Supervisors, requiring that the mayor's appointees serve only while he held office, electing the supervisors and canvassers of elections, and publishing the details of all financial transactions. In the meantime the Young Democracy was meeting to draft its own charter. By the end of February, they had nearly finished and Marble seemed optimistic. In a memo to Chamberlain he declared that the charter would abolish the Board of Supervisors, consolidate the city and county governments, and provide for a mayoralty election in the fall. Mayor Hall, he reported, had even promised to appoint the Young Democracy's nominees as soon as their charter passed.

At this stage of their partnership, the leaders of the Young Democracy seemed to be getting along well together. Creamer had a disturbing ambition to be mayor, for which his only noticeable qualification was that he controlled twenty-one votes in the Tammany General Committee. Beach was warning that the rural Democracy was expecting results from their brothers in the city and Tilden was urging Marble to launch personal attacks on the ring members. Nothing too serious, however, and Marble thought victory lay ahead. Beach would deliver the votes of the rural senators, Creamer could become mayor if necessary, and the *World* could "keep the ring members straight."

And happily, his colleagues were not such a bad lot after all. "Genet has the heaviest head of the lot. Morrissey has the heaviest character. O'Brien has the most votes and like Morrissey the purest purposes. Creamer is eaten up with ambition. Norton is a 'good fellow.' "[23]

It was not long, however, until Marble's confidence was disturbed. Just as it seemed that the Young Democracy would block Tweed's charter, the boss brought his hidden persuader, the bribe, into play. In all, Tweed spent nearly $1 million to pass his charter. He had just distributed the first $200,000 when Morrissey wired Marble of the situation. The boss, it seemed, had formed an alliance with the Republicans and had succeeded temporarily in blocking the Young Democracy's charter. Although Morrissey bravely predicted that "justice and peoples' rights will ultimately prevail," the situation was definitely grim.[24]

Still, the Young Democracy continued to fight. On Thursday, March 24, Norton succeeded in bringing the Young Democracy's charter before the Senate for referral to the Committee on the Cities, where he, Genet, and Creamer held a majority of one. In the Assembly, Kiernan had succeeded in getting the charter to a third reading. There the matter rested over the weekend, while the Young Democracy prepared to strike a final blow at the ring. On short notice they called a meeting of the Tammany General Committee, where they controlled a majority, to depose Tweed as county chairman.

Although things could not have looked worse for him, Tweed was equal to the occasion. Outnumbered on the general committee, he turned to his friends in the police department. On the evening of March 26, while the Young Democracy rallied their forces at Irving Hall, hundreds of policemen quietly surrounded Tammany. When the Young Democracy arrived, they were told that the meeting had been canceled because the Grand Sachems feared a riot might break out. Since all of this was strictly in accordance with the rules of the society, there was nothing more to do. Frustrated, the Young Democracy returned to Irving Hall to listen to their leaders denounce Tweed.[25]

Although the *World* announced that the Tammany proceedings foretold Tweed's doom, experienced politicians knew better. Tweed had successfully resisted the most vigorous efforts of his opponents and had also gained valuable time to distribute his largesse to doubtful legislators. Always willing to forgive his opponents, he even distributed some to Norton, Creamer, and Genet. It had a predictable effect. When the Young Democracy's charter came up for its third reading in the Assembly, its former supporters were nowhere to be seen. It was thus quickly disposed of and Tweed's brought again to the floor. In less than a week, the Tweed Charter had passed both houses.[26]

Marble never received any money from Tweed, and there is no evidence that any was ever offered. But Tweed probably realized that there was no need for it. With the other leaders of the Young Democracy safely bought off, Marble and Tilden had to beat a humiliating retreat back into his fold. No one was more thoroughly cowed than Tilden. Returning to the city on the day Tweed's charter passed the Senate, he warned Marble: *"don't mention my name in the paper till I see you."* Marble's retreat was somewhat slower. For the rest of April, he kept up a token support of the Young Democracy, but largely ignored city politics. After May 17, however, when Tweed's ticket swept the city elections, he bowed openly to the inevitable. On May 26 he sent Sweeny a note, asking for a conference. Sweeny arrived at his home, left, and returned a few days later accompanied by Tweed and Jay Gould.[27]

Marble's efforts at independent leadership were proving costly, both to his self-esteem and to his financial position. From a high point in 1868, the *World*'s profits had fallen in 1869 to a figure lower than those of 1867. Although daily circulation had increased by 1,500 over 1867, semiweekly and weekly circulation had declined by 9,150. This, combined with a falling off of weekly subscription revenues by $154 at a time when sales revenues were increasing, suggests that the out-of-town readers were the principal defectors. The rural Democracy was repaying Marble for his treachery to Seymour in 1868. Also of significance, campaign advertisements, which had totaled a high of $1,273 in 1867, had fallen to just $82 in 1869, suggesting that party members hesitated to identify themselves with the *World*. The effect of the battles with Tweed was revealed in the decline in corporation advertising from $14,265 in 1868, the lowest figure in the paper's history, to $7,588 in 1869.

Since Marble made peace with Tweed in mid-1870, it is difficult to estimate the financial impact of his flirtation with the Young Democracy. In 1870 corporation advertising rose to $43,527, nearly double the previous high. This suggests that the boss was willing to forgive Marble his past errors. It was largely because of this patronage that the *World* showed its second most profitable year. Others, however, seem not to have been so forgiving. Revenues from both sales and subscriptions declined, indicating that Democratic opinion was still suspicious of the journal. Independence, it seemed, exacted a high price.[28]

There was still another likely explanation for the falling off of business during 1870. In mid-July news arrived in the United States of war between France and Prussia. At once the press was thrown into a frenzy of activity as each newspaper tried to outdo the others in covering the conflict. As luck would have it, serious illness had forced Marble to leave for Newport a few days before the news arrived. Since he was unable to return, the responsibility for covering the event fell to his associate editors. Marble, however, had never bothered to establish a subordinate chain of command during the periods of his absence, so there was no one on hand to take charge. In theory the job should have fallen to Croly, but his personal differences with Marble had made it difficult for him to establish his authority. So the course of the *World* became a matter for group discussion.

Croly began by proposing to send to Europe a corps of six men, headed by city editor Lehman Israels and including ace reporter Stillson. He made his proposal to Nat Bangs, and while the publisher telegraphed Marble for instructions, Croly decided to leave for Saratoga to look after his sick wife. Probably he did not see Bangs's telegram, which was a model of ambiguity, giving the impression that Croly was proposing to send six men, including the best reporter, only to collect dispatches from European newspapers. Naturally, Marble rejected the plan, saying that either Stillson or Israels might go, but not both. He also directed Bangs to consult with Hurlbert.

It happened that Hurlbert arrived at the office just after Croly had left for Saratoga, so he got his information from Bangs. He opposed the idea of sending six men, but thought Israels, who read French, Dutch, and German, ought to be sent to edit foreign dispatches. They were discussing this plan when Marble's telegram arrived. Since Marble seemed to agree with Hurlbert, Bangs told Israels to be ready to leave for Europe in a few days. Israels did not like the idea, since it would cost him much outside income, and he protested so much that Bangs agreed to defer the assignment until Croly returned. Meanwhile, he wired Croly the latest developments. Croly at once opposed Hurlbert's plan, declaring that Israels should be sent only as the head of a corps and that if only one or two men were sent, they should be writers. Apparently he wrote to Israels also, because the city editor was soon telling Bangs that Croly could not spare him from the office.

On the evening of July 18, three days after the discussion had begun, Croly returned to the office to confer with Hurlbert and Bangs. Perhaps suspecting a plot by Hurlbert to undermine his authority, he refused to allow Israels to leave the office. Instead, he now suggested that the *World* send for copies of Europeans newspapers and make up its accounts at home. So forcefully did he argue that he convinced Hurlbert. Just in case any doubts remained, Stillson, learning that he was being considered for an overseas assignment and a cut in salary, suddenly reported that he had decided to take a trip west. So on July 21, nearly a week after the subject had first come up, Bangs sent to Great Britain for copies of the foreign press, and Croly, still annoyed at the publisher for having spoken to Israels behind his back, declared he felt ill and was leaving town for a week or two.[29]

The controversy left Hurlbert in control, and that, as it turned out, was disastrous. From the first, the war became important in American politics, with both parties courting the large German vote.

The issue was especially important to the *World* because a significant portion of the city Germans followed Oswald Ottendorfer, editor of the anti-Tammany *New Yorker Staats-Zeitung*. If Marble and Tilden ever hoped to overthrow Tweed, they would have to have Ottendorfer's cooperation as well as that of the anti-Tammany Germans among the rural Democracy. Under such circumstances, the *World*'s course should have been clear. With its reputation for party loyalty already in question, it should have done everything possible to avoid further suspicion. In short, the time seemed ripe for a few kind words about Prussian militarism.

At first it seemed that the *World* would follow such a course. Its first editorial on the war was decidedly anti-French. Recalling the episode of French imperialism in Mexico and accusing France of having favored the Confederacy, it suggested that it would welcome a French defeat. Soon, however, its sympathies changed. When President Grant issued a proclamation of neutrality, it wholeheartedly approved and urged all German-Americans, specifically, to do likewise. When some Republicans expressed sympathy for the Prussian cause, it denounced them and declared that the German-Americans would see through such a political scheme. During August and September, however, it forsook neutrality altogether and became outspokenly pro-French. On September 3, two weeks before the Democratic State Convention, it declared that "no true Democrat could rejoice at the prospect of a German invasion of France, threatening the sacrifice of French liberty and of French nationality to the ambitions of a German sovereign or of the German people." When news arrived of the collapse of the French monarchy, the *World* hailed the new republic as a fresh source of military strength and determination. As late as January, it was comparing the French resistance to that of Americans during the American Revolution and praising the French as "unfaltering" and "heroic." Also, it was warning its readers that Prince Bismarck was "by temper and policy a remorseless absolutist," whose rule of the German Empire would be "an oppressive, suffocating despotism."[30]

Such statements soon had their effect. When the *World*'s position became clear, Ottendorfer sought out one of Tilden's friends to warn against divisions in the party. Barlow also expressed concern, and Lieutenant Governor Beach was positively horrified. "The German democrats, especially in the country," he wrote Tilden, "are exasperated, not because the *World* does not sympathise with the cause of German unity, but because it is unmistakably *French*. Some of them say they will not vote this fall. A month hence they may go a step further. The Republicans will nominate one or more Germans at their State Convention and there is danger that before our convention is held the mass of the German voters will be committed against us." At the fall convention, the party passed resolutions praising the "heroic bravery and brilliant achievements of arms" of the Prussians and expressed the hope that they would establish a unified nation in Central Europe, "maintaining . . . the cause of civilization and progress."[31]

It is difficult to estimate precisely the effect of the war upon the *World*'s fortunes. Receipts from both sales and subscriptions were lower in 1870 than 1869, though an increase in advertising revenues allowed the paper to record high profits. Circulation figures for October 1 suggest, however, that the war may have injured it in the rural districts. On that day the daily circulation had increased by 500 over the previous year, while the semiweekly and weekly sales, which went out of town, had declined by 300. Also, the year's loss in revenue from sales amounted to 4 percent of the previous year's income, while the loss from subscriptions amounted to 14 percent. Undoubtedly, such figures resulted in part from the *World*'s giving up its attack on Tweed and thus gaining many city readers. By the same token, its alliance with Tweed probably alienated many rural Democrats, who had supported the Young Democracy. The observations of such astute observers as Ottendorfer, Barlow, and Beach, however, suggest that its editorials on the war also played an important role in keeping the rural Democracy at arm's length.[32]

Responsibility for the *World*'s Gallicism rested with Hurlbert and Marble. Since Marble was out of the city when the war broke out, Hurlbert steered the paper through the first weeks of the conflict and determined its policy. Long attracted to French culture, Hurlbert decided that the *World* should favor the French. Whenever objections arose to his course, he quickly assured Marble that there was nothing to worry about. After conferring with Ottendorfer, he reported that the German leader "cares for none of these things at heart and has been perfectly civil to the *World*." Barlow had objected, Hurlbert declared, only because he was organizing a German-American bank. As for the Germans themselves, in the east they were either safely Democratic or safely Republican and in the west they were all Carl Schurz Radicals. Such explanations seem to have been enough for Marble. Years later a story appeared that McClellan told Marble that the French would probably win the war and influenced him to kill a story predicting victory for the Prussians. Lacking contemporary support, the story is questionable. Still, it seems clear that in this instance Marble allowed his feelings of friendship, either for McClellan or for Hurlbert, to overcome sound political judgment.[33]

In the long run the war probably affected the *World*'s business more than its political influence. Although the paper kept expenses to a minimum by sending no correspondents to the battle areas, it still spent large sums for special telegraphic dispatches and for additional Associated Press reports. In the last three months of the year, these increases amounted to just over $15,000. Normally, such months were the paper's most profitable, especially during election years, which brought great demands for political news and much campaign advertising. In 1870, however, advertising gained only $8,000, leaving the paper with profits nearly $7,500 below those of the same period the year before. As early as mid-October, Bangs was warning Marble that the paper faced a difficult future. "I have not got a cent which belongs to us," he declared, "not enough to meet an immediate (to which it is liable) demand for money I have borrowed." By carrying forward certain debts into January and February, he hoped to keep the paper out of trouble, but he was none too optimistic. "It has taken all my *efforts* to take care of ourselves," he noted, "and [we] ain't out of the woods yet."[34]

In January and February business continued to languish, and Bangs was pushed to the limit of his ingenuity to keep the *World* from financial embarrassment. Under such circumstances, he and Marble agreed that expenses should be cut to the minimum, including those planned for improvements in the *World*'s format and news coverage.[35]

No one chafed under the restrictions more than David Goodman Croly. Although his imagination and skill had done much to promote the paper, he had not realized his ambition of making it the city's leading daily. Moreover, he had been forced to compete with Chamberlain, Hurlbert, and Bangs in determining the paper's policies. Over the years such competition and frustration bred in him a bitterness, which by 1871 had become obsessive. Thus when Bangs announced that the paper would continue to practice economy, he could no longer restrain himself. That June he decided to force Marble to a showdown.

Croly began by suggesting changes in the *World*'s format and news coverage. Noting that the management lacked clear lines of authority, he called for granting well-defined powers to specific editors, so the paper could more easily keep abreast of the daily events. He suggested that the paper start its daily press run late in the evening so as to include only the latest dispatches. He believed the display advertisements should be eliminated to draw more attention to the news stories. To make the *World* more a *news* paper, he suggested eliminating the market statistics and replacing them with feature articles. The articles should be enlivened with dogmatic assertions and brilliant, emotional appeals that would excite the reader's passions instead of merely appealing to his reason. Wider columns also would create a more attractive, and salable, format.

To inspire the staff with the enthusiasm necessary for success, Croly proposed that Marble abandon the wage system and replace it with an "industrial partnership" in which all would share in the paper's profits. Such an arrangement would involve no loss of control, for Marble would continue to own the stock of the company, but rewards would be apportioned according to the success of the journal. Men whose rewards depended directly upon such success, Croly argued, would work more effectively to promote it. Such a reform would also make the *World* popular with "the industrial and democratic masses."

From Croly's suggestions emerged for the first time the ideas that his famous son, Herbert, would popularize in the *Promise of American Life*. The time had come, he declared, for Marble to discard the traditional individualism of the Democratic party. "The old democratic talk that government has nothing to do with the business affairs of the community," he asserted, "is now replaced with the new democratic talk, the popular talk, that it has everything to do with them." Instead of preaching competitive individualism and laissez-faire, the *World* should support such reforms as the consolidation of the railroads, and government ownership of the telegraph. Also, the paper should attack the irresponsible behavior of the nation's business leaders. "There is no more popular thing that a newspaper can do today," Croly argued, "than to hold up these rich, selfish men to the scorn and contempt of mankind."

Croly's suggestions arose from more than his principles. His years with the *World* had left him jealous and contemptuous of his fellow editors. As he watched the influence of Chamberlain and Hurlbert increase, he gradually became unable to suppress his feelings. Thus he charged, correctly, that Chamberlain was writing many of his editorials while drunk, scoffed at Hurlbert's social and economic attitudes, and declared that they both were overpaid. "The evil genius of the N.Y. *World*," he declared, "is I. C., and the one new departure imperatively demanded is that he should depart for Europe and stay there a year."

It is possible that Croly's outburst also sprang from a final, suicidal impulse. An intelligent and perceptive man, he must have known that Marble would neither adopt his suggestions nor accept his charges. He also must have known that Chamberlain and Hurlbert prospered because they shared Marble's social and political prejudices and background. Marble could identify with Chamberlain's Whig-American upbringing and Hurlbert's genteel culture far more easily than with a reform-minded, self-educated, Irish immigrant.

In any event, this crisis was Croly's last. He stayed with the *World* for a year, occasionally sending in a memorandum and always meeting the same response. On November 25, 1872, he decided things had gone on long enough and submitted his resignation. Marble, who by then had become thoroughly disenchanted with his managing editor, quickly accepted it and appointed Stillson to the position.[36]

Although Marble's social attitudes and the *World*'s financial condition were largely responsible for Croly's departure, the political situation was also important. The failure of the Young Democracy had left Marble with no suitable political base from which to oppose

Tweed and had forced him to make peace with the boss. The winter and spring of 1870–71 found the two on amiable terms. In December and again in April, Marble negotiated with Sweeny to find jobs for friends and was promised that they would be taken care of. In May the *World* received notice that it would soon be printing corporation advertisements. Mayor Hall even told Bangs that a competing journal had, on Marble's request, been denied patronage. Under such circumstances, there seemed little reason or opportunity for Marble to adopt the stance of the reformer and oppose Tweed. In fact, during most of this period, the *World* actually praised Tammany as a reform organization.[37]

It seemed Marble's lot in these times, however, always to be in the wrong camp at the worst time. No sooner had he and Tweed formed a stable alliance than the *New York Times* brought forth its famous exposé of the boss and his ring. Beginning in July of 1871 and continuing into the fall, the *Times* published documentary evidence of the ring's mammoth frauds. As the charges grew ever more convincing, the Democracy was thrown into panic and indecision. Should the party repudiate Tweed, or should it continue to support him? Neither alternative seemed particularly attractive, because of Tweed's influence in the party. Repudiating him risked splitting the party organization, and supporting him risked losing popular support.

Typical reactions came from Chamberlain and Croly. Shortly after the first of the *Times*'s exposures appeared, Chamberlain declared to Marble that the state committee should request the ring members to resign. On August 8, however, he declared that the *World* should defend the ring out of "political necessity." Also, he cautioned Marble, who was in Newport for the summer, to stay away and to have "no ostensible agency and no personal hand" in the defense. Similarly, in August Croly denounced Marble for having accepted Tweed's patronage, and in September outlined a strategy for defending the boss.[38]

Although Marble's own thoughts are unknown, he did allow the *World* to defend Tweed. Throughout the summer the paper declared its faith in the innocence of the ring members and dismissed the *Times*'s evidence as irrelevant. In September when a mass meeting of outraged citizens gathered at Cooper Institute to protest the ring's deeds, the *World* wrote them off as custom-house officials, meekly doing the bidding of the custom-house newspaper, the *Times*. When the meeting organized a Committee of Seventy, it scoffed at the reformers' efforts. "It is a weak affair," it declared, "which will result in nothing beyond giving a few spavined individuals an opportunity to go through their paces in the eyes of the public."[39]

Shortly after the Committee of Seventy was organized, Marble returned to the city to canvass the situation. His findings could scarcely have pleased him. Friends had warned him that the *World* was suffering from its defense of Tweed. Bangs had declared: "the *World* is more on trial in the public mind than the Ring," and had suggested the paper begin a crusade for tariff reform in order to divert attention from the affair. Croly reported that Tilden and Andrew H. Green believed the *World* was defending Tweed out of fear that it would lose its corporation advertising. "The fact is, Mr. Marble," Croly wrote, "the *World* is under a cloud just now. Its defense of the ring is attributed to corrupt motives and what is almost as bad for the *prestige* of the paper it has wholly lost its reputation for editorial ability. Greeley gives the popular verdict in saying the editor must be a fool or his readers fools."[40]

If the *World* was to survive the crisis, Marble knew he must act quickly and wisely. It was imperative, therefore, that he work out a plan of action with the party leaders. Fortunately, he arrived in New York just as the crisis was coming to a head. Realizing that mere denials would not put off the citizenry, the ring had decided to sacrifice one of its number in hopes that the others would then survive. The problem was to find the sacrifice. When no one volunteered, Hall and Sweeny fearlessly nominated Comptroller Richard B. Connolly, whose office held the incriminating records. The vote to elect fell only one short of unanimity, and on September 11 Hall publicly requested Connolly's resignation. On September 12 Connolly refused.

At once the contest between Hall and Connolly became the focus for an intraparty intrigue. When he first learned of his plight, Connolly sought help from Tilden. Sensing that his moment of opportunity had arrived, Tilden offered the comptroller a cunning proposal. Although refusing to defend him, Tilden proposed that Connolly stay in office and appoint Tilden's close friend, Andrew H. Green, as deputy comptroller. Green would lend Connolly the support of an honest man, who would also keep the incriminating records out of the hands of the other members of the ring. Tilden, of course, was hoping to use this evidence later as part of a reform crusade that would destroy his enemies while keeping the Republicans from profiting from Tammany's embarrassment. On September 17 Connolly, who had no other choice, accepted the proposal and appointed Green.[41]

While Tilden was laying his plans, he kept his own counsel. When a *Times* reporter asked him about the removal of Connolly, he only replied, "I know nothing about it. I have had nothing to do with it. I don't think the remedy is powerful enough for the disease." Green said the same thing.[42]

Tilden's security was so air-tight that not even Belmont knew of his plans. This was unfortunate, since Belmont and Tilden were working at cross-purposes. While Tilden was conferring with Connolly, Belmont was conferring with Hall. The latter two decided to remove Connolly and to replace him with either Belmont himself or with General McClellan. It is unclear what Hall hoped to gain from such an arrangement, but he nevertheless agreed to it.[43]

This was the situation Marble encountered when he returned to

New York. At once he called on Tilden to learn his plans, but found that the mantle of secrecy excluded even him. Tilden would only assure him that the ring would be destroyed and replaced by a regenerated Democracy. Such slogans were of no use to Marble, and so he sought advice from Belmont, who told him of his plan and enlisted his support. He then conferred with Hall and Sweeny and received their promises to help remove all the members of the ring. Henceforth the *World* defended Hall, called for Connolly to resign, and attacked the appointment of Green. Even after Hall had failed to persuade McClellan to replace Connolly, the paper continued to call for "great changes both in the organic structure and the *personnel* of the city government."[44]

Connolly and Green remained in office and enabled Tilden to construct his famous case against Tweed. Thus Tilden—the man who for three years had shied away from Marble's efforts for reform—emerged as one of America's great reformers, while the *World*'s defense of Hall caused it to appear an apologist for the ring. Once again, in a time of political crisis, Marble found himself an outsider. For an aspiring president-maker, it was a most dangerous position.

Marble's isolation continued through the party's fall convention. Before the convention he again tried to learn Ti'den's plans, but again met only evasion. Tilden replied only that the rural delegates were coming "with sentiments so strong that they might require restraining but would not need exciting" and advocated "decisive measures which cannot be misinterpreted." Beyond that he refused to go.[45]

Judging from Tilden's performance at the convention, it is unlikely that he actually had a well-thought-out plan. Rather, he seems to have hoped that the rural delegates would join him in purging Tweed. Early in September he had sent out a circular letter, declaring that "wherever the gangrene of corruption has reached the Democratic Party, we must take a knife and cut it out by the roots." Four days before the convention, he declared to Marble that Tammany was disintegrating so rapidly that it might not be able to put a ticket into the field. If one did run, however, and if he led the "outside" vote, he believed the Democratic majority would be "immense."[46]

But as Marble could have told Tilden from his experience with the Young Democracy, it was unwise to be overconfident in dealing with Tweed. When the state committee met, Tilden, Seymour, Church, John A. Green, and Henry Richmond proposed a floor fight to unseat Tammany and to replace it with a reform delegation. William Cassidy, Delos DeWolf, and William A. Fowler proposed, however, to allow Tammany to claim its seats and then to withdraw on condition that no other delegation be allowed to replace them. Rather than use their majority on the committee to force the issue, Tilden and his friends allowed the meeting to adjourn without a decision.

This was their mistake, for while the committee was meeting, Tweed was arranging a combination with the state officeholders, the Canal Ring, and William Cassidy's *Argus*. By the time the convention met, the boss was prepared to put up a fight. Realizing Tweed's power, Tilden decided to back down rather than to risk an open party split. He acquiesced in the Tammany plan of allowing its delegates to withdraw without allowing the reformers to claim its seats. Although he did push through a resolution permitting the reform delegation to address the convention, he sat back while the convention dodged the reform issue by blaming all the problems on the Republicans and then proceeded to nominate all the incumbent state legislators. Only when it was too late did he attempt to save some of his honor by declaring that if the question of seating Tammany had been put to a vote, he would have voted to reject them. Also, he announced that he did not intend to vote for any of "Mr. Tweed's twenty-one members of the Assembly."[47]

Marble witnessed Tilden's performance with smoldering rage and growing frustration. It was bad enough to have been excluded from Tilden's plans, but to find those plans inadequate was more than he could bear. On October 11, no longer able to contain himself, he poured out his feelings to the Sage of Gramercy Park. Recalling his own attack on Tweed, he declared: "I struck at Tammany when Tammany was in the plenitude of her power. I had every reason to expect your concurrence, *tho'* the fight was hopeless." During the fight against the Tweed Charter, when it appeared that Tilden could bring the rural Democracy into the fight on the reform side, he had urged Tilden to go to Albany and "take the lead and win the victory." Instead, Tilden had maintained an air of "judicial neutrality," which fooled no one and allowed the charter to pass.

After the passage of the charter, the *World* had ceased to oppose Tweed in order to force the ring "to hold power at the price of decent integrity and tolerable economy," to give the charter a fair trial, and to maintain party unity for the fall elections. Once the *Times* published its evidence against the ring, however, the *World* had spared "no occasion great or small to develop and direct that new force into effective and permanent remedies."

But Tilden had hidden his plans from Marble and the result had been disastrous. Bitterly, Marble recalled the convention. "The only interview we had of the least moment," he recalled, "was one in which I listened to Henry Richmond cursing to your face the absence of all plan and all leadership in Wednesday's proceedings, and denied to his face by you the knowledge of plans which you said you had for Thursday's proceedings." He had left the convention the next day, after "all that was to be done on Thursday in the convention had been prearranged by those who had plans for Thursday as they had for Wednesday—men who hate corruption and corrupt men as cordially as you or I do—and who know how to execute their plans and who did execute them."

Marble hoped that his words would spur Tilden toward "organizing the Democracy of this city so as to send a complete delegation of honest men to the Senate and Assembly." Declaring "You can make the Democracy the nucleus of the honesty of New York and ensure the result," he urged Tilden to renew his attack. "It will add nothing to your efficiency," he warned, "to fancy that stabs in the rear may be dealt you by men than whom you have never had sincerer friends or stauncher allies for any war in which you were publicly enlisted. It will alter nothing in the public course of the *World* though you were to strike—fancying you were 'striking *back*'—those friends and allies—at least it would define relations which are scarcely susceptible of continuance whilst defined so differently by you and by Yours truly MM."

It was a good catharsis, and when he had finished the letter he set it aside and never mailed it.[48]

As things turned out, there was no need for him to have sent the letter. Even while he was drafting it, Tilden was writing to congratulate him on swinging the *World* behind Connolly. Five days later, Tilden reentered the campaign against Tweed by addressing an enthusiastic meeting of the anti-Tammany organization, Apollo Hall. Defeated in the convention, he had decided to attack Tammany from the outside. Without knowing it, he was following just the course Marble would have advised.[49]

In the November elections, Tilden and Apollo Hall swept to victory, and within six months Tilden had forced Tammany to its knees. Shrewdly, he then deserted Apollo and returned as the leader of a reformed Tammany. Marble had no role in these maneuvers. His name does not appear among the membership of the Apollo organization, and the *World* did not go out of its way to support the reformers in the campaign. Following the election, however, Marble tried to salvage some of his prestige by reading the results as an endorsement of the *World*'s policies since 1868. "The interests, nay, the existence of the Democratic party is staked upon its recognition of the soundness of our former advice," the *World* announced. But in 1871 such a claim rang hollow. It was too obvious that the reforming spirit of 1868 and 1870 had disappeared well before the *Times*'s attack on Tweed. In trying to claim credit as a reformer, Marble was expressing only an ambition and not a fact.[50]

In 1871, however, city politics was not the only field for the reformer, for that was also the year of the Liberal Republican revolt. Growing out of dissatisfactions with the patronage, tariff, and reconstruction policies of the Grant administration, the movement included such prominent Republican spokesmen as Carl Schurz, Charles Sumner, and George W. Julian. During 1871 these men looked for some signs of support from the Republican organization, and finding none, moved toward the formation of a third party.[51]

In New York the revolt drew its greatest support from the Barnburners. In 1870, with Grant's active support, Roscoe Conkling had seized the Republican organization from Reuben E. Fenton. This caused Fenton, a former Barnburner, to seek revenge. He was soon joined in his project by the *Evening Post.* In 1868 the *Post* had supported Grant, largely because Bryant and Godwin could not think of supporting Seymour. As it became obvious that Grant's attitude toward free trade and civil service reform was the opposite of their own, and as his southern policy brought forth disorder and military rule, the editors of the *Post* turned against his administration. By November 1870 the *Post* was openly opposed to Grant.[52]

Such developments offered the Democrats an almost heaven-sent opportunity. If they could combine with the Republican dissidents, they might at last be able to construct their majority coalition. To accomplish this, however, they would have to convince the Liberals that they were willing to accept the reconstruction amendments and the results of the war. Certainly, the Liberals seemed willing to be convinced. In the fall of 1871, Carl Schurz began organizing Reunion and Reform Associations in the West and South and visited New York to confer with the Democratic leaders.[53]

During 1871 a number of prominent Democrats seemed willing to meet the Liberals' terms. In the elections of 1870, the Missouri Democracy cooperated with the Liberals to win control of the state legislature and to send Frank Blair to the Senate. The Blairs thus at once became strong supporters of the Liberal movement. In May 1871 none other than Clement Vallandigham persuaded the Montgomery County, Ohio, Democracy to endorse a platform accepting the reconstruction amendments. The next month the full Ohio Democracy accepted the platform in its state convention. Also, Democratic conventions in Connecticut and Pennsylvania showed a willingness to accept the Liberals' principles.[54]

Since the *World* had argued for such a new departure for many years, these movements should have provided an opportunity for Marble to regain prominence in the party's councils. And in 1871 he was well-placed to capitalize on such an opportunity. He was on intimate personal terms with the leading free-traders in the Liberal movement. Long a free-trader himself, he was particularly close to David A. Wells, a founder of the American Free Trade League. Wells's dismissal as revenue commissioner by the Grant administration had spurred many free-traders to join the Liberal movement. Another free-trade leader was Horace White of the *Chicago Tribune.* White and Marble had been friends ever since 1866, when they had joined forces in the revolt against the Associated Press.

Relations between Marble and Wells, however, were the key to

Marble's involvement in the free-trade movement. The two had begun corresponding in 1869 and had kept up a frequent exchange of letters on the theory and strategy of the free-trade cause. By early 1871 Wells was showing great interest in the Liberal movement and sought out Marble to discuss "some topics political as well as social." In the spring he toured the West, speaking on free-trade and estimating the strength of the Liberal movement. In May he returned from conferences with "new departure" Republicans and Democrats, convinced that he had learned things that would "perhaps settle the next election." He had been so well received, in fact, that J. S. Moore believed he had developed a severe case of "presidential fever."

Although Marble was not a member of the Free Trade League, he kept in touch with its plans and proceedings through Wells and Moore. In 1870, for example, Moore reported on a meeting held in Washington to oppose Wells's dismissal as revenue commissioner, noting that "all felt the time had come, when so influential a paper [as the *World*], or rather the leader of it, should meet those in friendly council with whom he differs in party politics." Later, Moore reported of another meeting: "your suggestion of yesterday is certainly the plan they will adopt." In November 1871 Marble's association with the free-traders became more formal as he joined the Cobden Club.[55]

Further support for the new departure came from the New York leaders. Belmont, who had joined with Marble to advocate such a policy in 1868, encouraged the new departure in a letter to General George McCook, the Democratic candidate for governor in Ohio. "Mr. Vallandigham," he said, "has perfectly well understood the spirit of our people at the present juncture, when he advocated the adoption of the Amendments to the Constitution as *'faits accomplis.'* " It was now time for the Democracy to turn its attention to issues of tax reduction, free trade, and the limitation of federal power. Tilden also seemed to favor the new departure, and when Carl Schurz visited New York to deliver a speech on civil service reform, the two discussed the possibilities of a political alliance.[56]

Even more significant was the attitude of the upstate leaders. In 1868 the followers of Seymour had refused to accept Republican reconstruction and had fought the Chase movement. But by 1871 the party's inability to overcome Republican appeals to the "bloody-shirt" and Tilden's desire to capitalize on the "reform" issue to unseat Tweed had dictated a change of course. For all his failures at the state convention in 1871, Tilden did persuade the rural delegates to approve a platform supporting the new departure. The second plank declared: "We recognize the emancipation of the freedmen of the South and their enfranchisement and perfect equality before the law as the inevitable sequence of the Civil War and of the overthrow of the rebellion against the Union, and we hold it to be the duty of all to sustain them in the enjoyment of their established rights and to aid them in promoting their own welfare and the general prosperity of the country." Following the election he continued to support the new departure, declaring to a friend that "I am sure this is a ground upon which all at the North and the South can unite and stand and which I have not seen laid out."[57]

Thus at last the Democracy seemed to have come around to the course advocated by the *World* since the Seymour disaster. And the *World* itself continued to advocate the policy. In May 1871, when Jefferson Davis spoke fondly of the Lost Cause of the Confederacy in an Atlanta speech, the paper called upon Southerners to compare "the prophecies of this bankrupt politician, this blundering old man" with the new departure resolutions of the Ohio Democracy. When a personal friend of Davis suggested that Marble allow Davis to publish a letter explaining the speech, he received a sharp rebuff. "It was possible for Mr. Davis to have rendered one service to the South in its present condition," Marble replied, "he could have been silent. It has never been possible for him to do the Northern Democracy any service and is not now."[58]

During the year the *World* elaborated its new departure program. One of its principal aims was to persuade both North and South to accept the reconstruction amendments. In March it declared that the issue of Negro suffrage was no longer important nationally, because the expiration of the Reconstruction Acts had left the states free to change their state constitutions as they saw fit. To those who still opposed the amendments it pointed out that states could impose property or educational restrictions on suffrage without having to attack the amendments themselves. According to the *World*, only those Democrats living in states dominated by Negro majorities actually opposed Negro suffrage. Since their opposition only caused the Negroes to vote solidly Republican, thereby guaranteeing a Republican majority in their states, the *World* concluded that they should play no part in determining party strategy. After all, they could deliver no electoral votes.

Instead of worrying about Negro voters, the *World* urged the Democracy to worry about white voters. "The negroes are of little account if we can control the judgment of the white voters." Two-thirds of the country's population, the *World* explained, lived in states with overwhelming majorities of white voters. These states had cast the votes for the "misrule of the past ten years." To the "white majorities in the Northern States" the Democracy should now turn for support. Since the past elections had proved that many Democrats as well as Republicans in these states wished to continue the experiment of Negro suffrage, the party should cease to debate the issue. To do otherwise would be to court "inevitable, overwhelming defeat."

On November 18 the *World* presented its fullest statement of its new departure in an editorial written by Marble in consultation with Belmont. Although claiming to look to the future, the editorial was very much a product of the past, in effect summing up Marble's experience since Seymour's defeat. To a degree it also showed the lessening of his political independence, so proudly proclaimed three years earlier.

Marble counseled his fellow Democrats to set aside narrow sentiments of "party spirit and party prejudice" in order to encourage the support of all "honest" Republicans. Especially, the party should refuse for the moment to commit itself to a specific presidential candidate, but should cooperate with honest Republicans to select the best man. It should insist only that both sides agree to abide by the decision of the convention.

The Democracy should expand its crusade against corruption from a local to a national movement. "The overthrow of Tammany," Marble announced, "is a preliminary engagement which introduces the general battle against official corruption. It has demonstrated the possibility of sinking party differences in a joint effort to expose and dethrone fraud and punish its perpetrators." In the near future the movement should have a national impact.

The Democracy should support amnesty for former Confederates. The corruption of the southern governments had resulted, according to Marble, from the "vindictive, ostracizing policy which has excluded the property-holders and intelligent classes of the South from their due influence in local politics." Thus reform instead of racism should become the Democratic weapon against Republican reconstruction.

The Democracy should support the free-trade movement, which Marble considered "one of the most important bases of the new political combinations." Especially was it important to use the movement to secure western votes. Noting that in the last three years Republican newspapers in Chicago and Cincinnati had come out for free trade, Marble reminded his fellow Democrats that free trade and amnesty had carried Missouri for the Liberal Republicans.

The Democracy should make a special effort to attract German voters. Ever since Schurz's break with Grant, Marble had been striving with desperation, and no doubt with some embarrassing memories, to recover the support of Germans alienated by the *World*'s treatment of the Franco-Prussian War. As early as March, the *World* had declared that "the staunch adherence of the German Americans to their fatherland in the last momentous conflict has always had our admiring approval." In May it announced that "on all the live issues of the day . . . all intelligent Germans concur with the Democrats." Now Marble pointed to the German opposition to the Tweed Ring and to Schurz's favoring of amnesty for the South. Schurz's "vigorous sense and persuasive tongue," he declared, would help the reform movement win "the whole body of German voters."[59]

Several significant points emerge from the *World*'s program. It appears that Marble considered Reconstruction essentially a northern problem. The experience of the 1860s had showed the South unable to influence national policy. So long as northern voters were determined to stand by their commitment to Negro suffrage, the southern Democrats were powerless to oppose them. Continued Democratic opposition to Negro suffrage had brought only Republican majorities in the North and military rule in the South. Under such circumstances, it seemed better for the South to accept Negro suffrage and to hope that their northern colleagues could use other issues to defeat the Republicans. Those issues, it was hoped, would be administrative reform and free trade.

Both issues, of course, were conceived in response to northern conditions. In New York the attack on Tweed had literally forced Tilden and Belmont to become reformers in order to save their political careers. Nationally, reform and free trade seemed the most likely issues to use in effecting cooperation between the Democracy and the liberal Republicans. And the reform issue alone had another special attraction: maintaining party unity. Prior to 1871 the party had seemed able to unite only on opposition to Negro suffrage. Certainly, economic issues could not have been cohesive in a party containing Pennsylvania protectionists, Ohio greenbackers, and New York merchant-bankers. If, however, the party could unite upon a commitment to honest government and use that commitment to win converts from the Republican party, it made good political sense to replace the voice of the racist with the voice of the reformer.

Still, there were problems to solve. Especially important was the problem of finding a means of working with the Liberal Republicans. Although hostile to Grant, many Liberals still hesitated to break formally with their party, and others feared that an alliance with the Democracy would result only in their being absorbed into that party.[60]

Recognizing the Liberal hesitation, some Democrats suggested their party allow the Liberals to name the presidential and vice-presidential candidates in 1872. This method, known as the "passive policy," had been adopted by the Missouri Democracy in 1870 and had resulted in victory. As noted earlier, the Blairs had profited from this policy, and it was natural for them to be among its leading advocates in 1871.

A man with Marble's reputation for party irregularity might well have been expected to endorse the passive policy, and its supporters were quick to try him out. In February 1871 Montgomery Blair invited Marble to Washington for a conference, but Marble declined. In November Blair's friend and confidant, William Grosvenor, came to New York to discuss the passive policy with Marble. "If it is plain that a Democratic nomination cannot win," he declared, "the time has come to ask whether Grant cannot be beaten by union of all elements opposed to him, and I believe he can." Although Grosvenor had found much opposition to the new departure as a *"Democratic"* movement, he had found little opposition to an independent candidate.[61]

Surprisingly, however, Marble opposed the passive policy. On November 24 the *World* declared that "the Liberals must understand that it is we, and not they, whose hands are on the helm of the Democratic ship." While welcoming cooperation between Liberals and Democrats, the *World* declared that it was too early to estimate the importance of the Liberal revolt. Defections from the Republican party would help the Democracy only if they came as an "organized phalanx" and not merely as individuals. The *World* advised the Democracy to wait until after the Republican convention to see if the Liberals would be able to organize a phalanx.[62]

Shortly after the *World*'s editorial appeared, Marble expressed his own feelings to Montgomery Blair. He was still not convinced that the Liberals would "cut loose and burn their bridges." So far only Schurz and B. Gratz Brown had done so, and they were not enough. "Ten men," he declared, "could lead a triumphant revolt," but it was difficult to find ten audacious Republicans. "They may be reformers before Grant's nomination and beat him," Marble wrote. "If they wait to be bolters after it, they will be beaten, if indeed they dared to bolt." He did believe, however, that the Democracy would avoid its "crimes or follies" of 1864 and 1868, and thanked Blair for helping to dispose of the "hideboundness of the party and the reputation of it." He also thanked him for opening doors "which [Republican] voters will enter though their leaders don't."[63]

Although Blair continued to argue vigorously for the passive policy, he could not convince Marble. Apparently, Marble's unhappy experiments with independent reform had taken their toll. Bangs sensed the change and inferred from Marble's actions that the *World*'s policy was to accord with that chosen by the party leaders. Also, it should be noted that in Marble's letters to Blair he carefully pointed out that "in a large acquaintance among both the thinkers and the active politicians" he could find no support for the passive policy. "And," he emphasized, "I sought them patiently." The party was against the policy, and that was enough.[64]

Subsequent events proved the sincerity of Marble's objections. When the Liberal movement actually attained significant strength, he placed the *World* squarely behind it, even going so far as to endorse the candidacy of Charles Francis Adams. He probably would have attended the Liberal Republican convention in Cincinnati. He did not attend the convention, however, and took no active part in working out the Democratic-Liberal alliance because early in 1872 he was stricken with a serious illness.

Ever since his college days, Marble's health had been fragile. Hardly a year passed in which he enjoyed even moderately good health. Often as not, his summers in Newport were necessary to restore a constitution drained by a year of overwork. In December 1862, for example, Louisa Arnold inquired: "Are you as miserable as when you were here? I hoped a few days of rest might be of some benefit, although you need a much longer vacation." In the last two years his health seems to have grown weaker. Striving to place the *World* in the forefront of New York journalism and to expand its influence in the party, he drove himself beyond the limits of endurance. In the summer of 1870 he suffered a serious collapse, when long nights of reading by gaslight brought on an inflammation of his eyes, threatening him with blindness. For nearly five months he was forced to read nothing and to write only by dictation. We may well imagine that the events of 1871 further drained his vitality.[65]

So in February he collapsed. No evidence exists to tell of the exact nature of his illness, though it was serious enough to require months of rest in a warm climate. On February 21 Bangs secured passage on the U.S.S. *Missouri* to Havana. On March 8 Marble arrived in good spirits and requested "white waistcoats, case Ginger ale, quills, and three shirts." Five day later, however, he found the heat "too debilitating" and left for New Orleans. There he settled in a hotel to await news of the Liberal Republican convention.[66]

Before his illness Marble had committed himself to the nomination of the favorite among the Liberals, Charles Francis Adams. Marble's reasons for the choice are unclear, except that in 1868 he had favored John Quincy Adams, Jr., the only Adams to desert to the Democrats, for vice-president. It also seems likely that his choice was influenced by David A. Wells and August Belmont, both of whom were enthusiastic Adams men. Perhaps Marble was attracted by the political independence of the man, who in many ways must have typified his conception of noble manhood.[67] In any case, Adams was the logical choice for the Democrats, having consistently advocated a policy of leniency and understanding toward the South.

The news from Cincinnati, however, could scarcely have helped his recuperation. In the weeks preceding the convention, Adams remained aloof from the movement, publicly refusing to allow anyone to act on his behalf. His conduct, in fact, raised serious doubts about his availability for the nomination. His opponents were quick to take advantage of this. A week before the meeting of the convention, one of those opponents, Fernando Wood, arrived in Cincinnati with a statement that no Democratic congressman favored Adams.

Even more disquieting was news of a rising movement to nominate Horace Greeley. In March, J. S. Moore reported to Marble that Grosvenor had won Greeley to the Liberal cause. The victory, however, had come high; for Greeley had demanded that the Liberals give up their opposition to high tariffs and centralized government in exchange for his support.[68]

But the mere presence of Greeley was enough to horrify Marble; there were few men he despised more than the editor of the *Tribune.* Marble's hatred of Greeley stretched back over his entire career as editor of the *World.* In the fall of 1862, shortly after he had saved the paper from financial collapse, he had complained to Dr. Anderson of the "falsehoods" of the *Tribune, Times,* and *Herald.* A year later he showed that he had not forgotten those trying days. "When it would have saved me mental pain and pecuniary anxiety," he declared to Greeley, "I discovered that I could expect nothing from the *Tribune*'s fairness, justice, or generosity, towards me or the paper of which I am the editor." In following years his hatred was sustained by what he considered the *Tribune*'s misrepresentations of the *World.* During one controversy, such words as "intolerant and intolerable arrogance," "shabby quibbles," "false and calumnious," "false and libellous," "outrage," and "long series of malignant lies" filled his letters of complaint to Greeley. "How can I now believe," he wrote, "that you are anything else than the cunning, unscrupulous, 'honest' Mr. Greeley which those who have summered and wintered with you from your youth up declare you to be?"[69]

By 1872 Marble had not expressed such feelings for a few years, but neither had he retracted them. As he watched the movement to nominate Greeley gain momentum, his anxiety over the Liberal Republican enterprise grew. The day before the convention opened, he dispatched an impassioned telegram to Wells. "Don't regard talk of Democratic Congressmen or *Argus* against Adams. It is talk of trading politicians. Stick Stick Stick to your candidate and your free trade principles, and all politicians in both parties can't prevent your winning. Unquestionably the people will stand by you if you justify their highest hopes. Greeley's defection from platform will harm nobody and he will take good care it don't help Grant. For God's sake don't budge one inch from Adams and Free Trade." He also prepared a memorandum, probably for publication in the *World,* declaring that Wood's anti-Adams movement should be smashed and that the South "preferred Adams to any other man, whoever nominated him." He added, "Massachusetts expects every man to do his duty."[70]

Not every man did his duty, and when the Cincinnati convention adjourned, the nominee was Horace Greeley and the platform evaded the free-trade issue entirely. The news at once caused a volley of telegrams between Marble and Chamberlain. Marble's reaction was instinctive: "Of course no Democrat can or will endorse Greeley." If Greeley accepted the nomination and the Democracy nominated Adams, Marble believed Grant still might be defeated. At the moment, however, it seemed that a "straight Democratic nomination was doubtless inevitable." In any event, Greeley was out of the question. An hour later Chamberlain reported that Greeley would accept the nomination and assured Marble that the *World* was "strong against him."[71]

There the matter rested for about two hours. Then George W. Adams, the *World*'s Washington correspondent, sent Chamberlain a message from the Democratic congressmen, asking Marble to keep the *World* neutral. But Marble was in no mood for neutrality. To win the election, he declared, it had been necessary for the Liberals to insure a split in the Republican party and to nominate a man the Democracy could endorse. "The Damfool convention learned the first lesson, forgot second." Although the *World* would not hinder Greeley from helping to beat Grant, it would show the Democracy how to beat both. "Let the trumpet blow no uncertain sound," he declared, "though all the archangels beseech. Democratic patriotism displayed magnificently for [the] last few months. Its hoped-for allies have not risen to height of the great argument. Now it will do its utmost all for good government unaided and alone. God give us victory."[72]

Although Marble's opposition to Greeley was shared by such prominent Liberals as Wells, Bowles, Godkin, Schurz, and Bryant, it was not shared by the Democratic leaders. To the Democracy, it was necessary to accept even Greeley in order to defeat Grant. "The nomination is not what you and I wanted," Belmont declared to Bowles, "but the blunder is made, and if Grant is really to be beaten the ticket must be warmly and unanimously supported by *every organ* of the Liberal Republicans."[73]

And by every organ of the Democracy. Once again Marble's principles ran counter to party strategy. The party leaders could no longer allow the *World* the luxury of independence. They decided that the *World* should stop its opposition to Greeley and assume a skeptical neutrality until the Democratic convention had made its decision.

Perhaps in deference to his feelings, Marble was allowed to stay away from the paper during the campaign. After a few weeks' rest in the city, he retired to the Catskills. For those who wondered about his absence, his health provided a convenient excuse. During the campaign the *World* emphasized his poor health by reporting on the progress of his recovery.[74]

The job of guiding the *World* fell to Chamberlain, whose personal friendship with Greeley admirably suited him for the task. And he performed well. In the weeks preceding the Democratic convention, the *World* supported Adams, but once the inevitable nomination of Greeley had been made, it obediently fell into line behind him. It also supported the decision of the state party to draw up a joint ticket composed of Democrat Francis Kernan for governor and Liberal Republican Chauncy DePew for lieutenant governor.[75]

But even party unity could not keep the election from becoming a fiasco. Although Greeley conducted a surprisingly vigorous campaign, his candidacy obviously left the electorate bemused. Little else could have been expected in a campaign that saw a former Radical Republican protectionist supported by Democrats and free-traders. In New York Greeley's candidacy hurt the Democracy by preventing a full reconciliation with the Barnburners. Bryant's personal dislike of Greeley forced the *Evening Post* to support Grant, while the state Republicans, perhaps sensing their good fortune, wisely nominated the former Barnburner, John A. Dix, for governor. On election day, both Grant and Dix carried the state by over 53,000 votes.[76]

After the election Marble returned to New York to help repair the damage. On November 15 the *World* carried an editorial that probably reflected his preliminary conclusions. Despite the recent defeat, it declared, the future looked bright. The election had been the last contest for many of the founders and leaders of the Republican party; in the next election that party would have to rely on second-rate candidates. With the "Negro question" finally settled, the parties would at last be able to debate economic questions. For the Democracy, free trade still seemed the best issue, both because Great Britain had definitely committed herself to it and because it was supported by leaders in the science of political economy. To such men as Horace White, Samuel Bowles, David A. Wells, and Murat Halstead the Democracy should turn for its principles. And it was still necessary to "reunite all who held Democratic doctrines before the Republican party was formed, and reinforce them by the numerous recent converts to the same order of economic and political ideas." So despite the ferment of the last four years, the Democracy was still in need of reform. Left unanswered was the question of the means by which the *World* and its editor would attempt to accomplish that reform. And as it turned out, those who asked such a question would have many months to wait for their answer.[77] ✣

HARPER'S WEEKLY, *1870, Vol. 14*

MANTON MARBLE

AUGUST BELMONT, SR.

SAMUEL J. TILDEN

PHOTO BY ROCKWOOD, THE LIBRARY OF CONGRESS

MANTON MARBLE

SAMUEL BARLOW

HARPER'S WEEKLY, *1889, Vol. 33*

HARPER'S WEEKLY, *1881, Vol. 25*

IVORY CHAMBERLAIN

WILLIAM H. HURLBERT

HARPER'S MAGAZINE, *1878, Vol. 56*

CHAPTER NINE

Party Loyalty

In 1873 Marble spent the entire summer in New York. This was unusual, since he spent most summers in Newport with the Arnolds. But 1873 was an unusual year. The regular Democrats had led the party to defeat in 1868, and the new-departure Democrats had done the same thing in 1872. The problem was to develop another strategy, since the party seemed to have exhausted its alternatives. It was enough to keep any good Democrat in town for a hot summer.

The season was still young, however, when Marble reached a decision. On July 5 the *World* outlined a new strategy. The two previous defeats, it announced, had resulted from too great a willingness on the part of the New York Democracy to compromise its free-trade principles. From now on, whatever the needs of party unity, there would be no more compromise. "The Democratic party has no career as a party of expediency or of coalitions, no title to the allegiance of its hosts except as a party of principle, no use for defeats which are not precursors of ultimate victory, and no use for victory except those principles can be applied to the nation's sovereign ills." The time had come to stand fast for principle.

The time had also come to stand fast for party. In late August, when John Cochrane, representing the Liberal Republicans, sounded out the Democracy on the possibility of combining forces in the fall elections, the *World* commented: "The Democratic party of this state will adhere to its organization, maintain its discipline, and welcome all recruits who are willing to act with it from honest public motives. The party has had enough of coalitions, and in its present temper it cannot possibly be brought to act in a new one." In fact, so profound was the *World*'s aversion to allying with disaffected Republicans that it advised the party to ignore them entirely and to try instead to regroup its own forces. "What we need to make us strong in this state," it stated on September 2, "is not Republican recruits, but the recovery of our own stragglers." Coalitions with Liberal Republicans would not accomplish this, but would in fact "cause ten Democrats to stay at home for every Liberal Republican that could be induced to act with us." In order to rebuild its majority the Democracy needed only to retrieve "its reputation for honesty."[1]

For once Marble's thinking was in tune with that of the party leaders. A canvass of party opinions convinced Allen C. Beach that "the only sound policy this fall is to call a Democratic state convention, make a Democratic platform, nominate a Democratic ticket, and go on to win." Beach urged Marble to be on hand to help out with the strategy.[2]

Early in October Marble attended the state convention to work for a regular Democratic ticket and to draft a regular Democratic platform. Without even mentioning Reconstruction, the platform concentrated solely on issues of administrative and economic reform. In 1873 both issues held hope for the Democracy. The memory of the Credit Mobilier scandal was still fresh in many minds, as was the recent controversy over the "Salary Grab" by Congress. The shock and concern following the recent failure of Jay Cooke and Company indicated that economic questions would be a prominent part of American politics for at least the near future. Reminding the voters of the Credit Mobilier and the Salary Grab, the platform declared that public officials should be required to keep records that could be easily examined to reveal any wrongdoing. Officials should also be required to swear "at proper periods that they have not in any way been unlawfully benefited by their official action." Scoffing at Grant's economic policies as "the President's Pill for Panics," the platform demanded a revenue tariff and a return to specie payments: "the tried and historic principles of the old Democracy, applicable throughout our national, state, and municipal life." Liberal Republicans were invited to "unite with us in our efforts to restore pure government in our state and federal administrations."

Throughout the campaign, the *World* played upon the need for Democratic unity and traditional Democratic principles. When the ticket swept the state by nearly 15,000 votes, it found its course ringingly vindicated. "The people of the state have signified by their votes both their approval of the policy and of the honest boldness with which it is proclaimed," it announced. "Had the platform . . . been less explicit and courageous, we should have witnessed no such triumph as the people gave us yesterday." To Allen C. Beach it seemed that the election had accustomed "the Democratic party to a *real* Democratic platform," and Marble no doubt agreed.[3]

So by the fall of 1873, Marble had given up party independence. The state elections of 1872 had been especially disastrous for the party. Heading a Democratic-Liberal Republican coalition ticket, the regular Democrat, Francis Kernan, had been overwhelmed. His showing was especially poor upstate, where he captured only six counties, in contrast to Seymour's eleven in 1868. Undoubtedly, many

Democrats in the rural areas stayed home rather than vote for Greeley. It was there that the *World* had suffered most for its course in 1868 and during the Franco-Prussian War. It was there also that disappointment over the failure of the Young Democracy movement had been most widespread. Marble probably hoped to appeal to the rural Democracy in his effort to reestablish the *World*'s leadership in the party. During the campaign the paper emphasized with special pride the endorsement given Marble's platform by the rural Democracy.[4]

In other ways the *World* appealed for the farm vote. Realizing the political importance of the Granger movement in the Middle West, it tried to convince the farmer that antimonopoly and free trade were different sides of the same coin. Protection, it pointed out, required railroads to pay high prices for materials and caused them to increase the rates charged to farmers. The farmers, of course, were forced to pay the rates because of the monopoly power of the railroads. Both free trade and antimonopoly, therefore, benefited the farmer by lowering the cost of transportation. Both were also important because they opposed centralization. "It seems to be confessed, on all hands," the *World* declared, "that this growing centralization of the railroad power is the most alarming feature of the situation. It undermines the control of the separate states over their own railroads and destroys competition." To regulate the railroads effectively, while at the same time preventing an increase in the power of the central government, the *World* suggested that states enter into interstate compacts with the consent of Congress. It should also be noted that Marble's platform in 1873 included a plank calling for cheap transportation, and specifically for the New York farmer, lower canal tolls.[5]

But if Marble's party loyalty resulted from a desire to attract rural votes, his choice of party leadership remained, as in previous years, bounded by the circle of his personal friendships. For that leadership he was coming to look most hopefully toward Samuel J. Tilden.

One of the nation's wealthiest and most respected corporation lawyers, Tilden conducted his life as though he were preparing a brief. Thorough, dispassionate, and calculating, he acted boldly only when assured of success, fled when unprepared to meet a challenge, and usually kept to himself. His conduct toward Marble during the overthrow of Tweed is testimony enough about his conception of personal loyalty. Although his character alienated such men as Barlow and Belmont, it attracted Marble with an intensity that, as we shall see, caused the ambitious editor to risk his own manhood in the service of the Sage of Gramercy Park.[6]

In personality Marble was quite different from Tilden. With his friends he was outgoing and expressive, always ready to express his anger or joy, always ready with a compliment, bon mot, flowery allusion, or a declaration of sympathy. Sparkling and witty, he was at the same time loyal and affectionate in the best traditions of his gentleman's code. But he was also attracted to power, and of all his friends, Tilden seemed the most able to lead the party back to power in the state and nation. To an ambitious president-maker, who had been forced to set aside party independence, he seemed the party's best hope.[7]

And for Democrats everywhere these, indeed, were times of hope. As economic distress grew and spread and as scandal lingered over the Grant administration, the Democracy looked expectantly toward the elections of 1874. Allen C. Beach spoke for many New York Democrats when he declared to Tilden on July 20 that the party could win with "any decent ticket." The man most likely to lend the needed decency was Tilden, who throughout the summer of 1874 was receiving many requests to accept the gubernatorial nomination. By the time the convention assembled in mid-September, he faced only token opposition from the state's Canal Ring and easily secured the nomination. Second place on the ticket went to William Dorsheimer, a former Barnburner and Liberal Republican who had returned to the party. The platform merely summarized Marble's effort of the previous year.[8]

The campaign produced few surprises. Presenting Tilden as "the Hercules who slew the Tammany Hydra," the Democratic press did its best to contrast its candidate with the scandals of the Grant administration. Governor Dix, it was pointed out, had been president of the Union Pacific at the time of the Credit Mobilier frauds. Also, the governor had not opposed a third term for Grant. Democratic speakers also denounced Grant's reconstruction policies—S. S. Cox called them "crimes against the social order and human honesty"—and arraigned Grant's failure to combat the depression. The *World* summed it all up: "Every vote for Dix is a vote for Grant and Hard Times."[9]

It was, of course, a Democratic year. Twenty-three of thirty-five states went Democratic, returning the first Democratic majority to the House of Representatives since prewar days. In New York the Democratic ticket easily swept the state, electing large majorities in the state assembly and winning the governorship by over 50,000 votes. For the first time since joining the party, Marble found himself closely identified with a winner.

After the election Marble discussed its significance in an article for the *Weekly World*. Learning from the old Democracy, he wrote, the new Democracy was "making sound economic issues against the much more monstrous evils of our time." Those evils included a fluctuating currency that defrauded every buyer and seller and deprived farmers and planters of their just reward, a tariff that increased the price of a few domestic products instead of merely raising revenue, and centralization in government. Hard money, free trade, and home rule were the three cries of the Democracy, and though gains had been made toward securing these principles in government, it was still necessary to capture the Senate and the presidency. The revolution had begun, but it needed to be carried forward.[10]

It would be necessary to organize the Democracy to assure success. Much would depend upon the party's leadership, which in New York meant Samuel J. Tilden. As governor of the nation's largest and richest state, Tilden at once attracted attention as presidential timber. Thus he assumed a double responsibility. Not only would he have to influence the party's congressional leadership but would also have to demonstrate skill in leading his own state party. Upon his accomplishments would depend many things: the future of the New York Democracy, the hopes of the eastern wing of the party to establish its leadership, the possibilities for a Democratic return to national power, and the hopes and ambitions of Manton Marble.

It soon appeared that on the state level Tilden was to be in for a difficult time. Almost as soon as the election returns were counted, dissensions broke out. The first faction to cause serious trouble was Tammany Hall. By 1874 Tammany was securely in the hands of "Honest John" Kelly. In many respects Kelly was eminently qualified for his post. A youth spent in the poverty of New York's Hester Street had securely identified him with the working-class Irish who made up the rank and file of Tammany's organization, while a political career spent in opposition to Tweed easily qualified him to lead a "reformed" Tammany. But Kelly could not content himself with merely controlling Tammany. A driving ambition and an almost paranoiac jealousy instilled in him the determination to control the state organization.[11]

Kelly's ambition caused him to break with the Democratic mayor, William H. Wickham. A prominent diamond merchant, life-long Democrat, and member of the Committee of Seventy, Wickham also possessed excellent credentials as a "reformer." His lack of political experience, however, and his membership in the "swallow-tail" Democracy irritated Kelly and led the Tammany boss to conclude that the mayor should take orders from him.[12]

Further complicating the political picture in the city was Comptroller Andrew H. Green. A close friend of Tilden and also a spokesman for "reform," Green had assumed the comptrollership upon the overthrow of Tweed. At once he set out to demonstrate the virtues of "honest" government by launching a vigorous campaign to reduce city expenditures. Acting as though he feared even the slightest extravagance would be interpreted as a return to Tweedism, he carefully examined all bills and trimmed them wherever possible.

Although such practices eliminated any trace of graft, they created problems of a different kind. Workingmen, many of them loyal sons of Tammany, complained when their wages were cut or withheld altogether, uptown developers resented the curtailing of funds for expansion, and residents in settled areas complained when city services disappeared. In January 1875 the opposition to Green increased when Wickham and William R. Martin of the Parks Department began to call for freeing funds to develop the uptown area.[13]

Green's policies also alienated Marble. In the summer of 1872 the *World* billed the city for $50,000 for various corporation advertisements. Business had not improved, and Bangs was informing Marble that he would need all the money from the city account to pay the journal's obligations. Green, however, decided to reduce the claim by half and seemed willing to go to court to enforce his decision. Hoping to avoid the expense and delay of a lawsuit, Marble hired Martin to negotiate with Green and authorized Chamberlain to use political pressure against the comptroller. But Green would not yield. Marble then appealed to Tilden to have Green replaced; but Tilden remained loyal to Green and advised Marble to settle for whatever he could get. In the end that turned out to be only $28,000. In 1873, when the legislature established the *City Record* to print all corporation advertising at city expense, and allowed brief notices in two morning and two evening papers, Green appointed the *Times, Tribune, Post,* and *Commercial Advertiser,* all Republican papers.[14]

In January 1875 these problems led to a confrontation between Tilden and the city leaders. Under state law the mayor had to obtain the governor's consent to remove city officials. When Wickham sought to remove Corporation Counsel E. Delafield Smith, Tilden thought a plot might be underway to remove Green. When Kelly's stooge, Assemblyman Thomas Costigan, introduced a bill to deprive the governor of his removal power, he was convinced of it. With his usual caution, he set out to protect Green. Offering various excuses, he stalled the mayor on the Smith removal, while behind the scenes he rounded up opposition to the Costigan Bill.

As it turned out, both controversies were made to order for Tilden. Although Tammany was strong enough to push the Costigan Bill through the Assembly, they could not influence the Republican-controlled Senate, which wanted to be sure that Albany retained some power in New York City government. So Tilden was able to remain conveniently silent on the issue, while the Republicans killed the bill. When Wickham decided not to press the Smith removal, he was able to wait until the right moment and then settle the case on his own terms.[15]

Clearly Tilden was seeking to dominate the party. On April 2 he outlined his plans in a long conversation with the *World*'s managing editor, Jerome B. Stillson. "He indulged himself," Stillson reported to Marble, "in something very much like a tirade against Wickham, Kelly, and other Tammany compatriots. He affirmed, rapping the table violently with clenched fists, that he had felt himself to be in more danger from his friends in New York than from all his enemies together, and that he was glad to be so independent of them as he felt himself to be." Carefully Tilden outlined how he had kept himself free from the various "rings and snares" in city politics and how those rings and snares endangered the Democracy's popular appeal.

> He spoke of the government of New York City as a sham, calling attention (as he had done before, as I told you) to the fact that no striking reform measure had been introduced and that the only noticeable thing accompanying a change of Mayors had been a mere coarse redistribution of the local offices and spoils. He emphasized with particular force that New York City, the conspicuous political center of the country, ought to be foremost in starting Democratic reform. Everything in New York is discovered by the press; the radiation of example and intelligence from there is countrywide. New York has the greatest power for political suasion of the whole country; the Governor does not find that it has done anything to make that power felt for good.

Such was the ambition of Samuel J. Tilden. From a timid party regular he had emerged a ruthless chieftain, demanding obedience and loyalty. In return he promised little. When Stillson remarked that the governor's friends were finding fault with his delay in the Smith removal, Tilden replied that "he didn't care; he owed nothing to them." It was a statement that Marble might well have noted, since it showed the dangers confronting those who served the governor.[16]

Both controversies severely tested Marble's party loyalty. Undoubtedly he would have relished Green's removal. Still, he knew that to obtain such personal satisfaction he would have to risk injuring Tilden's prestige. And from his own experience he knew the fate awaiting those who threatened to divide the party. So he assumed the role of the compromiser. The *World* defended Tilden's right to remain silent on the Costigan Bill and declared that neither Wickham nor Kelly was "morally capable" of offering the "inducements" necessary to secure its passage. It dismissed the Smith case as a quibble over a "legal technicality." Privately, Marble offered Wickham his services as a mediator and urged Tilden to "smooth the ruffled feathers of the Tammany brave."[17]

While he was gaining mastery over the city, Tilden was also spreading his influence elsewhere in the state. Conscious of New York's influence in national politics, he sought to strengthen his image as a reformer. It was his desire to accomplish both aims simultaneously that led him to attack the Canal Ring.

For years the Canal Ring had robbed the taxpayers by rigging bids for repair work on the state's canals. Although the ring's existence was well known, its operations had been kept secret, largely because of its influence in both parties. In 1874, however, the ring's Democratic leaders had forfeited their influence by opposing Tilden's nomination for governor. After weeks of careful investigation, Tilden launched an attack on the ring with a special message, detailing its operations and cost to the taxpayers, and recommending specific reforms, among them the appointment of a special investigating commission. When his message received overwhelming public approval, he forsook his characteristic caution and ruthlessly pressed his attack. In less than a year, the ring was destroyed.[18]

In the early stages of the fight, Tilden revealed his motives to Stillson:

> The party needed a new departure . . . who was there to start on it but the Governor? In New York City the result of a Democratic victory at the polls was seen only in a division of spoils—a distribution of offices. *Something needed to be done!* The party needed revivifying. No party can get the country's attention, can win recruits, which don't *do something.* This *is* doing something, and no cries will avail against it. I have attempted to array and hold to the policy of arraying the transportation interest, the boatmen and the *taxpayers,* who include all classes of citizens, against the thieves, and the men who take the thieves' side cannot stand.[19]

Thus the Democracy was to take the road of administrative reform, and Tilden was to be its leader. Anxious to attract as many friends of reform as possible to the Democracy, Tilden assiduously courted the Liberal Republicans, especially the Barnburners. Among the ten members on his commission to propose reforms in municipal government were the Liberal Republicans E. L. Godkin, Simon Sterne, and William M. Evarts. His Canal Commission was headed by the former Barnburner, John Bigelow. Bigelow, who was to become one of Tilden's most enthusiastic admirers and who would author a hero-worshipping biography of the governor in 1895, was an especially important convert, having for many years been an associate editor of the *Evening Post.*

Tilden also appealed for the support of his old friend, William Cullen Bryant. Since the overthrow of Tweed, Bryant had been extremely cordial toward Tilden. In 1873 he had credited Tilden with "self-sacrificing courage, persistence, and far-seeing sagacity" in bringing Tweed to justice. In 1874, though not formally endorsing Tilden's candidacy, he had called him the Democracy's strongest candidate and had urged a reorganization of the parties. Soon after his inauguration, Tilden arranged a special reception in Albany to honor the famous editor. At the reception Bryant declared that the country would not be displeased to see Tilden run for president in 1876.[20]

Another editor whom Tilden hoped to beguile was Whitelaw Reid of the *Tribune.* Following the election of 1872 and the death of Greeley, Reid had kept the *Tribune* independent in politics, letting it be known that he would support the party that most sincerely favored reform. In 1874, when the New York Republicans refused to oppose a third term for Grant, he publicly announced his disgust and showed a willingness to listen to the Democracy. From that moment Tilden began to cultivate Reid's support. After the election, when Reid asked Tilden to bind the Democracy to accepting the results of the war, the Reconstruction Amendments, and the sanctity of the public debt, Tilden included just such a passage in his message to the legislature. When Tilden released the evidence against the Canal Ring, he allowed the *Tribune* reporters to get the information ahead of the others. When Stillson found out about this, he commented to Marble that the governor "was not, I think, displeased to add to the number of his newspaper 'organs.' "[21]

In the following months Tilden's friends continually solicited Reid's support. The governor's nephew, William T. Pelton, advised Reid about party affairs and William C. Whitney, Delafield Smith's replacement as corporation counsel, did his best to convince the editor that the Democracy was truly the party of administrative reform, even going so far as to suggest which Democratic candidates the *Tribune* ought to oppose.[22]

By the time the state convention met in the fall of 1875, Tilden had decided to go one step further by reviving the new departure coalition of 1872. From the convention emerged a ticket dominated by Tilden reformers. John Bigelow and John D. Van Buren, Jr., of the Canal Commission stood for secretary of state and state engineer, respectively; Charles S. Fairchild, a reform Democrat who had distinguished himself in prosecuting Tweed, stood for attorney-general; Lucius Robinson, one of the earliest of the Barnburner converts, stood for comptroller; and Daniel Magone, another Canal Commission member, replaced Beach as chairman of the state committee. "There is not a straight Democrat on the ticket," complained one of the party regulars, "they are every mothers son of them party renegades." Certainly, the endorsement of the entire ticket by the Liberal Republican convention seemed to bear out such a judgment.[23]

On election day Tilden's strategy paid dividends. After a campaign in which the Democracy emphasized the governor's reform program, the voters approved the entire ticket. The new departure, it seemed, had come into its own in New York.[24]

While Tilden was building a reform coalition in the New York Democracy, Marble was helping to build one nationally. His efforts began in the summer of 1875, when he put the *World* behind the efforts of Samuel J. Randall to capture the Pennsylvania Democracy. Randall had served continuously in Congress since 1863, establishing a creditable record and gaining considerable prestige. In 1875 he decided to capture control of the Pennsylvania party by attacking the state's "Treasury Ring," an organization in many respects similar to the New York Canal Ring.[25]

Randall's campaign was well advanced when he sought Marble's support. After some effort he persuaded Marble not only to support him but also to hire a special correspondent to cover the story on the reformers' behalf.[26]

In an early editorial on the Pennsylvania contest, the *World* spelled out its objectives. Looking toward the fall convention in Pennsylvania, it declared that "the Democracy craves not relative but positive strength in the candidate of this crisis. He must be a thoroughgoing reformer. He must be one who reflects the opinions and will imitate the conduct of the seventeen Democrats, headed by such men as Heister Clymer and James H. Hopkins and Samuel J. Randall, whose duty of reform and investigation is in another direction, and, no one doubts, will be effective." The *World* continued in a similar vein throughout the summer, so winning the confidence of the reformers that they suggested that Marble draft the currency plank in their state platform.[27]

But even before the Pennsylvania convention met, Marble began to lose interest in Randall's cause. After the first week in September, the *World* paid little attention to the Pennsylvania Democracy. There was, of course, the New York convention to attract its attention; but there was also another event of even greater national significance. That December, for the first time since the war, the Democracy would choose a Speaker of the House of Representatives. The choice would tell much about the party's course in 1876 and would thus shed light on Tilden's presidential chances.

One of the leading candidates for the speakership was Randall, whose career in Congress well entitled him to consideration. Other candidates included Fernando Wood and S. S. Cox of New York, and Michael Kerr of Indiana. Although for many the choice might have been difficult, for Marble it was easy. Randall's protectionism and uncertain currency views disqualified him as did Wood's copperhead past and support of the Salary Grab. Although Cox had been Marble's friend for years and had recently moved to New York, where he had established himself as a reliable member of the Democratic organization, his record in the House suggested that he had failed to qualify as a true leader.[28]

Thus Marble's choice was Michael Kerr. By no means, however, was his choice based upon a mere process of elimination; for Kerr possessed the very qualities of reform leadership that Marble and Tilden were seeking. Kerr had represented his district in southern Indiana from 1865 to 1873, when redistricting forced him to run unsuccessfully as an at-large candidate. In 1874 he had run successfully from his old district. In the Forty-Second Congress he had served as his party's floor leader and had held important committee assignments.

Also, he had consistently supported the low-tariff, hard money, and antisubsidy principles of the eastern reformers. Although not known as a forceful or dramatic leader, his simple honesty, integrity, and loyalty had gained him many important friendships, the strongest of which were among the leaders of the New York swallow-tail Democracy.[29]

Of Kerr's New York friends, none was more intimate than Marble. The nearly ten years of correspondence between them shows a consistent agreement on the issues of the day. During the campaign of 1868, Kerr had endorsed Marble's suggestion to change the national ticket "not because I believe it could give us victory, but because it would secure us and leave us (after defeat) a more compact and better organized party, and would secure us more representatives in Congress and in our state legislatures." In 1870 he had praised Marble's attack on Tweed, declaring that "the one chief peril that now everywhere besets our pathway is that of pervading political and personal dishonesty and corruption." In the same year he also supported Marble's agitation for tariff reform, because "all tariffs for *protection* are dishonest and immoral and breed injustice and corruption constantly." In 1871 he had enthusiastically endorsed the new departure, stating that "in that matter, vitally important to us as a party and to the country, the *World* was the leader, the pioneer. It was wise on that subject when the other press of the country were foolish."[30]

In the complicated maneuverings that accompanied Kerr's campaign for the Speakership, Marble's precise role is unclear. He did follow Kerr's advice and withhold the *World*'s endorsement until requested, but beyond that there is little evidence of his direct influence. Of course, since the *World* was recognized as a spokesman for Tilden, its endorsement alone contributed substantially to Kerr's cause. Still, there may have been more to his influence than that. Both Stillson and Hurlbert were in Washington for the Democratic caucus, and though no evidence remains to tell of their exploits, on the decisive ballot Kerr did receive enough support from former supporters of Cox and Wood to win the Speakership.[31]

Regardless of his role in gaining Kerr the Speakership, Marble did influence the early decisions of the new Speaker. Immediately after his election, Kerr urged Marble to come to Washington to help select committee members. He was especially concerned about Wood and Cox, since both desired the chairmanship of the Ways and Means Committee. A few days after receiving Kerr's letter, Marble traveled to Washington. There he seems to have convinced Kerr that neither Wood nor Cox should have the position. Marble's exact reasons for opposing Wood and Cox are unclear, though in regard to Cox he may have been concerned about his appointment's causing dissension in the party. While he was in Washington, he received a letter from a Wood supporter, declaring that the appointment of Cox would lead to an "increased bitterness in our local fights next year, extending to national matters." There is no evidence of his specific reasons for opposing Wood, though his long personal distrust of the former copperhead is perhaps reason enough. Kerr followed his advice and appointed William R. Morrison, a low-tariff man from Illinois.[32]

Some difficulty arose over appointing the chairman of the Banking and Currency Committee. Marble favored Henry B. Payne, an Ohio congressman whom he had met through Payne's son-in-law, William C. Whitney. Inflationist sentiment was rising again in the party, and the Ohio Democracy had adopted a soft money platform at its last convention. Marble hoped the appointment of Payne, a hard money advocate, would show the greenbackers that the party leaders were determined to oppose them. Although Kerr agreed with Marble's reasoning, he thought the position should go to S. S. Cox, whose seniority and prestige entitled him to it. The best he could do was to "put Paine [*sic*] next to" Cox on the committee. Marble accepted the arrangement, but thought it an "infinite pity."[33]

Kerr's election to the Speakership added significantly to the prestige of the eastern Democracy. Other favorable signs in 1875 were the state elections in Ohio and Pennsylvania. In both states the pro-Tilden forces had been unable to contain rising inflationist pressures, which forced the inclusion of soft money planks in the party platforms. Since Tilden's commitment to hard money was well known, the results in Ohio and Pennsylvania were watched closely to measure his leadership. To many observers, including Marble, it appeared that the Democracy was heading toward the same sort of disastrous split that had demoralized the party in 1868.[34]

In such an emergency the New Yorkers launched a desperate attack upon their inflationist rivals. In its first editorial on the Ohio platform, the *World* sneered at a "fiscal policy founded upon such ignorance and fabricated with such absurd coherence." Whatever course such Democrats should adopt, it promised that the "Democrats of New York, like the Democrats of Illinois, and the Democrats of most of the other States of the Union," would continue to demand "steady steps towards specie payments: no step backwards." As the campaign proceeded, the soft money advocates complained bitterly that the easterners were actually contributing financially to their hard money opponents. Whatever the truth of such charges, it is certain that the New Yorkers hoped for the defeat of the Democratic tickets in Ohio and Pennsylvania. Writing to Senator Thomas F. Bayard of Delaware, Marble declared that "if Gov. Allen [of Ohio] were to be elected this October I venture to predict that an inflation party will shortly exist, and that the Democracy will be beaten in 1876—by its own blundering as usual. But the only doubt I have of Gov. Allen's ignominious defeat arises from the fact that I distrust a judgment which my desires color."[35]

In both states Marble's hopes were realized as Republican candidates, running on hard money platforms, won narrow victories. In New York the results were a cause for rejoicing. The day after the

Ohio election, Marble wrote to Barlow: "it looks to me now more than ever, that what I told you before Uncle Sammy's name had been whispered for Governor would turn out true and he [will] go in over the ⅔ rule in '76. The Ohio business which looked a hindrance will be a help."[36]

With all the signs pointing in his favor, Tilden prepared to close in on the nomination. In the latter half of December, he closeted himself with Marble and his other advisers to prepare an annual message which would in effect be his national platform. Seeking to capitalize on the Ohio and Pennsylvania elections, he called for the resumption of specie payments as rapidly as possible without "creating at any time an artificial scarcity" of money. Although the statement bore the marks of Tilden's usual caution, it demonstrated his willingness to make the currency question his principal issue in seeking the presidential nomination.[37]

Yet, even as the legislature was listening to Tilden's words, signs were appearing that difficulties lay ahead. In fact, in both the state and the nation the Tilden organization was coming under severe attack, and many were wondering whether it would be able to survive.

Problems first manifested themselves in New York City, where the policies of Wickham's swallow-tail administration were proving politically disastrous. Believing that the elections of 1874 had given the Democracy a mandate to economize the city's expenditures, Wickham's administration held up work on a number of projects and reduced the wages of unskilled workers from twenty-five to twenty cents an hour. Both actions created a furor among the city workingmen. Already suffering from the depression, the workingmen organized protest meetings and petitioned the city to have the wage cuts restored and more jobs created. The administration, with the *World*'s support, refused. Following one protest meeting, the *World* declared the city officials had a duty to pay no more than "the market value" for labor. "As public officers they have no right at all to pay more out of the public money than the market rate of the labor they hire; and yet this breach of duty is what the disaffected workingmen not only expect, but 'demand' of them and denounce them for not committing. . . . The protest of the workingmen against the men who have refused to buy anything of them but their labor, and to pay no more than its value for that, is a gratifying testimony that we have some public officers who are not demagogues."[38]

Such logic, however, failed to convince the workingmen, who by the fall elections were ripe for political revolt. Sensing their opportunity, Republicans and disaffected Democrats organized an anti-Tammany movement, which in the fall elected thirteen of twenty-one assemblymen and four of five senators. Stung by the defeat, John Kelly, who earlier in the year had made peace with Tilden, began to reconsider his course. Writing to Marble in December, he laid Tammany's recent defeat squarely upon "the labor question" and questioned the advisability of retaining the superintendent of public works, who, interestingly enough, was Marble's old friend Fitz-John Porter. Although Porter eventually lost his job, Kelly remained dissatisfied, and early in 1876 came out against Tilden's presidential candidacy.[39]

While Kelly was causing trouble in the state, Congress was balking under Tildenite leadership. In the House, Democratic unity collapsed as the soft money wing of the party launched a determined campaign to repeal the Resumption Act which required the Treasury to resume specie payments on January 1, 1879. By February things were so bad that even August Belmont was suggesting that a compromise might be necessary to keep the party united in the presidential contest. "We have battering rams enough to strike down federal and congressional corruption, maladministration, usurpations and centralization without *hard money,* on which our antagonists are really less disunited than we are," he declared to Marble. Although in the end the hard money men were able to block the repeal, it was obvious that the stage had merely been set for the controversy to flare anew when the Democracy held its national convention.[40]

Such developments seriously jeopardized Tilden's chances for the nomination. By the end of March, Kerr believed that Tilden was out of the running. The West, he said, "does not intend this year to take a New York man. . . . The insanity that prevails there, and to a great extent in the South on the currency question is an impossible barrier in his way." It seemed that Thomas A. Hendricks of Indiana was the current favorite, but in the chaos that ruled the party, Kerr hesitated to make any final prediction. "Men are liable to be overthrown in a day," he observed, "and reputations to be so smirched as to destroy usefulness." The Democracy was "at sea without a guide."[41]

Kerr was not alone in this belief. The growing party strife had convinced many New York Democrats, including Barlow, Belmont, Church, Beach, Hoffman, and Sidney Webster, that Tilden could not be nominated. Many of them were turning to Senator Thomas F. Bayard of Delaware to lead the eastern forces. Although Bayard shared Tilden's views on most of the important issues, he had remained sufficiently aloof from the party squabbles to avoid making many enemies. Thus he seemed admirably suited for the role of a dark-horse candidate, to be trotted out when the convention had exhausted itself trying to reconcile its factional disputes. Although it required a good deal of persuasion, by May Bayard had come around to accept the role his New York friends had prepared for him.[42]

The pressures that turned so many of Marble's friends from Tilden also exerted themselves upon Marble. Yet his loyalty to the Sage of Gramercy Park never wavered. During the currency fight, for example, the *World* opposed all compromise with the soft money advocates. Commenting on a resolution introduced by Representative

Holman of Indiana to repeal the resumption-day clause in the Resumption Act, it charged that the westerners were threatening to throw away the presidential election "as their present Ohio and Indiana advisers have thrown away every presidential election since and including 1864." On February 28, when the hard money forces seemed most demoralized, it strengthened its stand by appealing to political realism. Presenting a table of states carried by the parties in the last elections, it declared that the Democracy could win the presidency without the help of the soft money faction. If the party could hold the 127 electoral votes of the South and the 12 votes of the Far West, it could win by capturing the hard money states of Connecticut, New Jersey, and New York. Thus it would not need the support of any soft money middle western states. "The success of the Democratic party, therefore depends," the *World* concluded, "upon the nomination at St. Louis, June 27, of a Hard Money Democrat upon a Hard Money Platform."[43]

Nor was Marble dismayed by the anti-Tilden sentiment among his friends. In May, when their support for Bayard was at its height, he wrote confidently to Barlow that "Tilden will be nominated I believe before three ballots."[44]

Under the circumstances, and in view of the past relations between the two men, Marble would have had just cause for deserting the governor. He could have conveniently recalled, for example, how Tilden had repudiated his suggestion to change the ticket in 1868; how he had encouraged him to attack Tweed and had then deserted him; and how he had allowed him to suffer in humiliating isolation when Tweed was at last deposed. Or he might have noted that Tilden's reorganization of the party had excluded many loyal supporters, or that the governor has sustained Green when he had favored his removal. Such a record, combined with the hazardous political scene of early 1876, might well have prompted the proud, sensitive, and ambitious editor to set aside the loyalties of friendship and to transfer his allegiance.

Undoubtedly, there had been a time when such circumstances would have occasioned such a response; but by 1876 that time had gone. Marble's pride, sensitivity, and ambition were as strong as ever, but they now operated in a different political context. He was no longer independent. The failures of 1868, 1870, and 1871 had destroyed his chances for personal leadership and had forced him into the service of others. His ambition was in effect shrinking to encompass a narrower field. Although he did not know it, it had been shrinking for many years. The young college graduate, filled with a desire to know the universe, had given way to the political journalist and gentleman, eager to lead his party and his paper to national power so his country might be guided by correct principles. Now that, too, was giving way to the party functionary, whose fortunes were intricately bound to those of a single man. "You are Tilden and he is Marble," Barlow told him that fall. "This is recognized everywhere." And so it seemed, for earlier that year Marble had committed the final act that cut him off from his days of party independence. He had sold the *World*.[45]

Marble decided to sell the *World* primarily for business reasons. Amid the tangled politics of Tweed's overthrow and the Liberal Republican coalition, the paper's income had fallen precipitiously. Weekly profits, which in 1871 averaged $1,373, had fallen in 1872 to $101. Since expenditures actually declined in 1872, the loss resulted solely from lost business, especially sales and advertising. Each fell off 19 percent from the previous year, sales losing $655 per week, advertising $1,074. These figures suggest that the *World* was losing popularity among the city Democrats. Other evidence also bears this out. Circulation figures show that the semiweekly and weekly editions actually gained during the year, while daily circulation on October 1, 1872, was 1,000 less than the previous year—a startling fact, since the figure was taken in the midst of the presidential campaign. The major loss of advertising revenues came from the daily account, while semiweekly and weekly advertising was slightly higher than the previous year. Early in 1873 Bangs declared that the advertising decline resulted mostly from the refusal of local Democrats to give the *World* their business.[46]

Little direct evidence exists to explain the paper's decline in popularity with the local Democracy. Possible reasons are the paper's support of Tweed and its hostility toward Greeley, both of which would have antagonized local party regulars. Whatever the specific reasons, it seems sure that politics had something to do with it. In 1874 Tilden told Bangs directly that the *World* "did not fill the requirement of the party."[47]

The *World* was already declining financially when the depression of 1873 delivered its shattering blow. From the onset of the depression, the history of the paper tells only of failure. Bangs's reports and letters to Marble tell a story repeated thousands of times in those years: of frantic searches for new sources of income, of new debts contracted to pay old ones, of a dozen economies and retrenchments contrived to reduce the mounting losses, and of crises so frequent as to recall the frantic times of 1862. Still, the losses increased. In 1873 they were $541 per week; in 1874, $735; and in 1875, $1,308.[48]

Throughout these years Marble struggled to save his paper. At first he attempted to increase sales. In 1874 Bangs employed a special agent to promote a subscriptions campaign. The effort may have helped, for by October subscriptions were higher than the last year. Next Bangs and Marble discussed ways to attract more advertising. By 1875 Marble had decided that advertising would not increase unless circulation increased. This would not occur unless the *World* could equal the best of its rivals, and this in turn meant changing the paper's format.[49]

Since it had first appeared, the *World* had been produced as a quarto sheet of eight 6-column pages, measuring 32 by 46 inches. Occasionally the paper appeared in a twelve-page, "triple-sheet" edition. Such editions were most frequent when Croly was given the freedom to suggest feature articles on social and cultural topics. After Croly's departure, the triple sheets appeared infrequently, and the paper concentrated on the staple political, economic, and literary features.

In 1875 Marble proposed to change the format by increasing the size of pages to seven columns, measuring 36 by 49, approximately the size of the *Tribune*. He also proposed to increase the number of triple sheets to two per week. These changes, he hoped, would increase circulation and attract more advertising.

Because the changes would increase the cost of production, Bangs and Marble spent much time discussing whether the extra expense would be worth the risk. According to Marble's calculations, the changes would add approximately $1,400 to weekly expenditures. By adding this sum to the current deficit of nearly $900, the paper would have to overcome a total increased cost of nearly $2,300. Calculating that at 3¢ a copy each 10,000 in circulation would return $1,141, he concluded that by adding 20,000 the *World* would show a profit. He was willing to take the chance.[50]

Bangs, however, was not. Using figures that resembled Marble's in only a few instances, he showed that Marble had underestimated the added expenses and that it was impossible to compensate for them. This advice and Marble's inability to persuade either Tilden or Belmont to help finance the changes forced Marble to give up the plan. By September 1875 the *World* was for sale.[51]

That month, the first buyers appeared when Barlow approached him on behalf of Stilson Hutchins and Montrose Pallen of the *St. Louis Times*. But Marble hesitated to sell. Believing that the Democracy was at last moving toward victory, he could hope that better times lay ahead for the *World*. Despite assurances from Barlow that the *Times* men were good Democrats, he seems to have been suspicious of their character. In a note to Barlow he referred to them as being connected with Grant, the Whiskey Ring, the Texas-Pacific Railroad, and soft money. Probably for these reasons, then, he set his price at $600,000, well beyond the reach of Hutchins and Pallen. By October 20 they had given up.[52]

But the *World*'s financial condition was too weak to allow Marble to hold out forever. As losses continued to mount, he was forced to the inevitable decision. Early in 1876 he undertook new negotiations, this time with his friend Hurlbert, who was by then the only one of the original editors still with the paper.[53]

Although Marble would undoubtedly have sold the *World* to Hurlbert without a second thought, his decision to do business with Hurlbert's financial backer shows the extent of his desperation. That backer was none other than Thomas A. Scott of the Pennsylvania Railroad, whose Texas and Pacific project was the essence of the subsidy-seeking he claimed to deplore. In the four years during which he had promoted the Texas and Pacific project, Scott had employed a number of devices to secure the necessary state and congressional legislation. Generally successful at the state level, he had been rebuffed again and again in Washington, where many important Democrats, true to the principles of their Jacksonian heritage, had opposed him. In 1874, when the Democracy captured control of the House, Scott needed more than ever to win friends within that party. In 1875 he had supported Randall for the Speakership, hoping to gain the support of the powerful and influential Pennsylvanian. Randall's defeat by the Tilden forces probably suggested the need for a new approach. Undoubtedly the opportunity to purchase Tilden's journalistic spokesman strongly appealed to him.[54]

The record of the negotiations among Scott, Hurlbert, Marble, and their representatives shows that Marble parted with the *World* with some reluctance. In mid-February, when it appeared that the sale would soon be completed, he suddenly changed his terms, and much to Hurlbert's exasperation, prevented it. Scott followed with a second offer, which was also rejected. Barlow then entered the negotiations with a suggestion that became the basis of the final settlement. Still, it required two more offers from Scott and a personal conference with Marble in April to conclude the deal. Early in May, after another delay while Marble settled with his creditors, the paper passed from his hands.[55]

The exact reasons for the delays are difficult to determine. Marble's distrust of Scott, his sentimental attachment to the *World,* and his hesitancy to risk losing his political influence may have played some part. Shortly before concluding the sale, he told one of his creditors that he was making "a very serious sacrifice of my own personal interests and ambitions." Hurlbert also stated that Marble finally decided to sell only after the party state convention had endorsed Tilden's presidential candidacy. Yet, during the actual course of the negotiations, Marble showed no such concerns. Rather, he hesitated to sell until he was certain he had received Scott's highest bid. His letters to Barlow dealt only with the amount of Scott's offers and with the value of the railroad securities that would comprise part of the payment. Since Barlow was Marble's closest adviser on the sale, it seems that Marble was primarily interested in getting his money's worth.[56]

In the final settlement, Marble received $100,000 in cash and $150,000 in railroad bonds. The cash payment consisted of $66,000 in checks and $34,000 in railroad bonds, which Scott promised to redeem at par within four years. The other bonds included $100,000 in the Indianapolis and St. Louis Railroad and $50,000 in the St. Louis, Vandalia and Terre Haute Railroad, both "high quality" issues bearing 7 percent interest. Most of these bonds Marble assigned to the *World*'s creditors, leaving himself approximately $44,000 in the Vandalia bonds.

These were the only sums Marble actually received from Scott. According to the terms of the sale, however, he might have received more. At Scott's suggestion, the agreement contained a clause binding him to pay Marble an additional $100,000 "within thirty days after the adoption by the Congress of the United States of any bill or bills securing the endorsement by the United States Government of the bonds of the Texas Pacific R. R. . . . or any other practical guaranty in subsidy to said road." Aside from the light it casts upon Scott's motives in purchasing the *World,* this "contingent clause" represents one more bit of evidence of Marble's growing identification with the world of affairs and men. Little by little his life seems to have conspired to rob him of his youthful idealism. Now it had advanced the conspiracy a small step forward by involving him in one of the decade's most notorious subsidy-seeking ventures. For one who had hoped to lead the Democracy in the ways of Thomas Jefferson and Herbert Spencer, it was at best an uncomfortable arrangement.[57]

Now politics alone remained to engage Marble's energies, and in politics the outlook seemed bright. Despite the dissatisfactions within the party, the state convention supported Tilden's bid for the presidential nomination and selected a delegation dominated by his friends. For the first time in his life Marble was among the delegates. In the weeks before the convention, reports arrived showing widespread support for Tilden's nomination. Less than a week before the convention, Barlow conceded that "Tilden stands by far the best chance both of nomination and election."[58]

Anticipating victory, the Tilden men prepared for it. One of their most important duties was to prepare a platform. It was indicative of Marble's position in the Tilden organization that he received the job of drafting it. Nine days before the convention, he met with Tilden's private secretaries and set himself to the task.

The document that emerged from the drafting sessions was well designed for Tilden's purposes. "We the authorized delegates of the Democratic Party of the U.S. in National Convention assembled," it began, "do hereby declare the Administration of the Federal Gov't to be in urgent need of immediate Reform." Itemizing the shortcomings of the Grant administration, it pictured the United States on the verge of economic, political, and moral collapse because of "abuses, wrongs, and crimes" in finance, taxation, public lands, diplomacy, and civil service. To emphasize the determination of the party to correct this dismal situation, the draft introduced each subject with "Reform is necessary. . . ."

Reform was necessary, first of all, to establish a sound currency and to restore the public credit. In sweeping style the draft denounced the "violations of the Constitution and of a wise fiscal policy" that had caused the enactment of "paper promises" to the American people. It further denounced the extravagant expenditures that had postponed accumulation of a reserve for the resumption of specie payments and called for "a judicious system of preparation, by public economies, by official retrenchments, and by wise finance, which shall enable the nation soon to assure the whole world of its perfect ability and its perfect readiness to meet any of its promises at the call of the creditor entitled to payment." At the same time, it promised to establish a system that would at "no time" create "an artificial scarcity of currency." Instead, it promised an "open and public and inspiring" system that would relieve industrial distress and bring recovery from the depression.

Reform was necessary "in the sum and mode of Federal Taxation." The present system of customs duties had only reduced revenues, impoverished many industries to protect a "rapacious, log-rolling few," denied the workingman the freedom to purchase goods in the cheapest market and to sell in the dearest, depleted the returns to American agriculture, fostered smuggling, enriched dishonest officials, and bankrupted honest merchants. To replace it, the platform demanded that "all customs house taxation shall be for revenue solely," complemented by a general reduction in governmental expenditures so that "a larger share of the results of their labor" would remain "in the hands of the people."

Reform was necessary in the civil service. "Experience proves," the platform declared, "that efficient economical conduct of the government business is not possible if its civil (unlike its military and naval) service be subject to change at every election, be a prize fought over at the ballot-box, be a brief reward of party zeal instead of posts of honor assigned for proved competency and held for fidelity in the public employ." More importantly, reform was necessary in the "higher grades of public service." Reminding the voters of the scandals of Grant's second term, the platform declared that the first step in reform would be the election of "honest men . . . lest the disease of one political party infect the body politic, and lest making no change of men, we get no change of measures."[59]

Other reforms were necessary, but they merely lengthened the indictment without adding to its substance. The platform was an important statement of swallow-tail principles and strategy, aimed primarily at furthering the cause of the Democracy's urban, upper-class leadership. Largely ignoring the constitutional, sectional, class, and racial issues that had marked previous campaigns, it appealed to the one great American class that embraced all others: the American taxpayer. To that class it promised an honest government, which in the "reform" language of the day meant a frugal government. Everywhere the promise was the same. Frugality would speed the resumption of specie payments; frugality would reduce the tariff; frugality would deny corrupt officeholders their ill-gotten rewards. Through frugality the government was to be returned to first principles, making it safe once more for honest men to administer and for honest men to support. "I shall hold to the policy of arraying the transportation interest, the boatmen, and the taxpayers, who include all classes of citizens, against the thieves," Tilden had declared, "and the men who take the thieves' side cannot stand." The platform was little more than a gloss on that statement.

Armed with their platform and their votes, the Tilden men traveled to St. Louis to seal their victory. On June 26 the full delegation caucused and decided that New York would cast its full vote for the governor under the unit rule. Marble attracted some attention when Belmont and a few others suggested that he represent the state on the resolutions committee. He declined, however, declaring that now was the time for concessions and his selection might suggest that New York was not willing to yield anything. The place went to Lieutenant Governor Dorsheimer.[60]

Marble's absence from the resolutions committee prevented his involvement in the convention's most heated debate. The failure of the hard and soft money wings of the party to compose their differences during the congressional session had all but guaranteed that the currency questions would be thrown into the convention. Convening early in the afternoon of June 27, the resolutions committee sat for nearly fifteen hours before reporting back to the convention. Over two-thirds of the time was spent in acrimonious debate between the two currency factions. By standing fast for their cause and by threatening not to accept certain resolutions even if they were approved by the convention, the soft money men eliminated statements declaring the greenbacks unconstitutional and "a lesson of disgrace to the youth of our land." Next they fought for a resolution favoring the repeal of the Resumption Act. So close was the division on the issue that at one point such a resolution was actually passed. Horrified, the hard money men rallied their forces, obtained a reconsideration of the resolution, and defeated it. Even then, however, they were forced to accept a compromise resolution for the repeal of the resumption date.[61]

At this point Marble attempted to salvage something for the hard money men. Called before the committee on revision to help prepare the platform for submission to the convention, he attempted to weaken the repeal clause by including it in a list of "hindrances" placed by the Grant administration in the path of resumption. Thus, when it was submitted to the convention, the platform denounced the administration for obstructing resumption by "annually enacting fresh hindrances thereto" and declared that "as such hindrance we denounce the resumption clause of the act of 1875 and we here demand its repeal."[62]

It was a poor compromise, which satisfied no one, but under the circumstances little else seemed possible. Thus, when the soft money men made one last effort for total repeal by bringing their case before the full convention, the exasperated hard money men did not hesitate to bring the controversy out into the open. Speaking for his faction, Dorsheimer stated the case clearly. "If you want to leave the hard money men some chance to carry their states," he declared, "then stand by the report of the committee—which was a compromise so great that a protest has been signed by every one of the Eastern Democratic states and to which I have put my signature. Here is a middle ground which does leave some hope, but if you declare . . . for a repeal forthwith, then abandon all your hopes."[63]

Dorsheimer's frankness inspired equally frank replies from Daniel Voorhees of Indiana, and the whole affair threatened to degenerate into the most embarrassing kind of public mudslinging until Henry Watterson moved the previous question and silenced the debate. The convention then approved the committee report by a vote of 550–219 and proceeded to nominate Tilden on the second ballot. Hoping to appease the soft money faction, it then nominated Thomas A. Hendricks for vice-president. In the excitement of the moment, it seemed to Marble that everything had gone supremely well. "Dorsheimer did magnificently today," he wired Tilden. "I did my work promised with Missouri. She set the bricks falling on second ballot. Nomination certain from that moment." It seemed that after a number of false starts, the president-maker was on the right track.[64]

As the campaign got underway, Marble found himself assigned a number of tasks. He prepared an article attacking a group of Albany Democrats who had turned against Tilden and opposed his nomination. He drafted a letter for Belmont, who had also opposed Tilden, giving the Sage his support. When Republicans charged Tilden with disloyalty during the war, he wrote a letter to the Democratic chairman refuting them.[65]

Most importantly, however, Marble tried to quiet eastern fears that the convention had conceded too much to soft money. Soon after the convention adjourned, reports were received that the soft money congressmen, egged on by Hendricks, were using the repeal clause to mount an all-out attack on the Resumption Act. Hard money Democrats feared their opponents might succeed unless Tilden and Hendricks could reach some agreement to stop them. "If Tilden and Hendricks cannot agree upon harmonious treatment of the currency question," Belmont declared, "we may as well give up at once."[66]

Facing the most serious crisis of the campaign, Marble sought to stiffen the courage of the hard money forces. "It is hoped that you will stand fast in your decision," he wrote Randall L. Gibson, a hard money member of the House Banking and Currency Committee. The repeal clause should be construed, he declared, as only one part of the entire currency plank, which committed the party to resumption. Since a repeal bill would never pass the Republican Senate, the House should leave the issue alone. "To press bare repeal does not appear to be the supreme stretch of human wisdom in shaping political issues. To do nothing this session is better than to do merely that. To do more is probably impracticable."[67]

Under the circumstances, such advice seemed all that was possible. Yet, it was no solution, and as the issue continued to vex the Democracy, Marble began to have second thoughts about the accomplishments of the convention. What had seemed so admirable in June became disastrous in July. Now it seemed that instead of salvaging under extreme duress all that the moment would have allowed, Dorsheimer had shown contemptible "weakness," yielding "without a struggle . . . as an ex-Republican might have been expected to do." If Dorsheimer had "fought there in the intrenchments, his citadel would not have been captured." Thus, in the resolutions committee he had hopelessly bungled his assignment. That had been the time for resolution and valor, and it seemed to Marble that if the decision had been his he would have fought it out to an easy victory. He would have pointed out that no repeal was possible so long as the Republicans controlled both the Senate and the Executive, and presumably, that would have been that. When he had thought it out in these terms, he could hardly forgive himself for yielding the place on the committee to Dorsheimer.[68]

For the moment, however, his task was to remedy the damage by finding some way of getting Tilden and Hendricks to reach an agreement on the currency question. With others he helped arrange a meeting between the two at Saratoga, where Tilden was vacationing. From the meeting came letters that showed the two were willing to compromise for the sake of party unity. Tilden's letter, though emphasizing the need for resumption, conceded that "the exact date would have to be chosen with reference to the then existing state of trade and credit operations . . . the course of foreign commerce, and the condition of exchanges with other nations." Hendricks's letter, though favoring repeal of the resumption clause, conceded that "there should be no hindrances put in the way of a return to specie payments." Soon afterward the crisis in Congress also subsided. Although the soft money men in the House forced through a bill repealing the resumption clause, the Senate took no action. When Congress adjourned, the currency question became a matter for local politicians to interpret as best suited their interests.[69]

While he was helping Tilden battle the inflationists, Marble was also considering his own future. At forty-one years of age he was by no means ready to take up a life of gentlemanly inactivity. Rather, he had decided to capitalize on his close association with Tilden to enter politics actively. Although some of his friends suggested that he wait until after the election and take a cabinet post or an ambassadorship, he had decided on a more independent course. The election that would make Tilden president of the United States would make him governor of New York.[70]

The state convention was to assemble on August 30, and in the weeks preceding it speculation was rife concerning Tilden's successor. The growing factionalism in the state party was producing a number of possible candidates. Kelly had decided to challenge Tilden's power by supporting Congressman Clarkson N. Potter. Another disgruntled group of New York Central and canal men were lining up behind Sanford E. Church. The Liberal Republicans leaned toward Dorsheimer or Abram S. Hewitt. Many party regulars, concerned over Tilden's intimacy with the Liberal Republicans, were determined to prevent a repetition of the 1875 convention and were looking toward the old stalwart, Horatio Seymour. With the party so divided and with advice flooding in from all quarters, Tilden remained silent.[71]

Thus it seemed to be anybody's race, and as speculation increased, Marble's name was added to the list of hopefuls. Early in August he began organizing an unofficial canvass to test his strength. On August 16 things were well enough along for Barlow to report that "with a vigorous effort you can be nominated." By August 26 Marble's hopes had risen to the point where he could declare to one of Tilden's private secretaries that "another friend of yours will have more votes in convention than Hewitt or Dorsheimer. Easiest combination on him with minimum favor."[72]

As Marble's letter suggests, he was working earnestly in his own behalf. His attacks on Dorsheimer's conduct at the national convention were no doubt inspired in part by his desire to discredit one of his principal rivals. Taking a page from Tilden's book, he was also attempting to make himself as attractive as possible to the Liberal Republicans. Many of the Liberals were voicing concern over the currency plank and were leaning toward the Republicans, who had stood behind the Resumption Act. The *Evening Post,* for example, declared that Dorsheimer had placed his candidacy in jeopardy by agreeing to the repeal clause. Marble, the *Post* declared, was in a similar position, because he had drafted the platform. Thus, despite his well-known support of hard money, it would be necessary for him to repudiate his own platform in order to win Liberal support. Marble recognized the seriousness of the *Post*'s statements and tried to answer them. The day after the paper's article appeared, he composed a letter "To a Pouting Liberal," in which he claimed he would have prevented the repeal clause from being adopted by the convention. Still, he declared, the platform would in no way prevent the Democracy from returning the country to specie payments.[73]

As the convention drew near, attention centered on Tilden. All realized that in a close contest his endorsement might prove decisive. Although the governor kept his opinions to himself, the actions of his friends were closely watched. Little was learned until two days before the convention. As the delegates were gathering at Saratoga, Abram S. Hewitt suddenly appeared as the leading contender for the nomination. A wealthy iron manufacturer and reform Democrat, Hewitt had cooperated with Tilden's attack on Tweed, had run successfully for Congress, and at the moment was serving as Tilden's campaign manager. That Hewitt's principal supporters were such intimates of Tilden as John Bigelow and Charles S. Fairchild led some to believe that the governor had made up his mind.[74]

Whether this was in fact the case is difficult to determine. After attending a meeting at Barlow's on August 28, Sam Ward reported that Tilden's choices in order of preference were Hewitt, Marble, and Dorsheimer. But John Bigelow, who was closer to Tilden than either Barlow or Ward, declared the same day that "I have not learned that the Governor has signified a partiality for any candidate." Both Ward and Bigelow agreed, however, that Tilden would have neither Potter nor Church. Probably he had decided to allow the convention to choose for itself from a number of acceptable candidates, including Marble.[75]

Whatever Tilden's actual views on the governorship, Barlow believed that he had chosen Hewitt and that the convention would narrow down to a contest between Hewitt and Potter. Thus he sought to dissuade Marble from continuing his fight for the nomination. "You can with great propriety go into the Cabinet if you desire to do so," he wrote, "but as Governor you add nothing to the ticket." In fact, it seemed to him that Potter would make the strongest candidate.[76]

But the day after Barlow offered his discouraging estimate, the situation suddenly changed completely. On August 29 it was learned that Hewitt had not lived in the state long enough to meet the residence requirements for governor. The choice of the Tilden men seemed to have narrowed to Marble and Dorsheimer. Determined to take advantage of his good fortune, Marble redoubled his campaign efforts, stopping delegates in the hotel lobbies, "submitting his buttonholes and bending his ears," one reporter observed, "to every earnest reformer who loves his country and wants a place."[77]

In opposing Dorsheimer, Marble's best argument was his faithful service to the party. Many of the regular Democrats disliked Tilden's favoring former Republicans with leading positions in his administration and were determined to see that one of their own headed the ticket. In canvassing the delegates, Marble could well present himself as such a candidate. He could point to his fourteen years of service to the party and especially to the last four years, during which he had played a major role in formulating party policy. Also, he could capitalize on his recent efforts as a peacemaker between Tilden and Tammany. Even after Kelly had turned against Tilden, he and Marble remained friends, and as the convention assembled there were reports circulating that Kelly supported Marble's candidacy.[78]

Indeed, it seemed to the reporters who covered the last hectic day of the preconvention canvass that in a contest alone with Dorsheimer, Marble would probably win. "To the delegates from New York, to a part of the delegates from Kings County, to a large number of delegates from the state at large," declared the *World,* "the nomination of Mr. Marble still presents itself as the best method of uniting the opposition to Mr. Dorsheimer."[79]

The proceedings of the convention bore out the reporter's predictions. From the beginning it was clear that the delegates were in no mood to endorse a Liberal Republican. Nevertheless, the Tilden men decided to support Dorsheimer. When the lieutenant governor's name was presented to the convention, it was greeted with loud objections and cries of "Give us a Democrat." Such cries, however, were no help to Marble. To counter his candidacy, his opponents had been busy reminding the delegates of the *World*'s record in 1868 and suggesting that Marble was not loyal enough to merit the nomination. So effective was their campaign that by the time the nominating speeches began Marble had decided to withhold his name. His withdrawal and the popular opposition to Dorsheimer set the stage for a major fiasco. Fearing that the convention might swing to Potter, the Tilden men panicked. Playing the game of their opponents in the 1868 national convention, they threw their support to a movement that led to the nomination by acclamation of no less a party regular than Horatio Seymour.[80]

Although Seymour's nomination unquestionably pleased a majority of the Democratic rank and file, it embarrassed the leaders. At sixty-six years of age and in poor health, the former governor had long since withdrawn from active political life. When a delegation from the convention attempted to persuade him to accept the nomination, he decisively refused. Out of the confusion that followed came a call by the state committee to reassemble the convention.[81]

His hopes for the nomination suddenly reborn, Marble was soon calling upon his friends to round up support. From the first to the last, however, the reports were discouraging. The proceedings of the first convention had reflected badly on Tilden's leadership, and there was little sentiment to nominate anyone closely associated with him. Marble seemed too controversial a candidate for a party desperately in need of unity. "Nothing will satisfy either side," Kelly wrote, "except a new man who hasn't been connected in any way with those troubles." Barlow's law partner, W. W. MacFarland, expressed the sentiments of all when he declared that he "would be more than delighted to see you Governor, but at this present I don't think you have the least chance."[82]

Similar advice was also reaching Tilden, who had decided to take a more active part in selecting the nominee. Shortly before the convention met, he and Bigelow canvassed a number of neutral candidates before deciding upon Comptroller Lucius Robinson. Although a former Republican, Robinson had transferred to the Democracy over ten years earlier and was well known as a hard money, reform Tildenite. In presenting him to those delegates who still leaned toward Potter or some other Tammany favorite, Bigelow summed up his appeal: "It was simply an issue between Copperhead Democracy strengthened by the baser elements of the party discontented with Tilden and reform on the one hand and the War Democracy of which Tilden is a representative, acting in harmony with reformers of all political denominations." Apparently it had been decided that Marble lacked such credentials.[83]

With Tilden actively involved, it required only one informal ballot to confirm Robinson's nomination. Kelly again supported Potter, but ran a poor second. Marble's name did not arise. For him it was a bitter defeat, denying him a reward he thought he deserved. For weeks he brooded over the result while his friends tried to comfort him. Early in October, when Barlow suggested he run for mayor of New York, he poured out his bitterness:

> As to the Governorship, it was Tilden's to indicate at either convention; Kelly's to indicate at the second convention provided he had limited himself to friends of Tilden. At the first convention Tilden indicated Dorsheimer who was the only man in the party except John Bigelow whom he couldn't nominate. At the second convention Kelly tried Potter, who was always impossible as any other opponent of Tilden was, when put forward by Kelly. . . . You were utterly wrong about the matter from the beginning to the end, and too lazy and indifferent about it for me to take the time and trouble to set you right, since you didn't accept the plain truth as I telegraphed it to you.

His friends had failed him. He could forgive many things, but not that. In his despair it no longer seemed as though politics was worth the effort. He cared nothing for the mayoralty, and when the presidential election was over "the last link will be broken that binds me to politics." After that he would have only a "languid interest . . . in seeing whether politics and policies so different from those which have made it possible for the Democracy to win, and inevitable that he should be nominated, can give an equal success hereafter to his party and him."[84]

Marble's wounds, though deep, were not fatal. He stayed on

through the campaign, writing editorials and party tracts. As election day neared, his spirits revived and his confidence returned. "I am beginning to think well of myself as a journalist," he wrote to a friend, "for I am not aware of a single article having been rejected by any of my late conferees, though none were recommended to them by name or repute of mine."[85]

For the most part, the campaign went smoothly. The Republicans waved the bloody shirt, attacked Tilden's war record and failure to pay his income tax, and warned against the Democracy's views on the currency question. The Democrats capitalized on the scandals of the Grant administration, the hardships of the depression, and Tilden's record as a reformer. They were disappointed, however, in their efforts to attract the *Evening Post* and the *Tribune*. Although Bryant personally favored Tilden, the publisher of the *Post* forced him to support Hayes, and Whitelaw Reid decided that the Republicans had reformed sufficiently to earn his support. Thus Tilden's overtures to the Barnburners and the Liberal Republicans were only partially successful.[86]

Election night found Marble in Bryn Mawr, Pennsylvania, eagerly telegraphing to New York for the latest returns. For two days messages traveled back and forth, each one showing a rising concern. At last, on November 10 came a final declaration: "Matter becoming serious. Advise strongly your returning without delay." The election, it seemed, was still in doubt.[87]

By the time Marble arrived in New York, the Republicans had apparently decided to convert a seeming defeat into victory by holding the states of South Carolina, Louisiana, and Florida, whose electoral votes, combined with a disputed one from Oregon, would give their candidate a one-vote majority in the Electoral College. To counter their opponents, the Democratic leaders had decided to send delegations of "visiting statesmen" to the South. When Marble arrived, arrangements already had been made to send delegations to Louisiana and South Carolina. At his own suggestion he was assigned to Florida.[88]

Marble left New York at once and by November 15 was in Tallahassee. Upon arriving he found himself in the midst of a complex and dangerous situation. The campaign in Florida had been hard-fought and highly emotional, filled with rumors, threats, and actual deeds of violence and intimidation by both parties. A split in the Republican party and new boldness on the part of the Democracy, which employed the tactics of the "Mississippi Plan" to keep Negroes from the polls, had raised Democratic hopes that Florida's "redemption" was at hand. As the vote came in, it appeared that those hopes would be realized, though by an extremely narrow margin. It was the closeness of the election that kept alive the passions of the campaign. Both sides feared that in the interval between the balloting and the official canvass, frauds would be committed to change the result. They also realized the need to have their forces strengthened by money and men from outside the state. The Republicans hoped, besides, to rely upon federal troops. At the request of the incumbent Republican governor, Marcellus Stearns, four companies of soldiers were dispatched to Tallahassee and were in position when Marble arrived on the scene.[89]

Marble set to work at once. Cooperating with local Democrats and the other "visiting statesmen," he began to gather evidence to present before the Board of State Canvassers. Believing that the Democracy had carried the state fairly, he and his fellow workers sought primarily to prevent Republican frauds. They sent men to the outlying counties to secure the returns before the Republicans could change them. They then tried to persuade the board to conduct its canvass as soon as possible, and to assume the authority to "purge" the returns of fraudulent votes.

Marble had three responsibilities. He made sure that each assignment was carried out. He exposed Republican frauds by preparing news dispatches for the northern press. And he telegraphed developments to Tilden's nephew, William T. Pelton, at the governor's home in Gramercy Park. Acting as the public and private spokesman for the Democratic operation, he came to think of himself as its commander. "Marble yesterday sent Thompson and Hay to Alachua to perfect our proofs," he wired. "Today Marble dispatched jurist to Manatee to fortify us thoroughly there, and others into two other counties Marble must not name." Indeed, he soon came to believe he had the situation well in hand. "Marble needs no further assistance," he declared, "except full powers which will be taken for granted till withdrawn."[90]

It was a sound strategy, and it worried the Republicans. To counter it, the Republicans first sought to postpone convening the Board of State Canvassers. Citing delays in receiving official returns from remote counties on the peninsula, the Republican secretary of state, Samuel McLin, refused to call the board into immediate session. The failure of the board to convene was then used by Governor Stearns as an excuse for claiming the power to canvass the returns himself. On November 19 he sent a letter to the chairman of the Democratic State Committee, requesting an opinion on the legality of such an act.[91]

Stearns's ploy greatly alarmed Marble. At once he relayed the news to New York, asking "shall I not ring fire-bell in the night?" Apparently he thought he should, for he prepared a dispatch to the *World,* exposing the governor's "flagrant usurpation." Although he had privately admitted there were both "law and precedent" for the governor's plan, he declared in his dispatch that the plan was illegal in every detail, and he appealed to "honest northern Republicans" to block it. "What a delusion," he wrote, "is the invitation of

President Grant to fair men of both parties to come hither and witness a fair count; and how well the muskets and the cannon of the Federal Government are planted to preclude and foil that honest supervision!"[92]

While Marble was sounding his "fire-bell," the other members of his group were working through the courts to check the governor. On November 20 they applied to the state circuit court for two orders: one to enjoin the governor from canvassing the returns and another to mandamus the returning board to proceed at once with its own canvass. Although the Republicans argued that the court lacked jurisdiction, the judge, a former Confederate officer, accepted the petitions and gave the parties two days to prepare their arguments. In the meantime, he issued a temporary injunction against the governor's canvassing the returns. The arguments were proceeding when word was received that the returns from the last three counties would arrive on November 27. Upon learning this, the Republicans gave up their plan, and on November 25 the chairman of the Board of State Canvassers announced the board would convene in two days.[93]

The Democratic forces had won an important battle, but their ultimate victory was far from assured. It had been apparent from the first that regardless of who canvassed the returns, the election would be decided by the narrowest of margins. Nearly 49,000 votes had been cast, and on November 27 Marble reported that the certified returns gave the Democracy a margin of only 100. The Republicans were claiming the same margin for their side. It was obvious that with only the slightest manipulation the board could decide the contest for either party. Nor could anyone doubt that the board would have ample opportunity for such manipulation, since the election had been attended by widespread charges and countercharges of intimidation and fraud. In such circumstances the Democrats had little comfort in the knowledge that two of the three members of the board were Republicans.[94]

As Marble saw it, the Democracy could carry the state only if the Republican board members judged the returns with strict impartiality, a quality that he had long since come to believe Republicans lacked. Perhaps, however, the will to honesty, if properly encouraged, was strong enough to bring at least one of the Republican board members around to the truth. As spokesman for the Democratic forces, and as a man to whom ambition, loyalty, and career left no alternative, he assumed the responsibility of providing such encouragement. On Sunday, November 26, the day before the board was to convene, he paid a visit to Secretary of State McLin.

Marble and McLin conversed alone and did not discuss the meeting until two years later, when they told different stories. According to McLin, Marble told him that the secretary's vote would decide the election and that if he could "rise superior to his prejudices" and declare the state for Tilden, "the Democratic party would be under everlasting obligations . . . for that service." According to McLin, Marble further said that Tilden had carried the state beyond doubt, but McLin would have to ignore the fraudulent claims of the Republicans in order to declare that fact. McLin admitted that he desired Hayes's election and would rather "die in the ditch" than give him up, provided the election returns showed him entitled to victory. Still, if it appeared that Tilden had carried the state, he would so declare. At this point, McLin recalled, Marble promised him: "there is no danger now, if you do right in this matter, of your dying in the ditch or your dying poor; the Democratic party can provide for you, and will do it." McLin interpreted this as an offer of a bribe.[95]

Although Marble denied ever having made such a statement, he probably did. General Lew Wallace, who was in Florida at the time representing Hayes, recalled that later the same day McLin reported Marble's statement to him. Still, it seems unlikely that Marble seriously intended to bribe McLin. At the time of the conversation, he had no authority to make such an offer, and in fact was not even responsible for handling the expenses of the Democratic operation. Nor was there anything in either his personal history or in the circumstances of that moment to warrant a bribe attempt. For all his experience in practical politics, Marble had always used ideas rather than dollars to win his battles. Since the board had not convened, there was still hope that the Republican members would be open to argument. It also seems that at the time McLin did not take Marble's remark too seriously. A month after the election had been decided, he wrote a series of letters to William E. Chandler, requesting a federal appointment. In recounting his many services to the Republican party, he never once mentioned having withstood Democratic efforts to bribe him into declaring Florida for Tilden.[96]

Marble apparently approached McLin convinced that the Democracy was fairly entitled to Florida's vote and determined to convince the secretary also. During the course of the conversation, he made a few remarks that suggested to McLin that the Democracy might be willing to offer money for a favorable decision. The remarks, however, only implied that in some undefined way the Democracy would reward McLin for an honest canvass. McLin mentioned the conversation to Wallace while its details were fresh in his mind, but soon afterward forgot about it. The visitor from New York had been a bit indiscreet, but little else. Perhaps in a few days he would be more specific.

On November 27 the board members met in private, established their rules of procedure, and adjourned. The next day they met to receive the returns. As the vote from each county was announced, notice was given by the leading attorney of one party or the other that the vote would be contested. By the end of the day, all of Florida's thirty-seven county returns were in dispute. It thus fell to the board to decide the vote of the entire state by December 6, when according to federal law the presidential vote was to be cast.[97]

Because he was not a lawyer, Marble took no part in the contests. He attended the sessions, however, and sent to New York public and private reports of the proceedings. During the early sessions, he felt confident that the strength of the Democratic case would prove overpowering and that Tilden would have no trouble carrying the state. Optimistically, he reported that the Democratic lawyers had persuaded the board to accept an "uncooked" return from a key county. When one of the visiting statesmen in Louisiana asked for his estimate of the Florida result, he reported the local odds were "about even," but added, "I cannot help distrusting that judgment."[98] Marble's confidence sprang in part from his belief that the Republicans would not dare to steal the election so long as he stood ready to expose them in the press. Convinced that his earlier "fire-bell in the night" had forced Governor Stearns to abandon his plan to count the votes himself, he was ready to ring the bell again at any moment. When the Republicans attempted to induce the board to accept an obviously contrived return from Alachua County, he was quick to take up the pen. On December 1 the *World* carried his account of the Alachua contest. In detail he described the forgeries of the signatures on the affidavits supporting the Republican claim and reported that two Republican poll inspectors had admitted that the Democratic return was the proper one. To emphasize the responsibility of the Republicans for this and any other frauds, he stated that the Republicans controlled the entire electoral machinery and were thus the only ones able to manipulate the returns. The Republicans, however, did not withdraw their Alachua claim.[99]

Strong though it was, Marble's confidence was not unshakable. The week the board was in session was filled with tension, born of countless rumors of plots and intrigues. Especially rife were rumors that one or another of the board members considered his vote for sale. To at least three of the Democratic visitors the rumors presented a fascinating temptation, which in the end they could not resist.

Two of the Democrats were Alexander Thain of New York and C. W. Woolley of Ohio, neither of whom played an important role in the main business of the Democratic delegation. Thain, in fact, seems to have spent most of his time seeking opportunities to suborn the board members. On different occasions he approached John H. Coyle, who was supervising the expenditures of the delegation, with information that the election could be secured for $200,000. Coyle, however, had been warned by Pelton against doing business with Thain, and according to his later testimony, rebuffed all Thain's offers. Like Thain, Woolley seems to have been concerned mostly with corruption. On December 1 his labors produced a wire to Pelton, declaring "Board fetch may make necessary expense half of a hundred thousand dollars. Can you say will deposit bank immediately agreed?" Pelton agreed.[100]

The third Democrat to be so enticed was Marble. It seems that since his visit to McLin he had kept himself informed about the possibilities of winning over the board with special appeals. Woolley, at least, had complained about Marble's "making propositions to the enemy" and had asked Pelton to put a stop to it, presumably in order to clear the field for his own machinations. But Pelton did not choose to put a stop to it, and on December 2, perhaps after a conversation with Thain, Marble sent word to New York that he had "just received a proposition to hand over at any hour required Tilden decision of Board and certificate for Governor for 200,000."[101]

That moment polarized the concerns of Marble's life. The path marked out by the years of commitment, struggle, and ambition had at last become clear. It had led from the Boston Athenaeum to Tallahassee, Florida. At its beginning had stood a young artist, determined to commit himself to other-worldly ideals, and at its end a middle-aged president-maker, determined to win a worldly prize by the most worldly of acts. Somehow the desire for noble manhood had become a desperate clutching at political office. But how, specifically? It had taken many things. There was his ambition for independence and success relentlessly pushing him onward, obscuring the difference between means and ends. There were the party leaders who had turned their backs on his advice and the voters who had rejected his appeals. There were the friends who had inspired his ambition and loyalty only to use them for their own purposes. There was the remorseless commercial and financial competition of his profession, made fatal by a fickle public and business cycle. And at that moment there was the awful possibility that Republican trickery would destroy the one hope he had left by stealing the presidency from the man he loved so selflessly. All these were with him in Tallahassee and in that moment moved the pen upon the telegraph paper as surely and decisively as his own hand.

Carrying out the bribe attempt proved more difficult than conceiving it. Pelton at once rejected Marble's suggestion, probably because the quoted price was too high. By the time Marble received the rejection, he had learned of the $50,000 price, which Woolley had reported earlier. He had not consulted with Woolley, however, and did not know of the latter's correspondence with New York. Hence he telegraphed the $50,000 figure to Pelton without mentioning Woolley. This alarmed Pelton, who apparently feared that the Democracy might wind up paying for the same vote twice, and he quickly telegraphed both Marble and Woolley to consult each other and to act together. What followed is uncertain. Marble later claimed that he destroyed Pelton's telegram and took no further action. Still, on

December 5, the day before the board was to announce its decision, he telegraphed Pelton: "Proposition failed. Finished yesterday afternoon responsibility Moses. Last night Woolley found me and said he had nothing which I knew already. Tell Tilden to saddle Blackstone." Assuming this to be an accurate translation, which Marble later denied, it would seem that he did in fact carry through the bribe attempt, only to fail. Whether he did or not, it is clear that he believed the board was for sale and thought seriously about making a bid.[102]

On the evening of December 5, the board met to decide the election. Shortly after midnight, it decided by a strictly partisan vote that the entire Republican ticket had been elected. Marble and his associates left town at once, pausing along the way north to send word of the result to New York and to draft an open letter to Samuel J. Randall, the new Speaker of the House, denouncing the decision and savagely arraigning the Republican party for allowing it. Commenting on the statement, which he drafted, Marble declared to Pelton: "you may think it harsh but compared to the facts it is milder than mothers milk."[103]

Marble thus arrived in New York angry and determined to checkmate the Republican efforts to steal the election. Frustrated by his own failure, he now looked toward Tilden to lead the party through the crisis. "I am confirmed . . . in the opinion . . . that everything now depends upon your nerve and your leadership," he declared, adding that "as there is no doubt of that, I believe order can and will be brought out of the present chaos."[104]

Judging from Tilden's past record in dealing with less immediate and less serious crises, it is likely that Marble's words expressed hope rather than confidence. The Sage of Gramercy Park had never shown himself to be a bold leader. Rather, his more representative traits, when faced by a resolute opposition, had been caution, timidity, and even cowardice. Only in his attack on the Canal Ring had he shown the least disposition toward vigorous leadership. As a close observer of Tilden's conduct and as one who had suffered from his weakness, Marble no doubt feared the battle would be lost unless he was able to toughen his leader's spirit.

If Marble returned with a specific plan of action, it has been lost. Indeed, his papers bear the signs of a careful pruning, suggesting that he did not care to allow history fully to witness his role. All that remains is the picture he would have liked: a man of honesty and principle determined to win legally what his opponents were conniving to take away illegally.

The basic problem confronting the Democracy was to find a method for counting the electoral vote in Congress. Following decisions favoring the Republicans in each of the three contested southern states, the Democracy had sent to Washington the votes of the Democratic electors and demanded that Congress count them. Because the Constitution did not fix the responsibility for counting the votes and because the Democracy controlled the House and the Republicans the Senate, it was impossible to predict the success of such a claim. Republicans declared that the president of the Senate, who would accept the Republican returns and seat Hayes, ought to count the votes. Democrats declared that the contested votes should be thrown out, leaving neither candidate with a majority and thus requiring the Democratic House to make the final decision. Soon after his return to New York, Marble closeted himself with Tilden and Bigelow to prepare a history of presidential election counts. The volume they produced early in January 1877 showed that each house of Congress had its own authority to count the electoral votes and might go behind the returns to do so. This would give the House sufficient authority to throw out the votes of Florida, South Carolina, Louisiana, and Oregon and to claim the right to settle the election itself.[105]

During December Tilden and his advisers worked out this strategy and pressed Democratic congressional leaders to adopt it. For once there seems to have been near unanimity within the circle of Marble's friends. Even Belmont and Barlow, neither of whom had been enthusiastic about Tilden's candidacy, gave their approval. Belmont even went so far as to call for public demonstrations to frighten the Republicans into accepting the plan. During the Christmas recess, when the party's congressional leaders journeyed to New York to confer with Tilden, they were met with a solid front.[106]

They were not, however, thoroughly convinced. Although impressed by Tilden's general determination, they came away from the meeting unsure of his dedication to his specific plan. This was unfortunate, since three of the congressional leaders, Hewitt, Bayard, and Allen G. Thurman, were considering the formation of a special electoral commission, which would bypass the House entirely. It seems that in their conversations Tilden, while preferring his own plan, spoke mostly in generalities, stressing especially the need to settle the controversy by peaceful "arbitration." Thus he apparently left the congressional leaders with the impression that they were free to work out such an arbitration by any means they thought best. "I don't know how you felt about all the talk that evening," Perry Belmont recalled a few days later to Bayard, "but it seemed very disappointing, and without much result in the way of arriving at any understanding."[107]

In the next two weeks, the election crisis resolved itself into a debate over the merits of the electoral commission plan. For Hewitt and others the plan became increasingly attractive. Most Republicans, Hayes included, continued to assert that only the president of the Senate could count the votes and opposed Tilden's plan without reservation. Thus there seemed little likelihood of Tilden's gaining the presidency in the way he had designated. At the same time, a few Republicans, including President Grant and Roscoe Conkling, seemed willing to accept an electoral commission. To the Democratic congressmen such a willingness seemed doubly attractive. Not only would it afford Tilden his only practical opportunity for obtaining a fair count, but it would also lead to his election. Both Grant and Conkling were thought to believe that Tilden had been fairly elected.[108]

The commission plan also seemed the most likely method of settling the crisis peacefully. Since election day, there had been much loose talk, largely in Democratic circles, of taking the presidency by force. In the highly tense atmosphere of those days, such statements aroused fears that the nation was again on the verge of civil war. Such a possibility horrified Democratic businessmen such as Hewitt, who after suffering through the depression longed for a return to stability. In mid-December business leaders of both parties met in New York to discuss the crisis. During the course of their discussions, it became plain that any settlement, regardless of its outcome, would be welcome so long as it was achieved without violence. "Democratic business men of the country," James Garfield reported to Hayes, "are more anxious for quiet than for Tilden." Such anxiety no doubt influenced Tilden to soften his commitment to his plan and also attracted Hewitt, Bayard, and Thurman to the commission formula.[109]

On January 12 the special House and Senate committees, which had been formed to find a solution to the crisis, held their first joint meeting. The next day Hewitt sent Tilden a copy of a bill creating an electoral commission and said he would arrive in New York the next day to discuss it. That night Marble found Tilden studying the bill and was invited to return the next day for the conference with Hewitt. Although Marble did not attend the conference, he soon learned that Tilden rejected the plan. Tilden especially objected to a provision that would have chosen some of the commission members by lot. He would not, he declared, raffle for the presidency. But he also declared that even if the obnoxious provision was removed he would still not support the bill. He still thought his plan the best. His opposition was in vain, however, and when Hewitt returned to Washington he worked for the passage of the commission bill. On January 20 a modification of the original bill was presented to the House.[110]

Up to this point, Tilden's protests had been made privately, mostly to Hewitt and to Hewitt's son-in-law, Edward Cooper. Thus, as the bill came before Congress, the country did not know he opposed it. If at that moment he had decided to reject it publicly, he undoubtedly would have killed it. But he did not, in part because his advisers began to have second thoughts on the subject. By January 19 Belmont was beginning to change his mind, largely because of

Bayard's arguments that the commission would undoubtedly seat Tilden. On January 20 he had completely changed his mind, declaring to Bayard that "your course is more than vindicated by events, and the country owes you and your colleagues a debt of gratitude." The next day he conveyed similar opinions to Marble. "The country and especially the financial community," he wrote of the commission plan, "have received it with great favor." Noting that such prominent Republicans as O. P. Morton and John Sherman opposed the bill and that Hendricks had declared in favor of it, he saw no alternative but for Tilden to accept it. Apparently Belmont's argument convinced Marble, for that same day Marble wrote Tilden that it was thought that the bill "beyond all question . . . will elect you and is meant to elect you." He also reported that Sidney Webster believed the Senate would probably defeat the bill if it was announced that Tilden favored it and for that reason they both believed "absolute silence" to be "the sound policy in every event." Marble slyly suggested, however, that "a 'record' might be convenient hereafter."[111]

Years later a controversy broke out between Marble and Hewitt concerning Tilden's attitude toward the electoral commission bill. Marble claimed that on January 16 Tilden dictated a telegram calling upon Democratic leaders to delay accepting the scheme. Marble admitted that Hewitt did not see the telegram, but claimed that by the time it had been deciphered in Washington the committee had approved the bill. Hewitt replied that such a telegram would have arrived in plenty of time to kill the bill. He argued, however, that on January 17 Pelton had returned to New York from Washington and had persuaded Tilden to accept the bill. From this he inferred that Tilden had suppressed the telegram before it could be sent.

Inconclusive evidence supports Marble's account. On January 18 Belmont wrote Marble: "I am afraid the mischief is done, and the Governor's telegram as well as mine come too late. All my hope is now that Judge Davis may be selected as the fifth Judge, because I am almost sure Congress will adopt the scheme." Belmont's remarks, together with a letter he wrote Bayard the next day saying his dispatch had called the bill a "departure from constitutional precedents," suggest his telegram had opposed the bill, and so, presumably, had Tilden's. Assuming Belmont knew all the facts, it would appear that Tilden did send off a protest against the bill—to little effect. Still, Marble's overall purpose, which was to discredit Hewitt's role in the electoral crisis, loses force when one notes how readily he, Belmont, and Tilden accepted the bill once the committee approved it.[112]

Marble's confidence in the electoral commission plan was probably strengthened by events in Florida. On the day the Board of State Canvassers returned its decision, the state Democratic party, on behalf of its gubernatorial candidate, George F. Drew, appealed to the state supreme court for a writ of mandamus ordering the board to reconvene and to recanvass the returns on their face. To their delight, the court granted the appeal, and after some quibbling, the board met on December 27 and declared Drew the winner. The news from Florida at once inspired hope in Marble and Tilden, who at once suggested that the decision be applied to the presidential canvass. The Floridians agreed to do their best.[113]

The steps to certify the Tilden electors followed two paths. First, the Tilden electors brought an action of quo warranto against the Hayes electors, claiming the latter had no legal title to their certificates. Second, a bill was introduced in the state legislature, authorizing the Board of State Canvassers to recanvass the presidential returns in accordance with the Drew decision. Since in the meantime Drew and his Democratic ticket had assumed office, it was certain that a new canvass would produce a Tilden victory.[114]

The proceedings carried on through the first three weeks of January. From Tilden's home, Marble kept in constant communication with the Florida Democrats. As the controversy developed, the New Yorkers increased their control of the Democratic operation, supplying their southern friends with advice and expert legal counsel. For once, everything went as planned. The legislature passed the bill authorizing the new canvass and the new board declared Tilden the winner by ninety-four votes. Shortly thereafter, the supreme court declared the Hayes electors were not entitled to their certificates. Governor Drew then issued new certificates to the Tilden electors. When the Electoral Commission began its hearings, it received three sets of Florida returns, two Democratic and one Republican.[115]

In the end, of course, all these efforts accomplished nothing. Near the end of January, Marble traveled to Washington to help Montgomery Blair edit the *Union,* a paper established especially to aid Tilden. There he observed the electoral controversy at first hand. But his observations brought him only pain. On every issue the commission, which so many had expected to make Tilden president, ruled in favor of Hayes and gave him the election. When it was all over, Marble's president-making had failed by one electoral vote.

As one reads through the record of these months, one last question occurs. What dealings, if any, did Marble have with Tom Scott or the Texas and Pacific lobby? As the modern account of the crisis of 1876–77 shows, Scott played a key role in the events of those days, using his political influence to aid the candidate who would support his Texas and Pacific project. In the end, of course, Scott's support went to Hayes. His relations with the Democracy, however, remain shadowy, largely because of insufficient evidence. For the moment the historian must conclude that Marble and Tilden remained aloof from Scott and his lobby and placed their hopes upon making an unshakable legal case before the Electoral Commission.

The biographer, however, must leave the question open. Marble's conduct in Florida had shown that his personal ambition and loyalty to Tilden could tempt him to engage in overt acts of corruption. It is difficult to believe that one capable of that would have ignored the opportunities to gain the support of a powerful railroad lobby. Also, it may be recalled that at that time Marble's own interests were linked to Scott's Texas and Pacific project by the terms of the *World*'s sale. Passage of a Texas and Pacific subsidy would mean $100,000 to Marble. Since he was in Washington early in February, he must have seen the role of the Scott interests in the election controversy. All of this is what makes so interesting one final bit of evidence. In the Marble papers is a note, written in Philadelphia to an unspecified addressee. It is dated January 27, 1877, and says: "I shall be happy to see you at my house today say 1 45 pm. The trains leaving N.Y. at 10 25 a.m. will bring you over in good time. Thos A. Scott." Since Marble first arrived in Washington on the evening of January 27, he might have been Scott's visitor.[116]

What was said at that meeting, whether in fact it even took place, we shall probably never know; Marble's sifting of his papers has seen to that. Perhaps Marble decided to put aside the temptations to involve himself again in the maneuverings of his Florida venture, and as the remaining documents would have us believe, put his trust in the law. Perhaps, however, there was a reason for the gaps that exist in his papers, and perhaps that reason had something to do with Tom Scott. It could be that when Marble was sifting through his papers he allowed that one note to remain as a reminder to himself and to future historians that president-making made its own special demands upon the manhood of those whose lives had become dominated by party loyalty. ✣

CHAPTER TEN

And Its Price

TILDEN'S DEFEAT left Marble's ambition, determination, and fighting spirit as strong as ever. Marble's years in politics had taught him to accept the past failures and to work toward a brighter future. In politics no defeat was final and each new election was a new opportunity. What had been lost in 1876 could be won in 1880, provided that the mistakes of the past were not repeated. The Democratic strategy for 1880 seemed clear-cut. The Republican theft of the 1876 election would be the principal issue, and it was up to the Tildenites to make sure that it would not be forgotten.

It was also necessary to rehabilitate Tilden's image. The governor's conduct during the election crisis had not argued well for his leadership. Many thought his indecisiveness had given the Republicans their chance to steal the election. Such a man seemed unworthy of renomination. August Belmont, for example, did not think Tilden was worth the effort. "Any movement connected with Tilden," he declared to Marble, "is doomed to defeat as surely as anything can be sure in this world." He thought Marble was wasting his time, not so much with the frauds of Louisiana and Florida as with "that worst of all frauds of Gramercy Park."[1]

Such party feeling was indeed a difficulty, but Marble thought it could be overcome. It would be necessary only to show that Tilden had been betrayed by his supporters in Congress. If the blame could be thus shifted, Tilden's renomination would be assured.

Fortunately, many Democrats seemed willing to be convinced. Following the seating of Hayes, a number of them began questioning the wisdom of the electoral commission plan. Tilden himself did his best to encourage such questioning. In July 1877 he spoke at length about the Electoral Commission with a *World* reporter. Declaring that he had never felt "any real confidence" in the commission plan, he said he had agreed to it only because the business community had desired a settlement at any price and because the joint committee had agreed to it. In private he declared that he had been betrayed by Thurman, Bayard, Lamar, Randall, and Hewitt.[2]

Indeed, Tilden was a principal architect of the strategy. In the Marble papers is an undated manuscript in Tilden's handwriting, discussing the Electoral Commission. The commission plan, Tilden wrote, had been a subterfuge designed by the Republicans to trick the Democracy into giving up "every positive power" in exchange for a "body of Republican partisans who decided by a party vote on every question that they had nothing to decide." History would show that "the grand error of the Democrats in Congress was in not making the House of Representatives the center of their battle, and gathering compactly around it all their forces." At least the party leaders in Congress should have demanded guarantees on the composition and procedures of the commission before agreeing to establish it. To those who argued that such a course might have driven the Republicans to military usurpation, Tilden replied that "a negotiator who would take no stand inviting risk of rupture against negotiators who would lose everything in detail from the defeat of the bill" had nothing to lose himself. This, he maintained, had been his position from the first to the last. Throughout the crisis, his leadership and determination had never wavered. "Mr. Tilden's conduct during these days was characterized by the same calm courage and undoubting confidence in the intelligence and moral sense of the people which he had manifested so confidently in the great contests through which he had passed." In other words, those Democrats who had trusted him in 1876 needed not to fear doing so in 1880.[3]

For nearly a year Tilden and his friends kept such opinions largely to themselves. Then in June 1878 the issue was suddenly thrust into the open. Henry Watterson, an ardent Tildenite who had been a member of the House during the election crisis and who believed Hewitt had allowed the Democracy to be bluffed out of the election, appeared in Washington to attend a Democratic Congressional Caucus. When Hewitt had Watterson excluded from the caucus, the volatile Kentuckian boiled over. Without thinking twice, he stormed to New York where he savagely attacked Hewitt's conduct during the election crisis. Declaring that Tilden had consistently opposed the Electoral Commission, he charged Hewitt, Randall, Bayard, and Thurman with base conduct and went on to single out Hewitt as a "red snake in the grass, falsifier, and charlatan."[4]

Watterson's outburst posed an embarrassing dilemma for Marble and Tilden. Although both had planned to use the issue to further Tilden's candidacy, Marble and Tilden hoped to use it without disrupting the party. In his public statements and in his unpublished manuscript Tilden had carefully refrained from the sort of personal attack Watterson had unleashed. Neither Tilden nor Marble wanted any part of the Watterson-Hewitt imbroglio. When an embarrassed and bewildered Watterson appealed to them for support, he was advised to drop the whole thing. Watterson should be satisfied, Marble wrote him, that the press had largely taken his side in the controversy.

"Is it not worth your consideration now, the expediency of dropping all allusions to [Hewitt] hereafter."[5]

By that time, however, things had gone too far. Eager to promote a rift in the Democracy, the Republican press gleefully seized upon the controversy and demanded an accounting from Tilden. Tilden's opponents within the party also took up the cry, hoping to discredit his leadership. As July passed, it became evident that silence would only invite disaster. So at the last minute, it was decided that the Tilden camp would issue a statement and that Marble would postpone his Newport vacation to draft it.[6]

Marble's statement, published later in pamphlet form as "A Secret Chapter of Political History," appeared August 5 as a letter to the *New York Sun.* Noting that "here and there a belief is current, or if not a belief, a suspicion that the rightful President might have become the President in fact, except for some act or omission of his own," Marble began by assuring his readers that "not anything Mr. Tilden did, caused, and nothing was omitted by him to avert, the success of the plot which in the winter of 1876–7, effected a revolution in the Presidential succession." To make clear that he intended only to praise Tilden's leadership and not to take sides in the Watterson-Hewitt controversy, he stated that Hewitt had not refused Tilden's request to publish the correspondence between them during the election crisis. He also included in a footnote Tilden's statement: "I have never questioned the good faith and patriotic purposes of Mr. Hewitt, or of any whose counsels and guidance he thought it his duty to follow."

His purposes established, Marble went on to recount the details of the Republican plot to steal the election. Emphasizing the venality of the Republican members of the southern returning boards, he declared that a number of such men, including the infamous McLin of Florida, had offered to sell their votes to the Democracy. They had found no buyers, however, because Tilden had decided to defeat the Republican conspiracy by legal means. Marble described Tilden's plan to have the House of Representatives assert and maintain its right to decide the election. He stated that at the December meeting with the House Democratic leadership, Tilden had "assured them that were their temper stiff and resolute, the conspiracy would break down in the process of execution; that in any event it was for the interest of popular elective government not to yield to the mere menace of usurpation all that actual usurpation could take for itself if completely successful." He then proceeded to show how Tilden's plan would inevitably have produced victory.

But Tilden's plan was not given a chance. Suddenly the electoral commission bill appeared, endorsed by the Democratic leadership. Popular attention focused on the bill as civic groups, trade associations, and prominent citizens gave it their support. When it became law, the Democracy's opportunity for success had been lost.

And it had not been Tilden's fault. Tilden's opposition to the electoral commission plan "was inherent and incurable." To show that Tilden's opposition had never wavered, Marble rehearsed the events occurring between January 14, when Tilden first learned of the bill, and January 17, when the congressional committees endorsed it. He reproduced telegrams between Tilden and Hewitt, conveying Tilden's opposition to one or another of the plans for establishing the commission. The last such telegram, sent the night of January 16, not only rejected the commission plan but also called upon the party to "stand on the Constitution and settled practice," meaning Tilden's original plan. To soften any imputation of bad faith against Hewitt, Marble declared that Hewitt had never seen this telegram. Still, he realized that such imputation was hard to escape. He concluded that "these proofs of the contemporaneous judgment, attitude and advice thereon of the elected Democratic leader could not (in the present currency of a false belief and of partisan misrepresentations) be withheld from the Democratic party, no matter in whose remembrance they may have chanced to repose, no matter in whom they shall inspire the reflection of a great doubt, a grave regret."

Marble left no doubt that a grave injustice had been done a great leader. Reviewing the character of Tilden's political leadership, he declared that all of Tilden's victories had been won by moral forces. Such forces would have carried the Democracy to victory in the election crisis, had they been allowed to operate. "In large political strategy as in military campaigns," Marble wrote, "the success or the failure of any untried plan must always remain a matter of reasoned conviction, not of actual proof. But at least the untried plan of Mr. Tilden was not more difficult than firmness and mere courage always are." To say that Tilden's plan could not have worked was, in his opinion, tantamount to saying that the American people could not govern themselves. Certainly the party rank and file had been ready to support Tilden. They had sustained Tilden before and were ready to do so again. Tilden was willing to trust their support. But Tilden had needed the support of the Democratic congressional leadership, and that support had failed.[7]

In making his case in this way, Marble showed as clearly as he was ever to do in these years the identification he had made between his youthful moral idealism and his political career. After sixteen years in the Democracy, his basic view of politics had changed little. Politics still demanded those qualities of courage, loyalty, and honor to which he had devoted himself in his early life. They also required a devotion to democratic government based on the assumption that people could be trusted to know the difference between right and wrong. To be sure, his party loyalty had seriously qualified his early beliefs: he thought of courage and loyalty as devices for maintaining party unity as well as universal traits uniting all good men; he suspected that loyalty to the Republican party clouded one's moral perceptions; and he felt most confident of the moral character of those in his own social class. Still, to him his commitment to moral principles was very real, and the contrast so often made in his time between the "politician" and the "good citizen" was not. Participation in politics, in fact, demanded the highest moral character and the noblest manhood, and those who were false to such ideals should pay a price for their infidelity. Little did he realize, as he composed his tribute to moral character, that the time was fast approaching when he too would pay that price.

Marble's defense of Tilden's conduct during the election crisis was one of two important moves made on behalf of the Sage of Gramercy Park. The other was made in May 1878, when the Democratic House of Representatives appointed a special investigating committee to examine the charges of Republican frauds in Florida and Louisiana in 1876. For a time Marble and Tilden thought of using the investigation to start a movement to remove Hayes from office. But such a plan received no support in the party and was soon given up in favor of simply strengthening Tilden's claim on the presidency in 1880.[8]

In the early months of its work, the committee, headed by Clarkson N. Potter, produced startling results. Some Republican witnesses admitted having allowed partisanship and the promise of reward to distort their honest judgment and others even admitted having committed fraud to give their states to Hayes. So successful was the investigation that by September Marble was telling Barlow that "it is getting so cocksure for Uncle Sammy that I was almost tempted to go off to Europe last Wednesday with my nieces, and loaf, and invite my soul."[9]

Then, in October the investigation took a distressing turn, as the *Tribune* startled the country with the publication of the famous "cipher dispatches." These dispatches—telegrams between the Democratic "visiting statesmen" in South Carolina and Florida—indicated that Tilden's lieutenants had tried to purchase the votes of the Republican members of those returning boards. Included were the dispatches of Woolley and Marble to New York and the replies of Havemeyer and Pelton. From these and other messages the *Tribune* constructed a tale of a monstrous *Democratic* plot to steal the election. Marble, it charged, had not only attempted to suborn the Florida returning board, but had also conspired to steal Oregon's vote.[10]

The dispatches created a sensation. At once, Republicans demanded that the Potter Committee take up the matter. Although the Democrats in the House used their majority to stall, they could not hold out forever against public curiosity and suspicion. On January 22, 1879, the House agreed to the investigation. Five days later the committee began taking testimony in Washington and made plans to send a subcommittee to New York. It was certain that Marble would be invited to testify.[11]

Marble was greatly alarmed. Long before the House resolved to investigate, he prepared a defense of his conduct in an open letter to the *Tribune*. Assuming an elevated moral tone, he declined to plead the *Tribune*'s jurisdiction and professed indifference to its verdict. "Your retractions and allegations," he declared, "are equally worthless to one who does not use your moral standards and is indifferent to any conclusions you reach from them." The *Tribune* had no business demanding explanations from him because it had inflicted "disgrace" upon "decent journalism" by obtaining and publishing "private missives." To avoid any suspicion of guilt, he would refrain from contesting the right of the *Tribune* to publish its evidence. He would object only to its ascribing to him telegrams he never wrote.

Suppose, he continued, that there actually had been a Democratic plot. What right had the *Tribune* to ascribe such a plot to Governor Tilden? And what right had the *Tribune* to censure Democratic frauds while ignoring Republican ones? "So long as thieves cry 'stop thief,' the theft will not be forgotten. And nothing is quite so important as that, till the ballot boxes of 1880 are set out, and the people of the United States are summoned to determine if they be sovereigns or dupes."

Filled with moral outrage and spiced with political cunning, the letter was worthy of Marble's best skills. It did not, however, squarely confront the evidence against him, and perhaps this fact dissuaded him from sending it. Passion without proof could hardly avoid arousing more suspicion. So, in the end, he contented himself with publishing a calm and straightforward denial of the charges, disputing the authenticity of only one irrelevant telegram that he declared he never wrote.[12]

Marble could hardly have expected that his denial would quiet the controversy over the cipher dispatches, and in the following weeks it remained annoyingly alive. Hardly a day passed without some comment from the *Tribune* about his inability to refute the evidence against him. Fellow Democrats offered to help. C. E. Dyke, a Florida editor who had told Marble about the $50,000 bribe offer, wrote a letter to the New York press declaring that Marble had refused to consider the offer. Other Florida Democrats and one of the "visiting statesmen" offered to refute minor points in the *Tribune*'s story. But the offers showed no clear proof of his innocence, and as the affair dragged on even his friends began to doubt him. "You were willing in this emergency," Barlow wrote, "to purchase the honest action of a Republican blackguard, who knew the right, but would still the wrong pursue unless he was paid for doing his duty." Barlow was disturbed only because Marble had failed to bribe the Republican and because he had conspired with such unsavory fellow Democrats. "To concoct even justice with the help of Johnny Coyle and Pelton is too much," he concluded. "Uncle Sammy deserved to be beaten for his choice of friends."[13]

Under such circumstances, it was obvious that the only way Marble could recover his reputation would be to confront the evidence against him. By the time the Potter Committee arrived in New York to take testimony, he had decided to appear as a witness. On the morning of February 7, carrying a large carpet bag filled with scrapbooks on the Florida election, he appeared at the Fifth Avenue Hotel to present his defense.[14]

By the time Marble took the stand, his case had turned alarmingly for the worse. Under vigorous cross-examination by the Republican committee members, Pelton had admitted that he had believed Marble intended to bribe one of the Republicans on the Florida returning board. He also admitted having approved the deed. Thus, when Marble took the stand, the most damaging evidence against him had been declared valid.[15]

But Marble had not come to the hearing to plead guilty; he had come to save his reputation and to impeach the reputation of the Republican party. For the most part he performed well. His answers were clear and calm, and only on a few occasions under insistently hostile cross-examination did he show irritation. Even the *Tribune*'s correspondent described him as a "good witness." He was also reasonably successful as a propagandist. Over the objections of the Republican minority he inserted in the record a number of his dispatches from Tallahassee accusing the Republicans of fraud.[16]

Marble also sought to discredit the *Tribune*'s account of his behavior. When confronted with the *Tribune*'s translations of his telegrams he occasionally disputed their accuracy or interpreted their significance to show how the *Tribune*'s partisan bias had led it into error. In this way he easily disproved the paper's charge that he had suggested stealing the vote of Oregon.

Everyone knew, however, that the *Tribune*'s case against him rested upon the telegrams of December 2 through 4 between him and Pelton. If he could explain these satisfactorily, his reputation would be saved. His examination had gone on for some time when chairman Eppa Hunton asked for his comment on the message: "Have just received a proposition to hand over at any hour required Tilden decision of Board and certificate of Governor for 200,000."

"That is substantially correct, I should think," Marble replied. "If I had relied upon my memory alone, I should have said that the amount signified was $250,000. I won't be absolutely certain that their translation is correct as to figures, but it was some preposterously large sum."

From whom did he receive the proposition?

"I don't remember. . . . I should be unwilling to state from whom it came."

It must, however, have come from a "responsible person."

"Yes; I thought it was a very significant fact, and I threw up a danger signal pretty quickly."

What about the reply from Pelton: "Warsaw here. Bolivia Brazil." Pelton had testified that he had rejected the proposition because the sum was too high.

Marble recalled receiving such a dispatch, but denied that it declared the sum "too high." Pelton must have been fatigued by the questioning of the Republican committee members; but in any case he was incorrect.

What about the telegram of December 3 to Pelton, reporting a proposition to turn over the vote for $50,000?

The translation was substantially accurate, and the proposition had been given him by C. E. Dyke. He had telegraphed Pelton on his own initiative, however, and did not involve Dyke any further. He could not remember who had conveyed the proposition to Dyke.

Did he tell Dyke that the proposition was merely a piece of strategy designed to get bids from both sides and that neither Tilden nor he would consent to it? A Republican objection, overruled.

"That is a precisely truthful representation of the substance of our conversation."

So far Marble's defense had been plausible enough. He had merely warned New York of various rumors that the returning board was for sale. But there was more to explain; for Pelton had obviously not interpreted his dispatches in this light and had replied on December 4 that the "proposition" was "accepted." When he received that dispatch, what did he do?

"I did nothing except to throw it in the fire. . . . I never mentioned it to a human being. . . . I put the dispatch into the fire, lit a cigar, smoked it, and went to bed."

Marble's defense was beginning to weaken. There was no one who could corroborate his statement, and there was one final bit of evidence that contradicted it. In order to exonerate himself he would have to explain it satisfactorily. It was a telegram of December 5, translated by the *Tribune* as reading: "Proposition failed. Finished yesterday responsibility (as) 'Moses.' Last night Woolley found me and said he had nothing, which I knew already. Tell Tilden to saddle Blackstone." The *Tribune* had interpreted the dispatch to mean that the bribery attempt had failed and that Tilden would have to resort to the law.

"Have you any remarks to make about that?"

First, in contrast to its usual practice the *Tribune* had printed only the translation of the message and not the original. Not until it prepared a special pamphlet edition of the dispatches did it print the original message. Second, its translation was false.

Could he provide a correct translation?

"I cannot do it; I am sorry. I wish I could; but it is enough that their translation is inaccurate, and that I find evidence of that in the dispatch itself." The dispatch showed only that he had believed the returning board would certify the Tilden electors. Because of this, he could not have reported that any "proposition" had "failed." The comment about "Blackstone" referred to Tilden's favorite horse, "and I meant to intimate to Governor Tilden my hope . . . that the Returning Board would decide in our favor according to the facts, and I meant to give 'Blackstone' that cud to chew while his master trotted him around the park." Thus, contrary to the *Tribune*'s interpretation, the message was harmless. That was all he had to say.

There followed a vigorous cross-examination by the Republican committee members, but it elicited no further clarification. Doggedly, Marble stuck to his story, swearing a number of times that he had never attempted to bribe the returning board. The next day Tilden appeared before the committee and denied that he had ever known about the cipher dispatches. After Tilden had completed his testimony, E. L. Parris, a New York lawyer who had been in Tallahassee with Marble, gave one bit of evidence in Marble's defense. Among the cipher dispatches had been one sent December 4, reading in part: "Marble says plan sent you Saturday must be acted upon immediately; otherwise unavailing. Plan unknown to undersigned." The *Tribune* interpreted "the plan" as being Marble's $200,000 telegram. Parris acknowledged having sent the message, but declared that he had never conferred with Marble about any bribery plan and that the dispatch had referred to C. W. Woolley and not to Marble. Since the name in the message had been a code word, Parris's testimony successfully cleared Marble on the point.[17]

There was other evidence of Marble's innocence. Neither of the Republican members of the returning board ever said Marble had actually approached them with a bribe offer. McLin had charged Marble with attempted bribery, but his evidence was flimsy and concerned an earlier period than the crucial one of December 2–4. Of even greater importance is a bit of contemporary evidence, overlooked by the committee. It is an unsigned and undated telegram to Pelton, printed in the appendix to the committee's report. Its translation reads in part: "May easily be cheated but Marble cannot help putting absolute faith in right result which I am promised midnight tonight." Although it is impossible to determine the author of the message, its reference to "midnight tonight" and other statements clearly show that it was sent December 5, the same day as the "proposition failed" dispatch. It supports Marble's claim that to the last he believed the returning board would certify the Tilden electors. It is also possible that Marble's explanation of "tell Tilden to saddle Blackstone" was accurate; he delighted in inventing such outrageously obscure phrases.[18]

Marble's testimony did have serious weaknesses. He had sent suspiciously specific "danger signals" and had followed Pelton's instructions by conferring with Woolley. Especially damaging was his unwillingness or inability to translate his "proposition failed" dispatch of December 5. Had he been able to provide a different translation, he could have argued convincingly that he had not followed up Pelton's approval of the bribery attempt. Indeed, Parris's testimony and the anonymous "absolute faith" dispatch would have placed the weight of evidence on his side. As it was, his failure to supply a different translation indelibly stained his reputation. It might have been enough for him to say that the *Tribune*'s translation was inaccurate, but for the historian it is not.

The available evidence does not conclusively convict Marble of attempted bribery. Even William E. Chandler, the Republican national chairman and leader of the Republican delegation to Florida, did not think the messages would prove any "overt acts" of bribery, only the willingness of the Democratic visitors to consider bribery. Certainly that is the worst that can be charged against Marble.[19]

To Marble's satisfaction, however, his friends refused to reach even that conclusion. "Mr. Marble was I think benefitted by the examination," wrote Sidney Webster to Thomas F. Bayard. Parris's evidence was "providential for him." Even William Springer, a Democratic member of the committee, was convinced of Marble's innocence. "I confess," Springer wrote Marble, "that when I entered upon the inquiry I supposed you guilty of the *Tribune*'s charge. But after hearing all the evidence, and especially the evidence of Mr. Parris, who gave the correct translation of the Woolley dispatch, and the clean and unequivocal statements and explanation of yourself, my mind was not only freed from doubt, but clearly convinced that your conduct in Florida was perfectly honorable, and free from taint."[20]

Such expressions of confidence no doubt comforted him. Still, they could not fully compensate for the embarrassment and the indignity of the affair. For the first time in his life, Marble had been subjected to sustained public abuse and censure on a matter of personal morality. His honor had been attacked and his manhood impugned. Moreover, the affair failed to achieve its ultimate purpose when Tilden, fearing that his failing health could not withstand the presidency, decided not to seek another nomination. Thus did another four years of president-making come to naught.

In these years, then, Marble paid a heavy price for his party loyalty. By 1880 both his honor and ambition had been blighted. Suddenly he found himself without purpose. "By the way," he wrote Barlow in September of 1880, "what is a Democrat now? What does he believe in? And what is the difference between him and an honest Republican, if that rare bird flies in American skies?" The man who could ask these questions had reached a turning point in his life. By 1880 only one thing seemed certain: president-making, for the time being at least, was over.[21] ✣

PART FOUR

The Political Economist

CHAPTER ELEVEN

Toward a Silver Summer

THE EARLY 1880s were an interlude of readjustment in Marble's life. The failure to renominate Tilden had set him adrift politically. His ambition, principles, and party loyalty had not changed, but his environment had been radically altered. Without Tilden, Marble's ambition lacked focus and direction. With the end of reconstruction and the restoration of "home rule" in the South, the major issues of his early political career had been resolved. Thus his problem was double: to find a new place for himself in the Democratic organization and to find new issues to lead the party to victory.

These were also years of readjustment in his personal life. In 1879 he remarried, taking as his wife Abby Williams Lambard, the widow of a New England railroad owner. They had met shortly after the death of Marble's first wife and had occasionally vacationed together in the Catskills. They were married in a private ceremony and honeymooned briefly in Europe before returning so Marble could manage Tilden's campaign for the presidential nomination.[1]

As a result of his marriage, Marble became a foreign traveler. Always in frail and delicate health, Abby suffered frequently from severe stomach pains and loss of appetite, a condition known in that day as "nervous dyspepsia." The summer heat sapped her strength and made her more susceptible to the affliction. Seeking cool summer climates, the Marbles began traveling to Europe and residing for long periods in Switzerland and Holland.[2]

Before his remarriage, Marble had not traveled abroad. His only recorded journeys outside the United States had been his Red River expedition to Canada and his short, ill-fated trip to Cuba. His reading in philosophy, literature, and political economy had acquainted him with European thought and society, but had failed to inspire him to travel. To become a European traveler in his late forties, then, was to disrupt his customary pattern of life.

It was natural, therefore, that his first extended trip to Europe found him intellectually unprepared. In May 1882 he and Abby sailed for Marseilles to begin eighteen months of travel, largely in France and Italy. The first months he spent observing his physical surroundings. His letters contain extensive descriptions of Cluny, Mont St. Michel, and the Rhone Valley. Piling detail upon detail, he tried his best to present graphic images of the sites. Occasionally he attempted to add clarity by providing sketches. At other times he gave up the effort altogether and merely referred his reader to an appropriate guidebook.[3]

Six months passed before he began to stuff his observations with critical comments. By the time he had arrived in Florence, however, he was scoffing at travelers who merely described the various sites without conveying what they "must have been feeling and thinking most." Florence revealed itself, he believed, only through history, not description. One needed a "sense of sequence" to convey "the atmosphere of the high and mighty days of Florence." So he turned to the past and began to reconsider his previous experiences. The result was a long letter to Tilden recalling a visit to the museum at St. Germain. The letter, however, was no more satisfactory than his earlier descriptions; for he discussed exclusively the exhibits of prehistory, "the tangible debris of our ancestors." Aside from illuminating the German invasions, Caesar's conquests, and the origin of the dolmen builders, prehistory led him no closer to understanding the French than had his detailed observations of Mont St. Michel. Indeed, prehistory afforded the excuse to avoid France's more recent past. Ever the moralist, Marble preferred the innocence of the prehistoric remains to the scandalous conduct of the French monarchs. The archeological fragments, he believed, left "a cleaner and more decent record with all its dung and its dirt, of the passage of the gentlemen of the caverns through their French vale of tears, than was left for example by the royal lover of Diana de Poitiers, or the French king of any other French mistress."[4]

To attract him favorably, history needed to be heroic, beautiful, and, above all, edifying. For all his experience in the world of affairs and men, Marble in Europe was still very much the young man in the Boston Athenaeum, hopefully seeking in culture a guide to noble manhood. European culture, however, was too remote from him to provide a simple, satisfying answer. Nothing better illustrated his problem than his experience in Rome. The Marbles arrived in late January and at once began the round of visits to the galleries, cathedrals, and historic sites. Marble tried his best to find inspiration in the city. "It is," he declared, "that all the past is here; it is that the overlaid, ruined, superseded, and surpassed city concludes within its bounding walls the gateways and vistas to all the world that antedates not alone the birth of Christ, but the redemption of mankind as well in 1492 and 1789. The world of history, of art, of literature is here."

But it was because Rome was overlaid, ruined, superseded, and surpassed that Marble could not feel at home in it. His attraction to material progress and its benefits was too great to allow him to bridge the gap between past and present. So despite the courage of his resolve, he was forced to admit that nineteenth-century America with its "11,000 miles of level iron road, and the webbed telegraphic wires, the intercommunication, the common consciousness, the various mastery and use of nature's secret ways" offered lessons "incomparably more marvellous" than the ancient ruins. Those lessons were impressed upon him that winter, as he shivered through the narrow, shadowy streets and the unheated galleries. "The floors and the walls," he complained, "radiate *freezure* to the marrow of your bones." The inconvenience of the season turned him inevitably toward the melancholy aspects of Roman history. Devastation and decay seemed the only lesson the city had to offer. His attention focused on the legions of the caesars and the "ceaseless northern hoardes." In the Coliseum the memory of thousands of citizens cheering their emperors could not compensate for the sight of crumbling arches and scraggy pines pushing their roots through the ruined palaces. Oppressed by somber skies and penetrated with bleak, wintery winds, Rome forced on him "that prodigious impression, which for immensity and force can have no second or similar in all the cities of the race of man—the impression of a momentous pregnant past, of unfolding catastrophes, and awful consummations, the crowding hastening history of a world, 'rerum magna parens.' "[5]

By October 1883 the Marbles had returned to New York, where amid friends and familiar surroundings they prepared to take up the affairs of society and politics. Marble's son Frank was to graduate the next June from fashionable Trinity School in upstate New York. First in his class, he had planned to attend Harvard until the opportunity appeared for him to enter the Naval Academy. Early in May Marble learned that Representative William Dorsheimer, his friend and political associate, was planning to nominate Frank to the academy. At once he set out to smooth his son's entry. He wrote to Captain F. Ramsey of the academy, praising the boy's excellent scholarship and leadership in military science. Through Dorsheimer and Perry Belmont he persuaded Secretary of the Navy William E. Chandler to postpone Frank's entrance examinations until September so the boy might have time to prepare adequately in modern history and geography. Everything went as planned, and Frank's appointment brought his father true happiness. Perhaps recalling his own youth, Marble wished for his son the same earnestness of purpose that he had brought to his own education. "May the lad justify your selection of him for the official service of his country," he wrote to Dorsheimer, "by a lifetime of fidelity, efficiency, and courage."[6]

Although this and other social affairs engaged his attention, politics remained his chief preoccupation. Marble had returned from Europe early enough to become involved in the coming presidential campaign. Since he no longer had a personal stake in the party's nominee, it seemed best to make the campaign a matter of principle, or more specifically of political economy. For years Marble had studied political economy avidly. He filled his library with all the standard works on the subject and became friends with such authorities as J. S. Moore, David A. Wells, and J. Laurence Laughlin. Within the Democracy his knowledge of the subject was so well recognized that as early as 1873 Congressman J. Proctor Knott of Kentucky had written him for advice on the theory of free trade.[7]

Marble had always been an enthusiastic free trader, and by 1884 it seemed that free trade would prove a serviceable issue for his party. During the early 1880s, sentiment for tariff reform had brought about the appointment of a Tariff Commission and the passage of a Tariff Act that reduced rates on such basic items as iron, steel rails, and copper. Such modest gains had inspired the low-tariff Democrats, led in the House by Speaker John J. Carlisle and Representative William R. Morrison, to redouble their efforts to effect a genuine reduction. To many observers, it appeared that they would succeed.[8]

Marble watched the tariff battle with great interest, hoping that the Democracy might at last emerge a full-fledged tariff reform party. This, he believed, was the free traders' only hope. "There is no instrument so powerful to carry our ideas into government," he wrote to Wells, "as the Democratic party. . . . To make another party is an infinitely harder task than to compel this one to accept the logic of its comparable creed. . . . Do not talk of disbanding. . . . Talk always of making the old party truly Democratic and insist upon staying in it and holding it up to its first, most necessary and most grand work."[9]

Marble urged Wells to cooperate fully with Carlisle and Morrison. To mark the Democracy as the party of tariff reform, the Democratic House must pass the proposed reductions. When Wells criticized the method of reduction, Marble replied that for political purposes "any reduction is a reform." Marble also encouraged Carlisle and the low tariff representatives by assuring them they were pursuing the best policy. "The Democratic House of Representatives," he told Carlisle, "is making the issues upon which majorities are to be declared."[10]

In the early stages of the debate, Marble thought the reform movement would succeed. As the final vote approached, however, serious weaknesses appeared in the Democratic ranks. David A. Wells passed along reports from Morrison, showing concern over party unity. Morrison especially worried that the protectionist forces, led by Samuel J. Randall, were being supported by the Tilden machine. On May 6 forty-one Democrats, largely from Pennsylvania and New York, voted against the reform bill and insured its defeat.[11]

The defeat of the bill seemed to doom any commitment to tariff reform in the coming election. Still, the reformers continued to hope and to plan. Speaker Carlisle urged Marble to meet with the reformers to plan their convention strategy, and Marble traveled to Washington to confer with them. Marble also arranged to attend the Democratic convention in Chicago.[12]

By the time the convention assembled, Marble and all other New York Democrats were committed to the nomination of Governor Grover Cleveland. Personally unattached to Cleveland, Marble took no hand in the governor's convention strategy. Nor did he influence the writing of the party platform. Like all other national platforms, the Democratic platform of 1884 was the work of the many men on the platform committee. The tariff plank, which for Marble was the key to the election, bowed noticeably toward protectionism. Marble's only contribution was to draw up the document for publication.[13]

When the convention adjourned, Marble no longer hoped to make free trade a campaign issue. Not only had the platform evaded the issue but the Mugwump bolt at Blaine's nomination had suggested that the campaign should emphasize personal morality rather than economic policy. So, when Wells sent him an article designed to promote the free-trade issue, Marble suggested that he hold back. "Blaine's character as a public man is the winning issue," he argued, "and we ought not to alter the issue as shaped by the exposures of him which nowhere else have been so formidable as in the *Evening Post*."[14]

In the campaign Marble served on the party's advisory committee. He received the place largely because of his friendships among the party's older leaders. The day after learning of his appointment he was contacted by Smith M. Weed, Cleveland's political trouble-shooter, who asked him to confer with Belmont and to see Dorsheimer, whose endorsement was needed to win the support of labor.[15]

Marble also drafted the address from the advisory committee to the party membership. Intended as a call to action, the address clearly showed the party strategy and Marble's willingness to abide by it. The address emphasized Cleveland's experience in local and state government, declaring that he had learned to execute the laws without regard to his personal interest or ambition. Blaine's public record contrasted darkly with Cleveland's. As Speaker of the House, Blaine had appointed friends of the infamous Credit Mobilier to head important committees and had suppressed the evidence against him in the Mulligan Letters. As secretary of state he had intervened in a controversy between Chile and Peru, jeopardizing the interests of peace in order to sponsor the financial claims of a disreputable French capitalist. Behind him stood a party in whose hands public office had ceased to be a public trust and had become instead a "private perquisite. . . . The public business has been neglected [the address concluded] or converted into an instrument for public plunder."[16]

Thus Marble acquiesced in the decision to keep economic questions out of the campaign. As he had done so often in the past, he subordinated his personal views to those of his party. By late September even Wells had acknowledged that the free-trade issue was dead.[17]

Cleveland's election, therefore, settled no questions of economic policy. Nor did it guarantee Marble a place of influence with the first Democratic administration of his political career. Cleveland entered the White House under few obligations to the Tilden machine. His political support in New York had come largely from Democrats who stood somewhat apart from the Tildenites: western New Yorkers, dissatisfied with eastern domination; Mugwumps; and the anti-Tammany County Democracy, led by Hewitt and William C. Whitney. Cleveland himself had avoided working closely with Tilden, so that throughout his governorship the two men had actually grown suspicious of each other. In fact Tilden had supported Cleveland's nomination only after realizing that his own candidacy was out of the question.[18]

In the weeks between the election and the inauguration, Marble fought to strengthen the influence of the Tildenites in Cleveland's administration and to hold together the elements of the victorious Democratic coalition. He tried especially to strengthen the alliance between the regular Democrats and the Mugwumps. In emphasizing Cleveland's spotless public record, the Democracy had specifically courted Mugwump support. When it came time for Cleveland to name his cabinet, the Mugwumps naturally looked for signs that their votes had been well cast. When Cleveland chose Tilden's upstate boss, Daniel Manning, as his secretary of the treasury, some of the Mugwumps began to doubt the president-elect's commitment to honest government.

When Cleveland asked William C. Whitney to become secretary of the navy, the Mugwumps were horrified. Although Whitney had made a good record as corporation counsel during the Tweed prosecutions, he was suspect because of his connection by marriage with the Standard Oil Company. It seemed that his appointment was merely a bow to the financial power of the nation's most conspicuous industrial monopoly. Horace White of the *Evening Post*, which had become a spokesman for the Mugwumps, characterized Whitney as "lazy" and an "intriguer," and predicted that his appointment would make it all the more difficult for the Mugwumps to accept Manning. Whitney's appointment was further complicated by Tilden's opposition. Over the years Tilden and Whitney had drifted apart, and with Cleveland's election, Tilden petulantly watched his own influence in the party decline and Whitney's rise.[19]

For Marble it was a delicate situation. To allow dissensions to break out so early in the victorious coalition would foredoom the administration and might destroy whatever influence he hoped to exercise in its councils. So, he tried to play the peacemaker. If Cleveland wanted Whitney, he was willing to go along. In January he held a dinner in honor of Speaker Carlisle and invited Whitney, Horace White, and E. L. Godkin. In writing to Cleveland later the same month, he referred to Whitney as "Secretary Whitney." To White he emphasized that the "main point" was the Mugwump attitude toward Manning and that Whitney was not important. When Whitney received his nomination for secretary of the navy, he at once sent his "hearty congratulations."[20]

Thus, as Cleveland prepared to enter office, Marble was on good terms with him and in a position to render him service. His opportunity came shortly before the inauguration. A sharp depression in 1884 had decreased the Treasury's gold supply, which by February 1885 was dipping near the $100 million thought necessary to maintain a stable currency. New York businessmen believed the depression resulted largely from the $200 million in silver put into circulation by the Bland-Allison Act of 1878. Faced with declining business prospects, holders of the silver dollars and greenbacks were turning them into the Treasury to receive a full dollar's worth of gold coin. Believing that the country faced a "great peril," Abram S. Hewitt and other New York politicians were urging Cleveland to take a stand against the silver coinage. Although faced with opposition from southerners and westerners, who wanted to maintain the silver coinage, Cleveland decided to follow the easterners' advice.[21]

Personally innocent of any knowledge of currency matters, Cleveland turned to Tilden for advice on his statement. When Tilden suggested that Marble should prepare the statement, the president-elect agreed. Politically, the choice of Marble made good sense. Although identified with the Tildenites, Marble had worked loyally for Cleveland in the campaign and seemed bent on maintaining the unity of the Democratic party. And his interest in the silver question was well known, for during the debate on the Bland Silver Bill in 1878, he had published an article on the silver coinage.

Marble's views on the silver question require some detailed consideration, since they were soon to become the basis for his political activities. By 1878 Marble had become convinced that questions of political economy should be decided by experts. He classified political economy with the "concrete" sciences, "dealing with that super-organic aggregate called Society." Specifically, political economy dealt with the "natural division of labor," corresponding to the "physiological division of labor among the mutually-dependent parts of animal organisms." Political economy was also unique in that its goal was "material well-being." So defined, it had as much claim to the status of an exact science as any study of society. Marble thought it necessary to define political economy in this way in order to meet challenges to its scientific precision. He thought it irrelevant to impeach its accuracy simply because its conclusions were affected by circumstances that did not affect the conclusions of the astronomer or the biologist. He also thought it irrelevant to point out that its conclusions were often disregarded by governments concerned with public opinion, or by moralists concerned with the "axioms of ethics" or the "behests of mere ten-commandment morality." The principles of political economy, he believed, were confirmed by man's historical experience, as exemplified by Britain's rise to prosperity through free trade. Like the principles of astronomy, they were true regardless of whether anyone decided to apply them.[22]

Marble also believed that the principles of political economy easily eluded the untrained mind. They involved "the intricacies and the principles of a science in which the experts are few." It was for the experts to debate the issues among themselves until a consensus could be achieved and laid before the public. Once this was done, he thought the common sense of the American voter would set the government upon the proper course, for as we have seen, he assumed that people could tell the difference between right and wrong. "The people's common sense, as in other cases outside their ken, may be trusted to estimate shrewdly and fairly the influence of authority in matters of opinion."

In 1878 Marble thought the experts agreed on the folly of reestablishing bimetallism in the United States. Attacking the Bland Bill, he quoted the French bimetallist Henri Cernuschi and the American S. Dana Horton, both of whom opposed the United States's coining silver without the other major nations' agreeing to coin it too. He then proceeded to attack a resolution offered by Representative Stanley Mathews of Ohio, calling for payment of part of the national debt in silver coin.

The value of money, Marble declared, lay in its purchasing power. Purchasing power in turn depended upon the market price of gold and silver, and it should be the goal of all monetary legislation to "find and fix an equality in market value and purchasing power between that quantity of gold and that quantity of silver upon which those acts confer the name 'dollar' and the quality of legal tender." To insure stable purchasing power under bimetallism, the legal ratio between gold and silver should equal the market ratio. So long as the law followed the market the currency would remain sound and stable.

Efforts to establish a legal ratio different from the market ratio would court disaster. This was clearly the case in the Bland Bill, which proposed to coin silver at a ratio of 16 to 1 at a time when the market ratio varied between 17 to 1 and 18 to 1. If the bill became law, gold would leave the United States and the country would be left with a silver standard, isolated among the advanced nations of the world.

The Mathews resolution was no less nefarious. Paying the national debt in 16 to 1 silver dollars would rob the creditor classes. And who were the creditor classes? They included the "wage-receivers, the industrious, saving poor," who deposited their money in the nation's savings banks, which in turn invested heavily in government securities and loaned to capitalists, who in their turn employed the original lenders. They included the life insurance companies, also protectors of the common man and agents for lending large sums to capitalists. "From these vast aggregates," Marble declared, "the silver bill will strike off ten per cent of the value," defrauding the most numerous class in the country.

The true remedy for the nation's financial problems was to create "loanable capital." But so long as Congress threatened to delay specie resumption and to reestablish bimetallism, no capitalist could be sufficiently confident of the stability of the dollar to borrow. "But if our captains of industry cannot hire capital, they cannot employ labor; and that implies hungry mouths unfed, shivering at cold hearths, and the wolves of poverty at a thousand doors."[23]

In 1885 Marble still held these views. Writing to Manning on February 19, he stated that currency reform should be the administration's top priority. While the executive patronage remained unspent, the administration should define its policy and carry it out to "make the issue upon which everywhere . . . we appeal to the people." Marble urged Manning to dramatize the issue by sponsoring a constitutional amendment, overturning the Supreme Court's decision in the Legal Tender Cases by making only gold and silver a legal tender. "If we do not thus at once undertake the reversal of the legal tender decision," he warned, "we shall be tarred with the ignominy of assent, and the restoration of a sound fiscal basis will have become forever impossible."[24]

Marble's draft of Cleveland's silver letter reiterated his stand against bimetallism. The letter was issued in reply to requests from ninety-four silver Democrats, led by A. J. Warner of Ohio, that the president-elect not yield to growing demands for suspending the silver coinage. While declaring his intention to answer the request "in the same friendly spirit in which it has been made," the letter left no doubt that Cleveland opposed the silverites. Charging that under the Bland-Allison Act the Treasury had burdened itself with heaps of eighty-five-cent silver dollars, he warned that the time was approaching when the government would be unable to redeem its obligations in gold. To prevent such an event and the subsequent flight of gold from the country, he called for suspending the purchases and coinage of silver. Without a suspension gold would be hoarded, the volume of currency would sharply contract, and the present depression would continue. Once the country had been forced on a silver standard, the purchasing power of the dollar would decline, further injuring the working classes. "From these impending calamities," he concluded, "it is surely a most patriotic and grateful duty of the representative of the people to deliver them."[25]

Marble also believed the Cleveland administration would face serious political problems unless Congress suspended the silver coinage. When he heard of a proposal to leave suspension to the discretion of the president, he quickly warned Cleveland against it. Although such an option would make the president the "centre of hope among sound money men and instructed men," it would also make him the "object of assault from all the unsound men with whose vagaries the country has been plagued since the first paper Legal Tender act was spawned." Hoping that the president-elect might be won to their cause, the silverites would bedevil the administration enough to prevent Cleveland's working out any satisfactory currency reform.[26]

Marble believed that Congress would suspend the silver coinage in response to Cleveland's letter. Two days after the letter appeared, however, the House refused to suspend. One hundred eighteen Democrats opposed suspension and only fifty-four approved. Nothing could have been more alarming to Marble and the other gold men; not only did the party remain divided but the silver forces controlled the majority.[27]

Still, Marble hoped Cleveland would win out. In April he suggested that the president call a special session of Congress to deal with the problem before his patronage power had been exhausted. An effort "backed by every ounce of the moral and political power at your command," he declared, "will be the more likely to succeed." It is interesting to note that eight years later Cleveland did follow such a course and succeeded in suspending the Treasury's silver purchases.[28]

In 1885 Cleveland did not call a special session, but he and Manning thought long and hard about the silver problem. The results of the lame-duck session showed that the administration desperately needed some formula to deal with the problem if it was to avoid four years of demoralizing party wrangling. In seeking a solution the administration was led, as had been others, to examine the possibilities of an international agreement. Following the passage of the Bland-Allison Act, the Hayes, Garfield, and Arthur administrations had attempted to persuade the nations of Europe to recognize the silver dollar in international trade and thus to prevent the draining of gold from the United States. For various reasons each effort had failed. The day before Cleveland's inauguration, however, the Senate resolved that international negotiations be resumed. To the harried members of the administration, such a course seemed to be at least worth a try.[29]

"Why not become a silver tramp this summer," Manning wrote Marble, requesting that he investigate the possibilities of Europe's agreeing to international bimetallism. The request must have brought Marble a few moments of pause. Although he wished to serve the administration and to influence its policies, he had not thought seriously of a diplomatic career. Earlier in the year, when Barlow had suggested that he become American minister to Great Britain, he had replied that "service of the public under official conditions would be hateful to me." Perhaps because Manning and Secretary of State

Bayard assured him that his mission would be confidential and because of the importance of the silver question he decided to accept.[30]

Marble's formal instructions called upon him to confer with the American ministers and the "expert advisers and statesmen" of the major European countries to learn their opinions on establishing an internationally fixed ratio between gold and silver coins, the free coinage of both metals at the mints of all, and the international use of both metals as an "unlimited legal tender." Shortly after he sailed, Bayard informed the American ambassador to France: "It is difficult to overstate the importance of the question and the momentous consequences to the American people which are involved in its solution." Bayard also instructed the American delegate to the conference of the Latin Monetary Union to refrain from meetings with government officials, so that he might in no way "embarrass" Marble's mission. It was hoped that secret diplomacy would redeem the failures of public conferences.[31]

Marble left for Europe sharing the administration's assumption that unless the United States could arrange an agreement on international bimetallism, it would have to suspend its silver coinage. Their interpretation of economic conditions in the United States allowed no other alternative. Decreasing revenues from a decline in imports was threatening the Treasury's gold reserve and endangering its ability to pay interest on the national debt. By continuing to coin silver dollars, the Treasury increased the danger. Still, the administration hesitated to suspend the silver coinage until it had exhausted all possible alternatives, for suspension would cause the collapse of the silver market and invite serious political repercussions. Thus Marble's mission was not merely a gesture to win political support for the gold standard. It was a sincere effort to find a solution that would be both economically and politically sound.[33]

It should be emphasized, however, that Marble left the United States a confirmed advocate of the gold standard. Nothing in either his published writings or private correspondence even suggests that he was sympathetic to international bimetallism or that he even thought it important.[33]

In mid-May Marble and his wife sailed for Europe. Arriving first in London, Marble spent three days instructing the American minister, E. J. Phelps, in the history of American silver legislation and the international monetary conferences. While they were conferring, the Gladstone ministry fell from power and was replaced by the Salisbury Conservatives. Realizing that the new ministry would need time to organize itself, Marble and Phelps decided to proceed slowly, relying upon a "social approach" to diplomacy. They spent nearly a month familiarizing themselves with London society. "Busy as a bumblebee," Marble set about meeting the proper people. Things went well, and with obvious relish he was soon reporting to Bayard all the details of his "social approach": Randolph Churchill's snubbing of the

Phelpses; the Prince of Wales's attitude toward a proposed American exhibition; the reception of the American singer, Mrs. Ronalds. Nothing pleased him more than the aid he received from Herbert Spencer, who helped him gain admission to the elite Athenaeum Club, social home of Britain's scientific and literary community. They were soon spending as much time together as their schedules would permit. After twenty years of admiring Spencer's philosophy, Marble was at last able to admire the man himself. "He gets through more and harder work than any man in England," he reported to Barlow, "and is the only being on the islands who might (if he thought of such a trifle) be quite sure of immortality of fame—if not a share of the dust-heaps of the Abbey."[34]

The month of social preparation paid its first dividends July 10, when Marble and Phelps attended a breakfast with the ex-Chancellor of the Exchequer George Goschen and the Liberal spokesman John Bright. There Marble heard for the first time a statement that would become a refrain among British leaders: Britain would never agree to any plan of international bimetallism. Goschen and Bright said that the subject no longer interested anyone in the country, save a few "queers."[35]

Two more weeks of investigation only confirmed the judgment. Ever diligent in his country's service, Marble interviewed leading merchants, bankers, politicians, and scholars and read everything available in pamphlets, books, and articles. The British were interested in the future of the American silver coinage, but that was all. Although Goschen told Marble that Britain favored a limited international circulation of silver, it preferred to leave the question to the discretion of "each state or group of states." Thus Marble could only conclude that "the hope of any cooperation of Great Britain with the government of the United States in any effort to effect an international establishment of bimetallic money at one fixed ratio is a baseless hope, a mere illusion, for which there is not substantial warrant of any sort whatever."[36]

To many an advocate of the gold standard, such evidence would have been enough. But Marble was determined not to allow his prejudices to cause him to conduct a hasty, one-sided investigation. He thought it especially necessary to investigate British opinion thoroughly, since Britain absorbed half of America's European trade. He was also careful because he thought the next elections would return the Gladstone Liberals to power.[37]

So, he seized every opportunity to pursue his mission. When the Salisbury ministry decided to appoint a special commission to examine the causes of a commercial depression in Britain, Marble arranged an interview with its supervisor, Lord Iddesleigh. Iddesleigh told him that the commission would probably hear testimony on the money question, but assured him that the ministry firmly opposed bimetallism.

At Marble's insistence, however, he agreed to bring up the question at the next cabinet meeting. After the meeting, he reported that "there is nothing doing, nor anything in immediate contemplation with respect to the currency and the standard of value questions." Still, Marble persisted until he had obtained a more explicit statement: "Her Majesty's present government have not had occasion to reconsider the policy adopted by their predecessors upon the subject."[38]

Although Marble's diplomatic efforts occupied most of his time, he had opportunities for social diversions. The official nature of his visit allowed him to mingle with the British social elite, and because his life among the American upper classes had drawn him to admire British society, he seems for the first time to have thoroughly enjoyed his stay abroad.

Marble especially enjoyed the privileges of membership in the Athenaeum Club. "One must have made his proofs, and then generally waits fourteen years before election," he informed Barlow. He found the whist especially good, "if you don't mind playing with octogenarians and an archbishop." Of the members he had high praise for Lord Bramwell, a leader of the bar. Marble found him "capable of cogency, logical to the last fibre of him."[39]

Other names crowd the pages of his letters: Lord Bryce, who provided letters of introduction to prominent economists; Thomas Huxley, Britain's foremost Darwinian; Lord and Lady Rosebery; and a host of lesser knowns. The Roseberys were particularly attractive. Calling upon Lord Rosebery to sound him out on bimetallism, Marble found himself and his wife the objects of a generous hospitality. "We dined at Lansdowne House gorgeously with the Roseberys," he reported to Barlow. "I enjoyed him vastly for a couple of days at Epsom and have plighted my faith and Mrs. M. hers."[40]

But only Herbert Spencer compared favorably with William Ewart Gladstone. The principles of British liberalism had long informed Marble's brand of Democracy, and he had eagerly looked forward to dealing with the Gladstone ministry. He arrived believing that "Mr. Gladstone has more ability to the square inch than all the rest of the members of both ministries and of both Houses put together." Although the Gladstone ministry fell shortly after he arrived, he still sought to confer with the ex-Prime Minister, believing that the next elections would return him to power.[41]

The two met July 15 at Gladstone's residence. In a shaded corner of the garden Gladstone seated himself next to Marble and opened the conversation. Two days later Marble recalled the scene as "almost startling. . . . Thin white hairs framed his large symmetrical head and his face with its sallow complexion, but these and his whole figure—still vigorous and alert, stood forth so to speak from the background of fresh and living green made by the lawn and its boundary of sloping turf and rising wall beyond; but high overhead and away—a spectral vision in the misty air, that leaped to the light whenever its glance was turned from the deep dark smouldering eyes which mark his genius more than any other external sign—arose the majestic towers of St. Stephen and Victoria, the scene of his splendid eloquence, of his long triumphs, and of his last defeat." Apart from a slight "graying about the eyes," Gladstone showed few signs of age. The skin on his hands "had the freshness and appearance and the texture of that of a man of thirty, even to the rosy finger tips and nails." His conversation suggested that age "had strengthened his powers of attention and invigorated his youthful capacity to command his whole memory and mental resources without delay."

All of this compensated for Gladstone's remarks on international bimetallism. All statesmen, he declared, believed any departure from the gold standard would be political suicide. Satisfied on this point, Marble took his leave. As he was saying goodbye to Mrs. Gladstone, she pointed to a corner window through which he could see Gladstone bending over a table in his library. "That's the way he does his work," she commented, "never losing a moment from morning till night." It had been a memorable visit. "Gladstone is much more than all my fancy painted him," Marble exclaimed to Barlow. "So incontestable is his superiority to all the people of his own party and of the other party, that Owen and Huxley would seem to need a new order of Primates."[42]

Finally convinced that Great Britain would never abandon the gold standard, Marble looked upon the remainder of his mission as anticlimactic. In neither France nor Germany did he anticipate any difficulty in confirming his conclusions. As he prepared to leave for Paris, he sent Manning a preliminary report. International bimetallism was impossible, and the United States should officially recognize that the major western nations were moving toward "a single and common standard of value in exchanges." The administration, he believed, should fight to adopt the gold standard not only by suspending the silver coinage, but also by retiring the greenbacks. Specifically, the Treasury should redeem the greenbacks with the silver already in the treasury vaults, valuing the silver at its market price.[43]

An hour with the French minister of finance only supported his conclusions. Although France was seeking to renew the Latin Union Treaty, which allowed silver and gold coins to circulate freely among the principal franc-using countries, it did not intend to resume the free coinage of silver. Indeed, the French had lost interest in the subject and because of approaching elections would continue to ignore it for the immediate future.[44]

Then he was off to Berlin, where he expected more significant information. Reasoning that France, "the defeated power" in Europe, could not initiate proposals for international bimetallism, he saw in Germany the only hope. Germany was, he reported to Bayard, "the key-stone of every bimetallic rainbow." There he would push the bimetallic cause to the limit. "No bimetallist among us," he declared, "no Bland, nor Warner . . . but shall admit that we have given the bimetallic baby all possible good nursing and every chance to live."[45]

He meant what he said. Conscientiously, he cultivated high-ranking German politicians and financial experts. Prince Bismarck was vacationing at Varzin when he first arrived, so he presented himself to the Prince's son, Count Herbert von Bismarck. Arguing the case for bimetallism as strongly as possible, he declared that even without Britain's cooperation the United States, France, and Germany could successfully absorb the world's increased silver production and maintain free coinage at a common ratio. He also warned that if the United States stopped its silver coinage the market value of German silver would decline seriously. Although the Count doubted that Germany would endorse a bimetallic treaty without the participation of Great Britain, he agreed to introduce Marble to all the prominent financial authorities in his country.[46]

Taking advantage of such generosity, Marble set out to test German financial opinion. After two weeks he had met with Privy Chancellor Schraut, Imperial Finance Minister Burchard, Imperial Bank of Germany President Dechend, the Rothschild agent Bleichroder, and Prince-Chancellor Bismarck.

Marble insistently put forward as many arguments for international bimetallism as he could contrive. The United States, he said, could mine or trade for all the gold needed for its circulation. If it stopped its silver purchases and saved the $24 million annually spent to transport the silver from Nevada to Washington, its currency would soon become the soundest in the world. "For," he pointed out, "no government paper dollar would need exist which was not represented by, or rather which was not the actual sole representative of, a gold dollar or enough silver to be equivalent to a gold dollar." So, his country had no more reason than any other to desire a bimetallic treaty.

He had to admit, however, that continued silver purchases would eventually endanger the American gold supply. For ten years the United States had sought a bimetallic union, and it now must know whether Europe really desired one or not. If Germany did not, Marble warned, President Cleveland would have to recommend that Congress stop the silver coinage, "whatever the consequence to other nations."

But so long as Britain rejected bimetallism Germany preferred a decline in silver prices to a retreat from the gold standard. The imperial finance minister did suggest that Germany would "look with sympathy" upon a bimetallic union between the United States and France. Marble knew, however, that such a concession showed only that Germany hoped to avoid a decline in silver prices by encouraging others to adopt bimetallism. When Marble replied that the United

States would never undertake such a project, the finance minister "expressed the hope" that it would at least not repeal the Bland-Allison Act. In return for such a favor, Germany might refuse to sell silver.

But Marble would have none of such a compromise. The United States, he replied, would accept nothing less than "free mintage for both metals at the old ratio of the great mass of European coins, 15.5:1, into coins of full legal tender." A fixed ratio was absolutely necessary so that silver could be used freely in international trade. To this, however, the finance minister would not agree. "It is an impasse," Marble concluded.[47]

There was only one hope left. All the experts agreed that the final decision lay with the Prince-Chancellor. On September 23 Marble stated his case directly to Bismarck. The experience was almost overwhelming. Throughout his mission Marble had flooded Bayard with long, discursive reports; but after his interview with Bismarck he outdid himself. In 2,700 words he led his reader through every stage of the interview, carefully setting the scene and providing personal asides that all but smothered the central theme. His customary heading, "private, confidential, not for department files," had never been more appropriate. The report clearly revealed a man for whom the distinction between personal and political had never existed.

At half past two in the afternoon, Marble arrived at the Prince-Chancellor's "palace"—a "spacious, comfortable residence"—surrounded on three sides by a large courtyard and guarded by a high iron fence. From the anteroom he could see a large garden, shaded by trees, "many of a noble size." Then he was ushered into the Prince-Chancellor's office.

"The door was thrown open, and there stood erect, in military uniform, the most famous *conditores imperiorum,* his great black hound alert beside him." The hound sniffed Marble's trousers, the two men shook hands, seated themselves, and began their conversation.

Marble probed for some sign that Germany might be induced to join a bimetallic union. When Bismarck declared that Great Britain was the key to Germany's policy, he replied that his own experience in Britain had given him no such impression. He reminded Bismarck that Germany would suffer if the United States stopped its silver coinage. He argued that abundant gold supplies and a favorable balance of trade would protect the United States against a decline in silver prices. He denied that an international bimetallic union would cause American silver production to increase dramatically. Indeed, some experts were predicting that silver production would decline in the next ten years.

The principal problem to be solved, Marble argued, was not Britain's devotion to the gold standard, but the depression in world trade. Referring to several studies by noted British economists, he declared that since 1873 prices had declined to their lowest level since

1850. Although Bismarck seemed to attribute the decline to a "gold famine," Marble argued that such was not the case.

Gradually Marble made headway with the Prince-Chancellor. He assured him that a bimetallic union would reduce monetary fluctuations to a minimum. A union "would be no subversion of economic laws," but rather "a fresh illustration of them by constituting a demand in the strictest economic sense commensurate with any conceivable supply." He then proposed another international monetary conference. Bismarck agreed. Although the German merchants and manufacturers favored the gold standard, he said, the farmers, "of whom I am one," favored bimetallism. He told Marble to work out the details with the president of the Imperial Bank

Marble came away encouraged and thoroughly impressed. In every way Bismarck had been a striking figure of a man. Marble remembered him as tall, erect, and almost thin. An unaggressive nose contrasted strangely with "his very impressive forehead and jaw, and his grave deep bloodshotten eyes." His reddish hair, thick eyebrows, weatherbeaten skin, gold shoulder straps, and dark blue uniform created "a striking color-picture." He had spoken English well, though deliberately, pausing, Marble supposed, to select precisely the right words. "Despite his unfamiliarity with the 'dismal science,' and with whatever it has proved, and excepting from the comparison Mr. Gladstone for whom that knowledge is an open book and in whom it is a charm to which I may be too susceptible, I distinctly say that Prince Bismarck, baptized though he be in blood and moulded of iron, is a more highly civilized and manly creature than any other political personage I met in Europe—a noble type and farthest removed from the savage primeval who begat us all."[48]

Bismarck's assurances, however, could not prevail against a reluctant financial community. In his interview with the president of the Imperial Bank, Marble learned that the Prince-Chancellor would be advised to call a monetary conference only on two conditions. First, Germany should not be asked to coin silver for several years, so it would run no risk of buying silver it would later have to sell at a loss. Second, it would have to call in all small notes and coins "to show to the timid and distrustful that there was a place for silver which indeed it would scarce suffice to fill." And even then, Germany would promise nothing. Marble had to conclude that Germany would not help to establish a bimetallic union. He would have to advise Cleveland to recommend the repeal of the Bland-Allison Act. The United States could not risk exchanging its gold for European silver.[49]

By the end of September, Marble's mission was complete and his conclusions firm. France would take no initiative; Germany would not act without Great Britain; and Britain was wedded to the gold standard. Throughout Europe inaction was the word for the day, and change seemed impossible.

But if Europe had not changed, Marble had. By the end of his mission he had become an international bimetallist. He had begun as a fact-finder, interested solely in eliciting information and none too eager to encourage bimetallism. In Great Britain and France his investigation, though insistent and thorough, showed only the care of a hard-working representative. By the time he arrived in Berlin, however, he had become an advocate. His reports, which at first had reported the opinions of others, began to record his own arguments on behalf of international bimetallism. "I replied" became a familiar phrase in his German reports, and Marble himself realized the change. "Do not be guilty of inferring from the above *currante calamo* narration," he cautioned Bayard, "that Herr von Burchard had not a fair share of the conference."[50]

The cause of the change is plain. The course of Marble's life had always been strongly influenced by others. In his youth John F. Rathbone had inspired his Christian faith and had made possible his college education. Martin B. Anderson had further shaped his ideals and had suggested his career. S. L. M. Barlow had saved that career and had introduced him to the New York Democracy. Samuel J. Tilden had been the focus for his president-making ambitions and energies. Now in 1885 there appeared the last of these men: Henri Cernuschi. Born in Italy, Cernuschi had moved to Paris during the revolutions of 1848. There he became a noted and successful banker, a political activist, and a recognized financial authority. He was still in Paris, living in retirement, when Marble visited him.[51]

The outline of Cernuschi's life is less important than his financial theory, which Marble came wholeheartedly to accept. A lifelong advocate of bimetallism (a word which he coined), Cernuschi had long opposed the trend in Europe toward the single gold standard. The free coinage of both gold and silver, he argued, if supported by an international agreement, would strengthen the world's financial system. Prior to 1871 French bimetallism had stabilized European trade and finance. Because France opened her mints to the unrestricted use of both silver and gold at the ratio of 15.5:1, monometallic countries were able to trade with one another certain that the value of their currencies would not fluctuate. Great Britain on the gold standard could trade with India on the silver standard by selling gold to France in return for silver francs, and India could merely reverse the procedure to obtain gold francs to pay Britain. France in turn could maintain bimetallism because the British gold standard and the German silver standard guaranteed a constant demand for both money metals. In 1871, however, Germany had adopted the gold standard. With the demand for silver sharply reduced, France faced the possibility of being forced to absorb all the excess silver *thalers*. Fearing that such an influx of silver would force it to adopt a silver standard, France began to retreat from bimetallism and in 1878 closed its mints to silver. The result was financial chaos. For example, India found it next to impossible to pay her debts to Great Britain, and Austrian bondholders were "nearly ruined."[52]

Cernuschi believed that the demonetization of silver was both harmful and unnecessary. It was at this point that he challenged the assumptions of the gold standard theorists, who argued that increases in silver production would destroy the value of that metal as money. According to Cernuschi, the value of money was unaffected by the market price of the metal. "Money," he declared, "is a value created by law to be the scale of valuation and a valid tender for payments." In other words, the act of the government and not of the marketplace determined the value of money. Thus bimetallism would not *necessarily* force a country to a silver standard. Only "discordant legislation" that established different monetary ratios for different nations could cause the values of the metals to vary and so create a preference for one over the other. Uniform legislation, establishing international bimetallism at a common ratio, would eliminate such discord.[53]

Cernuschi believed legislation guaranteeing "free coinage" would fix the value of the money metals by fixing their market price. Under "free coinage" all metal produced might be sold to the mint. This in effect established a guaranteed price for the metal. It was also a permanent price, for if a producer of the money metal demanded more than the mint price, the jewelers and smiths would merely melt coins, thus driving down the commercial price. Conversely, the jewelers and smiths would always pay no less than the mint price because the metal producers could always sell their product to the mint at the guaranteed higher price. Thus Cernuschi concluded that under "free coinage" the mint price would determine the commercial price, and the distinction between the metal as money and the metal as merchandise would vanish.

Legislation that abolished the distinction between money and merchandise would also abolish the distinction between gold and silver. Once the law had fixed a ratio between the two metals, nothing could change the ratio. The ratio merely stated a price: so many ounces of silver were worth so many ounces of gold. If the law declared, for example, that 15.5 ounces of silver were worth one ounce of gold, that price could become universal, since commercial dealings would not affect it. Since the price never varied, no one had any reason to prefer payment in one metal to payment in another. Gold had become silver and silver had become gold.[54]

It would be a mistake, however, to conclude from this that Cernuschi differed radically from orthodox economic thought; for in important areas he shared many generally accepted assumptions about money. Most significantly, he accepted the quantity theory of money, which held that the value of money lay in its purchasing power and that any significant increase in the quantity of money would reduce purchasing power. When he appeared before the United States Monetary Commission in 1877, Cernuschi declared unequivocally that "the value of money depends upon its quantity." A few moments later, he emphasized the point in the following exchange:

"Do you make a difference between 'value' and 'purchasing power,' as you use the term?"

"I do not make any difference. The purchasing power signifies the value of money."

It is important to understand this, because it significantly clarifies Cernuschi's earlier statement that "money is a value created by law to be a scale of valuation and a valid tender for payments." By this statement, Cernuschi meant only that governments could establish the *price of the money metals,* not that governments could regulate their *purchasing power.* He left no doubt that he opposed all government regulation of purchasing power. "The government gives no value to the money. The government adopts a monetary unit . . . but the government does not interfere in determining the purchasing power or the value of the dollar."[55]

Once the choice of the monetary unit had been made, the government stepped aside and allowed nature to determine the purchasing power by making available to the country a given amount of the money metal. Thus Cernuschi's statement that government price-fixing abolished the distinction between money and merchandise was not intended to endorse government regulation of the currency. In fact, Cernuschi's theory pointed in the opposite direction. Once he had destroyed the distinction between money and merchandise, Cernuschi could declare that there was no difference between coined money and the bullion itself. "A good and sound money," he told the Monetary Commission, "is that money the coinage of which is unlimited and unrestrained; so that the value of bullion and the value of the coin are always the same. It is not the stamp on the coin which creates the monetary value; that which creates the value [i.e., the price of the money metal] is the legal right of every one of having all his metal stamped and coined into conformity with the law." None of this had anything to do with the purchasing power of the money. That value lay in the quantity of the money, not just the quantity of the money *coined,* but the quantity of *bullion.* And the quantity of bullion was not regulated by the government, but by nature. Cernuschi really wanted the government to create the conditions for bringing into use a kind of natural money.[56]

Nothing better illustrates Cernuschi's opposition to government regulation of the currency than his attitude toward paper money. Had he relied entirely upon the power of law to establish monetary values, he certainly could not have opposed the government's using paper instead of gold or silver. But when he was questioned on this point by the Monetary Commission he left no doubt that he opposed paper money. Paper money, he declared, had no other guarantee than the goodwill of the government, while gold and silver "are issued by nature itself." Because paper money lacked the guarantee of nature, it did not circulate in international exchange. Nor did the promise of the government to pay gold or silver for the paper redeem its value, since paper money carried no promise of payment at a specific time. "A promise to execute with no date for executing, is not a promise." Paper money circulated only because the government required it to circulate by making it a legal tender. "Paper money," he concluded, "is not a credit paper but an enforced standard." Gold and silver were also an "enforced standard," but because they were issued by nature they were infinitely preferable to paper.

In many ways, then, Cernuschi sided with orthodox, hard money economics. His brand of bimetallism was so narrow and restricted that it fit quite well with the ideology of the gold monometallists, who also emphasized the primacy of natural laws and opposed government regulation of the currency. Indeed, the principal difference between himself and the gold monometallists was one of national perspective. The gold men favored a standard that would insure the leadership of the gold-paying financial centers of Western Europe; Cernuschi favored one that would encompass such silver-paying countries as India, China, and Mexico. The reasons for Cernuschi's perspective are obscure and irrelevant. It is enough only to note the orthodoxy of his theory, because that orthodoxy no doubt appealed to Manton Marble.[57]

Marble first met Cernuschi during his August visit to Paris. It seems that he was deeply impressed. In Berlin he more aggressively supported international bimetallism than previously. Moreover, his arguments revealed traces of Cernuschi's thought. He charged Europe's financial difficulties to the "blundering of Germany in 1871–73." He emphasized that bimetallism meant international bimetallism with free coinage at a common ratio. He declared that the American silver mines were "owned and worked by individuals toward whom the government had precisely the same and no other relation than that which it held towards the owners of farms, of iron mines, etc." It is possible that he held such views before, but there is little evidence of them and none that he considered them important as arguments for bimetallism. He revealed his principal source of inspiration shortly before returning to the United States, when he sent Bayard one of Cernuschi's pamphlets with the remark: "I trust that you will agree with me that it casts light upon the whole subject and is particularly suited to advance the controversy in the United States towards a beneficent solution."[58]

Unquestionably, Marble was attracted by the orthodoxy of Cernuschi's theory, which extolled natural forces and severely restricted government action. And his growing familiarity with international bimetallism probably influenced him. Still, it seems unlikely that Marble would have changed his ideas had it not been for Cernuschi himself. From the first, Cernuschi impressed Marble as a man of culture and refinement. His collection of Chinese and Japanese bronzes was magnificent, and his house contained "more and finer specimens of every age than all the other museums and private collections of all Europe and America put together." Cernuschi was also personally compelling. He told Marble that no one knew more of "the situation" in France than he. In return for such praise Marble bestowed his highest accolade. Writing to Barlow, he told of "speaking with a magnificent Frenchman with whom I breakfasted yesterday—a *man* in the desert of human beings."[59]

Early in October Marble prepared to return to America. His summer abroad had opened the way for a new period in his life and career. For the first time he had fitted in with European society. His mission had provided him with credentials that opened doors and made those close friendships that had always been so indispensable. He could be assured that on future visits there would be friends to greet him, entertain him, and make him feel at home. Where sightseeing and history had failed, diplomacy had succeeded.

But Europe had been more than a personal triumph, for it had left him with a new perspective on American domestic politics. In international bimetallism he had found the answer not only to the silver debate but also to the question of his role in the politics of the 1880s. He no longer doubted what the Democracy should stand for.

His trip had thus resolved and synthesized the conflicts and frustrations of the early decade. In so doing it had opened a new phase of his life: the president-maker, concerned with the strategies and tactics of domestic politics, was giving way to the political economist, set upon the goal of international bimetallism. The change was actually one of dimension or perspective, for Marble was by no means through with president-making. But it was still a change, and it had taken place during that silver summer. ✣

CHAPTER TWELVE

The Politics of Treasury Reports

As soon as he arrived home, Marble was off to Washington to report his findings. The last session of Congress had shown that the administration could expect trouble from the silverites in December, and the administration wanted to have its arguments ready. None was more anxious than Daniel Manning. Politics, not expertise, had made Manning secretary of the treasury, and he had come without the qualifications for drafting his report to Congress. Throughout the summer he had implored Marble to return early enough to help him.[1]

Marble found an interested audience. Bayard asked him to contribute a passage on the silver coinage for Cleveland's first message to Congress, and Manning received a promise of aid with his report. Marble then met with Speaker Carlisle to discuss committee appointments. He rounded out his visit by sending each member of Congress a pamphlet by Cernuschi containing his own card.[2]

Seemingly assured the role of chief financial adviser to the administration, Marble returned to New York and began drafting the messages. Convinced that international bimetallism was impossible at the moment, he hoped to persuade Congress to stop the silver coinage. He argued his case most fully in Manning's report, which went to Congress December 7.

Marble began by attributing American currency problems to the silver coinage and the continued circulation of $346 million in greenbacks. Without spelling out the problems, he went on to say that the necessary reforms could be effected without economic disturbance. Industry would not suffer, the dollar would remain stable, no new taxes would be needed, and nothing would stand in the way of a future treaty establishing international bimetallism. The reforms should excite no opposition, moreover, because all Americans agreed on the fundamentals of sound financial policy. All favored a paper money redeemable in coin; all favored using silver for subsidiary coinage. In this sense, all Americans were greenbackers and bimetallists. Their only differences were differences of degree.

The crucial issue at present was the silver coinage, and Marble employed Cernuschi's theory to argue against it. A workable bimetallism required a fixed ratio between gold and silver. But no one nation could establish a ratio for the rest of the world. Any nation not having the same ratio as the others would eventually lose one or the other of its money metals. Workable bimetallism required a "balance of demands," so that neither metal was in greater demand in one country than in another. Such a balance had existed in Europe prior to 1871, when Germany abandoned its silver coinage and forced France later to do the same. It was now the United States's turn.

Stopping the silver coinage, however, did not mean that the United States should demonetize silver. In addition to its fractional currency, the Treasury had issued $215 million in silver. Since these dollars were not receivable in Europe, since their commercial price was 20 to 25 percent less than their mint price, and since Congress should not be expected to withdraw them, they would have to remain as part of the country's money stock. "The fact, then, is that we cannot but be two-metallists."

If bimetallism was a fact in the United States, it was the responsibility of the government to guarantee that it operated effectively. Sound financial policy required that an "equivalence" be maintained between gold and silver. This, in fact, had been the historic goal of the American government. All currency legislation since 1792, Marble argued, had aimed at maintaining an equal demand for both metals. Even the Bland-Allison Act had maintained the tradition. Recognizing the "disparity" between gold and silver, it had limited the coinage of silver dollars and had made them inferior to gold dollars. Tradition, then, decreed that the $215 million in silver should be maintained at an equivalence with gold.

Marble believed this was possible if Congress discontinued further silver coinage. Businessmen and workingmen in all the large commercial cities, he declared, were calling for such a step. He urged Congress to heed their cries because "it is their interests first, and afterward the interests of the agricultural classes, which are endangered." Unless Congress acted, silver dollars would decline to their commercial value, a loss of 20 percent. Gold would then leave the country, and the United States would be forced on a silver standard. Congress, then, faced a choice between bimetallism and silver monometallism. He much preferred bimetallism.

Marble concluded with an appeal to the workingman. Some silverites had argued that an expanded currency would raise prices and create jobs. But, Marble wrote, prices responded not to legislation but to "the fluctuations of commodities and currencies in the markets of the world." International trade and labor-saving inventions, he argued, were indeed driving prices downward, but the decline had been neither sudden enough nor prolonged enough to create mass unemployment. It had actually been an "unmixed good" to the American workingman. If the silver coinage continued, prices would rise and wages would lose their purchasing power. "It is this gigantic sum, the wages of labor, which is assailed by every policy that would make the dollar of the fathers worth less than its worth in gold."[3]

Marble had used much the same reasoning in Cleveland's silver letter. He had appealed to the wisdom of the business classes and the interest of the workingman to stop the silver coinage. Still, there were significant differences. In the silver letter he had not suggested the possibility of international bimetallism and had written scornfully of the "eighty-five cent dollars" of the Bland-Allison Act. In the report he acknowledged the practicality of an international agreement and declared that an "equivalence" existed between the gold dollar and the silver dollars already coined. His European journey and his meeting with Cernuschi undoubtedly accounted for the first change. Probably his sense of practical politics accounted for the second. During his European mission, he had become optimistic about the prospects for repealing the Bland-Allison Act. Upon returning home, however, he found his hopes unwarranted. Manning thought the administration was making progress against the silverites, but not so much as Marble had seemed to think. "The worst is white," Manning had told him, "but the yellow also is dangerous and both should be avoided by all who wish to live long and reasonably happy lives."[4]

It soon became evident that Marble's conciliatory approach had not smoothed the road to repeal. Manning reported that many of the silver congressmen remained "emphatically and dogmatically firm—perhaps stubborn is a better word."[5]

So Marble decided that strong administration leadership was needed. On December 11 he urged Bayard to have Cleveland lead a crusade against the Bland-Allison Act. He was disgusted that some advisers believed the president ought not to interfere. "I will go along," he declared, "with any theory of the disjunction of Executive and Legislative power which leaves the President free to save his Administration and his party from wreck, and the country from a return to its Republican vomit, by using every ounce of his patronage and every hour of his time, and every atom of his moral and political force, in stopping the coinage now."[6]

But Cleveland would not lead. Faced with rising belligerence from the silverites and divided counsels from his cabinet, he publicly adopted the ultralegalistic stance of a powerless spectator and allowed the congressional Democrats to fight out the issue among themselves. Rapidly the situation in Congress deteriorated as various representatives put forward plans for currency reform. To the veteran politician Manning, it seemed as though the Democracy was about to collapse. "Our people in the House are all abroad on pretty much everything of importance to the administration," he confessed to Marble, "There is great lack of discipline. . . . I have not lost hope, but I certainly feel uncomfortable."[7]

If Cleveland would not lead the party, Marble decided to find someone who would. Secretary Manning was the obvious choice. Manning's political experience and sagacity were beyond question. There was also no doubt that he relied heavily upon Marble's advice. Indeed, theirs seemed a perfect partnership: Marble's intellect and skill in using ideas as political weapons combined with Manning's strategic office in the administration and instinctive sense of political reality.

If the administration was to repeal the Bland-Allison Act, it would need arguments and allies, and Marble believed that sound arguments were the only safe way to win them. His European trip and his thorough study of the subject had confirmed his belief that financial questions were best answered by experts. If this presented difficulties in a democracy, which permitted expression of many points of view, it also presented an opportunity. Equipped with a precise understanding of the issue, the expert could cut through the confusion of uninformed debate, and by the clarity and invulnerability of his argument, set the controversy to rest. As the swallow-tail Democrats of the Manhattan Club had sought to free their city from the grip of "irresponsible majorities," so the experts would restore unity and rationality to a divided and impassioned nation.[8]

Marble needed only the proper occasion to test his assumption. When Bland pushed through a resolution calling upon the secretary of the treasury to state his future silver policy, he believed his chance had arrived. He would prepare a reply that answered the arguments of the silverites and sustained the administration. Since it would come from Manning alone, it would place the secretary at the head of the administration. In a long letter to Sidney Webster he set forth his plans. "I have, of course," he began, "a most disinterested judgment in the matter, and no desire but to serve Mr. Manning, the cause and the party." Confessing that he had "resented bitterly" President Cleveland's course, he declared that he aimed at stopping the silver coinage and giving Manning "the most advantage" from it. Marble believed the silver controversy had arisen basically from the ambitions of western Democrats to destroy the power of "New York and the East." A "cool and conciliatory" argument, which undercut the position of the westerners and offered a sound and reasonable alternative, would be the best possible response.[9]

When Marble first proposed his strategy to Manning, the secretary opposed it, fearing it would only widen the split in the party. The western Democrats, he warned, were "as wild as Texas steers" on the silver issue. "I don't think that at your distance you can fully appreciate the heat of their tempers." But Marble kept hammering away, and finally Manning gave in. He would show the report to Cleveland

and would fight against any "mutilation," but he imagined he "already felt black and blue all over from the blows that are to come."[10]

On March 2 Manning sent the report to Congress. Although it answered a number of specific questions posed by the Bland resolution, its purpose was to justify the administration's attack on the Bland-Allison Act. Marble had decided to begin by giving the silverites an elementary course in monetary policy. Under existing law the Treasury had to choose between a forced circulation of silver and a forced accumulation of silver. To increase the circulation of silver dollars, the Treasury would have to force out of circulation other dollars: gold coins, greenbacks, and national bank notes. Silver circulated in one-dollar denominations, which the Treasury could not arbitrarily increase without affecting the other denominations. "Ones can be forced to do the work of tens, . . . and if the ones are forced into an unnatural use, the tens heaping up in the [Treasury] will practically measure the violence." Thus, forcing a large circulation of silver dollars would bring the country to a silver standard. This, of course, was no solution to the problem.

The alternative, forced accumulation of silver, was scarcely better. Forced accumulation required an annual tax on the American people of $24 million to purchase the silver. Postulating that a reduction in federal taxes unaccompanied by the elimination of the $24 million for silver purchases would also force the country to a silver standard, Marble argued that forced accumulation would preclude any tax reduction.

The report also opposed paying the national debt with the silver reserve. If the Treasury paid out all its cash reserves to cancel the debt, little would actually be accomplished. From 1877 to 1885 the debt had been reduced by $683 million, and further payments could reduce it by only an additional $65 million. Instead, Congress should stop the silver coinage and use its silver reserves to redeem the greenbacks.

Once this had been accomplished, the government could establish a truly bimetallic currency. "There is one way, and only one," the report maintained, "by which silver can be restored to its old ratio and value, namely, an international concert upon a common ratio with open mints to both metals at that ratio." Such a concert required the participation of the United States because the American ratio of 16:1 differed from the European ratio of 15.5:1. It was necessary, too, because the Bland-Allison Act permitted Europeans to believe they might one day be allowed to sell their depreciated silver to the United States in return for gold. American participation in an international bimetallic union would dispel this belief.

The report went on to attack the "delusion" that "the Government has authority to fix the amount of the people's currency." Government could only establish a unit of value and insure that all coins truly represented that value. The amount of the money, however, should be determined by nature. If nature was allowed to regulate the money supply, a bimetallic currency would be sound and stable.[11]

Marble hoped the report would silence the silverites and reunite the Democracy. For a time it seemed to be doing its job. A week after its publication, Manning reported that it had not split the party and was appearing to work "like a soothing potion." He reported also that though he seemed not to approve of it, Cleveland had allowed it to go to Congress unchanged. When debate on a free coinage bill opened on March 20, he assured Marble that the administration was stronger than at any time since the opening of the session.[12]

In the midst of the debate, Marble's plans suffered a serious blow. On March 23 Manning suffered a stroke. So seriously was he affected that some feared for his life. Although he survived, he had to give up the duties of his office and only Cleveland's refusal to accept his resignation kept him in the cabinet at all. The event brought Marble great sorrow. He had developed a warm personal affection for Manning, in whom he had found "a fine quality and strength of character." Now, however, Manning's life and career seemed shattered and with them Marble's own plans and hopes. "How much," he regretfully wrote, "hung upon that plain man's life and strength—now shipwrecked." Nor were things helped when a majority of House Democrats voted for the free coinage bill.[13]

Despite his sorrow, Marble's spirit and resolve remained firm. That summer, as he traveled in Europe with Abby, he continued to urge the administration to take a strong stand on the currency issue. Writing to Bayard in July, he declared that Congress had proposed no legislation that "the President ought not to rejoice at the chance of vetoing." Regretting that the Democracy had not committed itself to currency reform during the presidential campaign, he again urged the secretary of state to support a policy of "Thorough." Washington seemed to him the only capital holding the power "to restore the price of silver to its old ratio with gold, and bring back the monetary peace of the world."[14]

While he exhorted the administration, Marble also sought to rebuild his forces. By the end of the summer his old friend Sidney Webster had persuaded Manning to remain as secretary of the treasury. Marble then approached the influential House leader, William R. Morrison. It had become obvious that the administration needed leadership in Congress, and as chairman of the House Ways and Means Committee, Morrison seemed well placed to provide it.

For other reasons Morrison was an attractive man to approach. He and Marble had known one another well, having fought ten years for tariff reductions. Although a westerner, he opposed the silverites and had tried to cooperate with Manning and Marble to head them off. Realizing their strength in the House, he had proposed a compromise strategy, whereby the administration would agree to reduce the Treasury surplus by paying off the national debt in silver dollars, thus putting more silver into circulation without creating strong inflationary pressures. Manning had favored the proposal, but Marble, convinced that a sound dose of expertise would bring Congress to its senses, had rejected it.[15]

The experience of the first session, however, convinced Marble of the wisdom of some compromise strategy. So on December 3 he indirectly opened negotiations in a letter to Morrison's wife. Hoping to strike a spark of ambition in his subject, he asserted that New York was still the "pivotal state" in national politics and that Morrison would have to show himself to be "a satisfactory candidate to New York, whether in the first place or the second place . . . on the next national ticket." To establish a national reputation Morrison would have to win some dramatic personal victory in Congress. First, he should "ally himself with Secretary Manning" and fight for the proposals in his forthcoming Treasury report (which Marble and Sidney Webster were preparing). Next, he should accomplish a modest tariff reform. Marble believed a wholesale attack on the tariff would fail, so he suggested that Morrison aim at eliminating the woolens duties, which taxed the clothing of the American people. After that, he should attack the silver coinage, even at the risk of a floor fight. This would demonstrate his soundness to the easterners who would determine the party candidates in 1888. Finally, he should attack the Treasury surplus by calling for repeal of the laws allowing the issue and reissue of the greenbacks. Then the Treasury could expend its surplus to retire the greenbacks. This, once again, would satisfy the easterners and all other supporters of sound money.

Marble argued that the political situation required such a course of action. He especially emphasized the importance of organized labor. The Knights of Labor had supported Morrison's attack on the surplus but had opposed his attack on the tariff. Marble hoped a reduction of the woolens duties would allow Morrison to embody "the hostilities of corporate capital in the eyes of the wage-earners, corporate capital seeking to use taxation by tariffs for its selfish aggrandizement." Morrison's efforts for sound finance would please the capitalists. Marble feared only the West. If the West did not accept Morrison's leadership, "it's a bad lookout for them and him and all of us."[16]

By the time Morrison received the letter, Marble and Webster had finished Manning's second annual report. As Marble indicated, the report laid the ground for a new political departure. To preserve party unity while maintaining eastern leadership, it tried to synthesize the objectives of both East and West. It began by calling for repeal of the Bland-Allison Act and for a declaration favoring international bimetallism. It went on to propose a formula to combine reduction of the treasury surplus, lower tariff rates, and the elimination of the greenbacks. Reducing the treasury surplus by paying off the national debt would prove costly and inequitable, since it would force the Treasury to bid in the open market for bonds not due until 1891 and 1907. These bonds were circulating at premiums of 11 percent and 28 percent, respectively, so their retirement would benefit only a small class of bondholders while requiring that all Americans pay heavy taxes. Instead, the Treasury should reduce the surplus by replacing the $346 million in greenbacks with silver certificates, and if necessary, gold certificates.

While greenback retirement proceeded, the government would be able to reduce taxes, largely by modifying its tariff rates. Avoiding the stigma of free trade, which would have alienated the high tariff wing of the Democracy, Marble and Webster proposed to abolish only those tariffs that injured American foreign trade. This meant abolishing tariffs on raw materials. Such tariffs raised production costs and kept American manufacturers from competing in world markets. Once they had been eliminated, trade, production, wages, and employment would increase. At this point the report opened the door for Morrison's appeal to the American worker. To compete effectively in world markets, American manufacturers would have to pay high wages, for high wages attracted the most efficient workers, who in turn produced the most valuable goods. When high wages were paid, the percentage labor cost actually declined. Tariff reform also meant lower prices for life's necessities. Here the report focused on the raw wool tariff, which it claimed nearly doubled the cost of clothing. It saw no reason to withhold the benefits of free wool from sixty million Americans and called for the repeal of the duty.

The report was a masterful effort to unite the Democracy behind its eastern leadership. Silverites were promised free coinage of silver by international agreement, if they repealed the Bland-Allison Act. Those concerned about the Treasury surplus were promised satisfaction, if they agreed to retire the greenbacks. Workingmen were told their wages would be raised, if they supported lower tariffs and an expanded foreign trade. And behind the scenes, a western Democrat had been told that he would emerge as his party's new leader if he called for an end to taxes on the clothing of sixty million Americans.[17]

But as so often in the past, Marble's plans went awry. As the second session wore on, it became apparent that Morrison would not follow his advice. Indeed, he seemed anxious merely to serve out his term and then to retire to private life. Soon after the publication of the report, Marble learned that Morrison opposed linking surplus reduction to greenback retirement and that many other Democratic leaders shared his view. He also learned that no one contemplated tariff reform. In the House, Samuel J. Randall led the protectionists on a crusade to reduce the internal revenue taxes, thus diverting attention from the tariff. By mid-January even Morrison had given up the idea of tariff reduction. "The Protectionists command the game," Manning informed Marble, "which will open when they choose to call it." When the Congress adjourned, it had accomplished nothing.[18]

While the session was running its unproductive course, Marble's plans suffered an even more devastating blow. Still in feeble health and no longer strong enough to fight Marble's battles, Manning decided to retire from office. His imminent resignation distressed not only Marble but also Cleveland, who feared that Marble would use the occasion to attack his administration. Realizing the need for care, the president enlisted the services of a long-time Tildenite, Smith M. Weed.

Weed visited Manning and found that the secretary would not resign unless Marble approved his letter. Manning urged Weed to travel to New York to confer with Marble, and Cleveland agreed that he should go. Upon arriving, Weed found that Cleveland's fears were justified. Marble greeted him with a draft, which, according to Weed, would be unacceptable to Cleveland. After an all-night session, Weed returned to Washington with a draft, which still "cast several reflections upon the treatment of Mr. Manning by the President." Cleveland refused to accept it, and even Manning thought it contained several things that "had better be left out." So Weed returned to New York for another all-night session with Marble, another trip to Washington, another rejection, and another return to New York. On the third try he and Marble worked out a satisfactory draft, which Cleveland and Manning accepted with only one minor change. Perhaps Marble would have held out indefinitely if Weed and Manning had not urged him to complete a satisfactory draft as quickly as possible.[19]

The final draft cast no aspersions upon the administration. Omitting any comment on the policies of the president or his treatment of Manning, it merely declared that the duties of the secretary's office were too onerous and expressed the hope that Manning might continue "to follow [our party's] fortunes under your successful guidance, with a fellow-citizen's loyal pride." Cleveland smugly accepted it with "deepest regret."[20]

Although the resignation was a serious loss, Marble still hoped that Cleveland would name a satisfactory replacement. Even as he and Weed were struggling with Manning's letter, he was writing that "I do think the 'Old Guard' ought to unite upon a wise and practicable choice, stand shoulder to shoulder with . . . Manning, and by his and Whitney's aid, control the succession." In a postscript he concluded: "You cannot afford to fail."[21]

Perhaps Marble thought of himself as Manning's successor. Manning urged Cleveland to consider him, and there was some newspaper speculation that he would receive the position. Cleveland, however, would not consider Marble for a minute. His choice was Assistant Secretary Charles S. Fairchild.[22]

Fairchild's nomination encouraged Marble. Although not so well known in New York politics as either Manning or Marble, Fairchild had come up in the party as a loyal Tildenite and had served as Tilden's attorney general. He had no sooner taken his place than Marble was making overtures to him.

But Fairchild did not respond. His ties to the Tilden organization were in fact much weaker than Marble suspected. Primarily a businessman, he brought to his position an independence from partisanship that neither Marble nor Manning could have understood. A member of New York's Reform Club, he moved in the society of such independents as R. R. Bowker, Walter Hines Page, Richard Watson Gilder, E. L. Godkin, and George W. Curtis. He also bore Cleveland a personal loyalty and affection that Marble had never shared. Marble soon learned that he would be writing no more treasury reports.[23]

After Fairchild's appointment, Cleveland moved decisively to free himself from the Tilden organization. Carefully, he minimized the influence of the Tildenites without provoking an open split in the Democracy. His handling of Marble clearly illustrates his methods.

The summer of 1887 once again found Marble traveling in Europe, caring for his wife and acquiring more information on the prospects for international bimetallism. Before leaving he had told Bayard that he would keep abreast of the silver issue in Europe and would report anything "new or opportune." On August 30 he cabled Barlow that he had an "important suggestion" to offer the secretary of state. He was dismayed to learn, however, that the administration had already sent Edward Atkinson, a Mugwump, to sound out European opinion. Bayard complimented Marble on his "most excellent service" in 1885 and expressed confidence that Marble would continue to advise him on the subject "in a spirit of friendly fidelity." He was so confident of Marble's good faith, in fact, that he felt he no longer had "any *official* hold on him."[24]

In smaller ways Marble also came to realize that he was outside the administration's councils. Shortly after Manning's resignation, Congress created a federal judgeship in New York, and soon the two leading candidates for the appointment were Barlow's son, Olin, and William C. Whitney's former assistant, E. Henry Lacombe. The contest mirrored in microcosm the struggle for influence in the administration. Barlow represented the Tilden organization and Lacombe represented the County Democracy, a reform organization which included Whitney and Cleveland's personal friend, Francis Lynde Stetson. As Barlow's dearest friend, Marble worked hard for Olin's appointment, as did Manning and Tilden's one-time state chairman, Daniel Magone. During the contest, Marble's confidence in Whitney began to fade, and he began to complain bitterly of the

"Whitney-Stetson clique of County Democrats." With Manning no longer in the cabinet, he confessed "great solicitude" about the administration's course. Barlow shared his fears. "With Fairchild in the Treasury," he complained, "the State of New York is surrendered to Whitney and a mess he will make of it." Their fears were confirmed when after three months of maneuvering the appointment went to Lacombe. Marble tried to console Barlow by suggesting that Olin had escaped the controversy "unharmed and even advantaged." But in the next sentence he confessed that "the judicial habit of mind is the best of disciplines and possessions, in a world of ambitions and strifes."[25]

It was left to Cleveland to deliver the *coup de grâce* to Marble in his December message to Congress. Marble had always believed currency reform the most important administration project, and by the fall of 1887 his belief was as strong as ever. Upon returning to America, he conferred with Bayard about the advisability of sending another representative to Europe. Apparently at Bayard's request, he prepared a memorandum for Cleveland, rehearsing Cernuschi's monetary theory and suggesting that repeal of the Bland-Allison Act be deferred until the British Royal Commission on Gold and Silver had filed its report. Marble believed such a passage in Cleveland's annual message would hold off the silverites and enable the administration to work out an international bimetallic agreement by secret diplomacy.[26]

In fact, Marble believed the time had arrived for the United States to act decisively on behalf of international bimetallism, because Britain was moving toward bimetallism. Early in 1887 George Goschen had become chancellor of the exchequer. Believing that Goschen favored bimetallism and that he would help to "dictate or supervise the report of the majority of the Commission," Marble urged the administration to appoint another confidential envoy to pressure him by threatening the immediate repeal of the Bland-Allison Act. "The real fear today," he believed, "is that by our repeal of the Bland law, all the annual silver output will go to the London market, knock-down heavily the price of silver, double England's difficulties with the Indian budget and exports, and widen more the present disparity between the legal rating and the melting-pot value of the enormous coined silver stocks of European nations." If the administration moved rapidly it could influence the royal commission's report and bring Great Britain to bimetallism. Poised for action and perhaps hoping to undertake the confidential mission himself, Marble awaited the administration's reply.[27]

It came on December 6. In one stroke Cleveland dashed Marble's hopes. Ignoring currency reform entirely, he devoted his message to tariff reform. His daring and dramatic act immediately focused national attention upon the tariff and left Marble isolated and helpless.

As he watched the public response to the message, Marble could not suppress his bitterness. "Tariff-talk and tariff act with no profit to man or party is doubtless more important in Washington," he complained to Barlow, "than a treaty which the Senate would approve unanimously and the House confirm by legislation needed, unanimously."[28]

Had Marble been wholly a man of principle, he might well have broken with the administration; for he had been totally rebuffed. Years in politics, however, had given his conscience a certain elasticity. They had also taught him the realities of political power. Thus he knew that however many headlines Cleveland might capture with his tariff message, the president could not hope to be reelected without the support of the powerful New York Democracy. By 1887 many members of the Tilden organization had grown hostile to Cleveland, and rumors were afloat that Governor David B. Hill was thinking of contesting the president for the nomination. Even if Cleveland could overcome Hill, the prospect of a close, hard-fought election dictated that he pacify the New York leaders. These facts indicated that sooner or later Cleveland would have to approach the Tilden organization. It would be then that Marble would try to win back his lost influence and prestige.[29]

The opportunity came on May 27, 1888, when Whitney approached Marble about helping draft the party platform. "The situation," Whitney wrote, "needs formulating by an able hand such as you carry about with you." Marble hurriedly accepted the invitation and was on his way to Washington. When he arrived, he found that Cleveland had decided to modify his tariff stand. Hoping to avoid a party split, he was seeking to cover up the issue. The congressional session had embarrassed him when Roger Q. Mills, Democratic chairman of the House Ways and Means Committee, had attempted to remove protection from northeastern industry while protecting southern agriculture. If the Democracy went to the country with the Mills Bill in its platform, it would face certain defeat in key northeastern states.[30]

Hoping to work out a satisfactory platform, Cleveland had assembled John G. Carlisle, Arthur Pue Gorman, Whitney, and Marble. Each man represented a key faction in the Democracy. Carlisle was a low-tariff westerner and Gorman a high-tariff easterner; Whitney was a County Democrat and Marble a Tilden Democrat. These were the factions that needed to be reconciled if the president was to be reelected. For two days they worked on the platform. When they had finally agreed, Marble drafted the document for transmission to the national convention. The draft reaffirmed the party's platform of 1884 and pledged its devotion to "individual liberty, political equality, and impartial laws." Under the last heading, it discussed the protective tariff. Pointing out that "ninety-four percent" of "the industrious freemen of our land" received no higher price for their products as a result of "tax laws," it charged that those same people paid higher prices for many goods because of "tax laws." The mounting Treasury surplus showed the amount of unnecessary taxation. The Republican solution to the surplus was to increase appropriations. The Democratic solution was "to enforce frugality in public expense, and abolish unnecessary taxation." Colorless almost to the point of invisibility, the plank did not endorse Cleveland's tariff message, and in fact did not even mention the word "tariff."[31]

Although Marble did not attend the Democratic convention, he kept in touch with the proceedings via Gorman. He also lent his support by urging Henry Watterson and Richard Croker to cooperate with Gorman in writing the platform. The result was another disaster. In hot pursuit of his "star-eyed goddess" of tariff reform, Watterson refused to accept the administration's plank. Arguing through the night against the sacrifice of principle, he persuaded the platform committee to endorse Cleveland's tariff message and specifically to cite "tariff reform" as the central issue of the campaign. To make matters worse, in a separate resolution the convention approved the Mills Bill. Although much of the platform followed Marble's draft, the central issue had been thoroughly altered. "The change in the platform was so great," Gorman confessed to Marble, "that you could hardly recognize it."[32]

Marble took little part in the campaign. The summer heat once again dictated a trip to Europe with Abby. Before leaving he used his position as president of the Manhattan Club to have his platform draft adopted as the club's resolutions and distributed throughout the country. Then, expressing confidence in Cleveland's reelection, he sailed for Europe. Soon he was in southern Britain, relaxing in its fair climate, marveling at its scenery and history, and incidentally suggesting the need for a special mission to deal with the currency question.[33]

The news of Cleveland's defeat startled him and caused him to reconsider his political course. There was no doubt that he would continue to support international bimetallism. With tariff reform discredited, the way seemed clear to promote the currency question. But how was he going to promote it? Of his political allies, Tilden and Manning were gone and Barlow, too old to take an active role in politics, had but a year to live. Henry Watterson was still active, but he controlled no organization and was too wedded to tariff reform. The old Tilden organization was collapsing, and no one seemed capable of saving it. "We have too much neglected the building up of young men," Marble had remarked to Bayard in 1886. Now, in 1888, he found himself squarely confronted with that reality.[34]

Capable young men were about; but for Marble they had little appeal. William C. Whitney, for example, seemed to be reaching the height of his political career. But, though Marble and Whitney had maintained superficially cordial relations, Marble could not really trust the secretary of the navy. If, during the months following the election, Marble considered the possibility of joining with Whitney, the phrase "Whitney-Stetson clique" undoubtedly flickered in his memory and aroused suspicions about Whitney's reliability.[35]

If Marble had his doubts about Whitney and the other County Democrats, he positively loathed the Mugwumps. Throughout most of Cleveland's terms, he had been willing to accept the Mugwumps as allies because of their contribution to Cleveland's election. Late in 1887, however, his attitude began to change as it became apparent that the Mugwumps were opposed to international bimetallism. It also injured his pride to have the administration send Edward Atkinson to investigate international bimetallism when he was anxious for the assignment himself. When Atkinson reported, contrary to his findings, that the European states contemplated no major changes in financial policy, Marble's anger blazed. In a thousand-word letter to Barlow he answered Atkinson point-for-point, declaring that Atkinson did "not know this matter and naturally proclaims that that does not exist which he has not the trained vision to see." Marble also worried about the effects of Atkinson's report, since "Atkinson and his school of opinion have no political importance. . . . There is a shadow of danger [he concluded] that Atkinson and the *Post* are politically just clumsy babes enough to invite the return of past trouble."[36]

Marble's complaint against the Mugwumps, therefore, was twofold: they lacked expertise and political sense. Writing to Barlow, he declared: "White, Wells, Perry . . . and Godkin have never *studied* the silver question deeply nor have their economic studies been in a department which has equipped them for its successful study. Atkinson with still more genius than any of them has had still less training and least of the most requisite kind." He especially objected to the Mugwumps' belief that government policy could not affect the price of silver. So long as the market price of silver remained low, the Mugwumps treated the silver dollar as merely another kind of *fiat* money. Since Marble shared Cernuschi's opinion that international bimetallism would fix the price of silver at the legal ratio, he was forced to rate the Mugwumps weak in economic science.[37]

Marble deeply resented the Mugwumps' political meddling. Although he had had his moments of independence, Marble had spent most of his political career as an organization man. By 1887 he could not think of political principles apart from the organizations that were necessary to enact them. But the Mugwumps seemed to pride themselves on their independence from party and their devotion to principle. In Marble's eyes this made them contemptible creatures. Adopting the attitude of many of his era's professional politicians, he savagely attacked them. In an unpublished memorandum written during the campaign, he referred to the Mugwumps as "that chicken-livered breed" that saw national politics through a "pin-hole."[38]

So Marble knew whom he was against. But whom was he for? Two years earlier he had turned to a western congressman in an effort to provide the Democracy with a new kind of doughface leadership, a western man with eastern principles. Now he decided to employ the same strategy in an appeal to John G. Carlisle of Kentucky. Carlisle seemed an excellent choice. In 1889 the congressman was at the height of his political career, having served two terms as Speaker of the House. Although known most widely as a tariff reformer and supporter of the Mills Bill, he had also favored international bimetallism. Although most popular in the West, he had worked consistently for party unity. It was acknowledged that when the Fifty-first Congress assembled he would lead the Democratic minority.[39]

On December 23, 1889, Marble sent Carlisle a long letter, setting forth his plans. "There is possible, in my opinion," he began, "a sound and final solution of the silver question in which you but only you might lead the bulk of our party in Congress, obtain at any rate the support of a majority of both houses of Congress and avoid the veto of the Executive." The solution would benefit "all the mints and markets of both hemispheres," while rescuing the Democracy from its low-tariff trap. The party had lost the last election with the tariff as its issue, and for the next six to ten years Republican control of the Senate would block any tariff reform. If the party continued to emphasize tariff reform, it would merely tie itself to a futile and losing cause. "Must we all, you likewise," he wrote, but then crossed out, "take the vows of obedience, self-denial, and chastity?"

If Carlisle was willing to lead the party on the currency question, Marble had a specific plan to propose. He believed the silver issue should be raised during the second session of Congress, after the Republican majority had shown itself incapable of carrying out a sound currency reform. This would give the Democrats a claim to greater competence in the field and would help to determine the party's presidential candidate in 1892. Marble then slyly suggested that Carlisle might well be that candidate. Of course Carlisle would need the support of New York, and that would be difficult to obtain against both Cleveland and Governor David B. Hill. But Marble thought it could be achieved. If Carlisle was willing to play Cleveland and Hill off against each other, he could create a deadlock in the convention and open the door for his own nomination.

Marble was wise enough to realize that Carlisle might not respond to such an appeal. He knew, in fact, that the former Speaker favored Cleveland's renomination. So he closed his paragraph on tactics by proposing that Carlisle publish a letter inviting Cleveland to join him in the fight for currency reform. Marble probably believed that

Cleveland would have to follow initiatives taken by the party's congressional leaders. "You alone," he wrote, "*now* have the opportunity of an immense public service, and I am glad to believe that you cannot, will not, shirk your work, let whoever may hereafter bear off the palm."[40]

In later years Marble must have looked back on his letter with a certain ironic satisfaction. He had accurately forecast the rise of the silver issue in national politics and had urged his party to be the first to take advantage of it. Only one event marred his strategy. He had feared that the currency issue might arise during the first session of Congress. That would require "a more difficult and inconvenient choice in respect to New York's cooperation." As the session progressed, the issue did arise, and the Republican majority met it with the Sherman Silver Purchase Act.

The Silver Purchase Act did not dismay him so much, however, as did Carlisle's failure to respond to his letter. The Kentuckian received the letter, but misplaced it and did not find it again for eighteen months. Thus, as the silver controversy in Congress dragged into the summer of 1890, Marble decided upon an alternative plan of action. Late in August he interrupted his vacation in Switzerland long enough to send off another long letter, this time to Governor David B. Hill.[41] ✣

CHAPTER THIRTEEN

Making Issues and Winning Delegates

As everyone knew, David Bennett Hill was a professional politician. His had not been the kind of career to inspire public enthusiasm; it boasted no striking accomplishments, no fiery crusades, no acts of daring or of innovation. Examined closely, it revealed only the details of professional politics: distributing patronage, looking after the rank and file members, defending the party officeholders, ridiculing the opposition, getting out the vote, organizing caucuses and conventions; seeing all the while that his party lost no advantage. It was enough for Hill. By his own design the voters knew him best by the slogan, "I am a Democrat."

And Hill had good reason to be satisfied with his career, for it had taken him a long way. In 1882, ten years of loyal service to the Tilden organization won him the Democratic nomination for lieutenant governor behind Grover Cleveland. When Cleveland resigned to assume the presidency, he succeeded to the governorship and to the leadership of the Tilden organization. Skillfully, he used his talents to strengthen his party and to win election as governor in his own right. His support of labor legislation and opposition to prohibition satisfied the voters, while his deft patronage distribution and opposition to ballot reform satisfied the party managers. With the election of 1888, which coupled his own reelection with Cleveland's defeat, he became presidential timber.

As a presidential candidate, however, Hill had important weaknesses. Mugwump independents recoiled from his reputation as a spoilsman and his identification with certain unsavory scandals. Cleveland Democrats disliked his patronage policies. And both noted his lack of personal magnetism and his failure to identify himself with any national issue. By 1890 it was all too easy to dismiss him as just another political hack.[1]

But Hill's liabilities were Marble's opportunities. If Hill was a spoilsman, Marble knew the advantages of spoils politics. If Hill was opposed to Cleveland, so was Marble. If Hill championed no national cause, Marble did. If the Mugwumps distrusted Hill, Marble distrusted the Mugwumps. Like Daniel Manning before him, Hill presented just the sort of opportunity Marble was looking for.

Primarily Marble hoped to promote international bimetallism. By the summer of 1890, he was convinced that only the United States could accomplish the great reform. For a time he had hoped that Great Britain would lead the movement. Shortly after Cleveland's defeat, the Royal Commission on Gold and Silver had published its final report. While not recommending that Britain adopt bimetallism, it had accepted Cernuschi's theory that prior to 1873 France had maintained the ratio between gold and silver. On the wisdom of calling another international conference, the commission had divided six to six, but even the dissenters had recommended a conference to expand the use of silver. To Marble and Cernuschi, the report seemed a turning point, indicating at last that Britain was willing to initiate moves on behalf of bimetallism. Time now appeared to be on their side.[2]

Throughout 1889 Marble and Cernuschi waited hopefully for Britain to follow the report with more positive action. But Parliament refused to act. Apparently the British hoped the report would inspire other nations, most likely France or the United States, to take the lead. The final blow fell in April 1890, when Chancellor of the Exchequer George Goschen came out against silver coinage. The door had been shut on any future conference; it was necessary to develop a new strategy. Marble and Cernuschi set to work, and by June they had decided that in the absence of a European initiative, the United States would have to take the lead by establishing free coinage at 15.5:1. The United States would fill the role France had occupied prior to 1873, linking together the "free gold coinages of nations bordering the North Atlantic Seas and the free silver coinages of the rest of the world."

To accomplish this, however, the United States would have to change its current 16:1 ratio. As usual, Marble believed that Congress could be convinced. The change would prevent silver from leaving the country for Europe's higher price. It would grant a profit of 3 percent to all holders of silver coins. It would eliminate the $24 million in taxes annually collected for silver purchases. It would safeguard free bimetallic coinage by encouraging European countries to join in the change.

It was also the only course that was politically feasible. Marble formulated his proposal during the congressional debates over the Silver Purchase Bill. Closely following the progress of the bill, Marble and Cernuschi concluded that it was little better than the Bland-Allison Act and hoped that eastern Senators and Representatives would defeat it. The easterners, however, would approve free coinage at 15.5:1 because that would satisfy both western demands for more money and eastern demands for a dollar equivalent at home and abroad to the present gold dollar. President Harrison also would approve, since Secretary of State Blaine had long favored international bimetallism.[3]

Congress, however, refused to live up to his predictions. After a summer of debate, it passed the Silver Purchase Bill, and Harrison signed it July 14. The law required the secretary of the treasury to purchase each month 4,500 ounces of silver at the market price, issuing certificates of legal tender in their place. Although it provided for free coinage when the price of silver rose to the coining ratio, it did not establish free coinage. Nor did it seem likely that free coinage would ever result from it. Shortly after it went into effect, speculators, who had been hoarding silver in anticipation of its passage, dumped a sufficient amount on the market to send the price to a new low. But Marble did not wait to see the actual operation of the law. Two weeks after it went into effect, he began his correspondence with Hill.[4]

Before the summer of 1890, Marble and Hill had known little of each other. Marble's papers show no correspondence with Hill until that time. Marble doubtlessly knew of Hill's accomplishments and may have met him at some earlier time. There is no evidence to suggest, however, that the two had collaborated before that summer. Marble's letter shows only that Hill began the correspondence by asking his advice about the coming fall campaign.[5]

Marble believed the New York Democrats should enter the campaign with a well-formulated statement of principle, such as he had prepared for Tilden in the years from 1873 to 1876. Probing Hill's presidential ambition, he implied that the governor ought to look upon the campaign as the first of a series of steps toward the presidential nomination.

The first step should be to divert attention from Cleveland. Since the campaign of 1888 had identified Cleveland with the tariff, Marble thought Hill should treat that issue delicately. Hill could not afford to ignore the issue, lest the work of tariff reformers in Congress be interpreted as a Cleveland boom. Hill should treat it differently from Cleveland. Noting that Republican control of the Senate precluded any thoroughgoing tariff reform until the turn of the century, Marble suggested the issue be demoted in significance.

Once the tariff had been cast in its proper perspective, Hill should deal extensively with the silver question. Although the party had already thrown away one chance to pass a sound silver bill, events were pushing the country toward true bimetallism. The platform of the Farmers' Alliance, the condition of the Treasury, and the problems of taxation all showed that "monetary as well as financial questions will be pivotal in the politics of the next Presidential election." It was imperative, therefore, that the governor seize the issue and use it to its greatest political advantage. Hill should become the leading Democratic spokesman for bimetallism. "A New York Democrat dealing with these controlling issues now," Marble declared, "has the immense advantage that this time the West is right, and the East more than half persuaded." Hill could satisfy both sections and win much for himself in the process.[6]

Marble enclosed a draft of a public statement for Hill to issue in launching the fall campaign. The first two-thirds contained an indictment of Republican policies, which it declared had perpetuated the record of fraud begun in 1876. It charged the Republicans with purchasing votes in the last presidential election, rigging the federal census to increase their electoral vote, arbitrarily deciding contested elections for partisan purposes, and seeking to impose a Force Bill upon southern states and northern cities. Seeking to use the tariff issue to win support from the merchants of the East and the farmers of the South and West, it charged the Harrison administration with enhancing "the price of everything our farmers buy, but not the price of anything they sell" and with sweeping "our shipping off the high seas" to give "protection" to less than 7 percent of the American people. It further charged the administration with piling up a huge surplus to feed their corruption funds and increasing the national debt by issuing $54 million in new greenbacks.

The statement closed with a detailed indictment of Republican monetary policies. Instead of returning the country to hard money, the administration had merely created a "new-fangled legal tender" with its Silver Purchase Act. Instead of establishing free bimetallic coinage, it had sought only to withdraw silver from the commercial market. Moreover, it had continued to coin silver at 16:1, dimming the prospects of international bimetallism, setting the stage for future conflict over coinage ratios, and giving Europe the opportunity to profit from recoinage. It was the duty of all citizens to prevent further crimes and disasters.[7]

Marble waited nearly a month before receiving a reply. With pleasure he read Hill's words: "I am convinced after serious reflection and consultation with others whose advice I respect, that your suggestions are sound and that the ideas contained in your discussion of the silver question are both wise and timely."[8]

While Marble remained in Europe, Hill, true to his word, sought to follow his new mentor's advice. On September 23 he opened the Democratic campaign by issuing the manifesto of the state committee and delivering a speech in Brooklyn. The manifesto attacked various features of Republican misrule, emphasizing the McKinley Tariff and the Force Bill. The speech repeated the themes of the manifesto and added an extensive attack on the Silver Purchase Act, using much of the material Marble had provided in his August draft. To attract national attention Hill spent the last two weeks of the campaign stumping through other states.[9]

Marble arrived home in the wake of an overwhelming Democratic success. The congressional elections had produced a Democratic House and a nearly Democratic Senate. In New York the party had won the Assembly by such a large margin that it would be able to name the next United States Senator. The party could look into the future with real hopes of winning back the presidency.

Marble at once set to work. Now he believed Hill should speak out boldly, identifying himself with public sentiment on the great issues of the day. Reading the election returns as a repudiation of the acts of the last Congress, Marble urged Hill to demand that the outgoing Congress repeal its tariff and currency laws. To get the issues into the open he drafted a resolution for Hill to present to the state legislature in January.[10]

It soon became apparent, however, that Hill would have to do more than merely identify himself with great issues; for a serious problem at once developed over naming the next United States senator. The state election had given the Democrats a majority of two votes in the state legislature. Because of this, the selection of a candidate required great discretion, lest Hill's prestige suffer from a factional dispute. The situation especially strengthened the hand of Tammany, whose representatives comprised the major part of the party's strength. The Tammany men respected Hill enough not to demand that he support their candidate, Edward Murphy, but they gave no guarantees that they would support whomever the governor named. As weeks passed without a decision, immense pressure bore upon Hill. "Don't, for God's sake," Marble warned him, "send any man who cannot capture Washington's ablest men for *you—that* is all there is of it." But who was that man to be? Two days before the party caucus, Hill decided that he would accept the office himself.[11]

Together with Hill's other confidential advisers, Marble opposed his decision. Although he did not state his objections in writing, he probably agreed with those who saw the move as the "abdication" of Hill's presidential ambitions. It was well known that the United States Senate was a poor springboard for presidential aspirants. As Charles Dana of the *Sun* pointed out, no man had become president while serving as a senator, and it had required from eight to thirty-two years for a freshman senator to obtain the highest office. Marble probably noticed as well that of the Democratic papers only the *World* thought Hill had decided wisely.[12]

Marble also objected because the decision hampered Hill's speaking out on the tariff and currency issues. This especially disturbed him, because in Congress the silverites were waging a determined effort to pass a free coinage bill. In December Marble had traveled to Washington and had returned convinced that the silverites would win out and that "our true course both for freedom and for David was to try to prevail in this Congress—now." So confident was he that he cabled

Cernuschi £5,600 to purchase Indian rupees, anticipating that free silver in the United States would bring about a rise in silver prices. He urged Hill to speak out for free silver before Congress and prepared a statement declaring that since Britain blocked the way to an international agreement and Congress opposed stopping the silver purchases, the only alternative was for the United States alone to adopt free bimetallic coinage at 15.5:1. If Hill presented this to the New York State Legislature in the form of a resolution and urged its passage, the legislature would follow his lead and in turn would compel Congress to pass the free coinage bill.

Such a move was absolutely essential. The growing importance of the silver issue demanded that all who aspired to national leadership should declare themselves on it. Any Democratic presidential candidate who opposed free coinage or even appeared indifferent to it faced the loss of either the nomination or the election. For Hill the timing was especially crucial. If he delayed, he risked the loss of New York in the 1891 fall elections. It was essential for him to support a free coinage bill now, so the issue might be decided before it cost the party any necessary votes. Even if free coinage failed, Hill should have spoken out, so his case would be well made by the fall elections.

There were still other reasons. Even if free coinage failed in the present session and the Democrats lost the fall elections, the issue would come up again in the next Congress. If a coinage bill was passed by a Democratic Congress, Harrison would probably veto it, leaving the issue undecided as the presidential elections rolled around. "No other issue," Marble declared, "would be possible in the canvass of 1892, and vetoed then or not, no other candidate than yourself would be possible, in the event that you had spoken now, and staked all upon it." Once again, he urged Hill to bold and decisive action, and to show his confidence, increased his rupee holdings tenfold.[13]

While he was urging Hill to action, Marble was trying to organize Democratic congressional support for the free coinage bill. To Roswell P. Flower, Democratic representative from New York, he argued that the party could profit from the silver debate only if Harrison vetoed the free coinage bill. There was little chance of that, however, unless Democratic votes supplied the margin of passage. Marble urged Flower to fight for a bill that would coin silver at 15.5:1 and would use the new silver dollars to retire the greenbacks. Should either or both of these propositions fail, Flower still should vote for free coinage in order to prevent an East-West party split. "Even with a bad ratio," he wrote, "your vote for free coinage will be vindicated by the result." In the meantime, he suggested that Flower arrange with Senator Arthur Pue Gorman to trade votes for free coinage for the votes against the pending Force Bill.[14]

Flower tried his best to follow Marble's instructions, but with little success. Eastern Democrats would never agree to free coinage at any ratio unless some sort of bargain was reached to defeat the Force Bill. Also he feared that in any event the House would bottle up the Senate bill until the session expired. Faced with the prospect of a long delay and possible defeat, Marble renewed his efforts with Hill and sold his rupee holdings at a loss.[15]

But Hill would not accept Marble's advice. At first he hesitated because he feared he would only complicate the senatorial election problem. When the Senate passed the free coinage bill, he had not spoken. Even after the senatorship had been decided, he refused to speak out. Inexperienced in discussing the currency issue and cautious by nature, he hesitated to involve himself with a complex and controversial issue until he thoroughly understood its political implications.[16]

All of this was bad enough, but the situation soon became far worse. While Marble watched the opportunities for Hill and for free coinage slip away, Grover Cleveland suddenly seized the issue and the headlines for himself. On February 10, when it appeared that free coinage no longer had a chance, Cleveland published a letter denouncing the silverites, declaring that the pending legislation threatened the nation with "the greatest peril," and attacking free coinage as a "dangerous and reckless experiment." Although the letter at once drew bitter denunciations from the South and West, it focused national attention upon the ex-president. Once again Cleveland seemed on the way to establishing himself as his party's leader.[17]

Unable to contain himself, Marble drafted a reply to Cleveland. Cleveland, he declared, had shown that he "has never yet conceived precisely what free coinage is nor why those who demand free coinage will never accept anything except free coinage." Cleveland in fact had endorsed the Republican Silver Purchase Act, which would surely lead the country to a silver standard. Moreover, his statements repudiated the policy of his own party, for when the Senate had passed its free coinage law, every Democrat save one had favored it. Indeed, they ran counter to the announced policies of both parties in some fifteen western and southern states and to the recommendations of Manning, Tilden, himself, and even the Republican secretary of the treasury, William Windom. Faced with such general sentiment for free coinage, eastern Democrats had hoped to avoid discussing the issue in the coming elections. Now, however, Cleveland had forced their hand in a manner which threatened to divide the party. Marble thought it "illegitimate and unworthy" to bring up an issue that threatened "that old and firm alliance between the Democracy of New York and the Democracy of the Western and Southern States." Hoping to heal the breach, he declared that, in fact, free coinage was neither a sectional nor a class issue, but rather a technical monetary issue to be decided by experts in political economy. Thus the party should repudiate Cleveland's leadership and adopt free coinage. "I venture to think," he concluded, "the New York Democracy will now take up the unfinished labor of Samuel J. Tilden and as a solid united party carry free bimetallic coinage to victory, rather than join Mr. Cleveland's stampede to the Wall Street Republican policy of gold monometallism."[18]

Desperately, Marble urged Hill to issue the statement. If Hill refused to speak out now, Cleveland's views would become, by default, the official policy of the New York Democrats, and his power to win the presidential nomination would thereby increase. At a time when the "whole west is shivering for lack of a leader," Hill's opportunities were immense. "You have now to upheave the country," he wrote, "make the issues, keep your own state, threaten loss to Republican states, capture the whole Farmers' Alliance, satisfy hard money Democrats, compel your own nomination, and win your own election." Now was the time for Hill to consolidate his whole case and so to lead men's minds from "this apparent chaos and black night."[19]

It was no use. "I am rather inclined," came the governor's laconic reply, "to say nothing at present, publicly, upon the subject which we have discussed." So the session drew to a close without a word from him. What had begun so promisingly had come to a disappointing stage. Hill was clearly now at a disadvantage. Throughout the entire session he had failed to speak out on any major national issue. The Force Bill had been defeated, but the credit had gone to Gorman, who had his own presidential aspirations. Free coinage had been lost and the credit had gone to Cleveland. The McKinley Tariff remained in force. Moreover, Hill would soon enter the Senate, where his influence would be diminished and his image blurred. When Marble left for Europe in June, he may well have doubted the wisdom of continuing to support a leader who seemed so unwilling to lead.[20]

A few weeks travel and relaxation were enough to restore his spirits and soon he was reevaluating the political situation and formulating new strategy. He first decided to give up the fight for the 15.5:1 ratio. Even Cernuschi agreed that coinage ratios were too difficult to explain to the American people. They were even more difficult to change, since that required remelting all the present silver dollars. So the United States would have to establish free coinage at 16 to 1, wait until the price of silver had risen to 16 in London, and then press the European countries to adopt the American standard.[21]

With the problem of the ratios disposed of, Marble turned to work out a new strategy for Hill. Since Hill had decided to remain in the governor's office until a successor could be elected, he would still have the advantage of speaking as the leader of the nation's most prominent state. Marble believed the New York Democrats should repeat last year's strategy, stating their principles in their state platform and speaking boldly for them once the election had brought them victory. Although he thought it wise for Hill to remind the public of his views by publishing an article on silver, he believed the governor should not speak until the elections had indicated public sentiment. Anticipating Democratic victories in November, Marble called on Hill to rally the party again to the issues of 1890. Hill should concentrate on Republican misdeeds, emphasizing that free coinage was the only sound alternative to the Silver Purchase Act. Realizing that Hill's support of free coinage would anger Cleveland's Mugwump supporters, Marble planned for Hill to attack them in a second speech. Marble's hatred of the Mugwumps had grown over the years, and he welcomed the chance to strike at the "incredible absurdities" of their financial theories. As Hill's principal opponents, the Mugwumps needed to be answered and shown to be "ridiculous." "If you prefer to have *me* do this," he declared, "I will not hesitate one instant, but my judgment is that *you* should cut their controls."[22]

All of this would happen after the elections. For the moment, Marble thought it enough merely to write a satisfactory platform for the coming campaign. Here a problem arose because the party had decided to nominate Roswell P. Flower for governor. Marble feared that Flower's support of free silver in Congress might bring out the silver issue prematurely. So he drafted a vague and meaningless currency plank for the state convention.[23]

Things should have gone smoothly at the Democratic convention; Hill's forces controlled a solid majority and were agreed on their strategy. They encountered no difficulty in nominating Flower for governor and Hill's close friend, William Sheehan, for lieutenant governor. But then perhaps from overconfidence, they committed a colossal blunder. The subcommittee that drafted the coinage resolutions easily defeated efforts by the Clevelandites to write a plank opposing free coinage and adopted a modified version of Marble's plank. When it reported to the full committee, however, Boss Richard Croker of Tammany offered an amendment, declaring: "We are against the coinage of any silver dollar which is of less intrinsic value than any other dollar." Clearly designed to impugn the free silver movement, the amendment was presented at the worst possible time. Most of the Hill managers were out of the room, and Croker, who had been handed the amendment by a Cleveland supporter, had no idea of its significance. Before the Hill men could object, the amendment had been approved. Unexpectedly, the Clevelandites had scored a startling triumph. "It enthuses all Mugwumps and Democrats for the ticket," Timothy S. Williams reported to Marble. "The effect outside the state will be bad, as you can readily see. . . . Perhaps your fertile mind may suggest some way of counteracting the evil effects."[24]

For once, both Hill and Marble agreed that the platform blunder had forced Hill to declare himself on the coinage issue before the election. If he did not, a Democratic victory could be interpreted as a victory for Cleveland or as a repudiation of the South and West. Hill handled the situation in one speech. Appearing at Cooper Institute, he ignored the money plank and declared the platform had united "all Democrats upon the common ground of honest bimetallic coinage."[25]

The election was another sweeping Democratic victory. Flower and Sheehan were elected by margins of 50,000 and 35,000 votes, respectively, and the party captured both houses of the legislature. Marble returned from Europe the day before the election and was soon planning postelection strategy with Hill. Marble advised Hill to deliver an address that would anticipate the problems he would face in the Senate. Marble feared disaster if Hill should be forced to vote on a free coinage bill without having reconciled all critics and factions in advance. It seemed a large task, but as usual he thought he was equal to it.[26]

On November 30 Hill delivered the address at Elmira. Employing Cernuschi's monetary theory, he argued that the recent state platform approved of free bimetallic coinage. Indeed, Hill declared that he had been elected to the Senate because he favored free silver. New York, therefore, stood shoulder to shoulder with the South and West in support of bimetallism. Castigating the Republican party as the "seventy-five cent silver-dollar party," he declared that silver purchases could not solve the currency problem and that the only solution was free bimetallic coinage.

Hill then discussed Democratic policy in the coming session of Congress. Here he took a startling turn. Instead of calling for an all-out drive for free silver, he declared that the party should seek only to repeal the McKinley Tariff and the Sherman Silver Purchase Act. The issues of 1890, then, would indeed be the issues of 1892. The repeal efforts would undoubtedly fail, Hill went on, since both the Senate and the Executive were in Republican hands. Still, it was the duty of the Democrats to maintain their own unity and to rivet the attention of the American people upon the misdeeds that had led to the Republican downfall in the last congressional elections. Until the Democrats controlled the other two branches of the national government, they could enact no new laws anyway. Thus the speech ended with a ringing call to inaction.[27]

There was little new in the speech. Hill and Marble had developed the issues over a year before, and if Hill had followed Marble's advice the public would have been quite accustomed to them. Politically, however, it was a masterful document. By opposing the policy but not the theory of free coinage, it neatly excused Hill from championing the cause. Should a free coinage bill come to the floor, Hill could vote for it and still disclaim responsibility for its defeat. It even left him the option of refusing to vote altogether on grounds that the time was not yet appropriate. "This speech," Marble declared, "will convert your helpless imprisonment into victorious leadership. And though your advice be not taken, *you* will rise above the Congress that rejects it, and remain the people's hope at the convention."

Hill would not only remain a spokesman for free silver but also would gain in stature as a party leader. Rather than call upon the party to risk discords and divisions, he called upon it to remain united, to oppose Republican laws and to support traditional Democratic policies of currency and revenue reform. At the same time he had come out for free silver with a monetary theory sound enough for even the most conservative businessman. Neither East nor West could quarrel with such a position. "You withhold unwisdom on silver, and it will elect you."[28]

Marble's enthusiasm, however, did not prove particularly infectious. Republican newspapers, of course, attacked and ridiculed the speech. But so did Democratic journals, including the *World*. Marble was dismayed. He had counted on the *World*'s support, in part no doubt because of his friendship with its famous editor, Joseph Pulitzer. The two had met abroad during one of Marble's annual journeys and had become friends almost immediately. As recently as the spring of 1891 Pulitzer had invited Marble to accompany him to Norway. "I miss your intellectual suggestions," he had written, "and am hungry for information and reasons on the political possibilities—in which you are always fertile." Hoping to set things right, Marble visited Pulitzer, but found him incapacitated by illness. Thus, he could only sit by, trying to console Hill as best he could, and sending in articles which the *World* rejected.[29]

Hill's chances for the nomination hinged upon the support of the South and West. Thus, when Senator John T. Morgan of Alabama asked Hill to clarify his views, Marble complied. Proposing Democratic substitutes for the Republican tariff and coinage laws, he wrote, would only prolong the session, lead to certain defeat, and possibly cost the party the issues for the coming campaign. A tariff bill would be smothered by protectionist amendments in the Republican Senate, and if the party proposed a number of separate reform bills, they would give the Republicans the chance of accepting a few and of going to the country as tariff reformers. A free coinage bill would be just as dangerous, since it would surely be vetoed and might also worry eastern Democrats. Finally the strategy had carried New York, and the party had to carry New York to win the election.[30]

Marble had only one issue left to make. The Mugwumps must be read out of the party. As Marble saw it, this project went beyond discrediting enemies of Hill; it struck at those who had so often frustrated his ambitions. From the beginning of his political career, Democratic success had always turned, at least in part, upon Mugwump support. Whether known as Barnburners, Independents, Reformers, or Mugwumps, they had always been outsiders, whose selfish demands had often forced the Democracy to compromise its selection of candidates and issues. The result had only weakened the influence of the regular party members. In the past Marble had often favored such compromises, but he had also come to regret them. Recently the Mugwumps had separated him from the Cleveland Administration, leaving him without the political influence he had so long hoped to exert. Now they were opposing Hill's nomination and again threatening his ambition. The time had come to dispose of them, and Marble set out to do so in an article on "The Mugwumps and the Democratic Party."

For some reason, however, he did not finish the article. He began well enough, declaring that "the Mugwumps are contending in New York for the control of the Democratic party, bent on its rule or its ruin," by calling upon the party to repudiate Tammany and Senator Hill. But history showed the absurdity of their demands. In 1872 they had forced Horace Greeley's nomination upon the party, leading it to defeat. In 1876 most of them had opposed Samuel J. Tilden, who had reformed the Democracy. But he went no further. He suddenly changed the subject, recalling Tilden's role in the campaigns of 1880 and 1884. Before he had finished even that, however, he laid the manuscript aside and turned to other problems.[31]

The first of these problems was to gather as much Congressional support as possible for Hill's nomination. Marble was greatly encouraged when the House elected Charles F. Crisp of Georgia to the Speakership. Crisp won the position from Roger Q. Mills, the great tariff reformer of 1888. Thus his victory indicated that the party representatives hoped to avoid the issue that had cost them so dearly four years earlier. To emphasize their determination, they demoted Mills from the chairmanship of the Ways and Means Committee. Also, the election of Crisp, who was known primarily as a silver supporter, showed they were leaning Hill's way. For Marble, it was an occasion to rejoice. "Crisp wins. Speaker Crisp," he wired Hill. "Cordial congratulations." When Hill arrived in Washington to assume his seat, he was further gratified to learn of "the very kindly feeling" of many of the southern Senators.[32]

While these signs indicated that Hill was off to a good start as a senator, certain difficulties soon began to appear. Although Hill enjoyed a degree of respect, he could not influence the party's legislative program. From the first, the Democratic leadership in the House refused to follow the course he had suggested in the Elmira Address. Instead of trying to repeal the McKinley Tariff in one bill, the Ways and Means Committee reported out a number of bills, aimed at particular duties on such items as wool, cotton bagging, binding-twine, tin plate, and lead ore. Although the bills passed the House, they were bottled up in the Republican Senate and never came to a vote.

No doubt Hill and Marble were relieved by this, since Hill had argued specifically against such a tariff strategy. Had he been forced to vote, he would have had the unenviable chore of repudiating either his southern and western allies or his own advice.[33]

The tariff, however, was only a lesser evil during the session. Again failing to respond to Hill's advice, Chairman Bland of the House Committee on Banking reported out a free silver bill late in February. To Marble the silver bill portended disaster for Hill's presidential aspirations. Late in January he had written to William R. Morrison of Illinois, George L. Miller of Nebraska, and John P. Irish of California to learn how their states would react if Congress passed a free silver bill, President Harrison vetoed it, and the Democratic party went into the election with a free silver plank in its platform. From all quarters the reports were discouraging. Both Miller and Irish declared that free silver would lose their states in the fall. Morrison could not see that the issue would make any difference in Illinois, declaring that the tariff was the only important issue.[34]

With such information, Marble believed the silver bill would create a serious crisis. If the bill passed both Houses of Congress with Hill voting yea, Harrison's veto would attract all opponents of free silver to the Republicans. Then Hill would have to "fight for free coinage, tooth and nail, trying to save New York, Connecticut, and New Jersey, with the press incompetent or hostile, but yet you raising the ground swell and letting loose all the dogs of war, and saving your election by repairing eastern losses with western gains, between Ohio and Nebraska."

A careful examination of the political situation convinced Marble that Hill could win with such a campaign. To support his argument he prepared two tables, one showing the votes of the states in the elections of 1884, 1888, 1890, and the other analyzing the northern state platforms of both parties in 1890. The first table revealed two key groups of states: those that had voted Democratic in 1890, while voting Republican in 1884 and 1888, and those that voted Democratic in 1884 and 1890, but Republican in 1888. To these two groups, especially to the former, Hill would have to appeal. The second table exhibited the most recent party declarations on free silver in all the northern states. Marble's calculations indicated that with the help of the Farmers' Alliance a Democratic party commitment to free silver could capture Nebraska, Minnesota, South Dakota, and Kansas. In addition, he thought free silver would carry Wyoming, Idaho, Ohio, and Indiana, while the support of "one good Chicago Newspaper" would carry Illinois. Only in this way could Hill overcome the loss of the eastern states. Since there would be little margin for error, the risk would be great, and even Marble thought success would be doubtful. "I do not say it cannot be won," he wrote. "But the odds are heavy."[35]

With so much at stake, Marble urged Hill to bend every effort to block the silver bill. Both realized that Hill would have little success trying to accomplish this in Washington; as a freshman senator, he lacked both the stature and the personal influence with the party's leaders. So Marble proposed that Hill join with Speaker Crisp and Representative L. L. Livingston, leader of the Georgia Alliance, to issue a joint statement calling upon the party to postpone all action until the November elections had given "a renewed mandate" for free silver. Although at first interested in the plan, Crisp finally decided against it.[36]

Marble had also hoped that Hill would use his influence with the New York State Convention to pressure Congress against the Bland Bill. Ordinarily the convention would not meet until May, far too late to be of any use. This year, however, the convention was being held in February. In January Marble and other members of the state organization had urged an early convention in order to promote Hill's candidacy. At the time, the decision seemed wise. Hill had just persuaded the national committee to hold the convention on June 21, in Chicago, and appeared to have the support of Calvin Brice, the national chairman, and Arthur P. Gorman. Gorman's endorsement was particularly gratifying, since the Maryland senator was thought to hold presidential ambitions for himself. With Cleveland generally considered out of the race because of his stand against free silver, Hill seemed to have no eastern challengers. Since, however, there was always the chance a free silverite from the South or West might try to secure the nomination, it seemed advisable to get Hill's name before the country as early as possible to show the party where New York's sympathies and votes lay. Thus on January 26 the state committee called for the state convention to assemble in Albany on February 22.[37]

Even before the committee issued its announcement, significant opposition to the early convention was developing. As early as January 16, E. Ellery Anderson, a reform Democrat and Cleveland supporter, was meeting with William C. Whitney and Charles Fairchild to protest the action. More significantly, George Harvey, managing editor of the *World,* also opposed the move and traveled to Washington in an effort to convince Hill to change his mind. When he failed, Harvey returned to New York and wrote an editorial, entitled "Don't," declaring that the maneuver would divide the party and win support for Cleveland.[38]

Perhaps such opposition gave Hill second thoughts, for Marble was soon admonishing him to stand by the original decision. Playing down the importance of the *World*'s position, Marble declared that Whitney and Daniel Lamont had inspired Pulitzer to oppose an early convention so they could "get time for making difficulties which will enable them to force you to agree to send Whitney to England as minister or to Washington as Senator." Their actions merely showed their panic at being unable to renominate Cleveland. Having no candidate, they lacked political power and thus ought to be ignored.

To give in to them would make Hill and the state committee a "laughing stock" for having been "bull dozed" by the *World*. Rather than waste time worrying about such insignificant matters, Hill should consider really important issues, such as heading off a western candidate and making sure "the convention of New York precedes your action on a possible silver bill in the Senate."[39]

It was especially important that the convention deal with the silver question. Marble hoped the convention would resolve to postpone congressional action on free silver. When the proposal came before the party leaders, however, they unanimously opposed it, believing that the Bland Bill could be defeated quietly in the House or that the national platform could deal with a presidential veto. As T. S. Williams reported to Marble with amazement: "The assembled aggregation of intellects expressed the opinion that . . . free coinage need not necessarily, and probably would not, be an issue in the campaign—the national platform would fix that." Thus, though the convention supported Hill for the nomination and chose a slate of delegates pledged to him, it said nothing about free silver. Hill had to content himself with an acceptance speech, which reaffirmed his Elmira address. This, however, seems not to have disturbed Marble. When he reviewed the convention's work, he scarcely noticed the platform, except to mention some minor points of style and phrasing. When he cabled the results to Cernuschi, he was unreservedly enthusiastic. "Nomination unanimous. Platform perfect."[40]

For a time it seemed as though Marble's optimism was justified. Hill escaped having to vote on the Bland Bill when it was defeated in the House. Also, shortly after the convention, the *World* reversed itself and called upon the Clevelandites to close ranks behind Hill. These events elated Marble. Predicting that Cleveland's nomination was now impossible and that only Hill could carry free silver through Congress, he saw no important obstacle in Hill's path. Even the movement within the Farmers' Alliance to form a third party failed to disturb him. To Perry Belmont he declared that the Farmers' Alliance vote could only change the election result by throwing the decision into the House of Representatives. "But that," he declared, "is merely an insurance of Hill's election."[41]

Still, the weeks following the convention carried many danger signs. Clevelandite opponents of the early convention, calling themselves "anti-snappers," showed no signs of returning to the ranks. Instead, they redoubled their efforts for their candidate, calling an anti-snapper convention for May 31 to select a contesting delegation to the Chicago convention. Drawing support from the Mugwumps and other anti-Tammany groups in New York, they swelled their ranks so rapidly that by May 1 they were claiming the support of more than 120,000 voters.[42]

While the anti-snappers went about their work in New York, reports were reaching Marble that Cleveland sentiment was growing throughout the country. From Rhode Island, the first state to hold a convention after New York, Samuel R. Honey reported that the "social and financial influences" solidly opposed the Hill movement. So strong was the anti-Hill feeling that if Hill received the nomination Honey would "have to cease visiting houses in which I am now welcome. . . . No one [he warned] who has supplied us with the sinews of war would do so again." From Nebraska, George L. Miller at first reported some gains for Hill, but within a week was writing of a movement by the governors of Pennsylvania, Indiana, and Iowa to nominate Cleveland. From California, John P. Irish reported that seven-tenths of the Democrats he had interviewed favored Cleveland.[43]

As winter turned into spring, these premonitions started to come true. One state convention after another ignored Hill and named delegations supporting Grover Cleveland. The state elections in Rhode Island, where Cleveland had spoken on behalf of the Democratic candidate for governor, returned a Democratic majority and increased the ex-president's prestige. Even more discouraging was the response of the silver states of the South and West, where Hill had hoped to make his greatest appeal. The key state of Georgia sent an uninstructed delegation composed of twenty Cleveland men in a total of twenty-six. When all the southern conventions had been held, only South Carolina, controlled by Pitchfork Ben Tillman, had openly repudiated Cleveland. In Nebraska it was a similar story. The defeat of the Bland Bill, according to George L. Miller, "caused the pendulum to swing away from Governor Hill." When the state convention met, it refused to instruct its delegates, but passed a resolution endorsing Cleveland. It also narrowly defeated a resolution to endorse free silver. Miller reported that the delegation contained some members strongly opposed to Cleveland, some favoring Arthur P. Gorman, and some who would vote for Hill if they could be convinced that he would carry New York. A few days later he frankly admitted that he was "unable to see how Governor Hill can be nominated under any circumstances." All at once, or so it seemed, Hill's chances were evaporating. As the Cleveland bandwagon gathered riders, reports of disaffections from Hill increased. Perhaps Marble noted ruefully that when Pulitzer sailed for Europe in May he took ship with the William C. Whitneys.[44]

By mid-May all optimism had disappeared from Marble's correspondence. Now he was fighting grimly to prevent Cleveland's nomination. Although Cleveland's pledged support gave him a majority of the delegates, it left him short of the two-thirds needed to win him the nomination. If enough uncommitted delegates could be kept from him, perhaps Hill would still have a chance. The best way to accomplish this, it seemed, would be to convince them that Cleveland could not carry New York. So long as this element of doubt could be pressed into their minds, Hill could still hope. Writing to George L. Miller, Marble declared that the New York delegation could "at no time, under no circumstances vote for the nomination of any candidate whose nomination would again ensure the loss of New York and again ensure the election of a Republican President." The assault on the party by "thrice defeated revengeful Mugwumps allied with discarded local Democratic aspirants" had made Cleveland's nomination impossible and the nomination of any candidate aside from Hill inexpedient.

Following the anti-snapper convention, Marble urged the regular New York delegation to issue a similar statement. But the party bosses rejected this strategy and merely restated their support of Hill.[45]

Marble also urged Hill to speak again on behalf of free silver. Convinced that the defeat of the Bland Bill by an overwhelmingly Democratic House had caused the free silver men from the South and West to lose confidence in the Democratic party, he had proposed for months that Hill dramatically revive the issue. He had called on Hill to present resolutions supporting free silver and calling for a special session of Congress immediately after the inauguration to legislate it into effect. Now he again brought his proposal forward. "Your party, your state, your friends," he declared June 7, "should hear your voice this very day." For days Hill vacillated, fearing the possible consequences. On the last day before the Republican senators were to leave for their national convention, he went so far as to take the documents into the chamber. Adjournment came, however, before he could find an appropriate occasion to present them. When he told Marble that he had intended to speak, Marble refused to believe him. "I take no stock in the carriage of the typewritten documents to the Senate," he announced to Cernuschi. "*Intent* did not sit on the box and hold the reigns and whip."[46]

A few days later, Hill admitted the truth of Marble's charge. To placate his adviser he agreed to publish a letter to a Kansas Democrat declaring that if elected he would sign a free silver bill. But he thought it would not be of much help. "The question does not turn upon free coinage," he wrote, "but is, who can be elected?" So long as the New York delegation held firm, he believed, the convention would see that Cleveland could never carry New York. Then "either myself or some friend will be nominated."[47]

So it was that Marble accompanied the New York delegation to Chicago to press his last efforts at president-making. Upon arriving, he first sought out the anti-Cleveland men to see if they could agree on a strategy to stop the ex-president. When he learned, however, that Gorman and Daniel Voorhees of Indiana had gone over to Cleveland, and that Henry Watterson would not support Hill, he realized that the only hope lay in the strength of the New York delegation. Perhaps if New York remained firm, *something* would happen to stop Cleveland. In any case, it was the only hope left. So he prepared a manifesto, declaring that Cleveland's nomination would "imperil the success of the party" and cause the loss of New York. Seventy-one of the seventy-two New York delegates signed the manifesto, and the document was circulated throughout the convention. At the same time, Hill's managers searched out the backers of favorite son candidates and urged them not to desert to Cleveland.[48]

Of course, none of this worked. In the early hours of June 23, Cleveland received the nomination on the first ballot. Marble was not at hand to see it. As soon as his manifesto had been distributed, he bought a compartment on an eastbound train and returned to New York. Almost at once he and Abby were on the seas, bound once again for Holland. After nearly nine months of campaigning, the thought of a summer's rest was especially appealing. He had no way of knowing that it had been his last campaign, ending where it had begun twenty-eight years earlier, in Chicago.

The Dutch environment could restore him physically, but it could not relieve the anguish and frustration. As he had done so often in the past, he sought emotional relief by pouring out his thoughts to a trusted friend. So he wrote Cernuschi of the last few weeks of the campaign, elaborately defending his actions and finding others to saddle with the responsibility of defeat. As he recounted the important events of the campaign, discussing their causes, effects, and significance, one event held his attention. Hill's failure to present the resolutions calling for a special session to enact free silver legislation had caused the defeat. Carefully, Marble rehearsed all his arguments in favor of the resolution. To each argument Hill had replied, "I fear that I can get no votes for it except my own" or "I do not see that it will gain me a single delegate."

To Marble, Hill's attitude was nothing more than "the transfer of Albany methods to Washington, the habit of counting up individual delegates." By relying on the ability of the New York delegation to influence the convention instead of speaking out for free silver, Hill had caused Farmers' Alliance men in the South and West to desert to the Populist party, thus increasing the influence of the anti-silver Cleveland supporters. The contrast between the two was obvious. "My own methods have always been to make issues," Marble wrote. "His methods have always been to 'get the delegates.'" The Chicago convention had demonstrated the relative merits of the two approaches.[49]

Marble's judgment had its strengths. Certainly the defeat of the Bland Bill by an overwhelmingly Democratic House required some response from a presidential candidate who favored free silver. By remaining silent, Hill and his supporters lost the chance to reassert their leadership. Voters who thought free silver the paramount issue were not going to support a candidate who appeared to have forsaken their cause.

In another sense, also, Marble's judgment was appropriate, for issues were again coming to dominate national politics. That would become clear as the decade wore on and as class and sectional conflicts became more heated. To old-style professionals as Hill, Murphy,

Croker, Sheehan, and Cockran, however, issues had counted for little in national politics. Long accustomed to the politics maneuver, they had become masters at disguising issues instead of at clarifying them. Marble, of course, had come to realize the importance of the silver issue through his association with Cernuschi. His sensitivity to American opinion on the subject and his training in political journalism led him to understand its growing importance.

Perhaps, however, he was a bit oversensitive, a bit too willing to stake all on the silver issue. Free silver had its supporters and was growing in importance, but in 1892 it was only one among many issues being agitated in the West and South. If westerners and southerners were calling for free silver, they were also calling for government ownership of the railroads, a subtreasury for agricultural loans, a graduated income tax, postal savings banks, abolition of the national banks and land monopolies, the secret ballot, and lower tariffs. Hill's silence on these issues might well have kept the Alliance men from supporting him, regardless of his stand on silver. Also, Marble seems not to have appreciated the strength of sentiment among western and southern farmers for third-party action. By 1892 westerners were convinced that a third party would succeed in accomplishing their aims, and southerners were paying more attention to the statements of L. L. Polk and Tom Watson, who were urging their supporters to look outside the Democratic party. Had Marble understood this rising sentiment he might have appreciated the significance of the Confederation of Industrial Organizations' meeting in St. Louis, which took the first steps toward uniting various agrarian labor and reform groups into the People's party. He would have seen in the meeting's adoption of a broad-based reform platform that free silver alone would not hold the Alliance in the Democratic party. At the time of that meeting, however, he was too concerned with the Bland Bill and the snap convention, and too fascinated with his own theory of bimetallism.[50]

It was important that Marble should have understood the causes of Populism, because his strategy required it. By renewing his support of free silver and calling for a special session of Congress to enact it, Hill would have been challenging the decision of his own party, which had defeated the Bland Bill. Hill realized such a move would have given such powerful Senate Democrats as Gorman, Carlisle, and Voorhees the opportunity to defeat his resolution and so to repudiate his leadership. It also would have given the Cleveland men another argument to use among eastern anti-silver Democrats. In such circumstances, Hill's only hope would have been to appeal directly to the Farmers' Alliance, hoping the farmers would at once flock to his support in the state conventions. At a time when the Alliance men seemed to be leaving the Democratic party, however, one so devoted to party regularity as Hill naturally hesitated to take the chance. Even if he had decided to speak out, his chances of success, as indicated above, would have been questionable. Given the alternatives and the nature of the political situation, his was probably the wiser course.[51]

But for Marble July was no time for dispassionate objectivity. It was a time for justification, recrimination, and perhaps reassurance. It was time also to make contrasts, this time between the ward-heeling politician and the principled statesman, between making issues and winning delegates. So it was time to forget how the snap convention, designed with his approval to win delegates, had contributed to the loss and how he had made his issues for the purpose of winning delegates. It was time to remember only the issue, free silver at home and international bimetallism abroad. It was time once again to turn from political maneuvering to the great cause and to pursue it, wherever it led, to the end. ✣

CHAPTER FOURTEEN

"The Truest Friend That Ever Lived"

ON FEBRUARY 9, 1893, David A. Wells asked William F. Vilas for a copy of a recent speech on the silver question by David B. Hill. He was anxious to read it because he understood that his old friend Manton Marble had written it. He was also sure that Marble had written Hill's Elmira Address, because "nobody but Marble indulges in such rhetorical phrases." Obviously, Wells was interested in more than the speech, for he went on to comment upon the recent strange behavior of his friend. "I was formerly very intimate with Marble, who is undoubtedly a man of great ability; but he has become so morbid on this silver question, that he seems not to desire association with any of his old friends who do not agree with him in respect to the silver problem."[1]

It seemed all too true. Hill's failure to win the presidential nomination had only spurred Marble to a new dedication on his behalf. Through the fall of 1892 he devoted all his energies to devising a new strategy for Hill and for international bimetallism. By December he was back in New York with his plan fully developed. Realizing that Cleveland would attack the Silver Purchase Act, he urged Hill to head him off with an attack of his own. Cleveland intended to repeal the act in the name of the gold standard; Hill should repeal it in the name of international bimetallism. Hill should introduce a bill to repeal the act and at the same time deliver a speech declaring repeal a necessary first step toward bimetallism. In that way he could count on the support of the Clevelandites while he used their issue against them.[2]

As usual, Hill hesitated to follow Marble's advice. The senator was at the moment engaged in a struggle to elect his friend Edward Murphy to the Senate and feared that raising the silver issue would endanger his chances. Although he did introduce the repeal bill, he put off speaking until Murphy was safely elected. Not until February 6 did he feel free to speak.[3]

Hill's speech outlined the strategy that Marble and Cernuschi had worked out the previous fall. Believing that international bimetallism would never succeed without Britain's cooperation, they had decided to force Britain's hand by repealing the Silver Purchase Act. It was Britain's interest, they believed, to maintain near parity between gold and silver in international exchanges in order to maintain stability in the Indian Empire. The Indian economy rested upon the stability of the silver rupee. A sudden fall in the value of the rupee would impair India's ability to pay her debts to Britain and would in other ways damage India's economy. Marble and Cernuschi were convinced that repeal of the Silver Purchase Act would bring about such a fall. Marble estimated that repeal would decrease the value of the silver dollar from its present sixty-four cents in gold to thirty-three cents. Britain would be forced then either to close the Indian mints or to invite the United States to reestablish international bimetallism. Since public sentiment in Britain had been growing in favor of bimetallism, Marble expected Britain to choose the latter course.

By calling for repeal of the Silver Purchase Act as a step toward international bimetallism, Marble hoped that Hill would win the support of the silverites. But if he was to rally a united party behind his leadership, Hill would also have to appeal to the Cleveland Gold Democrats. The speech therefore included an attack on the monetary theory and practice of silver purchases. Although free coinage would abolish the commodity price of silver, the mere purchases of silver would have no such effect. "Silver purchased even if coined, monetizes no unpurchased silver, and if not coined monetizes none at all." Purchased silver dollars, if coined, at once depreciated in value. Thus they comprised a stock of "nonexportable money." If that stock increased too much, it would drive out the stock of exportable money. Silver purchases also injured the domestic economy by imperiling the stability of the dollar. This in turn weakened the resolve of businessmen to expand their operations and frightened foreign investors into liquidating their American holdings. These conditions created a premium on gold and pushed the United States toward silver monometallism.[4]

Once Hill had spoken, Marble set about to reap the political harvest. On February 12 he sent President-elect Cleveland a pamphlet copy of the speech and a letter explaining its political significance. "Money is pure science and politics more or less pure art. If one man among your actual or possible advisers knew both, I should not feel driven as I am to do so disagreeable a thing as obtruding counsel unasked." Still, such an obtrusion seemed necessary because the president-elect could not "extort" from Congress "the primary conditions of the first step toward monetary and fiscal reform" unless he took hold of the issue by the right handle, "right as to science, right as to politics." Hill's speech provided that handle.

So that Cleveland might capitalize on the opportunity, Marble enclosed a draft of an open letter from Cleveland to Hill. Praising the logic of Hill's argument against the Silver Purchase Act but reserving comment on the international consequences of its repeal, the letter fully endorsed Hill's attack on the silver purchases. "Every day's delay to repeal the Sherman law," it concluded, "increases the difficulties in our public finance and the dangerous hazards of all our private enterprise."[5]

Once again Marble had produced a political masterpiece. Hill's speech had permitted him to appeal to the Cleveland Gold Democrats by stressing the domestic failures of the Silver Purchase Act. It had permitted him to phrase a letter for Cleveland endorsing Hill's attack on the silver purchases without supporting international bimetallism. Both the speech and the letter had been written to allow Cleveland to appear to select a minor theme from Hill's argument and to use that theme to rally the party behind himself. Thus Cleveland could support Hill without appearing to sacrifice his party leadership, while Hill, if the repeal of the silver purchases did in fact drive Great Britain to bimetallism, would emerge the ultimate victor.

But once again the plan failed. Cleveland refused even to reply to Marble's letter. A few weeks later, the shock of economic collapse focused national attention on the domestic importance of the silver purchases and gave the president the chance to force through a repeal of the Silver Purchase Act free of any obligation to Hill. And that summer Great Britain, anticipating the repeal, closed the Indian mints.[6]

Thus was begun again the cycle that by now was so much a part of Marble's life: new discussions with Cernuschi to assay the prospects for international bimetallism, new discussions with Hill to determine the political forces at work in Congress, the combining of the two into a new political strategy "right as to science, right as to politics," and the inevitable failure. For the most part the sequence contained little that was new. There was, however, one important exception. In the fall of 1893, there crept into Marble's letters a note of nostalgia. The letters to Hill, though packed with the strategy of silver science and politics, contained laments for previous opportunities lost or imperfectly grasped. As the weeks and months rolled by, this theme swelled so that by July 1895 Marble's principal concern was with history.[7]

Little by little, as David A. Wells had seemed to realize, Marble was losing his grip on political reality. The American people, reeling under the blows of economic collapse, cared nothing for his finely spun theories. Even the gold men and the silverites cared little enough and debated the money question almost exclusively as a domestic issue. Nowhere could Marble find effective leadership for his cause. By May 1894 even Hill had deserted him, and he had no place to turn. "I have tried, my dear Cid," he wrote Webster the next year, "to give help to Governor Hill from your point of view, and from the new position which he has taken. It is quite impossible. I see a course for him most clearly, but you would not agree to it now, and he, not until three or four years too late. And I cannot at all help him just now on your lines."[8]

The following year brought only fresh disappointments. Desperately, Marble sought to attract Perry Belmont to his cause, but failed. In May death took Cernuschi, and in July William Jennings Bryan captured the Democracy. International bimetallism was dead.[9]

Of course Marble refused to acknowledge it. He continued to hope, to plan, and to urge. Following the election, he drew up another plan for Perry Belmont to use in capturing the presidential nomination in 1900. Hope flickered when Belmont replied that he "would be only too glad to submit" himself to Marble's guidance. But Belmont was soon engaged with other counsellors, and the hope vanished.[10]

Now he was completely without political influence or prospects. The year 1897 closed forever his hopes to be a president-maker. One of his life's greatest ambitions was to be denied him, and because of that his life would have to change. The contemporary, event-filled environment of the politician would have to be forsaken and a new environment created to sustain his final years. The time had come for new and final departures.

The first departure removed him from the United States. For years he and Abby had been spending only the winter months at home. Such a schedule had dovetailed nicely with his political activities and had permitted them both to keep up their personal relations with family and friends. In 1897, however, that schedule had to be given up. The previous year Abby had fallen seriously ill with influenza, and her doctor had prescribed a year-round warm climate. So Marble sold the Fifth Avenue house and settled with Abby on England's south coast in Brighton, where the mild winters would not threaten her delicate health.

There they lived for twelve happy years. Their house, after the addition of central heating, sheltered them well. Abby's health improved so markedly that they were soon traveling again. At home they could enjoy the view of the sea, which lay beneath the nearby cliffs, and the company of their neighbors. The dearest neighbor was Herbert Spencer, who had in fact encouraged them to settle near him. Often Marble and Spencer would walk together along a shaded path, guarded against the intrusions of the abominable automobiles that were coming to disrupt the life of the countryside, discussing philosophy and literature and generally enjoying each other's company. Always a true friend, Marble did his best to comfort and protect the aged philosopher. When a question arose over the American copyright of Spencer's publications, Marble hired his own lawyer to look after Spencer's interests. Henry James was another neighbor whom both the Marbles delighted in. "It isn't possible to express the delight we have," Marble told another friend, "when he comes over to stay with us. Nobody, nobody covers more brains with his hat, has keener discernment more refinement of soul. . . . I would rather be with him one day than eighteen months in each of all the Babylons. He is fooled by none of the phantasms. Him the idols do not obsess."[11]

So passed the years at Brighton. Gradually the old cares and controversies subsided. Marble kept up with international bimetallism for a few years, but by 1902 had seemingly lost interest. The coal strike in the United States provoked a brief note to Spencer in praise of George Baer, "the one strong man whom only a President could have constrained to tolerate his or any meddling." America's imperialistic adventures earned his scorn, and he branded the Supreme Court's decision in the Insular Cases "cutting up constitutions into cloaks for highwaymen."[12]

In these years his departure from politics to history was fully accomplished. With his removal to Brighton he seems to have decided to content himself with the role of political spectator. When Edward Murphy and Perry Belmont approached him about preparing a strategy to defeat Bryan's renomination in 1900, they received only one letter filled with generalities and after that nothing at all. When Bryan received the nomination, Marble seemed hardly to notice. "I find it impossible to flog my mind to a real interest in the contest," he confessed to Webster, "for the reason that contest there seems to be none." The only event that aroused his partisanship was Thomas B. Reed's attempt to gain membership in the Round Table. He had the satisfaction of blackballing the arch-Republican and thus keeping him out.[13]

"The politics of your life (so far) are closing," Webster had written; and so it seemed. In 1893 Marble had written to the prominent historian Worthington C. Ford that "no opinion in a controverted and political question, although an opinion expressing mere science, or history, should go into the melee except at the right time for good reasons." At Brighton his retreat from politics freed his historical interest and allowed him to relive in more comfortable circumstances the trials and struggles of his life.[14]

Over the years Marble had developed a true scholar's interest in history. He read scholarly books and periodicals and offered advice to the professionals within his acquaintance. A frequent correspondent during his years at Brighton was Ford, who was to become director of the Massachusetts Historical Society. Usually their letters touched upon topics of interest to the scholar. "How kind you are," Marble wrote Ford in 1906, "to answer my query as to the Monroe Correspondence Calendar by sending me the thing itself. . . . As soon as we return to Brighton I will send . . . all I can find of Mr. Wells's work; and you shall do what you please with it."[15]

On one occasion the scholars tried to persuade Marble to open his knowledge to them. In 1906 William A. Dunning wrote in hopes that he "might find time and have the inclination to make some contribution to the inside history of the Reconstruction era." Soon afterward Ford also asked him to tell what he knew about Andrew Johnson's acquittal in the impeachment controversy. Marble was tempted, and he composed a reply, hinting that the acquittal had been arranged by Tilden, Richmond, Belmont, and Seymour through a coalition of "Democrats" and "former Democrats." Beyond that, however, he would not go. "There was no contemporary record of all this," he said. "There can be no history of it." Then perhaps fearing that even this had been too much to say, he filed the letter and never mailed it.[16]

No doubt he found the scientific detachment of scholarship pleasurable. But it was not satisfying. Too much of the history had involved his ambition to be treated apart from that ambition. As the theory of international bimetallism had been made vital by the political controversies surrounding it, so history could become vital only by reaching out to touch his ambition. History, in short, would define his manhood. What did it show?

It showed that he had been consistent. "As to the Greenbacks," he wrote Webster in 1895, "from the first hour of their issue, for more than twenty years I had been conscious of their danger and constant in its exposure." He first assumed control of the *World* on the condition that he would be allowed to denounce paper money. He had "refused cooperation with the Chase movement in 1868" because Chase had fathered the greenbacks. In 1873 and 1874 he had put the resumption issue in the forefront of the state platforms. In 1875 he had "deliberately assailed Hendricks and his Rag Baby and openly endeavored the defeat of Bill Allen in Ohio because he had deserted his position with Hard Money Benton and gone over to the Greenbacker policy." He had worded the compromise plank in the 1876 platform "to save the day for Resumption which had been lost by poor Dorsheimer in Committee" and had consistently urged Manning to approve stronger statements against paper money in his treasury reports. "Come and tell me," he had written to Ford, "how it happened that the financial platforms of the Democratic party of New York from 1873 to 1892 are continuous, coherent, unswerving. That could never have happened if they had not been framed by one man and he never a delegate to a convention or chairman of a platform committee."[17]

History also showed that he had been master of his own fate. Even in old age he longed for that sense of personal self-determination that would assure him of his manhood. So whenever a challenge to his independence arose, he hastened to set the record straight. Nothing wounded him more than statements appearing from time to time in the *World Almanac* that Belmont and Barlow had taken the initial risk to save the *World* from bankruptcy and had installed Marble as their editor. "All the risk I took alone," he assured his old reporter, Montgomery Schuyler, "devising alone the ways and means." He had not known the members of the Democracy until after he had set the paper on its course with regard to "Gen. McClellan, Stanton, Arbitrary Arrests, and Federal Finance." His original purchase of the *World* had been made possible by John R. Ford and Francis N. Bangs, neither one a Democrat. He alone had saved the paper and he alone had controlled it during his editorship. Belmont had never owned a share of stock, and Barlow had received "his own price" when he finally sold his shares.[18]

History also showed that he had played a vital role in making political decisions. In 1895 when John Bigelow's biography of Tilden appeared with scarcely a mention of him, Marble responded with wounded pride. "Bigelow never knew anything at all of our politics," he complained to Webster. "You would think the *Evening Post* had something to do with Tilden's career. Much history there, but history of Bigelow." From 1895 on, he spent much time correcting Bigelow's judgments, mostly on matters that had concerned him. "Bigelow probably never was told of any work of mine for Tilden," he concluded, "and doubtless thought Tilden wrote his own platform in 1876." When Webster suggested that Marble prepare his own history of the period, Marble left no doubt that his historical interest was largely personal. "The difficulty," he wrote, "is always what we have once or twice considered. The platforms were so entirely mine as to offer no difficulty. They do but express the policy *created* after the Greeley fiasco and championed and conducted to success. Whatever of mine bore another signature."[19]

Marble's clearest and most detailed reminiscences were highly personal and shed little light upon the significant history of his time. When he touched upon the larger issues, he became mysterious and elliptical. He could recall in minute detail the scene at Greeley's funeral, but would only hint at the maneuvers that had won Andrew Johnson acquittal. He could reveal that Tilden had hoped to phrase his letter of withdrawal to the 1880 Democratic convention so as to keep the frauds of 1876 the principal campaign issue. But when it came to other conventions, he would only tantalize his reader. "Had you anything to do with the effort, through Dick Taylor and others," he slyly asked Webster, "to slide Hendricks off the St. Louis 1876 ticket and put Palmer (Ill.) on? Do you believe that Belmont and Barlow were in fact for Chase in 1868?" Those questions he would never answer.[20]

Why the mystery? Partly it was because he needed self-justification. The memory of the Chase fiasco no doubt embarrassed him, so he would rather not have been a part of it. Since he had been, however, his only recourse was to alter the record.

Still, there was a more fundamental reason consistent with his entire career and character. For all its importance in the world of public affairs, politics for him had always been intensely personal, because it had been so intimately bound to his friendships. Tilden, Belmont, and Barlow had been more than political allies; they had been true friends whose honor he felt duty bound to protect. "I should only be sorry," he once wrote, "to have given any man or woman a regret who was unreserved to me. I have made every other mistake in life but not that, to the best of my knowledge and belief."[21]

For this reason, one of Marble's chief activities during his years in Brighton was to burn much of his private correspondence. In 1874 he had stated his opinion on the sanctity of private correspondence: "Where is the treachery in the disclosure unless what is disclosed does dishonor instead of honor to the dead?" So as he sorted out his personal papers and reread the record of his life, he determined that none of that record should dishonor his friends. Much of the correspondence he burned before moving to Brighton and more after arriving. "How you would enjoy the holocaust here in my library fireplace," he declared to Ford. "For a moment I was tempted to send you a few letters out of the flames." But he did not: history meant little unless it preserved the duties of friendship.[22]

Besides his responsibilities to his friends were those to his family. There is little evidence of Marble's family life, but it is impossible to think of him as other than a proud, loving father and devoted husband. His own father had died in 1887 and his mother in 1898. His sister Susan lived at the family farm in Bedford, cared for by his daughter Delia. His stepdaughter Katrina lived a few miles north of Brighton at Allington Castle in Kent. She was the wife of William Martin Conway, noted mountain climber, geographer, and professor of fine arts at Cambridge. His son Frank had served aboard the cruiser *New York* in the Spanish-American War, had been an aide to Admiral Dewey in the Philippines, naval attaché to the American Legation in Japan, and in 1909 joined the staff of the Naval War College in Newport.[23]

In this environment, surrounded by history, friends, and family, Marble lived content. Undoubtedly he would have preferred to live out his days at Brighton, comforted by his memories and his loved ones. But such was not to be. In April 1909 Abby again contracted influenza. This time she no longer had the strength to resist its complications and pneumonia soon developed. As her husband and doctors helplessly stood by, she sank into unconsciousness and death. On April 10 Marble wrote Webster: "Early this morning the light of my life went out."[24]

He was alone and without plans. Only one thing seemed certain: he must leave Brighton. That summer he packed his belongings, gave up his lease, and traveled to Allington Castle to visit the Conways.[25]

At seventy-four years of age he was in need of comfort, and at the castle he found it. The Conways loved and cared for him and he returned their affection with a kindness and consideration that made him all the more endearing. Soon he was remarking to Martin that everyone should live within a moat and walls five feet thick. He had found his final home.[26]

The moat was not wide enough and the walls not thick enough, however, to protect him from one final tragedy. On the evening of February 13, 1911, his son Frank left his home in Newport, made his way to the offices of the War College, and in a washroom shot himself in the head. He was found the next morning, still alive, and was rushed to the hospital where he died at noon on the operating table. No one could understand why he had done it. He left no note and had shown his wife no signs of anxiety or depression. Some speculated that he had been worried about his health, which had suffered during his tour in the Philippines. Others suggested temporary insanity. But Marble would believe neither explanation. Frank "had a silent sweetness and high pride, incompatible with any such sad misgiving interpretations of his appalling act as, by those not near to him are unavoidable." It seemed to him that some "rush of blood to the head" must have suddenly plunged his son into despair. The "all-invading distress of the lost balance, with enough consciousness still fluttering to foreshadow the quite terminated ambition, the long burthen upon others' lives, the inevitable end: thus I read the incredible, the awful, mystery."[27]

After Frank's death, the record of Marble's life collapses into fragments. Letters in 1911, 1914, and 1915 are all that remain. Appropriately, they epitomize his last years. The first comments on a recent visit by Delia and shows the father's love. The second shows him reading Henry Cabot Lodge's memoirs and recalling his first visit with Charles Sumner. In the last he extends his sympathies to Worthington C. Ford after learning of the death of Charles Francis Adams, Jr., and in his quaint, flowery style reveals what had always been best in him—his loyalty to his friends.

> Neither we two nor any of the one or two thousand millions can harness sightless couriers, or suspend aloft visionary mirrors, for instant reception or transmittal to one another through our common atmosphere, of whatever we can silently shape to say. Nor can it be done with French nor by prayer and fasting. Yet look at all the inventions and the widespread faith in actual telegrams to the Throne of Grace; and all the submerged cables, suspended wires, steel rails, steam-engines, steamboats, and now the aeroplanes and £2,000,000 a day spending by Little Britain alone for sheer killing,

> whereas you must wait a fortnight nearly and I spend twopence to get a hearing across the unfordable abyss for my affection for—
> Worthington Chauncey Ford.[28]

He survived that year and the next. Gradually his strength began to fail and his memory to err. At Christmastime, 1916, he failed noticeably and was soon bedfast. There he lay for months, peaceful and happy, holding on to life ever so gently. Spring came and gave way to summer. In mid-July, he became painfully restless. Then on the morning of July 24, the pain subsided and for a few hours he waited in peace for death to claim him.[29]

All those who had known him best were gone. There seemed to be no one capable of gauging accurately the substance of his life, no one capable of cutting through the ambition, struggle, self-deception, and failure to reveal the true lineaments of the man. There seemed to be no one, in short, capable of saying whether or not in his eighty-three years he had achieved a noble manhood. Yet Martin Conway, who loved him, was equal to the task. Writing that fall to Timothy S. Williams, he was able to say of Marble all that the moment required: "He was the truest friend that ever lived, and he preserved the memory of his old friends as freshly to the last as if he had only just parted from them."[30] ❖

NOTES

Chapter One

1. *Who's Who in New York City and State,* 3rd. ed. (New York: L. R. Hamersly and Co., 1907), p. 908; Sarah Loring Bailey, *Historical Sketches of Andover, Massachusetts* (Boston: Houghton Mifflin Co., 1880), pp. 107, 117, 141, 147–48, 320; William A. Benedict and Hiram A. Tracy, *History of the Town of Sutton, Massachusetts, from 1704 to 1876* (Worcester: Sanford and Co., 1878), pp. 687–88; C. A. Wall, *Reminiscences of Worcester, 1657–1877* (Worcester: Tyler and Seagrave, 1877), pp. 337–38.

2. Charles Nutt, *History of Worcester and Its People,* 4 vols. (New York: Lewis Historical Publishing Co., 1919) 3:177–78, 4:810–11; Bailey, *Historical Sketches of Andover,* p. 117; Benedict and Tracy, *History of Sutton,* p. 687.

3. William Lincoln, *History of Worcester* (Worcester: Charles Hersey, 1862), pp. 257–58; Wall, *Reminiscences of Worcester,* p. 338.

   Sister Mary Cortona Phelan, using the federal census report for 1850, and a copy of the vital records of Worcester, gives Marble's birthdate as Nov. 16, 1835. Marble, however, consistently placed the date a year earlier. On the theory that Marble was closer to the sources of information, and that clerical errors could have accounted for the discrepancy in the official records, I have chosen the date Nov. 16, 1834. In support of that date, see Marble to Martin B. Anderson, Nov. 15, 1855, Anderson MSS, Rush Rhees Library, Rochester University; Marble to "Baron," Sept. 15, 1872, Marble MSS, Library, of Congress. Phelan's evidence is presented in *Manton Marble of the New York World* (Washington: Catholic University of America Press, 1957), p. 3.

   The federal census for 1850 also indicated that Manton Marble had an older brother, Francis C. Marble, a younger sister, Susan Antoinette Marble, and a younger brother, "Melvin" Marble. The evidence in the Marble papers indicates that Francis died sometime early in 1854. "Melvin," referred to by Manton as "Melville" and as "Frank," was drowned on a field trip while a student at Rochester University. Ben Baker to Marble, Feb. 23, Mar. 25, 1854, Marble MSS; Marble to Anderson, July 7, 1860, Aug. 1, 1861, Anderson MSS; Roswell Ward, *Henry A. Ward, Museum Builder to America* (Rochester: Rochester Historical Society, 1948), pp. 123–24.

4. The date of the move to Albany is based on the Albany directory, which does not list Joel Marble in its issue for 1839–40, but does list him as residing at 261 State Street in 1840–41. L. G. Hoffman, *Hoffman's Albany Directory and City Register* (Albany: L. G. Hoffman, 1842), p. 136; George R. Howell and Jonathan Tenney, *History of Albany and of Albany County, New York, 1609–1886* (New York: W. W. Munsell and Co., 1886), pp. 695–96.

5. Joel Munsell, *Collections of the History of Albany,* 3 vols. (Albany: Joel Munsell, 1870) 3:273; *New York World,* Dec. 18, 1887.

6. Phelan, *Marble,* p. 3; Marble to "Baron," Sept. 15, 1872, Marble MSS; *Annual Catalogue of the Officers and Students of the Albany Academy* (Albany: Joel Munsell, 1852), p. 14.

7. *Annual Catalogue of Albany Academy,* 1851–52, pp. 8, 26–27; 1852–53, p. 20. Manton won neither of the medals awarded for proficiency in mathematics or classical languages. These prizes, however, required four years attendance at the Academy, and he did not meet the requirement. Ibid., 1852–53, p. 24; William A. Miller to "Messrs. Marble, Sheldon, Strong, and others," Jan. 2, 1852, Marble MSS.

8. *Annual Catalogue of Albany Academy,* 1851–52, pp. 14, 32; ibid., 1852–53, pp. 6, 24; *Annual Report of the President of the Young Men's Association,* 1839–55; Henry Buell to Marble, Apr. 6, 1853; R. Merrifield to Marble, May 23, 1857, Marble MSS. At the closing exercises of the Albany Academy, Manton also delivered a poem entitled "Old Times and New Times." Program of the exercises in Marble MSS.

9. *Report of the Board of Commissioners of the District Schools,* 1852, p. 18; Marble to "Baron," Sept. 15, 1872; receipt from Rathbone dated July 11, 1855, Marble MSS.

10. John F. Rathbone to Marble, Jan. 24, 1853, Marble MSS.

11. Blake McKelvey, *Rochester: The Water-Power City* (Cambridge: Harvard Press, 1945), pp. 294–95; *Catalogue of Rochester Theological Seminary,* 1853–54, p. 4; Jesse L. Rosenberger, *Rochester: The Making of a University* (Rochester: University of Rochester Press, 1927), pp. 36–37; Meryl Frank and Blake McKelvey, "Some Former Rochesterians of National Distinction," *Rochester History,* vol. 21, no. 3 (July, 1959), pp. 8, 14; *Annual Catalogue of the Officers and Students of the University of Rochester,* 1854–55 (Rochester: A. Strong and Co.), pp. 21–22.

12. Rathbone to Marble, Jan. 24, Feb. 5, Mar. 1, June 15, 1853, Marble MSS.

13. The clearest statement of the aims of the classical curriculum is presented in the Yale Report of 1829, published as "Original Papers in relation to a course of Liberal Education," *The American Journal of Science and Arts,* vol. 15 (1829), pp. 297–351. See especially 300–302, 326–29. The report is summarized and ably put in the context of its times in Frederick Rudolph, *The American College and University* (New York: Knopf, 1962), pp. 110–35. For the Rochester curriculum see "Report of the Regents," *New York Senate Documents,* 1854–56.

14. Ashahel C. Kendrick, *Martin B. Anderson: A Biography* (Philadelphia: American Baptist Publication Society, 1895), pp. 207–17; Marble to "Baron," Sept. 15, 1872, Marble MSS.

15. Rosenberger, *Rochester,* p. 99; Kendrick, *Anderson,* pp. 165, 271; Timothy L. Smith, *Revivalism and Social Reform* (New York: Harper & Row, 1957), p. 48.

16. Rudolph, *American College and University,* pp. 86–109; Wilson Smith, *Professors and Public Ethics, Studies of Northern Moral Philosophers before the Civil War* (Ithaca: Cornell University Press, 1956), pp. 33–43; William C. Morey, ed., *Papers and Public Addresses of Martin B. Anderson* (Philadelphia: American Baptist Publication Society, 1895), pp. 125–26.

17. Rosenberger, *Rochester,* p. 117; Kendrick, *Anderson,* pp. 171, 282.

18. Marble to Anderson, Dec. 3, 1855, Anderson MSS.

19. This analysis is drawn from the *Rochester American,* Mar. 10, May 5, 13, 20, 1853, May 15, 23, 24, 30, June 3, Sept. 23, Oct. 6, Nov. 4, 1854.

20. C. P. Dewey to Marble, Aug. 6, 1854, Oct. 14, "October," 1855, Marble MSS.

21. Marble to "Baron," Sept. 15, 1872, Marble MSS; Marble to Anderson, Nov. 16, 1855, Anderson MSS.

Chapter Two

1. Marble to Anderson, Aug. 12, 1855, Anderson MSS.

2. Ibid., Nov. 10, 1855.

3. Ibid., Nov. 16, 1855.

4. Ibid., "1856."

5. Ibid., Mar. 30, 1856.

6. Ibid., Apr. 26, 1856; A. Kingman Nott to Marble, Mar. 10, 1857, Marble MSS; *Boston Traveller* files in New England Deposit Library, Cambridge, Mass.

7. *Traveller,* Jan. 16, Feb. 10, 17, 1857; Marble to Anderson, "1857," Anderson MSS.

8. Marble to "Baron," Sept. 15, 1872; Rathbone to Marble, Oct. 11, Dec. 31, 1856, Marble MSS; Marble to Anderson, "1857," Anderson MSS.

9. Marble to Anderson, Mar. 30, 1857, Anderson MSS.

10. Ibid., May 12, 1857; Rathbone to Marble, May 27, 1857, Marble MSS.

11. *Traveller,* June 4, 25, July 16, 21, Sept. 10, 1857.

12. Marble to Anderson, May 12, 1857, Anderson MSS; Rathbone to Marble, May 16, 19, July 13, 20, 1857; Elizabeth Stoddard to Marble, Sept. 19, 1857; Marble to "Baron," Sept. 15, 1872, Marble MSS.

13. Marble to Anderson, Sept. 8, 1856, Mar. 30, 1857, Anderson MSS; George S. Hillard to John Bigelow, Feb. 13, 1858; Charles Fitch to Marble, Aug. 17, 1858, Marble MSS.

14. Hillard to Marble, Dec. 28, 1857; F. W. Seward letter of recommendation dated Jan. 4, 1858; C. P. Dewey to Marble, Jan. 16, Feb. 1, 1858; Dawson to Marble, Feb. 28, 1858, Marble MSS.

15. Allan Nevins, *The Evening Post, a Century of Journalism* (New York: Boni and Liveright, 1922), pp. 207–41; Allan Nevins, *The Emergence of Lincoln* (New York: Charles Scribner's Sons, 1950) 1:381, n. 7.

16. Marble to Anderson, Mar. 8, 1858, Anderson MSS.

17. Ibid., July 21, 1858.

18. Ibid., May 21, 1859, Anderson MSS; Manton Marble, "Fraser River," *Knickerbocker* 52 (1858):331–40.

19. Marble to Anderson, May 21, 1858, Anderson MSS.

20. *New York Evening Post,* Oct. 7, 1859.

21. The foregoing account of Marble's western experience is drawn from his "To Red River and Beyond," *Harper's New Monthly Magazine* 22 (1860):289–311, 581–606, 23 (1861):306–22.

22. Marble to Anderson, May 21, 1859, Anderson MSS; J. R. Spalding to Marble, Jan. 27, Feb. 10, 23, 1860, Marble MSS.

23. See letters of recommendation by Anderson, Oct. 8, 1855, Mar. 7, 1856, Feb. 11, 1858; T. J. Conant, Mar. 19, 1856; C. C. Hazewell, Feb. 23, 1858; George Hillard, Feb. 13, 1858; James T. Fields, Feb. 12, 1858; Samuel Bowles, Feb. 15, 1858; Worthington, Flanders, and Guild, Feb. 15, 1858; William Cullen Bryant, Dec. 10, 1858, Marble MSS.

24. Marble to Anderson, Mar. 30, Sept. 8, n.d., 1856, Mar. 30, May 12, n.d., "1857," Anderson MSS.

25. Marble to Anderson, Feb. 18, May 21, 1859, Mar. 30, 1857, Anderson MSS.

26. *Traveller,* Jan. 15, 1857; Stoddard to Marble, Jan. 28, 1857, Marble MSS.

27. Marble to Anderson, "1857," Anderson MSS; Review in *Knickerbocker* 53 (1859):405–9.

28. A. B. Johnson to Charles Sumner, Feb. 11, 1857, Sumner MSS, Houghton Library, Harvard; Marble to Anderson, "1857," Anderson MSS.

Chapter Three

1. Spalding to Marble, Feb. 10, 1860, Marble MSS.

2. *World,* Oct. 12, 1872.

3. Charles Godfrey Leland, *Memoirs* (New York: Appleton and Co., 1893), p. 216; J. M. Bloch, "The Rise of the New York *World* during the Civil War Decade," unpublished doctoral dissertation, Harvard University, 1941, pp. 15–16.

4. *World,* June 14, 1864; Spalding to Marble, Feb. 23, 1860, Marble MSS; Bloch, "Rise of the *World,*" pp. 20, 55; William Cassidy to Samuel J. Tilden, Oct. 1860, Tilden MSS, New York Public Library.

5. *Herald,* June 9, 1860.

6. Bloch, "Rise of the *World,*" pp. 12–14, 586.

7. Marble to Anderson, July 7, 1860, Anderson MSS.

8. *World,* July 3, 1860, Feb. 25, Mar. 8, 12, 16, 1861; Bloch, "Rise of the *World,*" pp. 21–31.

9. *World,* Mar. 10, 1881; Ivory Chamberlain, *Biography of Millard Fillmore* (Buffalo, N.Y.: Thomas and Lathrops, 1856).

10. *World,* Jan. 19, Feb. 8, Mar. 1, 8, Apr. 10, 1861.

11. Marble to Anderson, July 7, 1860, Anderson MSS.

12. *World,* Nov. 23, 1860, Jan. 30, Mar. 2, 6, Nov. 8, 1861.

13. Marble to Anderson, Apr. 9, 1861, Anderson MSS; Glyndon G. Van Deusen, *Thurlow Weed: Wizard of the Lobby* (Boston: Little, Brown and Co., 1947), pp. 259, 261, 284; Bloch, "Rise of the *World,*" pp. 15–16, 58; cf. Marble's eulogy of Bangs in *Harper's Weekly* 29 (1885): 838; Rathbone to Marble, Dec. 31, 1860, Feb. 8, 1861; Samuel Greene Arnold to Marble, Jan. 8, Mar. 20, Apr. 15, June 3, 1861, Marble MSS.

14. Marble to Anderson, Apr. 9, 1861, Anderson MSS.

15. Marble to Anderson, June 11, Aug. 1, 1861, Anderson MSS; *World,* Mar. 1, 13, 25, Apr. 3, 1861; *Tribune,* Dec. 4, 1862.

16. Marble to Anderson, June 11, Aug. 1, 1861, Anderson MSS; Stedman and Gould, *Life and Letters of E. C. Stedman* 1:226; Arnold to Marble, June 22, 1861, Marble MSS.

17. Marble to Anderson, June 11, 1861, Anderson MSS; Arnold to Marble, June 22, 1861, Marble MSS.

18. *World,* July 1, 1861.

19. Marble to Anderson, Aug. 1, 1861, Anderson MSS.

20. Bloch, "Rise of the *World,*" p. 65; *World,* Aug. 28, 1861.

21. Bloch, "Rise of the *World,*" p. 66; Arnold to Marble, Sept. 15, 1861, Marble MSS.

22. Ford to Marble, Dec. 6, 1861; E. C. Stedman to Marble, Dec. 9, 1861, Marble MSS; *World,* June 14, 1864, Jan. 25, 1862.

23. *World,* June 14, 1864; Marble to "Baron," Sept. 15, 1872; Arnold to Marble, Jan. 23, 1862, Marble MSS.

24. Marble to Anderson, Mar. 6, 1862, Anderson MSS.

25. Ibid., May 12, 16, Oct. 19, 1862; Arnold to Marble, May 18, 1862, Marble MSS.

26. Marble to Anderson, May 23, 1862, Anderson MSS.

27. *World,* May 12, 1862.

28. Ibid., Mar. 5, Apr. 11, 23, June 3, 13, July 16, 22, 1862.

29. Ibid., Jan. 10, 18, July 10, 1862.

30. Louis M. Starr, *Reporting the Civil War* (New York: Collier Books, 1962), pp. 84–86; *World,* Feb. 27, 1862.

31. Starr, *Reporting the Civil War,* p. 77; Porter to Marble, Oct. 23, Nov. 22, 1861, Marble MSS.

32. Porter to Marble, Mar. 17, 1862, Marble MSS; *World,* Mar. 15, 16, 17, 1862.

33. Porter to Marble, Apr. 26, May 21, June 20, 1862, Marble MSS; *World,* June 21, July 4, 1862.

34. William M. Evarts to Marble, May 27, 1862; Arnold to Marble, June 12, 1862, Marble MSS.

35. Van Deusen, *Weed,* pp. 282–302; *Tribune,* May 2, 5, Sept. 18, Dec. 4, 1862; *Herald,* May 3, Aug. 12, 14, Sept. 14, Dec. 9, 1862; Marble to Raymond, July 18, 1862; Raymond to Marble, July 24, 1862; Arnold to Marble, Aug. 10, 16, 1862; Evarts to Marble, Aug. 18, 1862, Marble MSS; Marble to Weed, July 29, 1862, Weed MSS, University of Rochester; Marble to Anderson, Oct. 19, 1862, Anderson MSS.

36. *Herald,* Aug. 15, 1862; Marble to S. L. M. Barlow, June 13, 1868, Barlow MSS, Henry E. Huntington Library.

Chapter Four

1. H. W. Howard Knott, "Samuel Latham Mitchill Barlow," *Dictionary of American Biography* (New York: Charles Scribner's Sons, 1928–1940) 1:613–15; Allan Nevins, *The War for the Union* (New York: Scribner's, 1960) 1:24, 30, 49, 240, 303–4; 2:44, 49, 159; Marble to Anderson, Oct. 19, 1862, Anderson MSS; Barlow to Marble, June 15, 1868, Marble MSS; Marble to Barlow, Aug. 16, 1862, Barlow MSS.

2. *World,* Aug. 30, Sept. 3–11, 1862; Marble to Anderson, Oct. 19, 1862, Anderson MSS.

3. *Tribune,* Sept. 18, 1862; Ford to Marble, Sept. 19, 29, 1862, Marble MSS.

4. *World,* Sept. 10, 1862.

5. Sidney D. Brummer, *Political History of New York State during the Period of the Civil War* (New York: Columbia University Press, 1911), pp. 212–18; Stewart Mitchell, *Horatio Seymour* (Cambridge, Mass.: Harvard University Press, 1938), pp. 238–39, 244–48; *World,* Sept. 15, 1862.

6. Brummer, *New York during the Civil War,* pp. 218–26; *World,* Sept. 29, 1862; Marble to Anderson, Oct. 19, 1862, Anderson MSS.

7. Spalding to Marble, Oct. 6, 1862; Wayland to Marble, Oct. 13, 1862, Marble MSS; Marble to Anderson, Oct. 19, 1862, Anderson MSS.

8. Marble to Anderson, Oct. 19, 1862, Anderson MSS.

9. *World,* Sept. 11, 12, 15, 16, 30, Oct. 7, 29, 1862.

10. Belmont to Barlow n.d., but clearly 1862;? McMurray to Marble, Oct. 10, 1862; Ford to Marble, Oct. 14, 1862; Arnold to Marble, Oct. 10, 1862, Marble MSS; Marble to Anderson, Dec. 18, 1862, Anderson MSS.

11. *World,* Oct. 16, 17, 1862; Barlow to Marble, June 15, 1868; Wilson Barstow to Marble, Oct. 7, 1862, Marble MSS; Marble to Anderson, Dec. 18, 1862, Anderson MSS.

12. Brummer, *New York during the Civil War,* pp. 24–32.

13. Marble to Anderson, Oct. 19, Dec. 18, 1862, Anderson MSS; E. C. Stedman to Marble, Nov. 24, 1862; S. S. Cox to Marble, Dec. 5, 1862, Marble MSS.

14. Barlow to Marble, June 15, 1868, Marble MSS; Marble to Anderson, Dec. 18, 1862, Anderson MSS. Ben Wood retained a small share, which he gave up in Sept., 1863. Wood to Marble, Sept. 4, 1863, Marble MSS.

15. Marble to Anderson, Dec. 18, 1862, Anderson MSS; Calvert Comstock to Marble, Dec. 26, 1862; Comstock and Cassidy to Marble, Jan. 23, 1863; Barlow to Marble, June 15, 1868, Marble MSS; *Herald,* Oct. 8, 1863.

16. C. Comstock to Marble, June 20, 1863; Barlow to Comstock and Cassidy, June 25, 1863; William H. Bogart to Marble, July 14, 1863, Marble MSS.

17. Elon Comstock to Marble, July 15, 1863; Calvert Comstock to Marble, Sept. 11, 1863; receipts from scrip, dated Dec. 24, 26, 1863, Jan. 11, 22, Feb. 6, 1864, Marble MSS.

18. Circulars in the Marble MSS; *World,* Oct. 8, 1863.

19. Cox to Marble, Dec. 5, 1862; Bogart to Marble, June 16, 1863; Clipping from the Batavia, New York, *Spirit of the Times,* Dec. 26, 1863, Marble MSS; *Evening Post,* Feb. 7, 14, 24, July 14, 1863.

20. Seymour to Marble, Nov. 11, 1862, Marble MSS; Brummer, *New York during the Civil War,* p. 303; David Lindsey, *"Sunset" Cox: Irrepressible Democrat* (Detroit: Wayne State University Press, 1959), p. 72; F. L. Klement, *The Copperheads in the Middle West* (Chicago: University of Chicago Press, 1960).

21. Brummer, *New York during the Civil War,* pp. 303–19.

22. *World,* March 11, April 11, 21, 1863.

23. Mitchell, *Seymour,* pp. 293–94; *World,* May 6, 7, 9, 11, 22, 26, 1863.

24. Vallandigham to Marble, May 12, 15, 21, 1863, Marble MSS.

25. Pleasants, *Wood,* pp. 139–40; Brummer, *New York during the Civil War,* pp. 316–19; *World,* June 4, 5, 12, 13, 15, 1863.

26. Mitchell, *Seymour,* pp. 313–14; Eugene C. Murdock, "Horatio Seymour and the 1863 Draft," *Civil War History,* 11 (1965): 117–41; *Harper's Weekly,* Aug. 22, 1863; *World,* Feb. 2, Mar. 13, 23, Apr. 2, June 9, 11, 13, 14, 1863.

27. Brummer, *New York during the Civil War,* pp. 346–48; *World,* July 15, 17, 18, 20, Aug. 3, 17, Sept. 8, 14, 1863.

28. Cox to Marble, Aug. 17, 1863; Vallandigham to Marble, Oct. 4, 1863; Seymour to Marble, Sept. 17, 1863, Marble MSS.

29. Marble to William F. Allen, Oct. 29, 1863, Marble MSS.

30. *World,* Oct. 14, Nov. 5, Dec. 21, 1863; Vallandigham to Marble, Oct. 28, 1863, Marble MSS.

31. Seymour to McClellan, Feb. 25, 1863; McClellan to William G. Fargo, Mar. 13, 1863; Cox to McClellan, May 31, 1863, McClellan MSS, Library of Congress; Cox to Marble, June 1, 1863, Marble MSS.

32. Marble to Anderson, Dec. 8, 1862, Anderson MSS; McClellan to Barlow, Aug. 11, 1863, McClellan MSS.

33. Cox to Marble, June 1, 1863; McClellan to Seymour, Mar. 13, 1863; McClellan to William G. Fargo, Mar. 13, 1863; McClellan to Barlow, Mar. 16, 1864; Cox to McClellan, May 31, 1863; McClellan to Cox, June 8, 1863, McClellan MSS; Cox to Marble, June 27, 1863; menu of dinner for McClellan at Delmonico's, attended by Marble, S. G. Arnold, George Ticknor Curtis, William Butler Duncan, August Belmont, Samuel J. Tilden, William Henry Hurlbert, and S. L. M. Barlow, May 19, 1863, Marble MSS.

34. McClellan to Charles J. Biddle, Oct. 12, 1863; D. Salmon to Marble, Nov. 12, 1863; Marble to McClellan, Nov. 16, 1863, McClellan MSS; *World,* Oct. 13, 1863.

35. Mary Rathbone to Marble, Jan. 17, 1862; Louisa Arnold to Marble, July 19, Oct. 11, 12, 1863, Marble MSS.

36. Louis M. Starr, *Reporting the Civil War* (New York: Collier Books, 1962), pp. 259–62; George Wakeman to Marble, n.d., Marble MSS.

37. Barlow to McClellan, May 18 [probably May 19], 1864, McClellan MSS.

38. Starr, *Reporting the Civil War,* pp. 262–63.

39. *World,* May 23, 1864; Chester Dewey, memoranda notebook, May 25, 1864, University of Rochester; Cox to McClellan, May 25, 1864, McClellan MSS.

40. Seymour to Marble, Sept. 19, 1863, Apr. 23, 1864, Marble MSS; Marble to Seymour, Aug. 31, 1863, James Wright Brown Collection, New York Historical Society; Marble to Anderson, Dec. 8, 1862, Anderson MSS.

41. Marble to Comstock and Cassidy, May 20, June 16, 1864; Cassidy to Marble, May 21, June 25, 26, 1864, Marble MSS; Barlow to McClellan, May 18, 1864, McClellan MSS.

42. McClellan to Barlow, Mar. 16, 1864; John V. L. Pruyn to McClellan, June 9, 1864, McClellan MSS; Dean Richmond to Marble, June 16, 1864; Pruyn to Marble, June 15, 1864; Cassidy to Marble, June 25, 1864, Marble MSS.

43. McClellan to Barlow, Mar. 16, 1864; Barlow to McClellan, June 18, 1864, McClellan MSS; Cox to Marble, June 22, July 25, 1864; McClellan to Marble, June 25, 1864, Marble MSS.

44. Cox to McClellan, Aug. 4, 1864; George Morgan to McClellan, Aug. 4, 1864; McClellan to Prime, Aug. 10, 1864, McClellan MSS; Cox to Marble, Aug. 7, 1864, Marble MSS; Marble to Lyman C. Draper, Aug. 17, 1864, Draper MSS, Wisconsin State Historical Society; *World,* Aug. 19, 23, 1864.

45. Barlow to Marble, Aug. 21, 24, 1864, Marble MSS. See also Marble's reports from the Chicago Convention in the *World,* Aug. 28, 29, 1864.

46. Marble to Barlow, Aug. 26, 27, 1864, Barlow MSS; Barlow to Marble, n.d., Marble MSS.

47. H. S. Lansing to McClellan, Aug. 28, 1864; Barlow to McClellan, "Sunday," 1864, McClellan MSS; Marble to Barlow, Aug. 27, 1864, Barlow MSS.

48. Marble to Barlow, Aug. 29, 30, 31, 1864, Barlow MSS.

49. Barlow to McClellan, Sept. 3, 1864; Marble to McClellan, Sept. 12, 1864, McClellan MSS; Charles R. Wilson, "McClellan's Changing Views on the Peace Plank of 1864," *American Historical Review* 38 (1933): 498–510.

50. William Cassidy to Marble, Sept. 16, 1864; memorandum "Plan of Democratic Campaign for October, 1864," Samuel North to Marble, Sept. 28, 1864; William Miller to Marble, Sept. 27, 1864; George W. Adams to David G. Croly, Sept. 25, 1864, R. D. Rice to Marble, Sept. 24, 1864, Marble MSS; Barlow to McClellan, Sept. 23, 1864, McClellan MSS.

51. Marble to Joel Marble, Oct. 1864; letter for Rathbone, Oct. 1864, Marble MSS.

52. Marble to McClellan, Nov. 13, 1864, McClellan MSS.

Chapter Five

1. *World,* Dec. 3, 4, 5, 1863.

2. S. S. Cox to Marble, Jan. 13, 1865, Marble MSS; Samuel A. Pleasants, *Fernando Wood of New York* (New York: Columbia University Press, 1948), p. 162; LaWanda and John H. Cox, *Politics, Principle, and Prejudice, 1865–1866* (London: Free Press of Glencoe, 1963), pp. 1–30; *World,* Jan. 17, 1865; Edward L. Gambill, "Northern Democrats and Reconstruction, 1865–1868," unpublished Ph.D. dissertation, University of Iowa, 1969, pp. 6–9.

3. Cox to Marble, Dec. 7, 1864, Marble MSS.

4. *World,* Dec. 19, 21, 30, 1864.

5. Richmond to Marble, Jan. 23, 1865, Marble MSS; Cox, *Politics, Principle, and Prejudice,* p. 16.

6. Cox to Marble, Jan. 13, 1865, Marble MSS.

7. Ibid., Feb. 1, 1865; *World,* Jan. 17, 1865; Cox, *Politics, Principle, and Prejudice,* pp. 19–20. Barlow also opposed the amendment. Writing to Montgomery

Blair, who was trying to persuade him to approve the amendment, he expressed the fear that the measure might cause the southern people to "become more firmly united than ever before" and that abolition in the border states would cause the abolitionists to call for letting the remaining slave states leave the union. Barlow to Blair, Jan. 16, 1865, Barlow Letterbooks, Huntington Library.

8. *World,* Dec. 19, 1864, Feb. 1, 1865.

9. Cox, *Politics, Principle, and Prejudice,* pp. 51–55; William A. Dunning, *Reconstruction, Political and Economic (1865–1867)* (New York: Harper Torchbook reprint of the 1907 edition, 1962), p. 43.

10. Cox, *Politics, Principle, and Prejudice,* pp. 56–65.

11. Ibid., pp. 65, 71–73; *World,* Sept. 8, 12, 1865; *Times,* Sept. 7, 1865.

12. *New York Evening Post,* Sept. 8, 1865.

13. Notable works on the antebellum activities of the Barnburners include Herbert A. Donovan, *The Barnburners* (New York: New York University Press, 1925); Margaret Clapp, *Forgotten First Citizen: John Bigelow* (Boston: Little, Brown and Co., 1947); Alexander C. Flick, *Samuel J. Tilden: A Study in Political Sagacity* (New York: Dodd, Mead & Co., 1939), pp. 81–86; Stewart Mitchell, *Horatio Seymour* (Cambridge Mass.: Harvard University Press, 1938), pp. 34, 69, 71, 77, 82–83, 86, 89, 91–92, 106–8, 117, 123, 125, 137, 143, 147–48, 150, 166, 251; Richard Hofstadter, "William Leggett, Spokesman of Jacksonian Democracy," *Political Science Quarterly* 58 (1943): 581–94; Marvin Meyers, *The Jacksonian Persuasion* (New York: Vintage Books, 1960), pp. 185–205. Hofstadter and Meyers are particularly valuable for connecting the Barnburners with the Locofoco radicalism of the *Evening Post.*

14. *Post,* Sept. 8, Nov. 7, 1865.

15. *Herald,* Sept. 8, 1865.

16. *World,* Oct. 10, 17, Nov. 6, 1865.

17. *Post,* Oct. 11, 18, 1865.

18. *World,* Sept. 19, 20, Oct. 18, 1865; *Post,* quoted in the *Tribune,* Nov. 7, 1865.

19. Parke Godwin, *The Life of William Cullen Bryant* (New York: D. Appleton and Co., 1883) 2:123–27; David Dudley Field to James R. Doolittle, July 14, 1866, Doolittle MSS, Wisconsin State Historical Society; *Post,* Oct. 11, 1865.

20. *Tribune,* Oct. 10, 1865; *Post,* Oct. 12, 1865; *World,* Oct. 14, 1865. For many other examples of this attitude toward Johnson see Cox, *Politics, Principle, and Prejudice,* pp. 88–106.

21. Cox, *Politics, Principle, and Prejudice,* pp. 172–77.

22. *World,* Jan. 20, Feb. 10, 23, 28, 1866.

23. Barlow to Blair, Sept. 11, 1865; Barlow to Russell Houston, Oct. 28, 1865, Barlow Letterbooks.

24. Cox, *Politics, Principle, and Prejudice,* pp. 114–18; Tilden to Blair, Mar. 10, 1866; Marble to Blair, Mar. 10, 1866, Blair MSS, Library of Congress.

25. Eric McKitrick, *Andrew Johnson and Reconstruction* (Chicago: University of Chicago Press, 1960), pp. 394–420; Cox, *Politics, Principle, and Prejudice,* p. 120; Homer A. Stebbins, *A Political History of the State of New York, 1865–1869* (New York: Columbia University Press, 1913), pp. 83–84, 89–91.

26. Seymour to M. Blair, July 19, 1866, Blair MSS; Porter to William C. Prime, July 6, 1866, Porter MSS, Library of Congress; Porter to Marble, July 19, 1866, Marble MSS; Barlow to Belmont, June 29, 1866, Barlow Letterbooks.

27. *Post,* July 25, Aug. 15, 1866; Field to Doolittle, July 14, 1866, Doolittle MSS; Barlow to Smythe, Aug. 25, 1866, Johnson MSS, Library of Congress; John Van Buren to Tilden, Aug. 31, 1866, Tilden MSS, New York Public Library.

28. Hurlbert to Marble, Aug. 26, Sept. 1, 12, 1866; Joseph Warren to Marble, Aug. 29, Sept. 6, 1866, Marble MSS; Van Buren to Tilden, Sept. 3, 1866, Tilden MSS.

29. Marble to Warren, "End of August, 1866," Marble MSS.

30. Godwin, *Bryant* 2:357; Flick, *Tilden,* pp. 82–87, 92.

31. D. S. Alexander, *Political History of New York State* (New York: Henry Holt and Co., 1909) 3:156–57; Hurlbert to Marble, Sept. 1, 1866, Marble MSS; Barlow to M. Blair, Sept. 11, 1865, Blair MSS.

32. Stebbins, *Political History of New York,* pp. 100–109; Barlow to Francis P. Blair, Sept. 19, 1866, Barlow Letterbooks.

33. *Post,* Sept. 7, 13, 14, 25, Nov. 2, 1866.

34. *Times,* Sept. 13, 27, Oct. 2, 9, 1866; Tilden to Hugh McCulloch, Sept. 17, 1866, Tilden MSS.

35. *World,* Sept. 20, 25, Nov. 7, 1866.

36. *Rochester Daily Union and Advertiser,* July 10, 1866, clipping in Marble MSS. Marble to F. A. Macomber, July 8, 9, 1867; Macomber to Marble, July 9, 1867, Marble MSS.

Chapter Six

1. William H. Bogart to Marble, Oct. 13, 1868; Barlow to Marble, Feb. 12, 1868, Marble MSS; John Fiske to Abby Fiske, Dec. 23, 1869, Ethel F. Fiske, ed., *The Letters of John Fiske* (New York: Macmillan Co., 1940), p. 192; *New York Records of Assessments,* 1869, 2:180; *New York Evening Telegram,* Mar. 23, 1869.

2. Notice of Marble's election to the Century Club, Apr. 5, 1862; personal bill at Delmonico's for $447.84, Sept. 30, 1863, Marble MSS; John Fiske to Abby Fiske, Oct. 22, 1867, Dec. 23, 1869, Fiske, *Letters of John Fiske,* pp. 167, 192; *World,* Nov. 23, 1867, Dec. 16, 1865; George Ticknor Curtiss to Marble, Oct. 6, 1867, Marble MSS.

3. Henry Adams, *The Education of Henry Adams* (New York: The Modern Library, 1931), p. 373; Horace S. Merrill, *Bourbon Democracy of the Middle West, 1865–1896* (Baton Rouge, La.: Louisiana State University Press, 1953), pp. vii–viii.

4. The members of the managing committee were John Van Buren, Augustus Schell, William Butler Duncan, Manton Marble, George W. McLean, Henry Hilton, Hiram Cranston, William F. Allen, S. L. M. Barlow, August Belmont, James T. Brady, Horace F. Clark, Edward Cooper, Edward Corlies, George Ticknor Curtis, Andrew H. Green, John T. Hoffman, Charles O'Conor, Edwards Pierrepont, William C. Prime, Dean Richmond, Anthony L. Robertson, Samuel J. Tilden, Douglas Taylor, and Gulian C. Verplanck. A survey of relevant biographical dictionaries, county, city, and professional histories, directories, and newspapers revealed detailed information about all but Edward Corlies, who ran an auction house, and Douglas Taylor, who was a printer.

   As used here the name "swallow-tail" is a bit anachronistic. The name did not appear until the 1870s, when it was used as an epithet by "Honest John" Kelly and the lower-class Irish of Tammany Hall against the upper-class Democrats, who often appeared in formal dress and in other ways put on "airs." Since the upper-class Democrats had no other identifying name in the 1860s, however, and since some name is required to distinguish the city elite both from the Tammany rank and file and from the Regency, which included upstate leaders, I have decided to use the one that was most contemporary.

5. Belmont to Barlow, June 26, 1866; Barlow to Belmont, June 29, 1866, Barlow MSS; Marble to Joseph Warren, "End of Aug., 1866"; Nat Bangs to Marble, Nov. 18, 1874, Marble MSS. The swallow-tails' capacity for maneuver so enraged party ideologues that by 1868 they were known as the "policy" Democrats. See M. M. "Brick" Pomeroy to Marble, Jan. 3, 1868, Marble MSS.

6. George T. Curtis, "Speech at Philadelphia, September 30, 1864," *Handbook for the Democracy, 1863, '64,* n.p., 1864. The *Handbook,* which contains many pamphlets prepared by the Society for the Diffusion of Political Knowledge, is a mine of information about swallow-tail ideology during the Civil War years.

7. John Bigelow, ed., *The Writings and Speeches of Samuel J. Tilden* (New York: Harper and Brothers, 1885) 1:422–33.

8. Irwin Unger, *The Greenback Era: A Social and Political History of American Finance, 1865–1879* (Princeton, N.J.: Princeton University Press, 1964), pp. 126–62; Walter T. K. Nugent, *Money and American Society, 1865–1880* (New York: Free Press, 1968), pp. 34–38.

9. Seymour J. Mandelbaum, *Boss Tweed's New York* (New York: John Wiley and Sons, 1965), pp. 1–75; Frank J. Goodnow, "The Tweed Ring in New York City," in James Bryce, *The American Commonwealth* (London: Macmillan Co., 1889) 2:336–38; *World,* Mar. 19, Sept. 18, Nov. 5, 1869, Feb. 3, 5, Mar. 1, 9, 1870.

10. *World,* Feb. 3, 5, 1870.

11. Edward G. Riggs in the *New York Sun,* Apr. 23, 1892, quoted in Henry Watterson, *History of the Manhattan Club* (New York: privately printed, 1915), pp. xxiii–xxvii, 12–15.

12. Douglas Taylor in the *Sun,* Oct. 23, 1910, quoted in Watterson, *History of Manhattan Club,* p. 15; Augustus Schell, receipt of Marble's membership dues, Oct. 28, 1865, Marble MSS.

13. *World,* Dec. 29, 1865.

14. Marble to Anderson, July 7, 1860, Anderson MSS.

15. Marble to Anderson, July 7, 1860, Anderson MSS; Stedman to Marble, Dec. 9, 1861; McKelway to Marble, Sept. 1, 1869; Chamberlain to Marble, Dec. 30, 1865; Marble to Nat Bangs, Nov. 20, 1865 (?), Marble MSS; Stillson to Barlow, June 23, 1875; William B. Reed to Barlow, June 3, 1875, Barlow MSS.

16. Marble draft of letter for Rathbone, Oct. 1864; Marble sketch of his career for "Men of the Times," care of Thompson Cooper, Kennington Park, London, Oct. 1870, Marble MSS.

17. Marble to Anderson, Aug. 12, Nov. 10, 1855, Mar. 30, 1856, "1857," Mar. 30, 1857, Mar. 8, 1858, Anderson MSS.

18. Ibid., Mar. 6, May 12, 16, Oct. 19, 1862.

19. Marble to William Cassidy, June or July, 1864, Marble MSS; Marble to Anderson, May 12, Oct. 19, 1862, Anderson MSS.

20. Marble to Greeley, Jan. 6 [1864], Feb. 23, 1865, Greeley MSS, New York Public Library; draft of letter for Rathbone, Oct. 1864; Marble to "Baron," Sept. 15, 1872, Marble MSS.

21. Marble to Greeley, Dec. 28 [1863], Greeley MSS.

22. Ibid., Jan. 6 [1864]; Arnold to Barlow, Nov. 20, 1863, Barlow MSS.

23. Marble to Barlow, Sept. 13, 1867, Barlow MSS; Marble to Bennett, June 1, 1873, Marble MSS.

24. Marble to Greeley, Dec. 18, 1863, Feb. 23, 1865, Greeley MSS.

25. Erik H. Erickson, *Identity, Youth and Crisis* (New York: W. W. Norton, 1968), p. 50.

26. Chester Dewey, Memoranda notebook, May 25, 1864; Francis G. Fairfield, *The Clubs of New York* (New York: Henry L. Hinton, 1873), p. 156; Marble to Barlow, n.d., Barlow MSS.

27. Marble to Mrs. Belmont, n.d., Marble MSS; Marble to Barlow, July 13, 1864, Barlow MSS.

28. Marble to Henry A. Ward, Oct. 22, 1862, Ward MSS, University of Rochester; Thomas Boese to Marble, Apr. 6, 1866; Gideon J. Tucker to Marble, Apr. 7, 9, 1866; Marble to Mrs. Barlow, Apr. 12, 1866; Robert Minturn to Marble, July 23, 28, 1866; Marble to Lucy Rathbone, n.d., Marble MSS; Marble to Barlow, July 13, 1864, Barlow MSS; John Fiske to Abby Fiske, Oct. 22, 1867, Oct. 27, 1868, Fiske, *Letters of John Fiske,* pp. 167, 177.

29. Louisa Arnold to Marble, Feb. 18, 1862, Jan. 10, Mar. 29, May 6, Aug. 7, 1863, May 3, 1864, Marble MSS.

30. Belmont to Marble, Aug. 17, Nov. 6, Dec. 10, 1868, Apr. 21 [1869], Marble MSS.

31. *World,* Dec. 18, 1887; Marble to Anderson, July 7, 1860, Anderson MSS; see checks from Marble to his father, 1873; Marble to William Cassidy, May 19, 1865, Marble MSS.

32. Marble to Anderson, Apr. 9, 1861, Anderson MSS.

33. Ibid., Oct. 19, Dec. 18, 1862; Marble to Joseph Warren, "End of Aug., 1866"; Marble to McClellan, Nov. 13, 1864, Marble MSS.

34. Louisa Arnold to Marble, July ?, Dec. 4, 1863; Marble to Rev. H. G. Graves, June ?, 1864; Hurlbert to Marble, Oct. 15, 1868, Marble MSS.

35. Stillson to Marble, Apr. 20, 27, 1875; Marble to Stillson, Apr. 16, May 20, 1875, Marble MSS.

36. John Fiske to Abby Fiske, Mar. 14, 1864, Fiske, *Letters of John Fiske,* p. 122.

37. Marble to Anderson, Mar. 17, 1868, n.d., Anderson MSS.

38. Charles F. Wingate, ed., *Views and Interviews on Journalism* (New York: F. B. Patterson, 1875), pp. 216–20, giving the text of an undated lecture by Marble.

39. Marble to E. D. Beach, May 21, 1863, Marble MSS; *World,* Jan. 2, 1869.

40. *World,* Sept. 18, 1869.

41. Ibid., Jan. 30, Feb. 28, Mar. 16, 1867, Jan. 9, 1869.

42. *Real Estate Record and Builder's Guide,* May 18, 1889; Louis M. Starr, *Reporting the Civil War* (New York: Collier Books, 1962), pp. 39, 61, 266–70, 270–73; Horace White to Marble, Dec. 12, 1868, Marble MSS.

43. *World,* Mar. 10, 1881; Ivory Chamberlain, *Biography of Millard Fillmore* (Buffalo, N.Y.: Thomas and Lathrop, 1856); Chamberlain to Marble, n.d. (2); Croly to Marble, Jan. 13, 1876, Marble MSS.

44. Alvin F. Harlow, "William Henry Hurlbert," *DAB* 9:424; Lately Thomas, *Sam Ward: "King of the Lobby"* (Boston: Houghton Mifflin Co., 1965), pp. 230–32.

45. *Real Estate Record,* May 8, 18, 1889; Frank Luther Mott, *American Journalism* (New York: Macmillan Co., 1962), p. 507.

46. Marble to Anderson, Dec. 11, 1872, Anderson MSS.

47. Croly to Marble, Apr. 14, 15, 20, 21, 1864, Jan. 22, Feb. 29, 1868, Marble MSS. Marble relied upon Croly and publisher N. D. Bangs for information on salaries, so Croly's "ultimatums" did not result from Marble's opposition to granting salary increases. See Bangs's note appended to Croly to Marble, Jan. 22, 1868, Marble MSS.

48. Sidney Kaplan, "The Miscegenation Issue in the Election of 1864," *Journal of Negro History* 34 (1949): 274–343.

49. Croly to Marble, Oct. 26, 1866, Marble MSS.

50. Ibid., Nov. 27, 1871.

51. Ibid., Nov. 30, 1871.

52. Ibid., Nov. 11, 1864; Marble to Anderson, Oct. 19, 1862, Anderson MSS.

53. *Herald,* Aug. 11, 1866.

54. *World,* Aug. 8, 1866; *Herald,* Aug. 12, 1866.

55. *World,* Aug. 13, 21, 1866; *Herald,* Aug. 14, 1866.

56. *World,* Dec. 10, 11, 1866; D. H. Craig circular letter to the New York Newspapers, Nov. 9, 1866, Marble MSS; Oliver Gramling, *AP: The Story of the News* (New York: Farrar and Rinehart, 1940), pp. 63–68.

57. *World,* Dec. 3, 10, 19, 1866.

58. Minutes of AP meeting, Dec. 4, 1866; White to Marble, Dec. 11, 14, 17, 1866, Marble MSS; Victor Rosewater, *History of Cooperative News-Gathering in the United States* (New York: D. Appleton and Co., 1930), pp. 124–26.

59. Barlow to Marble, n.d.; Marble to Joseph Medill, Jan. 4, 1867; Marble to Prime, Jan. 8, 1867, Marble MSS.

60. *World,* Jan. 11, 12, 1867; Marble to Medill, Smith, and Halstead, Jan. 8, 1867, Marble MSS; Rosewater, *History of Cooperative News-Gathering,* pp. 127–29.

61. Bangs to Marble, Aug. 21, 1867; Horace White to Marble, Aug. 21, 1867; Marble to the General News Association, Dec. 2, 1867; Marble to the AP, Feb. 17, 1868, Marble MSS.

62. Elon Comstock to Comstock and Cassidy, Nov. 11, 1863; *World* circular, 1863, Marble MSS.

63. Elon Comstock to Comstock and Cassidy, June 15, 1864; E. Comstock to Marble, July 19, 1864; Marble to E. Comstock, July 4, 1864; Marble to "C" June 29, 1864, Marble MSS.

64. William Cassidy to Marble, Feb. 2, Mar. 23, May 17, 29, June 2, 1865, n.d.; Marble to E. Comstock, Feb. 13, 1865; Marble to Calvert Comstock, n.d.; Marble to William Cassidy, May 19, 1865; statement of the *World*'s financial history prepared by Charles O'Conor, Oct. 30, 1868, Marble MSS.

65. Barlow to Marble, Sept. 11, 30, Oct. 4, 1867, Feb. 12, June 15, 1868, Marble MSS.

66. Marble to Barlow, Sept. 13, 1867, June 13, 1868, Barlow MSS.

67. Marble to Barlow, June 13, Oct. 9, 1868, Barlow MSS; Charles O'Conor statement of the financial history of the *World*, Oct. 30, 1868, Marble MSS.

68. Barlow to Marble, Nov. 2, 1868; Marble to Chamberlain, Jan. 8, 1869; Marble to Belmont, Jan. 9, 21, 1869; Bangs to Marble, Jan. 21, 1869, Marble MSS.

Chapter Seven

1. Marble to James Buchanan, Feb. 25, 1867, John Bassett Moore, ed., *The Works of James Buchanan* 11:435; Eric L. McKitrick, *Andrew Johnson and Reconstruction* (Chicago: University of Chicago Press, 1960), pp. 460–62; *World*, Dec. 6, 1866.

2. Edward McPherson, *The Political History of the United States of America during the Period of Reconstruction* (Washington: Phillips & Solomons, 1871), p. 194; *New Orleans Crescent* quoted in the *Herald*, Jan. 9, 1867; McKitrick, *Andrew Johnson and Reconstruction*, pp. 465–66; James Ford Rhodes, *History of the United States* (New York: Macmillan Co., 1906) 6:5–9; John Forsyth to Marble, Oct. 13, 1866, Marble MSS.

3. Forsyth to Marble, Jan. 28, 1867; Chamberlain to Marble, Dec. 2, 1866, Marble MSS.

4. Edward McPherson, *The Political History of the United States during the Period of Reconstruction* (Washington: Phillips & Solomons, 1871), pp. 143–47, 352–53.

5. *World*, Jan. 2, 15, 21, 1867; Edward L. Gambill, "Northern Democrats and Reconstruction, 1865–1868," unpublished Ph.D. dissertation, University of Iowa, 1969, pp. 227–29.

6. Forsyth to Marble, Oct. 13, 1866, Marble MSS; *World*, Jan. 9, 1867.

7. *World*, Jan. 14, 17, 22, 23, 1867.

8. McKitrick, *Andrew Johnson and Reconstruction*, pp. 473–81; *World*, Feb. 14, 1867.

9. Marble to Buchanan, Feb. 25, 1867, Moore, *Works of Buchanan* 11:434–35; Marble to Montgomery Blair, Mar. 11, 1867, Blair MSS; *World*, Feb. 19, 1867; *Herald*, Feb. 6, 7, 1867.

10. *World*, Feb. 21, 23, 26, 27, Mar. 4, 1867.

11. McKitrick, *Andrew Johnson and Reconstruction*, pp. 483–84; Rhodes, *History* 6:86–87; Forsyth to Marble, Mar. 5, 1867, Marble MSS; *World*, Mar. 9, 1867.

12. *World*, Aug. 15, Sept. 30, 1867.

13. Zeb Vance to Marble, May 5, 1867; J. A. Englehard to Marble, May 10, 1867; R. D. Rice (introducing Eben F. Pillsbury) to Marble, July 28, 1867, Marble MSS.

14. Belmont to Marble, n.d., July 4, 1867; Marcellus Emery to Marble, June 1, 1867, Marble MSS.

15. Ellis P. Oberholtzer, *A History of the United States since the Civil War* (New York: Macmillan Co., 1917–37) 2:10–26.

16. *World,* Sept. 26, 1867; Homer A. Stebbins, *A Political History of the State of New York, 1865–1869* (New York: Columbia University Press, 1913), pp. 233–38; Alexander C. Flick, *Samuel J. Tilden: A Study in Political Sagacity* (New York: Dodd, Mead & Co., 1939), p. 160.

17. *World,* Oct. 4, 5, 14, 15, 21, Nov. 8, 1867; *Post,* Oct. 5, 17, 1867.

18. Oberholtzer, *History* 1:479; Stebbins, *Political History of New York,* pp. 184–211; *World,* Nov. 7, 1867.

19. *World,* Nov. 13, 22, 1867.

20. Buchanan to Augustus Schell, Nov. 9, 1867, Moore, *Works of Buchanan* 11:455; Curtis to Marble, Nov. 7, 1867; Tilden to Marble, Apr. 23, 1867; Chamberlain to Marble, n.d.; Forsyth to Marble, Dec. 19, 1867; Haldeman to Marble, Nov. 13, 1867, Marble MSS; *World,* Jan. 4, Mar. 30, 1868; Gambill, "Northern Democrats and Reconstruction," pp. 269–70.

21. *World,* Mar. 19, 1867; Irwin Unger, *The Greenback Era* (Princeton, N.J.: Princeton University Press, 1964), pp. 78–84; Robert P. Sharkey, *Money, Class, and Party* (Baltimore: Johns Hopkins University Press, 1959), pp. 97–101; Chester M. Destler, *American Radicalism* (Chicago: Quadrangle, 1966), pp. 32–43.

22. *World,* Nov. 19, 1867; Marble to Pendleton, Nov. 23, 1867; Pendleton to Marble, Nov. 24, 1867, Marble MSS.

23. Joseph Dorfman, *The Economic Mind in American Civilization* (New York: Viking Press, 1946), pp. 758–67; Unger, *Greenback Era,* pp. 126–31.

24. Marble to Anderson, Mar. 17, 1868, Anderson MSS.

25. Bogart to Marble, Jan. 15, 1868; Warren to Marble, Jan. 28, 1868, Marble MSS.

26. Stewart Mitchell, *Horatio Seymour* (Cambridge, Mass.: Harvard University Press, 1938), pp. 399–400.

27. Marble to Anderson, Mar. 17, 1868, Anderson MSS.

28. Charles H. Coleman, *The Election of 1868* (New York: Columbia University Press, 1933), pp. 54–57; *World,* Apr. 14, 1868.

29. *World,* Feb. 18, 22, 1868; Belmont to Marble, n.d.; Horace White to Marble, Feb. 26, 1868, Marble MSS; Belmont to Tilden, Feb. 19, 1868, Tilden MSS.

30. Wilbur F. Storey to Marble, Feb. 12, 1868, Marble MSS; *World,* Jan. 30, Feb. 1, 1868.

31. *World,* Mar. 13, 14, 1868.

32. John Bigelow, ed., *The Writings and Speeches of Samuel J. Tilden* (New York: Harper and Brothers, 1885) 1:395–420.

33. Marble to Anderson, Mar. 17, 1868, Anderson MSS.

34. Pendleton to Marble, Mar. 3, 1868; McLean to Marble, Mar. 22, 1868, Marble MSS.

35. Howard K. Beale, ed., *The Diary of Gideon Welles* (New York: W. W. Norton and Co., 1960) 3:121, 184–85; Francis P. Blair, Sr., to F. P. Blair, Jr., Nov. 2, 1867, Blair MSS.

36. William B. Hesseltine, *Ulysses S. Grant, Politician* (New York: Dodd, Mead and Co., 1935), pp. 89–103; Doolittle to Marble, Dec. 21, 1867, Marble MSS; Marble to Doolittle, Dec. 29, 1867, *Publications of the Southern History Association* 11 (1907): 6.

37. *World,* Jan. 2, 16, 22, 1868.

38. Marble to M. Blair, Mar. 11, 1867, Blair MSS; Beale, ed., *Diary of Welles* 3:223; *World,* Feb. 26, 1868; John Fiske to Abby Fiske, Feb. 27, 1868, Ethel F. Fiske, ed., *The Letters of John Fiske* (New York: Macmillan Co., 1940), p. 172.

39. Beale, *Diary of Welles* 3:295; *Cincinnati West and South* quoted in Horace S. Merrill, *Bourbon Democracy of the Middle West, 1865–1896* (Baton Rouge, La.: Louisiana State University Press, 1953), p. 51.

40. Warren to Marble, May 23, 1868; Bogart to Marble, May 8, 1868; Belmont to Marble, Aug. 25, 1874, Marble MSS; Frederick A. Aiken to Chase, June 25, 1868, Chase MSS, Library of Congress; John Fiske to his mother, July 18, 1868, Fiske, *Letters of John Fiske,* p. 174; Unger, *Greenback Era,* p. 90.

41. J. W. Schuckers, *The Life and Public Services of Salmon Portland Chase,* (New York: D. Appleton and Co., 1874), pp. 576–89.

42. Coleman, *Election of 1868,* pp. 103–4; Marble to Anderson, Mar. 17, 1868, Anderson MSS; *World,* Mar. 26, 1868.

43. Robert B. Warden, *An Account of the Private Life and Public Services of Salmon Portland Chase* (Cincinnati: Wilstock, Baldwin and Co., 1874), pp. 683–84; *World,* Apr. 14, 1868; Schuckers, *Chase,* pp. 578–79.

44. Hiram Barney to Chase, May 28, 1868, Chase MSS; Chase to Belmont, May 30, 1868, Marble MSS.

45. Coleman, *Election of 1868,* pp. 111, 114; Stebbins, *Political History of New York,* pp. 316, 325–26; James Dixon to Marble, May 30, 1868, Marble MSS.

46. Coleman, *Election of 1868,* pp. 126–27; Warren to Marble, May 30, 1868, Marble MSS; Church to Tilden, June 10, 1868, Tilden MSS.

47. John Fiske to his mother, July 18, 1868, Fiske, *Letters of John Fiske,* p. 174; Frederick A. Aiken to Chase, June 25, 1868, Chase MSS; Belmont to Marble, Aug. 25, 1874, Marble MSS.

48. *World,* June 3, 8, 1868.

49. M. Blair to Barlow, June 10, 1868; James A. Bayard to Barlow, May 27, June 10, 1868, Barlow MSS; M. Blair to Tilden, June 5, 1868; Arphaxed Loomis to Tilden, June 8, 1868, John Bigelow, ed., *Letters and Literary Memorials of Samuel J. Tilden* 1:229–30, 232–33; *World,* June 15, 1868.

50. Marble to Francis N. Bangs, Aug. 1868, Marble MSS; Marble to Anderson, June 17, 1868, Anderson MSS.

51. Marble to Bangs, Aug., 1868, Marble MSS; John Fiske to Abby Fiske, Oct. 27, 1868, Fiske, *Letters of John Fiske,* p. 177.

52. William W. Warden to Johnson, June 29, 1868, Johnson MSS; *World,* June 18, 19, 22, 1868.

53. Winston S. Pierce to Marble, June 15, 1868; Pierce to Tilden, June 20, 1868, Marble MSS; Hiram Barney to Chase, June 26, 1868, Chase MSS; Edmund Cooper to Johnson, July 2, 1868, Johnson MSS.

54. Coleman, *Election of 1868,* pp. 187–245.

55. Sam Ward to Marble, July 31, 1868; Joseph Warren to Seymour, Sept. 7, 1868; Warren to Marble, Sept. 7, 1868, enclosing clipping from the *Buffalo Courier,* Marble MSS; Horace H. Day to Seymour, Aug. 15, 1868; Warren to Seymour, n.d., Seymour MSS, New York Historical Society; Coleman, *Election of 1868,* p. 296.

56. Belmont to Marble, Aug. 17, 1868; to Tilden, Oct. 8, 1868, Marble MSS.

57. W. E. Smith, *The Francis Preston Blair Family in Politics* (New York: Macmillan Co., 1933) 2:422–24; Coleman, *Election of 1868,* pp. 345–47; Barlow to Tilden, Oct. 14, 15, 1868, Tilden MSS.

58. Barlow to Tilden, Oct. 15, 1868, Tilden MSS.

59. *World,* Oct. 15, 1868.

60. Marble later denied responsibility for the article, claiming it was written by Ivory Chamberlain during his absence. But other evidence contradicts his claim. None of Marble's correspondents at the time referred to Chamberlain and all credited Marble with the article. Also the reports of indecision at the *World* during Marble's absence in June show that none of the staff would have approved such an article on his own responsibility. Certainly Chamberlain, who actually had favored Pendleton's nomination, would never have suggested such a departure. Also the article of Oct. 15 was followed by a similar one the next day. If the first article was a mistake, Marble would surely have stopped it from happening again. See Chamberlain to Marble, three undated letters filed in the volumes for 1868, Marble MSS; *World,* Oct. 16, 1868. For Marble's claims see Marble to Charles O'Conor, n.d. [May, 1881], Marble MSS; *World,* Mar. 10, 1881.

61. Coleman, *Election of 1868,* pp. 351–53; C. R. Rowland to Marble, Oct. 15, 1868; Orlando Robinson to Marble, Oct. 15, 1868; Brinton Coscoe to Marble, Oct. 16, 1868; Edward Hamilton to Marble, Oct. 16, 1868; H. J. Billings to Marble, Oct. 16, 1868; John G. Mills to Marble, Oct. 17, 1868; Henry J. Hopper to Marble, Oct. 17, 1868; Ten Democrats from Chautauqua County, New York, to Marble, Oct. 20, 1868; Cassidy to Tilden, Oct. 18, 1868, Marble MSS.

62. Coleman, *Election of 1868,* pp. 354–56; *World,* Oct. 23, 24, 26, 28, 1868; John Fiske to Abby Fiske, Oct. 27, 1868, Fiske, *Letters of John Fiske,* p. 177.

63. Cassidy to Marble, Oct. 18, 1868, Marble MSS.

64. Belmont to Marble, Nov. 6, 1868; Kerr to Marble, Nov. 8, 1868; Pierce to Marble, Nov. 10, 1868; Beach to Marble, Nov. 25, 1868, Marble MSS.

Chapter Eight

1. Minturn to Marble, Apr. 2, 1869, Marble MSS.

2. Belmont to Marble, Dec. 10, 1868, Marble MSS.

3. *World,* Jan. 2, 20, May 17, June 25, 29, July 19, Aug. 16, 1869.

4. Ibid., Dec. 24, 1868.

5. Tilden to Marble, Dec. ?, 1868; Marble to Tilden, Dec. 25, 1868; Hiram Calkins to Marble, Dec. 29, 1868, Marble MSS; *World,* Dec. 24, 26, 1868.

6. *World,* Jan. 2, 5, 9, 12, 14, 1869; Marble to Anderson, Mar. 16, 1869, Anderson MSS.

7. Calkins to Marble, Mar. 17, 1869, Marble MSS; *World,* Mar. 20, 1869.

8. *World,* Apr. 8, 21, 1869; Marble to Anderson, Jan. 6, 1869, Anderson MSS.

9. *World,* Apr. 28, May 3, 6, 7, 13, 1869.

10. Marble to Cassidy, May 9, 1869, Marble MSS.

11. Cassidy to Marble, May 13, 1869, Marble MSS.

12. Beach to Tilden, July 5, 30, 1869; Bogart to Marble, July 30, 1869, Marble MSS.

13. Marble to Tilden, n.d.; Tilden to Marble, July 30, 1869, Marble MSS.

14. *World,* Sept. 11, 14, 18, 20, 1869. Alexander C. Flick, *Samuel J. Tilden: A Study in Political Sagacity* (New York: Dodd, Mead & Co., 1939), p. 201; John Bigelow, *The Life of Samuel J. Tilden* (New York: Harper and Brothers, 1895) 1:184.

15. Chamberlain to Marble, Sept. 16, 1869; Calkins to Marble, Sept. 16, 1869; Croly to Marble, Sept. 13, 1869; Tilden to Marble, Sept. 14, 1869, Marble MSS.

16. Matthew P. Breen, *Thirty Years of New York Politics* (New York: the author, 1899), pp. 188–89; Bigelow, *Tilden* 1:184; *Post,* Sept. 23, 1869.

17. *World,* Nov. 4, 5, 1869.

18. Breen, *Thirty Years,* pp. 191–94; Mark D. Hirsch, *William C. Whitney: Modern Warwick* (New York: Dodd, Mead & Co., 1948), p. 56; Mark D. Hirsch, "More Light on Boss Tweed," *Political Science Quarterly* 55 (1945): 272.

19. Belmont to Marble, Mar. 1, 1870; Barlow to Marble, n.d. [Feb. 26, 1870]; Tilden to Marble, Mar. 1, 1870; Marble to Chamberlain, Feb. 27 [1870]; Marble to Tilden, Mar. 3, 1870, Marble MSS.

20. Beach to Marble, Feb. 16, 19, 1870; Bangs to Marble, Feb. 21, 1870, Marble MSS.

21. *World,* Feb. 3, 5, Mar. 1, 9, 1870; Marble to Chamberlain, Feb. 27 [1870], Marble MSS.

22. *Tribune,* Feb. 3, 1870; M. R. Werner, *Tammany Hall* (New York: Doubleday, Doran and Co., 1928), pp. 171–72; Denis Tilden Lynch, *"Boss Tweed": The Story of a Grim Generation* (New York: Boni and Liveright, 1927), pp. 325–26; Frank J. Goodnow, "The Tweed Ring," in Bryce, *American Commonwealth* 2:343–44.

23. Breen, *Thirty Years,* pp. 195–96; *World,* Feb. 8, 9, 10, 11, 17, 1870; Marble to Chamberlain, Feb. 27 [1870], Marble MSS.

24. Hirsch, "More Light on Boss Tweed," p. 270; Morrissey to Marble, Mar. 22, 1870, Marble MSS.

25. Lynch, *Tweed,* pp. 329–30; Breen, *Thirty Years,* pp. 196–99; *Tribune,* Mar. 29, 1870; Hirsch, "More Light on Boss Tweed," p. 270.

26. *World*, Mar. 29, 1870; Breen, *Thirty Years*, pp. 199–200; Lynch, *Tweed*, p. 331.

27. *World*, Apr. 20, May 19, 23, 1870; Marble to Sweeny, May 26, 1870; Sweeny to Marble, May 26, June 1, 1870, Marble MSS.

28. *World* financial statement, 1863–75, prepared by Bangs, item no. 9346, Marble MSS.

29. Bangs to Marble, July 13, 15, 16, 19 (2), 21 (2), 1870, n.d.; Hurlbert to Marble, n.d. [July 19, 1870], n.d.; Bangs to Croly, July 16, 1870; Croly to Bangs, July 18, 1870; Marble to Bangs, on bottom of Bangs to Marble, July 15, 1870, Marble MSS.

30. *World*, July 18, Aug. 11, Sept. 3, 4, 5, 13, 18, 23, Oct. 17, 1870, Jan. 8, 9, 15, 17, 20, 1871.

31. A. H. Green to Marble, July 23, 1870; Hurlbert to Marble, July 29, 1870; Beach to Tilden, Aug. 26, 1870, Marble MSS; *Times*, Sept. 22, 1870.

32. Financial statement, no. 9346, Marble MSS.

33. *Real Estate Record and Builder's Guide*, May 4, 1889; Hurlbert to Marble, July 29, 1870, Marble MSS.

34. Bangs to Marble, Oct. 17, 1870, Jan. 24, 1871, Marble MSS.

35. Bangs to Marble, Jan. 24, [Feb. 8], 1871, Marble MSS.

36. Croly to Marble, two letters dated "June, 1871," Sept. 19, Nov. 10, 27, n.d. [Nov. 30], 1871, Nov. 25, 1872; Croly to Bangs, Dec. 24, 1872, Marble MSS.

37. Sweeny to Marble, Dec. 8, 1870, Apr. 26, 1871; Bangs to Marble, May 12, 1871, Marble MSS; *World*, Feb. 6, 1871.

38. Chamberlain to Marble, n.d. [July 1871], Aug. 8 [1871]; Croly to Marble, Aug. 17, 1871, n.d. [Sept. 1871], Marble MSS.

39. *World*, July 24, 27, 28, 29, 30, Aug. 4, 18, 23, Sept. 5, 8, 1871.

40. Bangs to Marble, Aug. 19, 1871; Croly to Marble, Aug. 17, 1871, Marble MSS.

41. Werner, *Tammany Hall*, pp. 222–28; Flick, *Tilden*, p. 217; *Times*, Sept. 18, 1871.

42. *Times*, Sept. 15, 18, 1871.

43. Ibid., Sept. 13, 15, 1871.

44. Marble to Tilden, Oct. 11, 1871; Belmont to Marble, n.d., Sept. 19, 1871, Marble MSS; *World*, Sept. 12, 18, 20, 22, 1871.

45. Tilden to Marble, Sept. 29, 1871; Marble to Tilden, Oct. 11, 1871, Marble MSS.

46. Flick, *Tilden*, p. 216; Tilden to Marble, Sept. 30, 1871, Marble MSS.

47. Flick, *Tilden*, pp. 218–20; Mark D. Hirsch, "Samuel J. Tilden: The Story of a Lost Opportunity," *American Historical Review* 56 (1951): 794–95; Seymour to Tilden, Oct. 8, 1871, Tilden MSS; *Herald*, Oct. 4, 5, 6, 1871; *World*, Oct. 10, 1871.

48. Marble to Tilden, Oct. 11, 1871, Marble MSS.

49. Tilden to Marble, Oct. 11, 1871, Marble MSS; Hirsch, *Whitney*, pp. 58–59.

50. Hirsch, "Samuel J. Tilden," pp. 796–800; *World,* Oct. 24, Nov. 10, 1871.

51. Earle D. Ross, *The Liberal Republican Movement* (New York: Henry Holt and Co., 1919), pp. 11–29.

52. Allan Nevins, *The Evening Post, a Century of Journalism* (New York: Boni and Liveright, 1922), pp. 389–94; William B. Hesseltine, *Ulysses S. Grant: Politician* (New York: Ungar, 1957), pp. 211–12; Ross, *Liberal Republican Movement,* pp. 17–18.

53. Ross, *Liberal Republican Movement,* pp. 48–50, 72–75.

54. Ibid., pp. 28–32, 50–51, 68–70.

55. Hesseltine, *Grant,* p. 193; Moore to Marble, Apr. 25, Nov. 22, 1870, Feb. 5, May 27, 1871; Wells to Marble, Feb. 28, May 14, Nov. 6, 1871; Horace White to Marble, Feb. 18, 1870, Marble MSS; Marble to Wells, Mar. 19, 1869, Apr. 4, 17, Nov. 15, 1871,Wells MSS, Library of Congress.

56. Belmont to McCook, June 5, 1871, Marble MSS.

57. *Herald,* Oct. 5, 1871; Stewart Mitchell, *Horatio Seymour* (Cambridge, Mass.: Harvard University Press, 1938), pp. 496–97, 498–99.

58. *World,* June 2, 1871; Samuel J. Butterworth to Marble, June 5, 1871; Marble to Butterworth, n.d., on back of Butterworth's letter, Marble MSS.

59. *World,* March 6, 7, 10, May 24, June 3, Nov. 18, 1871; Belmont to Marble, n.d. [Nov. 1871], Marble MSS.

60. Cf. Charles Davies to Marble, Dec. 15, 1871, Marble MSS.

61. Marble to M. Blair, Feb. 21, 1871, Blair MSS; Grosvenor to Marble, Nov. 8, 1871; Marble to Tilden, Nov. 22, 1871, Marble MSS.

62. *World,* Nov. 24, 1871.

63. Marble to M. Blair, Nov. 28, Dec. 10, 1871, Blair MSS.

64. Blair to Marble, Dec. 14, 23, 1871, Blair MSS; Bangs to Marble, Nov. 16, 1871; George W. Adams to Marble, Dec. 16, 1871, Marble MSS; *World,* Dec. 8, 1871.

65. Louisa Arnold to Marble, Dec. 3, 1862, Jan. 28, 1869, Nov. 19, 1870; Chamberlain to Marble, Aug. 2, 1870; Bangs to Marble, Sept. 16, 1870, Marble MSS; John Fiske to Abby Fiske, July 12, 1870, Ethel F. Fiske, ed., *The Letters of John Fiske* (New York: Macmillan Co., 1940), pp. 197–98.

66. Bangs to Marble, Feb. 21, 1872; Marble to Bangs, Mar. 8, 13, 1872; S. G. Arnold to Marble, Mar. 29, 1872, Marble MSS.

67. Cf. Marble to John Quincy Adams, Jr., Oct. 28, 1868, Marble MSS; Martin Duberman, *Charles Francis Adams, 1807–1886* (Boston: Houghton Mifflin Co., 1961), pp. 356–59.

68. Moore to Marble, Mar. 14, 1872, Marble MSS.

69. Marble to Anderson, Oct. 19, 1862, Anderson MSS; Marble to Greeley, Dec. 18, 24, 1863, Jan. 6, 29, Aug. 16, Dec. 28, 1864, Feb. 13, 23, 1865, Greeley MSS, New York Public Library.

70. Marble to Wells, Apr. 30, 1872; undated memorandum filed with the letter, Marble MSS.

71. Marble to Chamberlain, 4 p.m., May 3, 1872; Chamberlain to Marble, 6 p.m., May 3, 1872, Marble MSS.

72. Chamberlain to Marble, 8:35 p.m., May 3, 1872; Marble to Chamberlain, 10 p.m., May 3, 1872, Marble MSS.

73. Belmont to Bowles, May 7, 1872, Wells MSS.

74. Belmont to Marble, Aug. 19, 1872, Marble MSS; *World,* Sept. 6, 1872.

75. Chamberlain to Whitelaw Reid, Dec. 1, 1872, Reid MSS, Library of Congress; *World,* July 1, 2, 8, 11, Sept. 2, 5, 6, 1872, Mar. 10, 1881.

76. Nevins, *Post,* pp. 395–99; *Tribune,* Nov. 17, 1874.

77. *World,* Nov. 15, 1872.

Chapter Nine

1. *World,* July 5, Aug. 26, Sept. 2, 1873.

2. Beach to Marble, Aug. 9, 1873, Marble MSS.

3. *World,* Oct. 2, 4, Nov. 5, 6, 1873; Beach to Marble, Nov. 27, 1873; Calvert Comstock to Marble, Oct. 18, 1873, Marble MSS.

4. *Tribune,* Nov. 6, 1874; Stewart Mitchell, *Horatio Seymour* (Cambridge, Mass.: Harvard University Press, 1938), p. 474; *World,* Oct. 8, 1873.

5. *World,* July 5, 17, Aug. 30, 31, Sept. 13, Oct. 1, 4, 1875.

6. Alexander C. Flick, *Samuel J. Tilden: A Study in Political Sagacity* (New York: Dodd, Mead & Co., 1939), pp. 274, 525–30; John Bigelow, *The Life of Samuel J. Tilden* (New York: Harper and Brothers, 1895) 1:17–18, 93, 284.

7. Mark D. Hirsch, "Samuel J. Tilden: The Story of a Lost Opportunity," *American Historical Review,* pp. 796–98.

8. Flick, *Tilden,* pp. 242–45; Beach to Tilden, July 20, 1874, Tilden MSS.

9. *Tribune,* Sept. 29, Oct. 27, 1874; *World,* Oct. 1, 20, 28, 29.

10. Undated draft of article for the *Weekly World* in Marble's handwriting, Marble MSS.

11. Werner, *Tammany Hall,* pp. 277–79.

12. Seymour Mandelbaum, *Boss Tweed's New York* (New York: John Wiley & Sons, 1965), p. 112.

13. Ibid., pp. 89–91, 114–16.

14. William R. Martin, statement of the *World*'s claim against the city, Mar. 8, ?; Bangs's statement, n.d., Marble MSS; A. H. Green to Mayor W. F. Havemeyer, June 25, 1873, Mayors MSS, New York City Municipal Archives.

15. Mandelbaum, *Boss Tweed's New York,* p. 133; Mark D. Hirsch, *William C. Whitney: Modern Warwick* (New York: Dodd, Mead & Co., 1948), pp. 86–89; Reid to Tilden, Feb. 22, 1875, Tilden MSS; *Herald,* Jan. 20, Feb. 14, 16, 19, 1875; *Tribune,* Feb. 8, 13, 17, 18, 19, 1875; *World,* Feb. 18, 26, Apr. 1, 1875.

16. Stillson to Marble, Apr. 2, 1875, Marble MSS.

17. Stillson to Marble, May 6, 1875; Marble to Tilden, n.d., July 21, 1875, Marble MSS; Marble to Tilden, Aug. 23, 1875, Tilden MSS; John Bigelow, "Diary," May 1, 1875, Bigelow MSS, New York Public Library; *World,* Feb. 19, 26, Mar. 2, 1875; Flick, *Tilden,* p. 261; Hirsch, *Whitney,* pp. 91–92.

18. Flick, *Tilden,* p. 265; Bigelow, "Diary," Sept. 10, 1874, Bigelow MSS; George T. McJimsey, "The Governorship of Samuel J. Tilden," unpublished M.A. thesis, Columbia University, 1959, pp. 44–51.

19. Stillson to Marble, Mar. 25, 1875, Marble MSS.

20. *Post,* Jan. 6, Mar. 10, 1873; Sept. 7, 24, Oct. 26, 1874; Allan Nevins, *The Evening Post, a Century of Journalism* (New York: Boni and Liveright, 1922), pp. 401–2.

21. Royal Cortissoz, *The Life of Whitelaw Reid* (New York: Charles Scribner's Sons, 1921) 1:276–300; Stillson to Marble, Mar. 25, Apr. 9, 1875, Marble MSS.

22. Whitney to Reid, Mar. 19, May 2, June 30, July 1, Oct. 9, 31, Dec. 31, 1875, Apr. 14, June 3, Oct. 8, Nov. 27, 1876; William T. Pelton to Reid, Sept. 21, 25, 1875, Reid MSS.

23. Flick, *Tilden,* p. 270; *Tribune,* Sept. 15, 18, 1875; *Times,* Sept. 15, 1875; J. S. Moore to Thomas F. Bayard, Sept. 20, 1875, Bayard MSS.

24. Flick, *Tilden,* pp. 270–72; McJimsey, "Tilden," p. 66.

25. Albert V. House, "Men, Morals, and Manipulation in the Pennsylvania Democracy of 1875," *Pennsylvania History* 23 (1956): 248–66.

26. Randall to Chauncey F. Black, June 30, 1875; Reed to Black, June 30, July 7, 21, 26, 1875; J. M. Cooper to Black, July 8, 10, 17, 1875, Jeremiah Black MSS, Library of Congress; Black to Reed, June 21, 26, 27, 1875, Marble MSS.

27. *World,* June 10, 19, July 19, 21, Aug. 2, 3, 1875; Reed to Marble, n.d., Marble MSS; House, "Pennsylvania Democracy," pp. 261–63.

28. Albert V. House, "The Speakership Contest of 1875: Democratic Response to Power," *Journal of American History* 52(1965):256–57, 259.

29. Ibid., pp. 257–58.

30. Kerr to Marble, Nov. 8, 1868, Mar. 17, Apr. 10, 1870, May 30, 1871, Marble MSS.

31. Kerr to Marble, two letters Nov. 28, 1875; Stillson to Marble, Dec. 5, 1875; Hurlbert to Marble, Dec. ?, 1875, Marble MSS; Randall to Chauncey Black, Nov. 8, 1875, J. S. Black MSS; Heister Clymer to Bayard, Dec. 1, 1875, Bayard MSS; House, "Speakership Contest," pp. 269–71.

32. Kerr to Marble, Dec. 7, 13, 1875; Hiram Calkins to Marble, Dec. 16, 1875, Marble MSS.

33. Kerr to Marble, Dec. 13, 18, 22, 1875; Stillson to Marble, Dec. 19, 1875; Marble to Stillson on back of Stillson's letter, Marble MSS; Hirsch, *Whitney,* pp. 33–34, 105; House, "Speakership Contest," p. 272.

34. Irwin Unger, *The Greenback Era* (Princeton, N.J.: Princeton University Press, 1964), pp. 268–69, 273; Marble to Thomas F. Bayard, Aug. 21, 1875, Bayard MSS.

35. *World,* June 18, 1875; Unger, *Greenback Era,* pp. 281–82; Marble to Bayard, Aug. 21, 1875, Bayard MSS.

36. Unger, *Greenback Era,* pp. 280–81; Marble to Barlow, Oct. 14, 1875, Barlow MSS.

37. Marble to Barlow, n.d., Marble MSS; John Bigelow, ed., *The Writings and Speeches of Samuel J. Tilden* (New York: Harper and Brothers, 1885) 2:282–92.

38. Mandelbaum, *Boss Tweed's New York,* pp. 126–27; *World,* June 22, 1875; Petitions from workingmen, Jan. 27, 1875, "1876," Mayors MSS, Municipal Archives.

39. Mandelbaum, *Boss Tweed's New York,* pp. 136–37; Kelly to Marble, Dec. 17, 1875, Marble MSS.

40. Unger, *Greenback Era,* pp. 304–5; Belmont to Marble, Feb. 14, n.d., 1876; Payne to Marble, Mar. 1, 1876, Marble MSS.

41. Kerr to Marble, Mar. 31, 1876, Marble MSS.

42. Barlow to Bayard, Feb. 1, Mar. 25, Apr. 26, May 19, 1876; Belmont to Bayard, June 9, 1876; Perry Belmont to Bayard, June 2, 1876; Marvin Bovee to Bayard, May 25, 1876, Bayard MSS; Bayard to David A. Wells, May 27, 1876, Wells MSS.

43. *World,* Feb. 22, 28, Mar. 1, 21, 1876; Theodore F. Randolph to Marble, Apr. 7, 1876, Marble MSS.

44. Marble to Barlow, n.d., Barlow MSS.

45. Barlow to Marble, Sept. 14, 1876, Marble MSS.

46. *World* financial statement, item no. 9346; Bangs to Marble, Feb. 28, 1873, Marble MSS.

47. Bangs to Marble, Nov. 18, 1874, Marble MSS.

48. *World* financial statement, item no. 9346; Bangs to Marble, Oct. 6, Nov. 18, Dec. 3, 8, 1873; Feb. 26, Mar. 14, Apr. 28, June 29, July 2, Sept. 26, Oct. 9, 15, Nov. 18, Dec. 31, 1874; Mar. 18, May 6, July 9, 1875, Marble MSS.

49. Bangs to Marble, Mar. 25, Oct. 9, 1874, Marble MSS.

50. See undated sheets of paper, items no. 9356, 9358, 9359, 9360, Marble MSS. Marble's calculations are a bit unclear. In some instances he has added $400 to the cost of newsgathering and in others has excluded it. Also, he is not clear in his figures and written comments whether he thought a profit would result from making up the *deficit,* including added costs, or from making up the *total costs,* which were, of course, higher than the deficit alone. In fact it is clear from his figures that it would have required an *added* circulation of 20,000 to make up the total costs. Marble is also unclear as to the role advertising revenues would play in increasing the *World*'s profits. In one place he suggests they would increase and in another he says they would not. It seems that in his calculations he did not anticipate a rise in advertising revenues. See also Marble to Belmont, June 30, 1875, Marble MSS.

    When all this has been noted, it must still be emphasized that Marble believed the *World* could be saved by changing its format and that he was willing to make the change.

51. Belmont to Marble, June 30, Sept. 11, 12, 1875; Marble to Belmont, June 30, Sept. 11, 1875; Bangs to Marble, June 30, July 9, 16, n.d., 1875, Marble MSS.

52. Barlow to Marble, Sept. 7, 8, 9, 1875; Marble to Montrose A. Pallen, Sept. 9, 1875; Pallen to Marble, n.d., Oct. 18, 1875; Stilson Hutchins to Marble, Oct. 15, 20, 1875, Marble MSS; Marble to Barlow, Sept. 9, 1875, Barlow MSS.

53. Bangs to Marble, Mar. 16, 1876, Marble MSS.

54. C. Vann Woodward, *Reunion and Reaction* (Garden City, N.Y.: Doubleday, rev. ed., 1956), pp. 73–106.

55. Scott's various offers are summarized in Marble to Sidney Webster, [Apr.] 21, 1876, Marble MSS. The progress of the negotiations is shown in Scott to Hurlbert, Feb. 12, 19 (three telegrams), 1876; Hurlbert to Scott, Apr. 11, n.d., 1876; Hurlbert to Marble, Feb. 15, 16, 17, 18, Mar. 8, Apr. 19, 1876; Barlow to Webster, Apr. 21, 1876, Marble MSS.

56. Marble to James Stokes, n.d. [Apr. 22, 1876], Marble MSS; *World,* May 22, 1876; Marble to Barlow, three undated letters, probably in Feb. and Mar. of 1876, Barlow MSS.

57. The details of the payment are recorded in two undated memoranda, one of which is in Marble's handwriting, and in Bangs to Marble, May 10, 1881, Marble MSS. The terms of the contract are in an undated statement by Hurlbert with additions by Barlow, also in the Marble MSS.

58. Flick, *Tilden,* pp. 283–86; Unger, *Greenback Era,* pp. 303–4; Barlow to Bayard, June 21, 1876, Bayard MSS.

59. Drafts of the platform in the handwriting of Marble, George Smith, and Joseph Hance, no. 10024–10046, Marble MSS. The drafts by Smith and Hance are undated, but Marble's bears the notation, "First rough sketch, June 18 '76," Marble MSS.

60. Flick, *Tilden,* pp. 286–87; *World,* June 27, 1876; Marble to G. W. Smith, June 27, 1876, Marble MSS.

61. Memorandum of the controversy by Thomas Ewing, Jr., dated 1876, Ewing MSS, Library of Congress; *World,* June 29, 1876.

62. Marble to Tilden, n.d. [July, 1876], Marble MSS; Kirk H. Porter and Donald Bruce Johnson, eds., *National Party Platforms* (Urbana, Ill.: University of Illinois Press, 1956), p. 50.

63. *World,* June 29, 1876.

64. Unger, *Greenback Era,* p. 309; Joseph F. Wall, *Henry Watterson, Reconstructed Rebel* (New York: Oxford University Press, 1956), p. 133; Marble to Tilden, June 28, 1876, Marble MSS.

65. Marble to the *World* on the "Albany Cabal," June, 1876; letter for Belmont, undated but published in the *World,* July 15, 1876; Marble to Abram S. Hewitt, Aug. 15, 1876, Marble MSS.

66. William R. Morrison to Marble, July 4, 1876; Randall L. Gibson to Marble, July 5, 13, 26, 1876; David A. Wells to Marble, July 12, 1876; Belmont to Marble, July 23, 1876, Marble MSS.

67. Marble to Gibson, July 12, 1876, Marble MSS.

68. Marble to Tilden, n.d. [July, 1876], Marble MSS; Marble, "To a Pouting Liberal," *World,* Aug. 26, 1876.

69. Morrison to Marble, July 4, 1876; Marble to Morrison, July 12, 1876, Marble MSS; *World,* Aug. 5, 1876; Unger, *Greenback Era,* pp. 311–18.

70. Belmont to Marble, July 23, 1876, Marble MSS.

71. Flick, *Tilden,* p. 305.

72. James B. Craig to Marble, July 26, 1876; Barlow to Marble, Aug. 10, 1876; Marble to Joseph Hance, Aug. 26, 1876, Marble MSS.

73. *Post,* Aug. 9, 1876; *World,* Aug. 26, 1876. The *Post,* however, was not convinced. *Post,* Aug. 26, 1876.

74. *Tribune,* Aug. 28, 29, 1876; *Times,* Aug. 29, 1876.

75. Ward to Bayard, Aug. 28, 1876, Bayard MSS; Bigelow, "Diary," Aug. 29, 1876, Bigelow MSS.

76. Barlow to Marble, Aug. 28, 1876, Marble MSS.

77. *Tribune,* Aug. 30, 1876.

78. Belmont to Marble, May 10, 1876; Marble to Joseph Hance, Aug. 26, 1876, Marble MSS; *Tribune,* Aug. 30, 1876.

79. *World,* Aug. 30, 1876; *Times,* Aug. 30, 1876; *Tribune,* Aug. 30, 1876; *Post,* Aug. 30, 1876.

80. *Tribune,* Aug. 31, 1876; Mitchell, *Seymour,* pp. 522–23.

81. Flick, *Tilden,* p. 306; Mitchell, *Seymour,* pp. 524–26; *World,* Sept. 1, 3, 4, 1876.

82. Alice Barlow to Barlow, Sept. 4, 1876; Barlow to Marble, Sept. 4, 5, 1876; Kelly to Marble, Sept. 4, 1876; Belmont to Marble, Sept. 7, 1876; MacFarland to Marble, Sept. 7, 1876, Marble MSS.

83. Bigelow, "Diary," Sept. 11, 12, 1876, Bigelow MSS.

84. *World,* Sept. 14, 1876; Marble to Barlow, Oct. 3, 1876, Barlow MSS.

85. Marble to Dr. A. G. Mercer, Nov. 5, 1876, Marble MSS.

86. Nevins, *Evening Post,* pp. 402–5; Cortissoz, *Reid* 1:324–28.

87. Marble to G. W. Smith, Nov. 8, 1876, Tilden MSS; Marble to Smith, Nov. 10, 1876; Smith to Marble, Nov. 8, 1876; "B" to Marble, Nov. 10, 1876, Marble MSS.

88. Wall, *Watterson,* pp. 140–41; "Testimony taken by the Select Committee on Alleged Frauds in the Presidential Election of 1876," *House Miscellaneous Documents,* 45th Congress, 3rd Session, no. 31, part 4 (Washington: Government Printing Office, 1879), pp. 221–22. Hereinafter cited as *House Investigation* with the part and page numbers following.

89. W. W. Davis, *Civil War and Reconstruction in Florida* (New York: Columbia University Press, 1913), pp. 687–714.

90. Marble to Pelton, Nov. 16, 17, 19, 21, 1876, *House Investigation* 4:224–25, 229–30; *World,* Nov. 20, 21, 1876; Davis, *Reconstruction in Florida,* pp. 715–16.

91. Marble to Pelton, two telegrams Nov. 19, 1876, *House Investigation* 4:224–25.

92. *World,* Nov. 21, 1876.

93. Davis, *Reconstruction in Florida,* pp. 269–71, 626–27; *World,* Nov. 22, 24, 25, 1876.

94. Marble to Pelton, Nov. 27, 1876, *House Investigation* 4:234.

95. Ibid. 2:134.

96. Wallace's testimony is in ibid. 1:513–14; for Marble's version see ibid. 4:264. See also McLin to William E. Chandler, Dec. 24, 1876, Jan. 2, 3, 9, 12, 16, 25, Mar. 21, June 13, 1877, Chandler MSS, Library of Congress.

97. Davis, *Reconstruction in Florida,* pp. 717–18; Marble to Pelton, Nov. 28, 1876, Tilden MSS.

98. Marble to Pelton, Nov. 28, 30, 1876, Tilden MSS; Marble to William Bigler, n.d. in reply to Bigler to Marble, Nov. 29, 1876, Marble MSS.

99. *World,* Dec. 1, 1876.

100. *House Investigation* 4:300, 302–3, 306–8; Woolley to Pelton, Dec. 1, 1876; Pelton to Woolley, Dec. 1, 1876, *House Investigation* 4:178.

101. Woolley to Pelton, Nov. 30, 1876; Woolley to Havemeyer, Dec. 1, 1876; Marble to Pelton, Dec. 2, 1876, *House Investigation* 4:175, 237, 310.

102. Marble to Pelton, Dec. 3, 5, 1876; Pelton to Marble, Dec. 3, 4, 1876; testimony of E. L. Parris, *House Investigation* 4:238–40, 179–80, 242, 291–92. William E. Chandler, who was in Florida representing the Republicans at the time, seems to have known nothing about overt attempts by Marble or Woolley to bribe the board members, and he later admitted that the evidence revealed only "the artifices of thieving shysters anxious to make money out of Tilden or Marble." Chandler to Whitelaw Reid, Sept. 28, 1878, Reid MSS. C. E. Dyke, who reported the $50,000 proposal to Marble, later declared that Marble refused to follow it up. Dyke to the New York Press, Oct. 24, 1878, Marble MSS.

103. Davis, *Reconstruction in Florida,* pp. 727–28; *House Investigation* 4:246–47; Marble to Pelton, Dec. 7, 1876, Tilden MSS.

104. Marble to Tilden, n.d., Marble MSS.

105. Flick, *Tilden,* pp. 354–55.

106. Belmont to Marble, n.d. probably written Dec. 25, 1876, Marble MSS; Barlow to Bayard, Jan. 10, 11, 1877, Bayard MSS; Flick, *Tilden,* p. 366.

107. Belmont to Marble [Dec. 25, 1876], Marble MSS; Perry Belmont to Bayard, Dec. 31, 1876, Bayard MSS; Flick, *Tilden,* pp. 357, 366.

108. James C. Welling to Marble, Jan. 10, 1877, Marble MSS; Flick, *Tilden,* pp. 366–67; William B. Hesseltine, *Ulysses S. Grant: Politician* (New York: Ungar, 1957), pp. 418–19.

109. Harry Barnard, *Rutherford B. Hayes and His America* (New York: Bobbs-Merrill Co., 1954), p. 362; Garfield to Hayes, Dec. 12, 1876, quoted in C. C. Tansill, *The Congressional Career of Thomas F. Bayard* (Washington, D.C.: Georgetown University Press, 1946), p. 154. For Hewitt's views see *House Investigation* 3:631–32.

110. Flick, *Tilden,* pp. 368–71; Marble, *A Secret Chapter of Political History,* pamphlet copy of a letter written to the *New York Sun,* Aug. 3, 1878, p. 15, claims he was present when Tilden and Hewitt discussed the plan. Hewitt many years later denied that Marble was present. "Secret History of the Disputed Election, 1876–77," in Allan Nevins, ed., *Selected Writings of Abram S. Hewitt* (New York: Columbia University Press, 1937), pp. 167–68.

111. Marble, *Secret Chapter,* pp. 20–22; Belmont to Bayard, Jan. 19, 20, 1877, Bayard MSS; Belmont to Marble, "Sunday"; Marble to Tilden, "Sunday,"

Marble MSS. Although the last two letters cited are undated, their contents make it plain that they were both written on Sunday, Jan. 21, 1877.

112. Marble, *Secret Chapter,* pp. 21–22; Bigelow, ed., *Letters and Literary Memorials of Samuel J. Tilden* (New York: Harper and Brothers, 1908) 2:533–34; Nevins, ed., *Writings of Hewitt,* pp. 187–90; Belmont to Marble, Jan. 18, 1877, Marble MSS; Belmont to Bayard, Jan. 19, 1877, Bayard MSS.

113. Davis, *Reconstruction in Florida,* pp. 733–34; R. B. Hilton to Marble, Dec. 31, 1876, Tilden MSS.

114. Bigelow, ed., *Writings and Speeches of Samuel J. Tilden* (New York: Harper and Brothers, 1885) 2:463, 469.

115. Davis, *Reconstruction in Florida,* p. 736; R. B. Hilton to Marble, Jan. 4, 7, 1877; Wilkinson Call to Marble, Jan. 5, 6, 7, 8 (3), 10 (2), 12, 17, 18, 19, 20, 23, 1877; Charles P. Thompson to Tilden, Jan. 4, 1877; George F. Drew to Marble, Jan. 5, 1877; Samuel Pasco to Marble, Jan. 8, 1877; E. A. Perry to Clarkson Potter, Jan. 22, 1877; Marble to E. L. Parris, Jan. 22, 25, 1877; Clarkson Potter to Tilden, Jan. 26, 1877; Marble to Call, Jan. 5, 10, 12, n.d., 1877; Hewitt to Tilden, Jan. 8, 1877, Tilden MSS.

116. Scott to ?, Jan. 27, 1877, Marble MSS; Marble to Samuel J. Randall, Jan. 27, 1877, Randall MSS, University of Pennsylvania Library.

Chapter Ten

1. Belmont to Marble, n.d., Marble MSS.

2. Alexander C. Flick, *Samuel J. Tilden: A Study in Political Sagacity* (New York: Dodd, Mead & Co., 1939), pp. 412–13.

3. Tilden's undated manuscript, Marble MSS.

4. Allan Nevins, ed., *Selected Writings of Abram S. Hewitt* (New York: Columbia University Press, 1937), pp. 391–92; Joseph F. Wall, *Henry Watterson, Reconstructed Rebel* (New York: Oxford University Press, 1956), pp. 168–69.

5. Watterson to Tilden, July 2, 1878; Watterson to Marble, July 2, 1878; Marble to Watterson, n.d., Marble MSS.

6. Marble to Tilden, July 30, 1878; Perry Belmont to Marble, Aug. 4, 1878; Marble to Charles A. Dana, n.d., Marble MSS.

7. *Sun,* Aug. 5, 1878.

8. George L. Miller to Marble, May 30, 1878; Julius L. Brown to Tilden, June 13, 1878; Marble to Tilden, n.d., Marble MSS; Marble to Mrs. Barlow, June, 1878, Barlow MSS; W. W. MacFarland to Bayard, May 26, 1878; Perry Belmont to Bayard, June 25, 1878, Bayard MSS; Flick, *Tilden,* p. 427.

9. Nevins, *Hewitt,* pp. 395–96; Marble to Barlow, Sept. 1878, Barlow MSS.

10. *Tribune,* Oct. 10–16, 1878.

11. Flick, *Tilden,* p. 432.

12. Marble to the *Tribune,* n.d., Marble MSS; *Tribune,* Oct. 16, 1878.

13. Dyke to the New York Press, Oct. 24, 1878, enclosed in Dyke to Marble, Oct.

24, 1878; Samuel Pasco to Marble, Nov. 12, 1878; George W. Guthrie to Marble, Oct. 15, 1878; C. Gibson to Marble, Oct. 17, 1878; Barlow to Marble, n.d., Marble MSS.

14. *Tribune,* Feb. 8, 1879.

15. *House Investigation* 4:213–17.

16. *Tribune,* Feb. 8, 1879.

17. The foregoing has been taken from the published testimony taken by the committee in New York. Marble's testimony is in *House Investigation* 4:221–71; Tilden's ibid. 4:272–89; Parris's ibid. 4:289–92.

18. Marble to Tilden, n.d., Marble MSS; C. A. Cowgill to W. E. Chandler, Feb. 11, 1879, Chandler MSS; *House Investigation* 4:357.

19. Chandler to Reid, Sept. 28, 1878, Reid MSS.

20. Webster to Bayard, Feb. 12, 1879, Bayard MSS; Springer to Marble, Mar. 7, 1879, Marble MSS.

21. Marble to Barlow, Sept. 9, 1880, Barlow MSS.

Chapter Eleven

1. Marble to Sidney Webster, n.d., Marble MSS; *Tribune,* July 11, 1879.

2. Marble to Tilden, n.d., Marble MSS; Marble to Barlow, Sept. 9, 1880, Barlow MSS.

3. Marble to Tilden, July 7, Oct. 7, 1882, Marble MSS.

4. Ibid., n.d. [Dec. 1882].

5. Ibid., Feb. 1, 1883.

6. Marble to Capt. F. Ramsey, May 7, 1884; Perry Belmont to Marble, May 14, 15, 16, 1884; Marble to Dorsheimer, May 18, 1884; Marble to P. Belmont, n.d., Marble MSS.

7. Knott to Marble, July 3, 1873, Marble MSS.

8. Wells to Marble, Mar. 22, 1884, Marble MSS.

9. Marble to Wells, Mar. 15, 1884, Wells MSS.

10. Ibid., Mar. 27, Apr. 18, 1884; Carlisle to Marble, Apr. 7, 1884; Marble to Carlisle, Apr. 25, 1884, Marble MSS.

11. Marble to Bovee, Mar. 21, 1884, Barlow MSS; Morrison to Wells, Apr. 25, May 1, 1884; Wells to Marble, Apr. 25, 1884, Marble MSS; Edward Stanwood, *American Tariff Controversies in the Nineteenth Century* (Boston and New York: Houghton Mifflin Co., 1903) 2:221.

12. Carlisle to Marble, Apr. 7, June 17, 25, 1884; E. K. Apgar to Marble, June 23, 1884; Draft of Tilden's letter to the chairman of the New York Democratic Committee, n.d., Marble MSS.

13. Marble to Bovee, June 19, 1884, Barlow MSS; Marble to ?, n.d., Marble to Tilden [June 1884], Marble MSS; Stanwood, *Tariff Controversies* 2:222–23;

Who's Who in the State of New York, 1907, p. 908; Allan Nevins, ed., *Selected Writings of Abram S. Hewitt* (New York: Columbia University Press, 1937), pp. 452–53.

14. Wells to Marble, Aug. 27, 1884, Marble MSS; Marble to Wells, n.d., Wells MSS.

15. William H. Barnum to Marble, Aug. 22, 1884; Weed to Marble, Aug. 23, 1884, Marble MSS.

16. Draft of the address, Aug. 1884, Marble MSS.

17. Marble to Fanny M. Green, Feb. 15, 1885; Wells to Marble, Sept. 28, 1884, Marble MSS.

18. Horace S. Merrill, *Bourbon Leader: Grover Cleveland and the Democratic Party* (Boston: Little, Brown and Co., 1957), pp. 17–21, 47–49.

19. Allan Nevins, *Grover Cleveland: A Study in Courage* (New York: Dodd, Mead & Co., 1930), p. 195; Mark D. Hirsch, *William C. Whitney: Modern Warwick* (New York: Dodd, Mead & Co., 1948), pp. 249–51; White to Marble, Jan. 29, Mar. 1, 1885, Marble MSS.

20. Clipping from the *New York Citizen,* "January, 1885"; Marble to Cleveland, Jan. 27, 1885, Cleveland MSS, Library of Congress; White to Marble, Mar. 1, 1885, Marble MSS; Marble to Whitney, Mar. 4, 1885, Whitney MSS.

21. Hewitt to Cleveland, Feb. 2, 1885, Cleveland MSS; Nevins, *Cleveland,* pp. 201–4.

22. Manton Marble, "Reason and Authority in Political Economy," unpublished letter to the *New York Sun,* Jan. 11, 1878, Marble MSS.

23. Manton Marble, "Currency Quacks and the Silver Bill," *North American Review* 126 (1878): 156–70; Irwin Unger, *The Greenback Era* (Princeton, N.J.: Princeton University Press, 1964), pp. 352–60.

24. Marble to Manning, Feb. 19, 1885, Marble MSS.

25. Allan Nevins, *Letters of Grover Cleveland* (Boston and New York: Houghton Mifflin Co., 1933), pp. 56–57.

26. Marble to Cleveland, Feb. 15, 1885, Cleveland MSS.

27. Ibid.; Nevins, *Cleveland,* p. 204.

28. Marble to Cleveland, Apr. 13, 1885, Cleveland MSS.

29. Jeanette P. Nichols, "Silver Diplomacy," *Political Science Quarterly* 48(1933): 568–74.

30. Manning to Marble, Apr. 29, 1885; Bayard to Marble, Apr. 30, 1885; Marble to Barlow, Mar. 9, 1885; Marble to Bayard, May 3, 1885, Marble MSS.

31. Bayard to Marble, May 13, 1885; Bayard to Robert McLane, May 14, 1885, Manning MSS, Library of Congress; Bayard to McLane, May 28, 1885, Marble MSS.

32. Marble to Bayard, Aug. 28, Sept. 14, 1885, Bayard MSS.

33. *Real Estate Record and Builder's Guide,* Nov. 14, 1885; Marble to Bayard, Aug. 17, 1885, Bayard MSS.

34. Marble to Bayard, July 9, 17, 1885, Bayard MSS; Marble to Barlow, Aug. 5, 1885, Barlow MSS.

35. Marble to Bayard, July 10, 1885, Bayard MSS.

36. Ibid., July 17, 1885.

37. Ibid.

38. Iddesleigh to Marble, July 22, 28, Aug. 3, 1885; Marble to Iddesleigh, July 30, 1885, Marble MSS; Marble to Bayard, July 29, Aug. 16, 1885, Bayard MSS.

39. Marble to Barlow, Aug. 5, 1885, Barlow MSS.

40. Marble to Henry Sidgwick, July, 1885; Bryce to Marble, Aug. 7, 1885; Marble to Lady Rosebery, July 10, 1885, Marble MSS; Marble to Barlow, Aug. 5, 1885, Barlow MSS.

41. Marble to Bayard, July 9, 1885, Bayard MSS.

42. Ibid., July 29, 1885; Marble to Barlow, Aug. 5, 1885, Barlow MSS.

43. Marble to Manning, Aug. 8, 1885, Marble MSS.

44. Marble to Bayard, Aug. 28, 1885, Bayard MSS.

45. Ibid., Sept. 14, 1885.

46. Ibid.

47. Ibid., Sept. 16, 19, 21, 24, 25, 1885.

48. Ibid., Sept. 23, 1885.

49. Ibid., Sept. 25, 1885.

50. Ibid., Sept. 16, 1885.

51. Henri Cernuschi, testimony before the United States Monetary Commission, Feb. 8, 1877, *Report of the United States Monetary Commission* (Washington: Government Printing Office, 1879) 2:473.

52. Ibid. 2:497–98, 505–6.

53. Henry Cernuschi, *Nomisma: or Legal Tender* (New York: D. Appleton and Co., 1877), pp. 110–11, 114–15.

54. Ibid., pp. 118–19, 125.

55. *Report of U.S. Monetary Commission* 2:476–77.

56. Ibid. 2:506–7.

57. For a fuller discussion of the differences between international bimetallists and gold monometallists see Walter T. K. Nugent, *Money and American Society, 1865–1880* (New York: Free Press, 1968), pp. 191–98.

58. Marble to Bayard, Sept. 16, 19, 23, Oct. 1, 1885, Bayard MSS.

59. Ibid., Oct. 1, 1885; Marble to Barlow, Aug. 24, 1885, Barlow MSS.

Chapter Twelve

1. Tilden to Marble, Aug. 17, 1885; Manning to Marble, Sept. 6, 1885, Marble MSS.

2. Marble to Cernuschi, Oct. 31, 1885, Marble MSS.

3. *Report of the Secretary of the Treasury on the State of the Finances for the Year 1885* (Washington: Government Printing Office, 1885) 1:xiv–xxiv.

4. Marble to Manning, Sept. 10, 1885; Manning to Marble, Nov. 22, Dec. 14, 1885; Warner to Marble, Nov. 16, 1885; Marble to Tilden, Nov. 24, 1885, Marble MSS.

5. Manning to Marble, Dec. 14, 1885, Marble MSS; Allan Nevins, *Grover Cleveland: A Study in Courage* (New York: Dodd, Mead & Co., 1930), pp. 285–86.

6. Marble to Bayard, Dec. 11, 1885, Bayard MSS.

7. Manning to Marble, Jan. 6, 18, 21, Feb. 6, 1886, Marble MSS.

8. Marble to Bayard, Dec. 11, 1885, Bayard MSS; Marble to Webster, Feb. 24, 1886; Marble to Bayard, Mar. 2, 1886, Marble MSS.

9. Nevins, *Cleveland,* p. 271; Marble to Webster, Feb. 24, 1886, Marble MSS.

10. Manning to Marble, Feb. 8, 12, 15, 23, 26, 1886, Marble MSS.

11. "Circulation of Standard Silver Dollars," *House Executive Documents,* 49th Congress, 1st Session, vol. 30, no. 100.

12. Manning to Marble, Mar. 9, 20, 1886, Marble MSS; Nevins, *Cleveland,* p. 273.

13. Sophie M. Walker to Marble, Mar. 24, 1886; Thomas Brennan to Marble, Mar. 29, 1886; Marble to Tilden, "March," 1886, Marble MSS.

14. Manning to Marble, July 17, Aug. 2, 1886; Manning to Webster, Aug. 30, 1886; Marble to Bayard, July 20, 1886, Marble MSS.

15. Manning to Marble, Jan. 19, 21, 1886; Morrison to Marble, Feb. 9, 21, 1886, Marble MSS; "Circulation of Standard Silver Dollars," pp. 6–8.

16. Marble to Mrs. Morrison, Dec. 3, 1886, Marble MSS.

17. *Report of the Secretary of the Treasury on the State of the Finances for the Year 1886* (Washington: Government Printing Office, 1886), pp. xix–lviii.

18. Manning to Marble, Dec. 10, 20, 24, 31, 1886, Jan. 9, 12, 1887, Marble MSS.

19. Weed to Lamont, Feb. 14, 1887, Cleveland MSS. See also a typescript memorandum, undated, giving Weed's account of his dealings with Marble over Manning's resignation, Manning MSS, Library of Congress.

20. Manning to Cleveland, Feb. 14, 1887, Cleveland MSS; Allan Nevins, *Letters of Grover Cleveland* (Boston and New York: Houghton Mifflin Co., 1933), pp. 131–32.

21. Marble to Weed, Feb. 13, 1887, Marble MSS.

22. Manning to Webster, Feb. 24, 1887, Marble MSS; undated newspaper clippings, items 25–30, book number 43, Marble scrapbooks, University of London.

23. Nevins, *Cleveland,* pp. 420, 451; Marble to Mrs. Fairchild, Apr. 6, 1887, Fairchild MSS, New York Historical Society; Marble to Fairchild, Nov. 16, 1887, Marble MSS.

24. Marble to Barlow, July 12, Aug. 30, 1887, Barlow MSS; Barlow to Marble, Sept. 6, 7, 1887, Marble MSS.

25. Barlow to Marble, Mar. 1, 15 (2), 17 (2), May 5, June 6, 1887, Marble MSS;

Marble to Barlow, n.d., July 12, 1887, Barlow MSS; Mark D. Hirsch, *William C. Whitney: Modern Warwick* (New York: Dodd, Mead & Co., 1948), p. 229.

26. Marble to Bayard, Nov. 16, 1887, Marble MSS; Marble to Bayard, Nov. 24, 1887, Bayard MSS; rough draft of memo, undated, Marble MSS; Bayard to Marble, Nov. 19, 25, 1887, Marble MSS.

27. Marble to Barlow, Dec. 2, 29, 1887, Bayard MSS.

28. Ibid., Dec. 20, 1887.

29. Nevins, *Cleveland,* pp. 394–95, 398, 400.

30. Whitney to Marble, May 27, 1888; Marble to Whitney, May 27, 1888, Marble MSS; Nevins, *Cleveland,* p. 389; Edward Stanwood, *American Tariff Controversies in the Nineteenth Century* (Boston and New York: Houghton Mifflin Co., 1903) 2:232–34; Horace S. Merrill, *Bourbon Leader: Grover Cleveland and the Democratic Party* (Boston: Little, Brown and Co., 1957), pp. 123–25.

31. Platform draft in Marble's handwriting with comments by Arthur P. Gorman, in folder "Democratic Party—Convention," New York Historical Society.

32. Marble to Gorman, June 2 or 3, n.d., 1888; Gorman to Marble, June 4, 12, 1888; John Sargeant Cram to Richard Croker, n.d., Marble to Watterson, n.d., Marble MSS; Nevins, *Cleveland,* pp. 400–402; Kirk H. Porter and Donald Bruce Johnson, eds., *National Party Platforms* (Urbana, Ill.: University of Illinois Press, 1956), pp. 76–77.

33. Copy of resolutions in Marble MSS. See also Douglas Taylor to Marble, July 17, 1888; Barlow to Marble, Sept. 28, 1888; Marble to Bayard, Aug. 28, 1888, Marble MSS.

34. Marble to Bayard, Mar. 30, 1886, Bayard MSS.

35. Marble to Whitney, Dec. 5, 1885, Mar. 9, 1886, June 29, 1888, Whitney MSS; Hirsch, *Whitney,* p. 353.

36. Henry B. Russell, *International Monetary Conferences* (New York: Harper and Brothers, 1898), pp. 348–49; Marble to Barlow, Dec. 29, 1887, Bayard MSS.

37. Marble to Barlow, Dec. 2, 1887, Bayard MSS.

38. Unpublished draft, "Delay in Confirmation of Chief-Justice Fuller," 1888, Marble MSS.

39. James A. Barnes, *John G. Carlisle, Financial Statesman* (New York: Dodd, Mead & Co., 1930), pp. 35, 76, 102, 137, 139, 163–64.

40. Marble to Carlisle, Dec. 23, 1889, Marble MSS.

41. See note on bottom of above letter, saying that Carlisle did not find the letter until May of 1891, when he called on Marble to express his apologies.

Chapter Thirteen

1. Herbert J. Bass, *"I am a Democrat": The Political Career of David Bennett Hill* (Syracuse, N.Y.: Syracuse University Press, 1961).

2. Henry B. Russell, *International Monetary Conferences* (New York: Harper and Brothers, 1898), pp. 350–53; Cernuschi to Marble, Nov. 10, 1888, Marble MSS.

3. Cf. Marble's miscellaneous memoranda on silver, including drafts of letters to the *Times* of London, Apr. and June, 1890, and to the *World,* June 25, 1890; Cernuschi to Marble, June 7, 16, 18, 19, 20, 21, 24, 1890, Marble MSS.

4. Russell, *International Monetary Conferences,* p. 367. The act went into effect Aug. 13. Marble's first letter to Hill was Aug. 27.

5. Hill's private secretary Timothy Shaler Williams also stated that Marble and Hill did not begin to correspond until 1890. See undated typescript ms. in Hill MSS, New York State Library, Albany.

6. Marble to Hill, Aug. 27, 1890, Marble MSS.

7. Draft of public statement, Aug. 27, 1890, Marble MSS.

8. Hill to Marble, Sept. 22, 1890, Marble MSS.

9. *New York Times,* Sept. 24, 1890; Bass, *Hill,* pp. 162–64.

10. Marble to Hill, Nov. 5, 7, 1890; draft of resolutions dated 1890–1891, Marble MSS.

11. Bass, *Hill,* pp. 166–71; Marble to Hill, Jan. 9, 1891, Marble MSS; T. S. Williams ms. account of Hill's decision, Jan. 28, Feb. 1, 1891, Williams MSS, New York Public Library.

12. Bass, *Hill,* pp. 171–72.

13. Marble to Cernuschi, Dec. 16, 17 (three cables), 1890; Marble's draft, undated, is in the Marble MSS and is identified by references to it in Marble to Hill, Jan. 11, 1891, Hill MSS; Marble to Hill, Jan. 18, Feb. 2, 1891; statement of account with M. Corgialegno and Co., Jan. 14, 1891; Cernuschi to Marble, Jan. 14, 16, 1891, Marble MSS.

14. Marble to Flower, Jan. 14, 17, 1891, Marble MSS.

15. Flower to Marble, Jan. 18, 21, 1891; Marble to Cernuschi, Jan. 20, 22, 23, 1891; Cernuschi to Marble, Jan. 22 (three cables), 23, 1891; Marble to Hill, Jan. 30, Feb. 2, 1891; statement from Corgialegno, Jan. 28, 1891, Marble MSS.

16. Williams to Marble, Jan. 11, 30, 1891, Marble MSS; Bass, *Hill,* pp. 184–85.

17. Allan Nevins, *Grover Cleveland: A Study in Courage* (New York: Dodd, Mead & Co., 1930), pp. 465–70; Horace S. Merrill, *Bourbon Leader: Grover Cleveland and the Democratic Party* (Boston: Little, Brown and Co., 1957), p. 155.

18. Draft of comment on Cleveland's silver letter, Mar. 5, 1891, Marble MSS.

19. Marble to Hill, Feb. 19, 20, 1891, Hill MSS; Marble to Hill, Feb. 25, 1891, Marble MSS.

20. Hill to Marble, Mar. 2, 1891, Marble MSS.

21. Cernuschi to Marble, July 25 [1891], Marble MSS.

22. Marble to Hill, July 18, 25, 26, 27, 1891, Marble MSS.

23. Marble to Hill, Sept. 11, 12, 1891, Williams MSS.

24. Williams to Marble, Sept. 17, 1891, Marble MSS.

25. Marble to Pulitzer, Oct. 3, 1891; Marble to Williams, Oct. 1, 1891; Marble to Hill, Oct. 9, 1891, Marble MSS; Bass, *Hill,* pp. 189–90.

26. Marble to Hill, Nov. 29, 1891, Marble MSS.

27. Bass, *Hill,* pp. 202–5.

28. Marble to Hill, Nov. 29, 1891, Marble MSS.

29. Pulitzer to Marble, Sept. 9, 1889, Mar. 22, 1891, n.d.; Marble to Hill, Dec. 16, 1891, Marble MSS; Marble to Hill, Dec. 7, 10, 12, 1891, Hill MSS; Bass, *Hill,* p. 84.

30. Marble's draft of letter from Hill to John T. Morgan, Dec. 17, 1891, Marble MSS. See also press clipping of letter from Senator William Stewart of Nevada to Hill, Jan. 2, 1892, and draft of reply, 1892, Marble MSS.

31. "Mugwumps and the Democratic Party," n.d., filed with papers of 1892, Marble MSS.

32. Bass, *Hill,* p. 211; Ellis P. Oberholtzer, *A History of the United States since the Civil War* (New York: Macmillan Co., 1917–1937) 5:147; Marble to Hill, n.d.; Hill to Marble, Jan. 11, 1892, Marble MSS.

33. Edward Stanwood, *American Tariff Controversies in the Nineteenth Century* (Boston and New York: Houghton Mifflin Co., 1903) 2:306–11.

34. Marble to Morrison, Miller, and Irish, Jan. 21, 1892; Miller to Marble, Jan. 26, 1892; Morrison to Marble, Jan. 27, 1892; Irish to Marble, Jan. 29, 1892, Marble MSS.

35. Marble to Hill, Feb. 14, 1892, Marble MSS.

36. Marble to Hill, Mar. 6, 21, 1892; Hill to Marble, Mar. 8, 21, 1892, Marble MSS; Bass, *Hill,* p. 228.

37. Bass, *Hill,* pp. 215–19; George Harmon Knoles, *The Presidential Campaign and Election of 1892* (Stanford University Publications, History, Economics, and Political Science, vol. 5, no. 1, 1942), pp. 11, 15–17.

38. Mark D. Hirsch, *William C. Whitney: Modern Warwick* (New York: Dodd, Mead & Co., 1948), p. 382; Knoles, *Election of 1892,* p. 17, note 41; Bass, *Hill,* pp. 218–19.

39. Marble to Hill, Jan. 25, 1892, Marble MSS.

40. Hill to Marble, Feb. 22, 1892; Williams to Marble, Feb. 23, 1892; Marble to Cernuschi, n.d., Marble MSS; Marble to Williams, Feb. 25, 1892, Williams MSS.

41. Bass, *Hill,* p. 222; Marble to Irish, Feb. 22, 1892; Marble to Perry Belmont, Feb. 26, 1892; Marble to A. J. Warner, Mar. 29, 1892, Marble MSS.

42, Knoles, *Election of 1892,* p. 21.

43. Honey to Marble, Feb. 27, 1892; Miller to Marble, Feb. 26, Mar. 1, 15, 1892; Irish to Marble, Mar. 1, 1892, Marble MSS.

44. Bass, *Hill,* pp. 229–31; Knoles, *Election of 1892,* pp. 22–29; Hirsch, *Whitney,* p. 385; Miller to Marble, Apr. 14, 15, 20, 27, May 5, 1892; P. Belmont to Marble, Apr. 7, 1892, Marble MSS.

45. Marble to Miller, May 14, 1892, Marble MSS.

46. Bass, *Hill,* p. 232; Marble to Hill, June 3, 4, 7, 10, 13, 1892; Marble to Cernuschi, July 25, 1892; draft of resolutions, June, 1892, Marble MSS.

47. Hill to Marble, June 16, 1892, Marble MSS; Bass, *Hill,* p. 233.

48. Knoles, *Election of 1892*, pp. 77–79; Marble to Cernuschi, July 25, 1892, Marble MSS.

49. Ibid.

50. John D. Hicks, *The Populist Revolt* (Lincoln, Nebr.: University of Nebraska Press, paperback reprint, 1961), pp. 205–37, 435–39.

51. Marble to Cernuschi, July 25, 1892, Marble MSS.

Chapter Fourteen

1. Wells to Vilas, Feb. 9, 1893, Vilas MSS, Wisconsin State Historical Society.

2. Cernuschi to Marble, Nov. 11 [1892]; Marble to Hill, Dec. 7, 1892, Marble MSS.

3. Hill to Marble, Dec. 7, 9, 1892; Marble to Cernuschi, Dec. 9, 1892, Marble MSS.

4. *Congressional Record*, 52nd Congress, 1st Session, pp. 1226–35. See also Marble's draft of an article for the *New York Sun*, Sept. 27, 1892; Cernuschi to Marble, Nov. 11, 18, 1892, Marble MSS.

5. Marble to Cleveland, Feb. 12, 1893, Cleveland MSS.

6. Horace S. Merrill, *Bourbon Leader: Grover Cleveland and the Democratic Party* (Boston: Little, Brown and Co., 1957), pp. 174–82; Cernuschi to Marble, June 27, 1893, Marble MSS.

7. Marble to Hill, Sept. 17, Dec. 10, 1893; Marble to Webster, July 2, 15, 21, 1895, Marble MSS.

8. Marble to Webster, July 21, Aug. 14, 1895, Marble MSS.

9. Marble to Webster, Sept. 17, 1896; Marble to Constantine Cernuschi, May 11, 1896, Marble MSS.

10. Marble to P. Belmont, July 9, 1897; P. Belmont to Marble, July 30, 1897, Marble MSS.

11. Marble to A. S. Frissell, Jan. 15, 1897; William Durrell to Marble, Mar. 26, 1898; Marble to the chairman of the Board of Customs, May 5, 1898; Marble to Richard Wood, Jan. 3, 1899; Marble to P. Belmont, Mar. 25, 1900; P. Belmont to Marble, Mar. 26, 1900; Herbert Spencer to Marble, Mar. 25, 29, 1900; Marble to Spencer, Mar. 29, Nov. 3, 11, 12, 1900; Marble to Richard Wood, Nov. 26, 1902; Marble to "Baron," June 22 [1905]; Marble to John Hone, Mar. 14, 1907; Marble to Delos McCurdy, n.d., Marble MSS.

12. Marble to Spencer, Feb. 28, 1903; Marble to Webster, Dec. 3, 1901, Marble MSS.

13. Murphy to Marble, Feb. 19, 1898; Marble to Murphy, Feb. 3, 1899; P. Belmont to Marble, July 15, 22, Aug. 16, Nov. 3, 1899; Marble to Charles H. Marshall, Jan. 25, 1900; Marshall to Marble, Jan. 30, 1900; Marble to Webster, Aug. 2, 1900, Marble MSS.

14. Webster to Marble, July 5, 1898, Marble MSS; Marble to Ford, Aug. 29, 1893, Ford MSS, New York Public Library.

15. Marble to Ford, Aug. 12, Sept. 12, 1906, Ford MSS; Marble to Ford, Nov. 12, 1907; Marble to August Belmont, Oct. 21, 1906, Marble MSS.

16. Dunning to Marble, Apr. 21, 1906; Marble to Dunning, n.d., Marble MSS; Marble to Ford, Aug. 12, 1906, Ford MSS.

17. Marble to Pulitzer, Apr. 21, 1908; Marble to Webster, Dec. 17, 1899, Marble MSS.

18. Marble to Schuyler, Dec. 14, 1906; Marble to Pulitzer, Apr. 21, 1908, Marble MSS.

19. Marble to Webster, July 15, 1895, Aug. 3, 1897; Webster to Marble, July 21, 1897, Marble MSS.

20. Marble to Ford, Aug. 12, 1906, Ford MSS; Marble to Webster, July 15, 1895, Aug. 29, 1897, Marble MSS.

21. Marble to Webster, July 15, 1895, Marble MSS.

22. Marble to Mme. Potertad, Mar. 17, 1874; Marble to George W. Smith, May 24, 1906, Marble MSS; Marble to Ford, Apr. 17, 1906, Ford MSS.

23. Marble to "Baron," June 22 [1905]; Marble to Henry Harisse, May 23, 1908, Marble MSS; *New York Times,* Feb. 16, 1911.

24. Marble to Webster, Apr. 10, 1909, Marble MSS.

25. Marble to Ford, Nov. 2, 1909, Ford MSS.

26. Marble to Ford, Nov. 2, 1909; Martin Conway to Ford, Sept. 3, 1917, Ford MSS; Conway to T. S. Williams, Oct. 12, 1917, Williams MSS.

27. *Times,* Feb. 15, 16, 1911; *Tribune,* Feb. 16, 17, 1911; Marble to Mrs. Sidney Webster, Mar. 27, 1911, Marble MSS.

28. Marble to Mrs. Webster, Nov. 24, 1911; Marble to Mr. Rives, May 29, 1914, Marble MSS; Marble to Ford, Apr. 6, 1915, Ford MSS.

29. Conway to Ford, Mar. 1, Sept. 13, 1917, Ford MSS; *Times,* July 25, 1917.

30. Conway to Williams, Oct. 12, 1917, Williams MSS.

BIBLIOGRAPHICAL ESSAY

THIS BIOGRAPHY has been written largely from manuscript sources. The principal source has been the Manton Marble MSS in the Manuscript Division of the Library of Congress. The Marble MSS contain nearly 14,000 items, including many copies of letters written by Marble. The collection, though generally complete, shows signs of pruning. Especially lacking are items dealing with Marble's life prior to joining the *World,* the election controversy of 1876, and Marble's family life. Still, the collection is quite revealing, both of its subject and of events that attracted his attention. Other valuable collections include the Martin B. Anderson MSS, Rush Rhees Library, University of Rochester, which contain almost fifty letters written by Marble between the years 1855 and 1862, a period for which the Marble MSS are disappointingly scanty; the Thomas F. Bayard MSS, Library of Congress, which are indispensable for Marble's silver mission and the politics of the Cleveland administration; the S. L. M. Barlow MSS, Henry E. Huntington Library, which contain many items relating to Marble's personal life and political activism; and the David B. Hill MSS, New York State Library, valuable for the years 1890 to 1892. Other collections containing valuable Marble items are the Francis Preston Blair Family MSS, Grover Cleveland MSS, George B. McClellan MSS, and David A. Wells MSS, all in the Library of Congress; the Worthington C. Ford MSS, Horace Greeley MSS, and Timothy S. Williams MSS in the New York Public Library; the Henry A. Ward MSS, Chester Dewey MSS, and Thurlow Weed MSS in the Rush Rhees Library, University of Rochester; Samuel J. Randall MSS, University of Pennsylvania Library; and the Lyman C. Draper MSS, Wisconsin State Historical Society. Indispensable for understanding the events Marble participated in are the aforementioned collections and the William E. Chandler MSS, Salmon P. Chase MSS, James R. Doolittle MSS, William M. Evarts MSS, Thomas Ewing Family MSS, Andrew Johnson MSS, Daniel Manning MSS, Fitz-John Porter MSS, Jeremiah Black MSS, Whitelaw Reid MSS,

Henry Watterson MSS, and William C. Whitney MSS, Library of Congress; John Bigelow MSS, New York Public Library; William H. Seward MSS, Rush Rhees Library, University of Rochester; and James R. Doolittle MSS, State Historical Society of Wisconsin. A useful published source is Ethel F. Fiske (ed.), *The Letters of John Fiske* (1940). A few other collections of lesser importance are cited in the footnotes.

Marble's published works are few, but reveal much. Political matters are discussed in *A Secret Chapter of Political History* (1878); "Currency Quacks and the Silver Bill," *North American Review* (1878); and "Freedom of the Press Wantonly Violated," *Papers from the Society for the Diffusion of Political Knowledge* (1864). His western adventure is recounted in "To Red River and Beyond," *Harper's New Monthly Magazine* (1860–1861). His literary interests are revealed in "English and Scottish Ballads," the *Knickerbocker* (1859), and in his review of Samuel Greene Arnold's *History of Rhode Island*, the *Knickerbocker* (1859). His views on journalism were published in Charles F. Wingate (ed.), *Views and Interviews on Journalism* (1875).

The second single most important source for this work was the *New York World*. All the evidence indicates that though Marble conferred with party leaders and his friends, the paper's editorial judgments were his own. The *World*, of course, discussed many subjects not treated in this book. In an effort to keep an already large manuscript from getting completely out of hand I have used the paper to illuminate issues that dominated Marble's personal correspondence.

For the years prior to Marble's joining the *World*, I have used the *Rochester American*, the *Boston Journal*, and the *Boston Traveller*. For the later years I have relied most heavily on the New York press, especially the *Herald*, *Evening Post*, *Times*, and *Tribune*. The files of the *Albany Argus* were also sampled to obtain the opinion of the Democracy's upstate leaders.

When I began my research on Marble, the first book I read was Sister Mary Cortona Phelan's *Manton Marble of the New York World* (1957). A brief account that concentrates on Marble's "political thought," the book is well researched and suggestive on many points. Although I have occasionally disagreed with its interpretations and have tried to provide a broader context for Marble's life than it offers, I have profited from reading it.

I have also profited greatly from the work of other scholars who have provided invaluable information on the men and events that surrounded Marble's life. Since a full bibliography is provided in the notes, I would here like to recognize only the works that have helped me the most.

For Marble's career as a journalist I have been greatly aided by a Harvard University doctoral dissertation by J. M. Bloch, "The Rise of the *New York World* during the Civil War Decade" (1941). Covering the years 1860 to 1868, the dissertation was particularly useful for tracing the financial history of the *World* and in assessing David Goodman Croly's role as managing editor. Also helpful were Louis M. Starr, *Reporting the Civil War* (1962); Oliver Gramling, *AP: The Story of the News* (1940); and Victor Rosewater, *History of Cooperative News-Gathering in the United States* (1930).

My understanding of Civil War politics has benefited from Sidney D. Brummer, *Political History of New York State During the Period of the Civil War* (1911); Frank Klement, *The Copperheads in the Middle West* (1960); and William Frank Zornow, *Lincoln and the Party Divided* (1954). Special studies that were helpful included Sidney Kaplan, "The Miscegenation Issue in the Election of 1864," *Journal of Negro History* (1949); Eugene C. Murdock, "Horatio Seymour and the 1863 Draft," *Civil War History* (1965); and Charles R. Wilson, "McClellan's Changing Views on the Peace Plank of 1864," *American Historical Review* (1933).

The most helpful work on the Reconstruction period is LaWanda and John H. Cox, *Politics, Principle, and Prejudice, 1865–1866* (1965). Although my account shifts the perspective of their study, it confirms their conclusion that the issue of Negro civil rights dominated New York and national politics in the years immediately after the Civil War. Also of great value are Eric L. McKitrick, *Andrew Johnson and Reconstruction* (1960), and Charles Coleman, *The Election of 1868* (1933). A superb doctoral dissertation is Edward L. Gambill, "Northern Democrats and Reconstruction, 1865–1868," University of Iowa (1969). I have also benefited from the findings of Homer A. Stebbins, *A Political History of the State of New York, 1865–1869,* and W. W. Davis, *Civil War and Reconstruction in Florida.*

In studying relations between the "swallow-tail" Democrats and Tammany Hall, I have relied heavily on Mark D. Hirsch, *William C. Whitney* (1948), and "Samuel J. Tilden: The Story of a Lost Opportunity," *American Historical Review* (1951). A work of great originality and insight is Seymour Mandelbaum, *Boss Tweed's New York* (1965). Also useful were Alexander B. Callow, *The Tweed Ring* (1966), and Matthew P. Breen, *Thirty Years of New York Politics* (1899).

Useful biographies for the Civil War and Reconstruction years include Alexander C. Flick, *Samuel J. Tilden* (1937); Stewart Mitchell, *Horatio Seymour* (1938); Allan Nevins, *Abram S. Hewitt: With Some Account of Peter Cooper* (1935); Joseph F. Wall, *Henry Watterson* (1957); and William E. Smith, *The Francis Preston Blair Family in Politics,* 2 vols. (1933).

Two outstanding books greatly simplified my task of understanding the monetary controversies of the Reconstruction era. Irwin Unger, *The Greenback Era* (1964), expertly untangled the political history, while Walter T. K. Nugent, *Money and American Society,*

1865–1880 (1968), illuminated the ideological and international aspects.

Two articles by Albert V. House, "Men, Morals, and Manipulation in the Pennsylvania Democracy of 1875," *Pennsylvania History* (1956), and "The Speakership Contest of 1875; Democratic Response to Power," *Journal of American History* (1965), came to my aid at important points in my narrative.

The history of monetary policy in the years following Reconstruction needs attention. Useful for the international aspect of the subject were Jeanette P. Nichols, "Silver Diplomacy," *Political Science Quarterly* (1933), and Henry B. Russell, *International Monetary Conferences* (1898). For the domestic aspects I have been aided by James A. Barnes, *John G. Carlisle, Financial Statesman* (1930), and Allan Nevins, *Grover Cleveland: A Study in Courage* (1931).

My understanding of David B. Hill's campaign for the Democratic presidential nomination in 1892 was sharpened by Herbert J. Bass, *"I am a Democrat," The Political Career of David Bennett Hill* (1961), and George Harmon Knoles, *The Presidential Campaign and Election of 1892* (1942).

INDEX